# The Battle for Boston

*POLIS: Fordham Series in Urban Studies*

Edited by Daniel J. Monti, Saint Louis University

POLIS will address the questions of what makes a good community and how urban dwellers succeed and fail to live up to the idea that people from various backgrounds and levels of society can live together effectively, if not always congenially. The series is the province of no single discipline; we are searching for authors in fields as diverse as American studies, anthropology, history, political science, sociology, and urban studies who can write for both academic and informed lay audiences. Our objective is to celebrate and critically assess the customary ways in which urbanites make the world corrigible for themselves and the other kinds of people with whom they come into contact every day.

To this end, we will publish both book-length manuscripts and a series of "digital shorts" (e-books) focusing on case studies of groups, locales, and events that provide clues as to how urban people accomplish this delicate and exciting task. We expect to publish one or two books every year and a larger number of "digital shorts." The digital shorts will be 20,000 words or fewer and have a strong narrative voice.

# THE BATTLE FOR BOSTON

How Mayor Ray Flynn and Community
Organizers Fought Racism and Downtown
Power Brokers

DON GILLIS
Foreword by Mayor Bill de Blasio

Fordham University Press
NEW YORK   2025

Fordham University Press has no responsibility for the persistence or accuracy of
URLs for external or third-party Internet websites referred to in this publication
and does not guarantee that any content on such websites is, or will remain,
accurate or appropriate.

Fordham University Press also publishes its books in a variety of electronic
formats. Some content that appears in print may not be available in electronic
books.

Visit us online at www.fordhampress.com.

For EU safety / GPSR concerns: Mare Nostrum Group B.V., Mauritskade 21D,
1091 GC Amsterdam, The Netherlands, gpsr@mare-nostrum.co.uk

Library of Congress Cataloging-in-Publication Data available online at
https://catalog.loc.gov.

Printed in the United States of America

27 26 25   5 4 3 2 1

First edition

For
Megan Gillis, Sally Gillis, and Ilana Schwartz
The new generation of community organizers

# Contents

*Photos follow page 206*

# BOSTON NEIGHBORHOODS MAP

MAP 1. Boston Neighborhoods Map

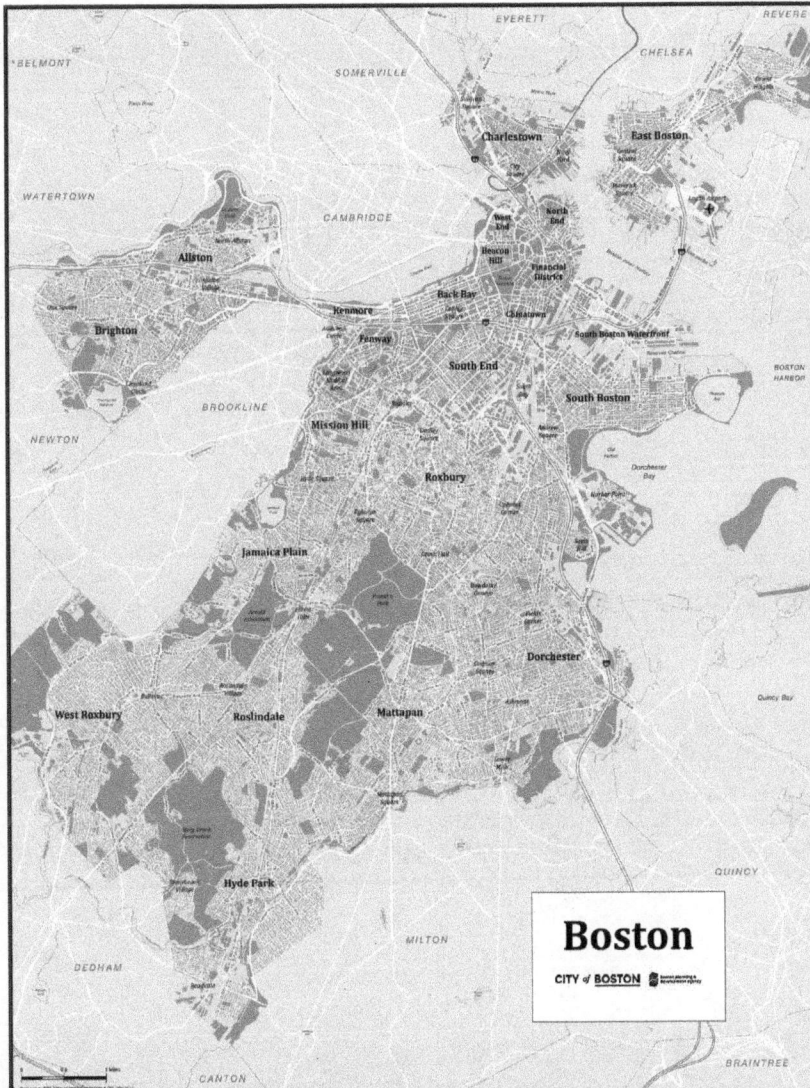

Source: Boston Planning and Development Agency

# Charts and Tables

# FOREWORD BY MAYOR BILL DE BLASIO

I grew up in the Boston area in the 1960s and 1970s. I remember the thrill of watching the Red Sox games. I continued to be a Red Sox fan throughout my life, much to the chagrin of my Yankees constituents! I watched from across the Charles River the issues of race and class play out in the city of Boston—school desegregation and busing in 1974 and the inability of Mayor Kevin White to manage the racial conflict. I graduated from Cambridge Rindge and Latin School in 1979 and developed an early interest in politics. I followed Boston politics closely and was thrilled in 1983 when Mel King and Ray Flynn were in the final election, beating out the business-backed candidates. I remember the excitement and hope that filled the city when Flynn was inaugurated. He worked tirelessly to unite the city and empower its neighborhoods. These experiences helped shape my understanding of urban politics and progressive leadership.

The turning point in my progressive journey was a moment of profound personal reflection. It was 1977, and my older brother Steve Wilhelm—like Don Gillis, the author of *The Battle for Boston*—was arrested while protesting the Seabrook nuclear power plant. This event, a pivotal juncture in steering America away from nuclear power, filled me with an overwhelming sense of pride for my brother. As I sat on the steps of my high school building, this realization washed over me: "I'm supposed to be a progressive." This personal epiphany marked a significant shift in my life's trajectory.

This experience and my work on the David Dinkins mayoral campaign ignited my passion for public service. In 1990, I was fortunate to secure a position in city hall. Dinkins, the first African American elected mayor in New York City's history, ran a campaign that pledged racial healing. He famously referred to New York City's demographic diversity as 'not a melting pot, but a gorgeous mosaic.' Inspired by Dinkins's vision, I was eager to contribute to this journey of uniting the city. The author, Don Gillis, was doing the same for Flynn, the mayor at that time.

When I was elected mayor of New York City in 2013, the first Democrat in twenty years, it was the same year Marty Walsh was elected Boston's fifty-fourth mayor. Marty, Ray, and I share a deep commitment to our cities' poor and working people. Marty and I served on the US Conference of Mayor's Cities of Opportunity Task Force. We prioritized addressing "the tale of two cities," economic and educational inequality. Inspired by the vision of our predecessors, we were eager to contribute to the journey of uniting our cities.

In NYC, we achieved universal pre-K, a publicly funded prekindergarten for all New York City children, serving ninety thousand three- and four-year-olds. Boston did the same under Walsh. We built thousands of affordable housing units, created jobs in emerging industries, and worked tirelessly to reduce income inequality, raise wages, and improve race relations—as Flynn and Walsh did in Boston. We created a guaranteed healthcare system, NYC Care, the nation's most extensive and comprehensive plan to guarantee healthcare for every New Yorker. Flynn launched Boston's first Immigrant Rights Unit to help the city's many immigrants with free healthcare and legal services. We both believed health care is a fundamental human right, not a privilege for those who can afford it. Like Flynn, I took on the downtown power brokers. The results were a redistribution of the benefits of growth. We had a measurable impact in reducing income inequality. While the problems persist, we made them the issues that future mayors can't ignore.

I first met Gillis when I was in Boston for a US Conference of Mayors meeting with other mayors from around the country to discuss strategies to attack income inequality. Gillis had his progressive trajectory. He started organizing tenants against displacement and the scourge of arson in the Fenway neighborhood. Later, as a youth street worker and public housing tenant organizer he joined the Flynn campaign and the mayor's office after the 1983 election. Flynn tapped him to lead neighborhood services and economic and workforce development efforts for his administration.

Gillis's book takes a deep dive into efforts to tackle the challenges faced by the city in terms of inequality, racism, and creating shared economic prosperity, primarily by Flynn, but also by Mayors Tom Menino, Marty Walsh, and Michelle Wu. He was uniquely positioned as a senior adviser to Flynn for a decade in city government. He skillfully portrays the political dynamics that led to the rejection of the business-backed growth machine coalition and the reduction of racial conflict, marking a profound realignment of power relationships in the city.

Gillis incorporates the voices of community organizers and neighborhood leaders, who bravely fought these battles from within the government and in the streets. The voices he captures bring to life efforts to respond to bank redlining and mortgage lending racial discrimination, to control spiraling rents and condominium conversions, and the never-ending struggle to improve public education. Flynn created the first-in-the-nation appointed school board, not an uncontested endeavor as Gillis describes, a practice New York later followed in 2002. He also ended stop-and-frisk search practices by the police and instituted community policing, as we did in NYC two decades later. Confronting racial conflict and inequality is a requirement for mayors. Flynn needed to deal with eliminating the chronic racial violence he inherited and the impact of the Carol DiMaiti Stuart murder and its aftermath. I dealt with the killing of Eric Garner. Marty Walsh and I confronted the ramifications of the George Floyd murder. Gillis explores the role race played during these periods.

The book's theme is how cities can be progressive and raise the voices of those often left behind. Boston's community organizers have a long history of fighting against racism, educational inequality, urban renewal programs, and highway expansion, and expanding tenants' rights. The courts ordered busing to integrate Boston's public schools, put the city's public housing developments in receivership, and forced the cleanup of Boston Harbor. How Flynn took back control and led these agencies is part of the city's story Gillis recounts. Flynn's administration waged powerful grassroots campaigns against the growth machine alongside residents, community organizers, and activists. The book studies how these policy battles enlisted neighborhood, labor, tenant, and small business groups and how they paved the way for progressive policies.

The story of progressive city leaders, often overlooked in urban social history courses, is crucial to understanding urban politics. As an undergraduate urban studies student at NYU, I couldn't find books like Don Gillis's. The book provides a historical account and road map of how cities like Boston became progressive and the key elements that sustain progressive policies. Drawing upon a rich scholarship, oral history, and archival research, Gillis concludes with a comprehensive analysis of Flynn's contributions to Boston and the invaluable lessons we can learn from them. *The Battle for Boston* helps us understand the challenges in urban

America today and the role of progressive leadership in city politics. It is a must-read for students of urban politics and lovers of cities. It proves that progressives can win and put their vision into action.

*Bill de Blasio*

Bill de Blasio

# PREFACE: A CITY IN THE TWENTY-FIRST CENTURY

*The Boston we love is a city that takes care of each other, where hard work meets big dreams with grit and resilience. But for too many, it's been impossible to dream when you're fighting to hold on. Fighting to afford to stay. Fighting for our kids. Fighting a system that wasn't built for us, doesn't speak our languages, doesn't hear our voices.* (Michelle Wu, as a candidate for mayor)

On November 2, 2021, Boston achieved a transformative moment, electing the first woman and person of color as mayor in its two-hundred-year history. Forty-six White men had led Boston since it was incorporated in 1822. Most were called "Yankees" or were of Irish descent. Before incorporation, Boston was led by many White selectmen since being settled in 1630.[1] In 2021, Boston voters elected Michelle Wu as mayor. She won a decisive and historic victory on a progressive platform promising to bring the benefits of growth to Boston's long-forgotten residents and respond to climate change, lack of affordable housing, inequality, transportation, and racism. Her platform would build considerably upon the unfinished business initiated forty years earlier by progressive mayor Ray Flynn.

Harken back to the final mayoral election in 1983 between two progressive candidates: Mel King of the South End, the first African American to reach the final election, and Ray Flynn of South Boston. When the 201,000 ballots were counted, 70 percent of the electorate, the largest turnout since 1949, voted for a new direction in Boston. The downtown power brokers were defeated, leading to decisive changes in the political structure. Flynn was elected Boston's fifty-second mayor in 1983 and would go on to lead the city for nearly a decade. This book is about the inspiring journey to transform Boston under Flynn into a progressive city where its poor and working-class residents would have a fair shot in a rapidly changing economy.

Boston has a well-deserved reputation for racial and ethnic hostility and inequality. This book is drawn from many of the stories of Bostonians who helped change the story and the city's unlikely champion who led the transformation to a more equitable, progressive Boston. The pivotal role of community organizers and neighborhood leaders in Flynn's election underscores the political dynamics that led to the rejection of the growth machine coalition and the racial politics of the past. These marked a profound realignment of power relationships in the city and were a testament to the indomitable spirit of these progressive activists and elected officials. This case study captures a crucial period in the city's history that paved the way for a progressive city in the late twentieth century.

This book is not a series of detached observations but a testament to my deep involvement in these issues. I was there. My work with tenants, young people in Boston's neighborhoods, and public housing tenants revealed to me the growing divide in the city. I felt a personal responsibility to contribute to the change that was needed. I led neighborhood services and economic and workforce development efforts in Flynn's administration, providing me with a unique vantage point into the workings of Boston City Hall and the activism in every neighborhood. This book is a product of that history.

As the book recounts, Flynn implemented an economic justice and progressive social policy agenda as mayor. His successor, Tom Menino, who served for twenty years, abandoned many of Flynn's policies and set a different course for the city. The next mayor, Marty Walsh, was in the Flynn mold. He centered his administration on addressing class and race issues, but Boston was so different by then that most people had forgotten Flynn's achievements. Following Walsh, Wu campaigned on a progressive platform for a very different city that continued to have significant economic and racial inequalities. Boston had increasingly become a tale of two cities. When Wu was elected, the wealthiest 5 percent of Boston residents had 25 percent of total income, while the bottom 60 percent had only 22 percent.[2] The shortage of affordable housing exacerbated the widening gap. Flynn had a redistributive agenda—a social contract with Boston that when the city moves ahead, everybody moves ahead together.

Peter Kadzis, a WGBH reporter who covered Boston politics, compared Boston's previous five mayors to Wu in her first year in office. "Michelle Wu has more in common with Ray Flynn's first year than people might think. That's because when Ray Flynn became mayor, Boston was still recovering from the intense racial animosity from Boston's school desegregation. Michelle Wu took over when the city, as was the nation, was still recovering from George Floyd's murder. Ray Flynn beat Mel King, the first Black politician to compete city-wide for mayor, and Wu faced a multi-ethnic field of opponents. There is a common thread of Black power for Flynn and Wu."[3] Race would be a defining issue for Flynn and virtually every Boston mayor during their terms in office. Mayors Walsh and Wu each told me that the legacy of racial injustice in the city is part of every policy consideration.[4]

While the book is framed through several theoretical lenses, its sociological underpinnings include ethnographic interviews with more than seventy people who were kind enough to speak to me. In the interviews, which sociologists call retrospective autoethnography, I used past personal experiences to identify and analyze sociologically relevant events and archival and historical records. I tried to be sparing with the theory, providing a greater exposition of the theoretical frameworks and a comparison with several other cities in the appendices for those readers wanting to delve deeper. The stories are woven together in what I hope is a comprehensive portrayal and analysis of what happened, why, and what it meant during the late twentieth century and into the next century in the city. It doesn't cover every bit of history or answer every question, but still, it gives the reader a portrait of the progressive challenges and opportunities during that era.

When Flynn took office, he cracked down on racial violence and expanded linkage—a fee on commercial office development—to fund affordable housing. He created the first-in-the-nation job training component to linkage and required developers to hire Boston residents, people of color, and women. He heard the same objections from the real estate and development community that Marty Walsh and Michelle Wu also rejected. "Shortsighted business lobby groups and their political allies should not have a monopoly on what it means to be pro-business. A healthy business climate is one in which people can afford to pay for decent housing, work in safe conditions, have adequate health care, and breathe clean air. Government's role is often to ensure that businesses live up to this responsibility."[5]

Mayors Walsh and Wu have supported and expanded Flynn's progressive initiatives. They, and Menino, supported the appointed school committee Flynn put in place, avoiding a return to a decentralized bureaucratic political governance model that has historically operated in the interest of adults—not children. Their redistributive agenda included increasing linkage fees and inclusionary housing, mandating low- to moderate-income housing as part of each development, and each proposed a transfer tax on multimillion-dollar real estate sales, which would have produced, between 2019 and 2022, almost $384 million to build affordable housing.[6] Wu also proposed a rent stabilization ordinance, which has widespread support from Boston[7] and statewide,[8] as shown in polls. The proposal has been the victim of legislative inaction. Flynn, too, was hampered on rent control by a conservative city council. While he controlled the mayor's office, the growth machine controlled the city council. Now, too, it looks like they control the State House.

Wu had an early opening to get results. As a progressive mayor with a like-minded city council and overwhelming support from the people of Boston, enacting these proposals seemed within reach. As Wu acknowledged, "City Government has always been a place where we try and solve hard problems; this political moment is quite intense in a combination of so many different issues that are so urgent to our families."[9]

Wu and her administration, however, need to more effectively organize to get the overwhelmingly Democratic legislature to support her key initiatives. According to Joan Vennochi, writing in the *Boston Globe*,

> Michelle Wu's success or failure as mayor won't depend on members of the Boston business community—but on her ability to stick with what she believes in and build the coalitions necessary to turn her progressive promises into progressive policies. If there's a constant, the same old argument is that rent control and affordable housing requirements will stifle growth. It didn't then, and it won't now. To press that argument, Wu needs the same tools as Flynn. She needs continued support from the grass-roots activists who believed in her campaign for mayor. She needs allies in the business community who are willing to publicly dismiss the propaganda that progressive policies are bad for business. She also needs allies in the Legislature who will back her plan to reinstate rent control and reorganize the city's planning structure. Flynn thought like a community organizer. Every battle for a policy was a campaign.[10]

Together, these progressive initiatives could be a meaningful victory for the people of Boston, with campaign promises and long-sought dreams fulfilled for poor and working-class families and the city's children. By listening to and championing their voices while promoting meaningful engagement of Boston's community organizers, activists, and residents, the city's progressive leadership can learn from the past and know that a more just and equitable "city on a hill" is within reach. This book looks at how we might get there again.

# THE BATTLE FOR BOSTON

# Introduction: Can Cities Be Economically and Socially Progressive?

*None is as enigmatic a political figure as Ray Flynn of South Boston, a man described simultaneously as a conservative, a liberal, and a socialist, for whom the most accurate label may be "populist." (Maria Karagianis)[1]*

The history of big-city mayors in the twentieth century focuses on how they seek to promote their cities' economies and address problems like housing, racial conflict, income inequality, jobs, and essential public services. Mayors have different visions of what a "healthy economy" looks like. Some want the overall economy to grow, hoping its prosperity will trickle down to the needy and vulnerable. Some mayors pursue policies that enrich the growth machine's interests through policies and official actions. Other mayors seek to use the government to redistribute resources from the haves to the have-nots, relying on a solid economy to ensure success. Their path depends on their values, the electoral coalition that helped get them into office, and the relative influence of different interest groups in the political culture, including business, labor, community and civic organizations, and people of color. It also depends on the political skills of the mayor in forging coalitions that can influence other politicians in the city, county, state, and national governments.

Local officials do not have complete control over the shape of the economy. Global and national forces influence where and what kind of private investment occurs. Similarly, mayors must deal with the formal government structure and the informal networks of businesses that often operate outside the established system. Business lobby groups can give campaign contributions or wield other kinds of direct influence. Still, they can also urge private companies to withhold investment if they think politicians are being unduly harsh when holding businesses accountable for practices that may endanger workers, consumers, community residents, and the environment. So politicians often walk a tightrope when it comes to challenging the priorities and prerogatives of businesses. They can be successful or be held hostage by efforts to promote their cities' economies and respond to many economic structural issues such as housing, income inequality, and jobs.

This book primarily focuses on three mayoral regimes. Kevin White's sixteen years in office (1968–1984), Ray Flynn's nine and one-half years (1984–1993), and Tom Menino's twenty-year mayoralty (1993–2014) helped refashion the city during this period through their unique brands of governance. Each approached the challenges of urban management in diverse ways. I hope readers will better understand the dynamics that led to those differences and the consequences for Boston and its residents.

Boston's Ray Flynn was fortunate because he came to the mayor's office in 1984 when the city's economy was growing. The prosperity was not benefiting most residents, particularly people with low incomes, renters, service-sector workers, Blacks and Latinos, and working-class Whites. This story is about how the Flynn administration challenged the growth machine they inherited from White to channel the city's prosperity toward more significant equity, and the book provides some brief highlights of how the subsequent three mayors—Menino, Marty Walsh (2013–2021), and Michelle Wu (2021–present)—dealt with these issues. The book provides a historical roadmap that can help inform current and future city leaders.

A successful mayor promotes economic development and works hard to keep the city's economy and tax base growing. When promoting and deciding on economic development projects and growth, questions often arise about where in the city this will happen and who will benefit most from these initiatives. For a city's economy to work, businesses and residents must actively participate in civic life and continuously work together to promote racial and economic progress.

Economic progress in a city provides the underpinnings for social peace. However, social problems can prevent economic progress. That is why most books about big-city mayors talk about economic development as if its principal beneficiaries are businesspeople and well-to-do institutions, residents, and visitors. It's good for elites but not so much for the little guy. They speak this way because dealing effectively with social and cultural issues is much more complicated than building an expressway.

I argue that Flynn reversed the economic development and social equation. He succeeded in promoting Boston's economy by working overtime and very publicly to bring the city's different populations together in ways previous mayors either failed at doing or did not care to try. Flynn indeed

CITIES: ECONOMICALLY AND SOCIALLY PROGRESSIVE? / 3

failed sometimes—and the economic justice policies on Flynn's agenda weren't always successful. But the social piece was critical to Flynn. The social part of Flynn's agenda drove the economic development piece, not vice versa. That made Flynn special, so we must read about him and the mayors who preceded and followed him.

## Research Questions

The central question addressed in this book is whether and how cities can be progressive in adopting policies that redistribute wealth, income, and power and significantly reduce the harsh suffering of many urban residents by confronting the growth machine and its allies. The growth machine is defined in this book as the alliance of development, real estate, and banking interests in the city—those who make money from land and buildings.[2] The question reflects three overarching issues the city faced during this period: *economic challenges*, including affordable housing, income inequality, and access to jobs; *governance challenges*, which focus on mayoral leadership in public education, fiscal management, and urban infrastructure; and *cultural issues*, from immigration and the assimilation of newcomers to racial discrimination, animosity, and conflict.

The book describes through the voices of those on all sides of each issue how politics and the public policies and governance decisions responded to racial conflict, inequality and uneven economic development, and wholesale structural changes in the city's economic base during the late twentieth century. Boston was in turmoil politically and racially at the end of Kevin White's sixteen-year administration, with political contests centered on the city's growing poverty, inequality, and racial unrest.

The 1983 mayoral election, which brought Flynn into office, was what political scientists call a "critical election," defined as "profound readjustments in the relations of power within the community."[3] It transformed the city's electoral dynamics.

For the first time in the city's history, an African American was in the final runoff, and the two finalists repudiated the growth machine coalition and the racial politics of the past. Flynn's election, the book argues, began the progressive transformation of economic policies in Boston to heal racial divisions. After he resigned in 1993 to become President Bill Clinton's ambassador to the Vatican, Tom Menino, the city council president—who became mayor when Flynn left and was elected four times— left many redistributive policies Flynn enacted intact. However, Menino gradually returned to the growth machine economic development model, fueling significant class and income inequality in Boston.

The policies of each mayor and the activities of the city's religious, cultural, business, and neighborhood organizations changed Boston in significant ways, leaving it more culturally tolerant and racially diverse but in some ways just as economically unequal and perhaps more unequal than at any time since the end of the nineteenth century. The lessons embedded in the story of politics and public life in Boston at the end of the twentieth century are their legacy and a guide that other public leaders would be wise not to ignore.

## What This Book Is About, and What Future City Leaders Can Learn

When Ray Flynn ran for mayor in 1983, the familiar hypothesis was that you can't fight city hall. For many, it seemed like the city government for decades ignored the neighborhoods and the struggles of poor and working-class families. Dozens of organizations emerged to fight for tenant rights and racial, educational, and economic equality and against airport and highway expansion into the neighborhoods. While they each achieved some measure of success, it was as if they were *always* fighting city hall. But what if you populated city hall with progressive activists, community organizers, poor people, and people of color and tackled significant issues—inequality, racism, and control of the city's economy by the downtown power brokers? Now you *are* city hall—but how do you govern? That was the challenge and opportunity Flynn brought to city hall in 1984. The chapters that follow recount a number of those struggles.

This book also seeks to uncover the critical elements in building and sustaining a progressive city. When Tom Menino was elected mayor in 1994, was the progressive era something of the past? With Marty Walsh's election in 2013 and Michelle Wu's in 2021, could they continue to build on successful progressive initiatives? Is Boston better off economically, socially, racially, and democratically today, or does a new generation of activists need to fight city hall or become city government again? The book argues that each succeeding mayor built upon a legacy established by Boston's fifty-second mayor, Ray Flynn, and continued significantly by Mayor Marty Walsh and Mayor Michelle Wu. Wu's election was a new chapter in Boston politics. Before this moment, all of Boston's mayors elected were White men—mostly Irish (except Tom Menino, Boston's longest-serving Italian mayor). For the first time, a woman and person of color (Wu has a Taiwanese background) was elected mayor of Boston as a strong progressive. Boston was changing, and many people living in the city at the time of Wu's election weren't in Boston during busing, which was a significant period of racial conflict. The city has changed, and new leaders need to answer the question as to how and why—what is good about the changes and what still needs to be fixed, not only by city hall but by residents, businesses, and civic, religious, and neighborhood organizations.

This book challenges critics who contend that cities operate globally and that there is little or nothing a mayor can (or should) do to try and redistribute the benefits of growth. They argue that cities are handicapped in their ability to be progressive because of the power of big business in urban politics and the fiscal limits of cities to raise revenue and spend it on providing essential services and creating more economic justice. As you will learn, leaders in cities across America have shown that they can adopt policies, even without sufficient federal government support, to improve city residents' lives and incomes, build affordable housing, create jobs, and address inequality and racial conflict. How urban policies can and did, in considerable measure, respond to poverty, unemployment, racial conflict, and the shortage of affordable housing is presented in the following chapters, along with considerations of Boston's structural, governance, and social and cultural forces.

While much of the research for this book is based upon interviews and research for my doctoral dissertation, it is being written in the context of a divided nation and the most severe income and wealth inequality in the nation's history. Policies and the personal practices of former president Donald J. Trump and his administration since his election in 2016 further exacerbated inequality and inflamed racial conflict, to name just two of the more severe problems his elevation to the presidency had caused.

Trump abandoned the "blue cities" and was downright hostile to urban America and their leaders. He joined those who portray cities as unsafe and evoke the "savage other" to characterize urban populations. He tweeted numerous times to denigrate cities and their leaders. "Our streets are riddled with needles and soaked with the blood of innocent victims," he said. "Many of our once-great cities, from New York to Chicago to LA, where the middle class used to flock to live the American dream, are now literal war zones. Every day there are stabbings, rapes, murders, and violent assaults of every kind imaginable."[4] In one tweet, he attacked Speaker Nancy Pelosi: "Speaking of failing badly, has anyone seen what is happening to Nancy Pelosi's district in San Francisco? It is not even recognizable lately. Something must be done before it is too late." In another tweet, he said, "Nancy Pelosi's district in California has rapidly become one of the worst anywhere in the US regarding the homeless and crime. It has gotten so bad, so fast, she has lost total control and, along with her equally incompetent governor, Gavin Newsom, it is a very sad sight! We can't have our cities going to hell."[5] He didn't stop with his nemesis Pelosi and called Congressman Elijah Cummings's Baltimore district "a disgusting, rat and rodent-infested mess. If he spent more time in Baltimore, maybe he could help clean up this very dangerous and filthy place."[6] Politics played no small part in Trump's condemnation of cities. Although he hails from New York, in the 2020 presidential election, he lost New York City by a margin of four to one and lost San Francisco 86 percent to 12 percent. What he missed—intentionally, no doubt—is that members of Congress do not run cities; mayors and other local elected officials do.

Trump even went on in his quest for the 2024 presidency to propose building ten brand-new "freedom cities" on federal land with flying cars to "create a new American future."[7] While as president, he neglected America's cities, and in the 2020 election, he attacked Vice President Joe Biden, tweeting, "Why would Suburban Women vote for Biden and the Democrats when Democrat-run cities are now rampant with crime (and they aren't asking the federal government for help) which could easily spread to the suburbs, and they will reconstitute, on steroids, their low-income suburbs plan!"[8] However, Trump's ill-conceived proposals were not how to solve the urban crisis. Over the past several years, levels of investment—including funding for infrastructure, health care, and climate—have dramatically increased, mainly through the American Rescue Plan, from which funds went directly to the city governments. President Joe Biden noted, speaking to the National League of Cities' municipal leaders, "We're so successful because the Rescue Plan went directly through the cities and towns without having to pass 'Go,' without having to go to the statehouses."[9] The results were millions of new jobs and unemployment at its lowest level in decades. Major infrastructure and health-care investments touched every corner of the country—and every city.

The campaign by the Republican candidates in the 2024 presidential election showed the challenges ahead. "The rural-urban divide is one of the defining features of the American electorate: Democrats dominate in cities, while Republicans rule in rural areas. But we've gotten used to Republicans describing our cities as repulsive and frightening for so long that it no longer strikes us as unusual. When Trump says that in America's cities, 'You can't walk across the street to get a loaf of bread. You get shot. You get mugged. You get raped,' it's easy to dismiss the ham-handed hyperbole, but we know that millions of Americans believe it. That's because conservative media's efforts to regularly portray cities as chaotic and more dangerous amplify a long antiurban tradition in America that dates back to the nation's founding. You don't have to be steeped in scholarship on race to grasp the racial subtext to the GOP attack on urban America and the people who live there."[10]

Now, with the 2024 national elections in the rearview mirror, the result will likely significantly impact Washington's investment in cities. All major urban centers voted overwhelmingly for democratic Vice President Kamala Harris, albeit Trump made small gains from 2020. Pro-urban policies will again be out of favor in a new Trump administration, as they were in his previous one. Many democratic cities are well-positioned, however, as drivers of their regional economies to employ strategies to address inequality and poverty, improve public education, and respond to the housing crisis. Boston, too, has a long history of standing up for its immigrant neighbors, and if Trump's anti-immigrant rhetoric is to be believed, it will be needed again. The future direction of progressive politics and policies of cities can be informed by successful strategies employed in Boston and elsewhere over the last several decades. City dwellers are counting on it.

## Role of the Author

On January 3, 1984, I walked from the Park Street subway station toward Boston City Hall. Heading down Washington Mall, I paused to view the sun's reflection off the building where I would soon be working. While I was not thinking about it then, I had stopped near the spot where Ted Landsmark, a Black man, was attacked by a White man using a flagpole bearing the American flag as a spear only eight years earlier, on April 5, 1976, during a protest over school desegregation in Boston. The school desegregation program, which had produced so much anger and violence, was still on many people's minds. This chapter in Boston's history was not closed.

I worked at the West Broadway Housing Development (D Street) in South Boston the previous day, where I led the community organizing and multiservice center programs. As part of the Tenants United for Public Housing, a citywide tenants' group I had cofounded, we had organized a citywide public housing inaugural celebration for the newly elected mayor of Boston, held January 2, 1984, at the Condon Community School on D Street. Following his swearing-in at the Wang Center in downtown Boston earlier that morning, Flynn traveled to meet with public housing tenants, telling them, "The name is still Ray, and I'm still going to come down to D Street to play basketball." At the same time, he, his wife, Cathy, and their children watched local youth perform a play called "The D Street Troll."[11]

The issue of race played out on the new administration's first day. Although the public housing tenant celebration included a racially and ethnically diverse group of tenants from across the city, its being held in the predominantly White South Boston neighborhood caused a change in the new mayor's schedule.

Accompanied by Mel King, the African American mayoral candidate he defeated in the mayoral election, Flynn traveled to the Franklin Hill housing development in Dorchester at the urging of King, where tenants handed him petitions with over a hundred complaints about sanitary code violations. King commented, "People don't want to be used as a symbol if Flynn's commitment is not real."[12]

I had known King, having worked on his campaigns for state representative while a housing organizer at the D Street housing project and living in the Fenway neighborhood of Boston. I probably knew King better than Flynn. We had discussed public housing integration on more than one occasion. He had told me his plan for integrating the projects was to move half the White residents to the minority developments and half the minority residents to the White developments, like busing. Mel might have been serious, but I wasn't sure that was the best way.

At the end of Inauguration Day, January 2, 1984, the new administration offered me a job in the Mayor's Office of Neighborhood Services. Never having sought or conceived of a position in government, I asked Tom "Alex" Bledsoe, Flynn's campaign field coordinator and the future head of the new office, how long I would have to think it over and decide. Alex responded, "Well, you will start tomorrow morning." I had been at D Street for years. I loved being a community organizer and leader of the project's multiservice center, where the tenants had made considerable progress in improving the housing conditions at the development and strengthening the social capital networks of the residents. I also knew this was an opportunity to be part of a new team and a journey to make a difference in the city.

I walked into city hall that first day of my new job, not knowing what to expect. I joined a hastily called staff meeting led by the new mayor to demonstrate to the public that the new administration was on the job running city hall. As Lucy Ferullo, an East Boston community activist who would join the administration representing the mayor in East Boston, the North End, and Charlestown, said to me on the first day, "I'm not sure if I want to be on the outside throwing stones at him or be on the inside trying to make the change." Like me and many other progressives and neighborhood activists in Boston's neighborhoods, we went to work and participated in the governance of Boston for the next decade.

I had come to know Flynn while working in public housing in South Boston. I was not initially involved in Flynn's campaign. However, I was present when he announced his candidacy for mayor at the housing development because I was then serving as the director of community organizing at the housing project's multiservice center. I met Flynn on several occasions, including when he ran the Boston Marathon in 1982; he jogged to the top of Mission Hill to view a documentary film I was producing on public housing. The film *Down the Project: The Crisis of Public Housing*, directed by Richard Broadman,[13] was about race and housing policy and chronicled the demise of the D Street and Columbia Point housing projects. On the ride home (he could barely walk down the three flights of stairs, having frozen up after his marathon run), Flynn asked me my thoughts on the issues facing the city's neighborhoods and about my work in public housing. He told me he planned on running for mayor and hoped I would support him. He struck me then as a person who cared about the poor and the oppressed, and that impression would propel me to get involved in his campaign later that year as the coordinator of the Mission Hill neighborhood where I lived. As the neighborhood campaign coordinator, I was responsible for bringing together the neighborhood's diverse population to support Flynn's candidacy. Mission Hill was populated by long-term Irish residents and a large population of Latinos and African Americans, some of whom lived in the neighborhood's two public housing developments. The Irish–Puerto Rican–African American neighborhood coalition did the campaign work of door knocking, candidate events, and poll work that helped propel Flynn into the final election in November 1983. Flynn lost Mission Hill to King, 71 percent to 29 percent in the preliminary election, and 56 percent to 44 percent in the final, improving his showing considerably. We engaged a broad cross-section of the community in the effort.

"The Gillis and Flynn relationship goes back many years to when Flynn was a city councilor, and Gillis worked with public housing tenants. As Flynn describes him, Gillis is a 'link' between the thousands of voices in the neighborhoods and the mayor," Jim Gomez from the *Boston Globe* wrote about their connection.[14]

During his nearly ten-year mayoralty, I served in several positions, first in the mayor's office and later as economic development director. During this time, I participated and saw firsthand much of what is described in the book.

## Chapter Outline and Organization of the Book

*The following chapters aim to weave Boston's story in the late twentieth and early twenty-first century in three areas of inquiry: mayoral leadership and community power, inequality and economic development and distribution, and racial conflict and public-school governance. It utilizes newspapers as "civic diaries" and the participants' stories. My voice echoes through those who told their stories to me or others.* (Don Gillis, author)

In the introduction (this section), I describe how I came to this project as the progression of a journey over my life and outline the sociological research questions I seek to answer. I explain what this book is about and why it is important, as well as my role as researcher, community organizer, and author, and provide a chapter outline.

In the first chapter, I answer the question "Can mayors make a difference?" by broadly exploring a few of Boston's political contemporaries nationwide, highlighting several other cities' successful and unsuccessful strategies. Coupled with the Boston story, these cities challenged Paul Peterson's assertions that "city politics is limited politics," and mayors can't solve structural economic issues, reduce poverty, create jobs, implement redistributive strategies, increase civic participation, or effectively respond to immigration and racial conflict. [15] I explore the limits and possibilities of municipal government and the forces—including structural, economic, housing, and cultural—and conflicts central to urban America.

Chapter 2 provides a brief social, economic, and political history of Boston to set the stage. This history frames the period under study with a backdrop of the key milestones that led to structural economic, political, governance, and social changes. This history touches on the Brahmin versus Irish battles and the post–World War II era when the business community consolidated its power through the federal urban renewal program and urban redevelopment, creating the growth machine in the city. Changing demographics and the emergence of community opposition and organizing are highlighted.

Chapter 3 begins with the mayoralty of Kevin White and his evolution from a liberal reformer to a business-oriented, often-called-corrupt mayor. It also discusses the resentment that White caused because of his policies and arrogance. White set the stage for the fundamental realignment of the city following the 1983 race for mayor of Boston. Ray Flynn and Mel King are introduced along with the key actors in the mayoral contest and the dynamics of their respective campaigns, their political constituencies, and the significant issues they tackled. I explore the political environment that led to the 1983 election and the issues and forces that shaped it. What made the 1983 election historically significant was that it was the first repudiation of the business community since 1949, when the growth machine mayors took over. Finalists Flynn and King, the first African American to be a final candidate in the city's history, were united in embracing the need to promote social and economic justice for all Boston's residents and heal a city divided along racial lines.

Chapter 4 follows Flynn as mayor in 1984, moving into city hall with his "pockets of coalitions" that were the foundation of the governing coalition he put in place to transition to a progressive urban regime. Building the governing regime was challenging in representing all these interests. Whether you were a bricklayer or a social worker in the Flynn administration, you became a "community organizer." The chapter concludes with Flynn's governing coalition's approach to handling race and class issues.

Chapter 5 begins a series of case studies of Flynn's different governing and policy challenges. Fighting inequality, for decent and affordable housing, and against gentrification and displacement were some of the administration's first tasks. The 1950s', 1960s', and 1970s' policies were analyzed and disassembled in many cases. The chapter highlights the housing policy and affordability challenges, including rent and condominium controls and housing production, which were on Flynn's to-do list.

The case study in chapter 6 traces the redlining, blockbusting, and racial discrimination in lending practices that affected the city and its neighborhoods. The federal government's Home Owners Loan Corporation (HOLC), initiated in 1933, is partly responsible for implementing some of the discriminatory practices that continue today. These and other economic factors led to the scourge of arson for profit and the city's aggressive response.

Chapter 7's case study chronicles the transformation of significant development policies to "manage growth." Notable is the battle with the downtown power brokers over linkage, a tax on commercial development. The chapter describes and analyzes several innovative neighborhood initiatives, including the Dudley Street Neighborhood Initiative and the Parcel-to-Parcel linkage effort in Roxbury. Both were designed to foster neighborhood and minority empowerment and capital formation in the redevelopment of their communities and create a new "social contract." The role of community development corporations and neighborhood organizations in rebuilding Boston is explored. The development policies discussed were accompanied by strategies to put residents, people of color, and women to work both in the construction industry and the broader growing economy.

Chapter 8 focuses on the politics of race, a topic central to Boston's troubled past. The turbulence engendered by the 1974 federal court decision to implement school desegregation through busing and its aftermath and the racial climate in the city are investigated alongside the roles played by White, Flynn, and Menino. Supporters of Mel King's mayoral campaign in 1983 sought to frame the race issue as a contest between redistributive and transformative populism, whereby redistributive populism sought to unite the community based upon class solidarity and shared economic benefits and the transformative populism upon race and diversity through a consciousness-raising and empowerment strategy. The debate on this issue led to conflict between the various progressive activists.

Chapter 9 traces the response of the Flynn administration in fighting racial violence through the Community Disorders Unit of the Boston Police Department and the response to an upswing in gang activity with the controversial stop-and-frisk policy. The traumatic event, the so-called Stuart incident in 1989, which was framed as symbolic of a city where racial divisions are ingrained in the public consciousness, is discussed. Efforts to integrate the historically segregated public housing developments and the divisive succession campaign called "Mandela" are recounted.

The historic challenges the Boston Public Schools have confronted, from leadership to academic achievement, and a case study about the transition from an elected school committee to one appointed by the mayor in 1992 are chronicled in chapter 10. Those interviewed uniformly discussed the impact the 1974 court-ordered busing had on the city's social fabric and education system. The racial conflict that followed received national attention, and the iconic busing era Pulitzer Prize–winning photo by Stanley Forman of Ted Landsmark, speared with the American flag on City Hall Plaza, is imprinted in the memories of Bostonians of that era and is often referred to in noteworthy events of racial cleavage or change today. The governance transformation of the school committee sharpened the racial and political cleavage in the city. After the structural change was implemented, voters ratified it five years later. Most Black Bostonians (71 percent, according to poll data by Suffolk University in July 2013) would support a return to the elected committee today. The poll showed that 64 percent support a return to an elected school committee, with only 24 percent supporting the mayoral-appointed board.[16] These numbers were even higher from the results of a 2021 nonbinding referendum when 79 percent of voters supported returning to an elected school committee.[17]

City finances and rebuilding the city infrastructure are highlighted in chapter 11. Municipal finance is not generally the subject of sociologists or progressives but is essential to the running of a city and the ability to achieve a progressive agenda. It is a central factor that can catalyze the business community to lose confidence in the city and was an early test for Flynn. Efforts to respond to the environmental challenges he experienced when he entered office, including the Boston Harbor Cleanup, are discussed.

Chapter 12 deals with poverty and homelessness in Boston, summarizing important national and local policies and programs and the leadership response of Flynn and his administration to these challenges. Homelessness was an issue for Flynn and subsequent mayors, with data indicating that homelessness continues on the upswing. In the decade between 1992 and 2002, Boston's homeless count went from 4,414 to 6,210, a 30 percent increase, and continues to rise today.[18]

Chapter 13 presents the story of the 2013 transition from Mayor Thomas Menino to Mayor Marty Walsh, followed by Mayor Michelle Wu. The racial and political dynamics of these contests are explored. After two hundred years of forty-six White male mayors in Boston, would 2013 and 2021 be a time of change? How Flynn's approach affected what voters expected and what future mayors did, and how they differed from Flynn's approach, is explored.

The concluding chapter presents key findings and the lessons for progressives from the Flynn experience. I argue that the period under study was a transformative time in Boston's history. I revisit the three themes and the advantages and disadvantages of the four theoretical approaches used to make sense of those themes. Policies from 1984 have led Boston to where it is today. I explore lessons for cities pursuing progressive social and economic justice agendas. I also examine Boston's current economic, political, and social conditions. With Menino's mayoralty ending in January 2014 after twenty years and Walsh after seven years, what are the unaddressed needs and legacies they left behind? How has Wu begun to address these challenges, and what are the early results?

This book is a systematic, qualitative analysis of this period's governing regimes using a grounded theory approach to make the analysis directly from the data collected.[19] It explores what constitutes an urban "progressive" regime in a large and diverse urban metropolis. The analysis presented in the following chapters differs from more descriptive presentations about the history of Boston's political actors. It is a complex story that is both an oral history of the period and an analysis of challenges for the future.

The results of this study should help current and future political and civic leaders understand the impact of past, present, and future policies and how they can create opportunities to make Boston a city that includes all of its citizens through shared prosperity, participatory democracy, and racial harmony.

# 1 / City Limits and Opportunities

> *I have met with popes, presidents, and prime ministers, but the most important things I have done were for the people of Boston. My life has been about promoting racial, economic, and social justice.* (Mayor Ray Flynn interview)

Much has been written about cities, mayors, and urban governing structures since urban areas' emergence and prominent role in the late nineteenth century. The governing styles of mayors—from the ward boss who drew upon ethnic coalitions to govern the unwieldy city to law and order, liberal, progressive, conservative, and redistributive mayoral approaches have evolved across the American urban landscape. While each style may differ in some respects, mayors are still responsible for the details of city governance: police and fire departments, picking up the trash, and removing the snow. Mayors must attend to infrastructure, build and repair roads, maintain playgrounds and schools, and keep their city financially solvent. So, what approach do progressive or populist mayors take that may differentiate them from their more conservative or liberal counterparts? What are the potential and limitations of an urban governing regime? This is the battle waged between progressives and conservatives in many urban areas.

Progressivism in the United States arose in the late nineteenth century. It continued until the early twentieth century as a direct response to the urbanization and industrialization of the period characterized by massive immigration, population growth, and a growing divide in the country. Progressives sought greater democratic participation in the political process they believed was being corrupted by both major political parties. Major policy thrusts of the progressive movement included strengthening the national government; addressing growing income inequality and poverty; supporting unions and fair wage laws; using regulations to require businesses to take responsibility for the dangers their practices caused for workers, consumers, community residents, and public health; and increasing political rights for those historically left out of the mainstream social, economic, and political institutions. While the progressive movement was not necessarily unified in its goals and tactics, it was the response to the social and political ills associated with the problems of urban-industrial life. Progressivism was not a singular philosophy or political party but the framework for collective action in response to the day's politics.

In cities, progressivism took on unique qualities. For example, in Boston, it was seen as the response to the institutional structures of government and corporate life. "It would emerge as the central motif of politics in twentieth-century Boston, employed by immigrant spokespersons as readily as Yankee business leaders or middle-class settlement workers. Progressivism was a public language open to manipulation by those with access to the public sphere, including ethnic civic leaders and politicians."[1]

During the post–World War II period, progressive cities, broadly defined, were characterized by the grassroots response to urbanization policies. During the 1960s, 1970s, and 1980s, these policies included highway incursions into inner-city neighborhoods, urban renewal, and expansive downtown development. They faced challenges involving issues such as deteriorating race relations or outright racial conflict, immigration, the quality of public education, high housing prices, and lack of participation in municipal decision-making. With growing class and income inequality during this period, reminiscent of the early Progressive Era, neighborhood organizations and political activists sought to change the nature of economic relations in cities across America. Reforms centered on redistributive policies, from sharing the benefits of downtown development with the neighborhoods through linkage to produce more affordable housing and controlling the existing rental housing stock through rent control and limitations on condominium conversions. Greater participation in planning and decision-making over development and basic city service delivery were some of the various strategies the progressive urban reformers sought.

The cities referenced in this book each had different priorities and trajectories. Still, they were unified in seeking fundamental change and greater control of their city during the period under study in Boston. Some cities pursued local election strategies to put more progressives on the city council or, in some cases, the county commission. Most cities described focused on changes in the city's chief elected official—the mayor.

The theoretical and thematic frameworks highlight examples of progressive mayors who governed in the twentieth and twenty-first centuries and are here fundamentally the story of one city—Boston. Several mayors led Boston—Kevin H. White, for an unprecedented sixteen years from 1968 to 1984; Raymond L. Flynn, from 1984 to 1993; and Thomas M. Menino, who outdid White by remaining in office for over twenty years. I also offer observations of the policies of Marty Walsh, who resigned near the end of his second term in 2021 to become secretary of labor in the Biden administration, and the city's next mayor, Michelle Wu, who was elected in 2021.

The story starts with the transformation of American society from rural to urban. Many scholars thought that this evolution was the beginning of the national downfall. Economic change was believed to have led to the social ills of the nineteenth and twentieth centuries—slums, poverty, crime, and general social disorganization that was not seen in the nation's rural and agricultural past.

The United States continued the process of urbanization throughout the twentieth century. In 1900, cities held 40 percent of America's population, compared with 60 percent in rural areas. By 1950, the balance flipped, with cities having 60 percent of America's population, compared with 40 percent in rural areas. The urban-suburban/rural transformation continued, and by 1980, cities held 74 percent of America's population, compared with 26 percent in rural areas. The size and nature of employment changed dramatically during this period as well. In 1900, the US workforce was 24 million; in 1999, it had burgeoned to 139 million. At the beginning of the century, 38 percent of Americans were employed in agriculture, and by the end, only 3 percent. Similarly, those in goods-producing industries like manufacturing went from 38 percent of the workforce in 1900 to 19 percent by the end of the twentieth century. By far, the most significant increases in employment during the twentieth century were in the service and retail sectors, which helped fuel urban growth.

The 1950s and 1960s were the heyday of urban influence in national politics. Congress was dominated by city representatives, supplanting the influence of small towns and agricultural interests. However, cities' influence gradually waned as Americans lived increasingly in the suburbs. In 1992, for the first time in US history, suburbanites represented most voters in a presidential election.[2] A similar trend occurred in state legislatures, where suburban interests began to dominate urban areas. For example, the Boston delegation in the State House was reduced significantly between 1950 and 2000 due to suburban population shifts in Massachusetts. The story of cities is, out of necessity, the story of the political relationships and the leaders who forged their brand of coalitions to govern, from machine politics prevailing in the nineteenth century—and reemerging in many cities throughout the early twentieth century—to the progressive and liberal reformers who paved the way for a new breed of politics in the growing urban areas. Occasionally, out of the reformers emerged a transformative progressive populist or political leader who tapped into the ever-increasing urban unrest. Public education, long seen as the critical socializing ingredient in cities, rapidly expanded and, with its multiple constituencies and problems, became a central and contested institution within the study of progressivism.

The redistributive populist agenda of one leader, Flynn, is chronicled and analyzed in the context of the growth machine: the alliance of development, real estate, and banking interests in the city. Appendix 1 briefly describes similarities across the nation of this new governing approach, from large cities like San Francisco, Chicago, Baltimore, and Cleveland to smaller cities like Santa Cruz, California, and Burlington, Vermont.

While all cities are influenced by national events, politics, the economy, and social issues, many cities have emerged with governing structures that challenge conventional wisdom, particularly the notion that there is only one way—the growth machine model. Of course, all cities (and suburban and rural areas) look to promote a healthy economy, jobs, and a steady tax base. The benefits of the Industrial Revolution, technology, and innovation across America are uneven. Capitalism works in diverse ways in various places while benefiting from a national affinity for the economic imperative of growth. Wealth accumulation and income inequality are assumed to be rational traits of our national experience. However, their assumptions are sometimes challenged, resulting in experiences promoting greater equality. While the book primarily focuses on Boston from 1980 to 2000, it is helpful to look at other cities during this period and their experiences with the three significant frames under investigation: *economic challenges*, including affordable housing, income inequality, and access to jobs; *governance challenges*, which focus on mayoral leadership in public education, fiscal management, civic participation, and urban infrastructure; and *cultural issues* from immigration and the assimilation of newcomers to racial animosity and conflict.

## What Can Cities Do and What Can't They Do?

History shows that cities are, in many ways, tightly controlled by federal and state policies and institutions. In the case of Boston, the legislature historically has regulated the city government's use of tax and fiscal policies. Cities cannot, absent state authority, tax the income of residents or businesses. On the other hand, cities can raise revenue through property taxes and the differential assessments of commercial/industrial and residential property. As Massachusetts and other states around the country demonstrate, taxing powers can be limited by proposals to do just that. In Massachusetts, Proposition 2½, enacted in 1980, limited tax increases to 2.5 percent per year. In California, Proposition 13, passed in 1978, also provided a 2 percent annual increase cap on property tax from the base values established and was the first such effort in the United States, to be followed by varying tax-limiting laws in forty-six states, according to the Tax Foundation.[3]

## Theoretical and Thematic Frameworks

> Sociologically, research based upon the traditional definitions of an urban place has had very little relevance to the actual, day-to-day activities of those at the top of the local power structure. Those priorities set the limits within which decisions affecting land use, the public budget, and urban social life come to be made.[4]

The research discussed in the book falls into four major theoretical approaches to city governance: urban regime, growth machine, progressive city, and government communalism. Using the urban sociological dichotomy of urbanization and urbanism, three primary themes explain how Boston worked under the different mayoral administrations during the period under study.

Race's dominance in urban political theories can be seen in urban America. It is necessary to clarify race's relationship in each economic, governance, social, and cultural challenge that cities experience.

This study employs each of the theories below to analyze the data from the Boston experience. The concluding chapter explores how Boston fits within these theoretical frameworks. A more detailed discussion of each theory employed in the book's analysis is in Appendix 2.

## Urban Regime Theory

Urban regime theory is the view that city governance results from a coalition between public and private actors. In another approach to urban regime theory, Peter Dreier, John Mollenkopf, and Todd Swanstrom[5] distinguish the characteristics of progressive, liberal, and conservative regimes to show variations in urban regimes and their attention to issues of equity and justice. Scholars have differing views about the precise nature and structure of growth politics. Clarence Stone theorizes that urban regimes govern through collaboration of institutional leaders, government, business, labor, religious, and nonprofit institutions.[6]

## Growth Machine Theory

Growth machine theory emerged from the Chicago School of urban sociology and the social science field of community power studies. The main power studies frames were the power elite—the capitalist class was in total control of the economy and decision-making—and the pluralist model, where power was dispersed among competing governmental, business, and civic groups. Growth machine theory, formulated mainly by Harvey Molotch, is composed of the local power structure, led by real estate interests, or "place entrepreneurs," which joins with other corporate interests, banks, landlords, developers, government, and, to a lesser extent, organized labor (mainly in the construction unions) to promote the fundamental transformation of the city.[7]

## Progressive City Theory

Progressive city theory, developed by Pierre Clavel in the 1970s and 1980s, is an outgrowth of the civil rights and antiwar movements decades before. Urban political and community leaders were fostering the creation of a new type of social organization in many cities centered on redistributive and participatory reforms.[8]

## Government Communalism Theory

"Government communalism" is a term coined by Daniel Monti,[9] who uses it to describe one prominent way Americans "do community." Monti argues that the principles of government communalism are exclusivity, accountability, and tolerance. Only some persons are deemed worthy to be welcomed as citizens (exclusivity). Those allowed in are expected to treat others in public in a way that respects other citizens' needs (accountability). People who make it as citizens are treated more leniently than those who do not (tolerance).

## The Urban Sociological Framework

Through scholarly research, analysis, and examination of Boston, the evidence uncovered the city's different governance models through the eyes and experiences of those who participated in the period's governing regimes and civic life.

Urban sociology asks two central questions: First, urbanization, or how do cities and metropolitan areas develop? This question focuses primarily on demographic and economic factors but also includes creating large institutions to manage and make local populations more productive. Growth machine and progressive city theories fall under this category. Second, following Wirth's "Urbanism as a Way of Life" (1938),[10] urbanism analyzes how people live in urban places. The emphasis here is on the size and density of the urban population. This question focuses on various levels of group life, informal and formal, including large institutions, and how they enable people to adapt, primarily because of their heterogeneous character.[11] The urban regime and government communalism theories fall under this category. To understand Boston during the period under study, data about the city's urbanization (the housing, development, and city building policies) and urbanism (the way of life and changing nature of power, race, class, and ethnic relations) from Boston's key civic actors between 1980 and 2000 are explored.

The most prominent research in urban sociology involves studies of city problems, such as poverty, juvenile delinquency, racial conflict, gangs, and prostitution. These have shaped the foundations of our understanding of urban America in many ways.[12]

The field of urban sociology, which emerged in the late nineteenth century at the University of Chicago, reflected the period's antiurbanism, which originated from concerns about the social disorganization believed to be the byproduct of industrial capitalism in large cities.[13] The connections between urban sociology and social reform movements of the early twentieth century can be understood partly as a way to identify how cities evolve and to find solutions to avoid civil unrest (between Blacks and Whites) and class conflicts (between business and labor). Reformers viewed public education as the mechanism outside the family to assimilate immigrants, the poor, and others into the mainstream culture, which they hoped would be an antidote to the problems of poverty, cultural conflict, crime, and class antagonisms. Cities and their educational institutions were portrayed as the laboratories in which the sociological issues of class, inequality, culture, power, and stratification have been aired and addressed. How can we understand how decisions in Boston affected the city and established the economic, political, and cultural framework for twenty-first-century Boston? Was poverty reduced? Did economic development decision-making change to be more inclusive? Were race relations improved? These are the quantitative and qualitative measures explored.

An examination of the coalitions that formed within city hall and the governing regime and the private interests of business, community, religious, and nonprofit leaders in Boston sheds light on how the regime was built, who the key members were, and how they differ significantly from today. An understanding of what happened during this period and the insights learned are drawn from the data of interviews, the stories of the civic and political leaders, autoethnography, and archival and historical sociological analysis drawing upon the "urban diaries" of the period.[14]

## Thematic Analysis

The four theoretical frameworks described above help make sense of three areas of inquiry crucial to understanding how the city works and the different approaches each mayoral administration takes: mayoral leadership and community power, inequality and economic development and redistribution, and race relations and conflict, including public-school governance. Each framework is more helpful for one of these three problems. Mayoral leadership and community power were framed by urban regime theory; inequality and economic development and redistribution draw upon growth machine theory and theories about progressive city governments; immigration, race relations, and conflict, including public school governance, explore government communalism and regime theory as a theoretical guiding framework. Each thematic framework is summarized below and draws upon academic literature to help explain sociologically how Boston became today's city.

## Theme One: Mayoral Leadership and Community Power

The study of mayoral leadership and urban regime theories emerges from contests between the liberal and neoliberal urban frameworks. Liberal and neoliberal tenets include tolerance for diversity, maximization of individual liberties, an unfettered market that protects private property rights, and a minimization of the role of government.[15] Sociologists or even political scientists do not widely research mayoral leadership. Theories that speak directly to how we have come to view cities in terms of power and governance and the internal and external forces at work, including how the factors that shape urban policy are internal to the city, are contested by Paul Peterson in his well-known work *City Limits*, in which he states. "City politics is limited politics."[16]

Community power literature shaped the discourse on city politics, including the conflict between political machines and reform movements, comparative urban policy, and federalism. The debate on community power can help shape Boston's exploration of this question.

Community power can be understood in three broad areas: the "power elite," comprising business and political leaders and, to some lesser extent, certain organized labor groups;[17] "pluralists," who see competition between these groups for power;[18] and a third group that sees political power as diffuse, with an "invisible elite" that keeps issues off local agendas.[19] The exercise of community power is a contested field of study, including Clarence Stone's and Dreier, Mollenkopf, and Swanstrom's framework of urban regime theory.[20]

The machine-reform conflict is often described as a class-based conflict "between the 'ethos' of the machine, which represents working-class immigrants, and the 'ethos' of the reformers, who represent upper-class, silk-stockinged, Anglo-Saxon businessmen and professionals."[21] The reformers of both cities and schools sought to run the city like an efficient business, with a corporate board of directors, and where cities and schools would serve the interests of the business elites.[22] The comparative urban policy approach seeks to understand city politics in terms of political variables often hampered by wide variations in urban governance structures from city to city. The federalism theory of urban politics suggests that intergovernmental relationships are complex and often have contested roles and responsibilities.

In his study of Atlanta, based on the regime theory framework he formulated, Stone posits that governing capacity is created and maintained through coalitions of government actors and economic and business leaders. He takes a political economy approach, drawing from Peterson: "Exploring the middle ground between, on the one side, pluralists with their assumption that the economy is just one of several discrete spheres of activity and, on the other side, structuralists who see the mode of production as pervading and dominating all other spheres of activity, including politics."[23]

Stone's regime theory thesis suggests an alternative social production model of power ("power to" rather than "power over"), in which the government is one of many actors and not the critical broker in urban decision-making. In regime theory, public policies are shaped and implemented by coalitions that include the government and political actors, but in which the government is not the only or the most influential of the coalition partners. Stone categorizes four ideal types of urban regimes: *maintenance regimes*, which support the status quo and focus on the delivery of basic services; *development regimes*, similar to the growth machine model, which use public action to promote private investment;

*middle-class progressive regimes*, which seek to negotiate community benefits as part of the development process; and *lower-class opportunity regimes*, which pursue a redistributive agenda to alter the actions of the private sector without stifling investment. The redistributive agenda has been the central strategy of progressive regimes.[24]

Dreier, Mollenkopf, and Swanstrom, drawing from Stone and others, classify urban regime ideal types as liberal, progressive, and conservative—which may more accurately reflect the basic operational tenets of how regimes are ideologically constituted in cities. In his case study of Cleveland under the mayoralty of Dennis Kucinich from 1977 to 1979, Swanstrom seeks to uncover the political side of growth politics in that city.[25] Richard Gendron and G. William Domhoff conduct a similar analysis of Santa Cruz, arguing that the fundamental conflict is between exchange values, promoted by the growth machine, and use values, promoted by advocates comprising neighborhood groups, community leaders, and environmentalists. They suggest that maintaining the progressive city coalition is challenging and often complex because most social movement activists focus on class-based and social justice issues. In contrast, neighborhood and environmental activists have a primary, if not sole, concern with land use values.[26]

Richard DeLeon studied San Francisco in 1992, during the same period under study in Boston. He argues that opposition to the growth machine led to an antiregime approach: "Proposed development projects were blocked at every turn by angry progressives who stadiums or hotels would not crowd out." He suggests that then-mayor Agnos "learned too late that democratic process and citizen empowerment were integral to the progressive agenda."[27] Interestingly, Mayor Flynn attended the board of supervisors meeting when San Francisco approved the controversial Downtown Plan in 1985 to pick up pointers for Boston's linkage and growth management approach, which locally had its genesis in Boston by Massachusetts Fair Share. DeLeon observed a different strategy. "Although Boston modeled its comprehensive linked development policies on San Francisco's earlier pioneering efforts, growth-control measures such as San Francisco's Downtown Plan, which many thought would stop development, continue to be perceived by Bostonians as politically dangerous and economically unnecessary," he said.[28] John Connolly, Flynn's development adviser, was obsessed with not having San Francisco's moratorium on downtown development occur in Boston. "We are trying to derive benefits from downtown to spend in the neighborhood and make downtown development pedestrian-scaled," according to Bart Mitchell, his assistant.

These theories and approaches are central to the insights, understandings, and analyses that follow for Boston. While these studies have made significant theoretical and analytic contributions to the urban regime, growth machine, government communalism, and progressive city theories, Boston must be examined as unique. Boston's historical, economic, cultural, and political development and the governing coalitions between 1980 and 2000 followed a different trajectory. They achieved results different from those of San Francisco, Santa Cruz, Cleveland, and Atlanta.

What is true, however, is that after two decades of struggle to balance the interests of business and neighborhood residents, particularly low-income and working-class citizens, each city mentioned now confronts widening income inequality with its resulting conflicts and social problems.

## Theme Two: Inequality and Economic Development

This book chronicles Boston's redistributive development policies, the questions of participation (whose voices were heard) and redistribution (who benefited), and the conflicts or the concession between the growth machine and the city government. Growth machine theory frames much of this analysis in Boston. For Peterson, cities compete for development with pro-development policies "to the advantage of the city as a whole because the benefits of the policy are widely distributed."[29] He maintains that redistributive policies negatively impact the city with pernicious economic consequences. Sociologist Dan Monti, too, believes that everyone profits overall from economic development, and "even when business leaders' interests are confined largely to matters of rebuilding cities, some corporate and business leaders can do a better job of spreading the wealth around than most persons expect."[30] While a handful of business leaders may ascribe to redistribution as a moral code or believe it is necessary to maintain the business's legitimacy as a player, most business leaders resist higher taxes and fees and stronger regulations, which are the crux of "redistribution" policies.

It is debatable whether the benefits from urban economic development are widely distributed to the needy and vulnerable.[31] John Logan and Harvey Molotch suggest that the government, the most influential of the coalition partners, affects urban fortunes, and therefore, developers are "structural speculators who must influence government decisions if they are to maximize returns from their holdings and also make campaign contributions (or bribes) to public officials."[32] In many cities, businesses are much more potent than municipal elected officials, partly because state "pre-emption" laws weaken the authority of cities to adopt redistributionist policies, like property and business taxes, rent control, and minimum wages.

The growth machine model extends beyond who governs to explore "For what?" and "For whom?" Logan and Molotch argue that "elites use their growth consensus to eliminate any alternative vision of the purpose of local government or the meaning of community."[33] They "construct a sociology of cities based on a sociology of urban property relations," in which places are commodities for which the goal is achieving the maximum economic value.[34] While Peterson, Stone, Clavel, Logan, Molotch, Gendron, Domhoff, and Dreier provide insights on the development or growth imperative, each approaches the political economy of place differently.[35]

Progressive urban regimes can implement redistributive policies that manage growth and exact concessions from the corporate and real estate development communities.[36] An example in Boston is "linkage," a tax on large-scale commercial development through which over $58 million was collected to build 6,000 units between 1984 and 2000. Of these, 4,812 (80 percent) were affordable for low- to moderate-income residents of Boston's neighborhoods.[37]

According to Peterson, city officials risk undermining cities' economic base when they adopt redistributionist policies. He argues that "city politics is limited politics," owing more to federalism and the global economy than local influence. In contrast, Clavel and Dreier say that cities have and can implement successful redistributive policies.[38]

Boston's downtown and neighborhoods look like they do today because of the "political choices on the physical city."[39] Evidence refutes Peterson's argument regarding experiences in several cities while being cognizant that progressive policies and redistributive efforts may come and go with changing regimes. As a result, where cities are on a path to reducing poverty and increasing opportunity, new leadership can quickly derail such policy objectives explicitly or implicitly. We will explore those choices, in part, for Boston.

## Theme Three: Racial Conflict, Segregation, Public Schools, and Policing

Government communalism is a theoretical framework that analyzes how the government can help build community and be more inclusive of those individuals left out of the mainstream civic culture. Politicians use the government to make rules that favor the rights of individuals not otherwise protected from harm.[40] How Boston's civic culture was shaped by its political, business, religious, and community leaders is essential to the city's history and impacts how its citizens get along today.[41] As Lyn Lofland observed, "In the obviously anonymous and impersonal world of the city, someone had located not only social life but a socially important life."[42]

The 1970s was a turbulent period for race relations in Boston. It was ignited by June 21, 1974, when the federal court issued a desegregation order for schools and the subsequent busing of students between Boston's Black neighborhood, Roxbury, and White neighborhood, South Boston. After this, Boston's racial climate was volatile. The US Department of Justice's Community Relations Service regional director, Martin Walsh, managed the DOJ's role in the Boston busing case. He identified Boston's school desegregation ordeal as "an exorcism, following which the resolution of other stubborn civil rights problems became possible."[43]

School desegregation was not the only arena of racial conflict in Boston. Residential blockbusting and racial discrimination in housing had been occurring throughout the city, exacerbated by bank policies and the federal housing, transportation, and urban policies of the 1950s and 1960s.[44] The iconic image of the time was captured by *Boston Herald* photographer Stanley Forman in his 1976 Pulitzer Prize–winning photograph of a Black man attacked with an American flag on City Hall Plaza. "The Soiling of Old Glory" would define Boston in the eyes of the world.[45]

## Boston's and Other Cities' Emergence in the Late Twentieth Century

In looking at other cities during the later twentieth and early twenty-first centuries, there are many parallels to the Boston experience. Reform mayors led large cities as diverse as San Francisco, Chicago, Baltimore, Philadelphia, and Cleveland and small cities such as Santa Cruz, California, and Burlington, Vermont.[46] (See Appendix 1 for more details on each city.)

The literature on growth machines focuses on the primary goal of expanding the overall economy. The real estate, business, construction unions, and newspapers coalition wants more jobs, people, wealth, and profits. The coalition is less interested in the distribution of economic prosperity—the quality and wages of jobs, housing affordability, public schools' success, and the environment's health. Only when these latter issues pose problems for business success do elements of the growth machine seek to join forces to address them. This book examines how regime and growth machine theories align with the experiences of critical actors in Boston. Exploring political, community, and governmental actions and decisions during the study period will help better explain why Boston's physical and socioeconomic profile is where it was at the end of 2024.

## Methodology of the Book

This book was written more than three decades after most of the events described. I accessed documents from that period, among them reports and memos I authored or could access only because I worked on the mayor's staff. I have contacts from those years and people on the scrimmage line and sidelines during the controversies described herein. (Some liked what Flynn was doing; others mostly did not.) I also have recollections of meetings and events that some of these people attended or had a hand in shaping.

I wrote much of this book for a PhD in sociology and later did additional research and interviews. I collected stories through interviews, retrospective participant observation, and autoethnographic techniques. Either I was there, or the people who have shared their recollections with me were there. Archival research was also involved: memos, reports, and news accounts. Some of the data included here is from official sources. Other data reflect my and others' impressions, recollections, and assessments of what happened and what it meant then and means now.

As noted earlier, I approach this book as having been a part of the Boston city administration from 1984 until 1994. I portray the public perceptions and the concrete realities of the impact of the Flynn administration and the other governing regimes of the period under study on selected areas of city life in Boston. While disposed to believe that there were positive accomplishments during the period that I worked for city government, I sought to discover and incorporate alternative views about the success or failure of Boston's governing coalitions to make a significant impact on the following areas of city life: racial discrimination and conflict, immigration, poverty, education, and economic inequality. How did each governing regime in Boston respond to and shape race and ethnic relations, inequality, economic development policy, and public education governance? There was a time when mayors made a difference, and I sought to find out how.

I uncovered many of the municipal government's successes and failures in promoting social and economic justice, reducing poverty, improving public education, reducing racial conflict, and increasing economic opportunities for city residents. Focusing on these issues, a sociological analysis identifies policies that led to transformative moments in Boston's history. The book draws upon extensive previous scholarship, interviews, and firsthand experiences.

Key interviewees included former and current city policymakers and business, religious, and neighborhood leaders through purposeful sampling methodology. All the people quoted here either allowed the use of their names or are quoted from already published accounts such as news stories. None of the more than seventy people interviewed refused to be identified. Several people were interviewed more than once and, in some cases, multiple times. I traveled to San Francisco, Washington, DC, South Carolina, Cape Cod, and other sites. I conducted interviews in people's homes, offices, coffee shops, bars, and, in one case, an airport. I included the mayors who had been in office since 1984. I also interviewed several candidates for the mayor's office in 1983, including civil rights icon and state legislator Mel King.

The central focus of the late twentieth century into the twenty-first century is described and analyzed using information gathered through all these means and sources. I use primary and secondary sources, including census and newspaper accounts from the archives of the *Boston Globe, Boston Herald, New York Times,* and community newspapers. I chose subjects that could shed light on the following questions: What did city political and civic leaders do during this period to respond to racial conflict, economic development, poverty, and public school governance? How have important areas of urban life—the economy, public education, immigration, race, and politics—changed how urban dwellers view themselves and others? How did newcomers assert themselves during this period of transformation? What were the significant points of animosity during this period? How were these transformations managed, and how did the public respond? In addition, I examine these additional questions: How could Ray Flynn and Mel King defeat the growth of machine banking, real estate, and business interests to become the two finalists in the 1983 election for mayor of Boston? What was the nature of the progressive, conservative, and union coalition that led to the election of Flynn? How did his administration retain political power over three election cycles, and was there an accommodation with the business community? What were the divisions within and between city hall and the progressives who formed the foundation of Mel King's Rainbow Coalition? How was the governing regime organized and managed? Through general interview questions regarding the period under study, I undertook a "guided conversation" rather than a static set of questions.[47] I asked each interview subject about their experiences and recollections during the mayoral regimes concerning race relations and conflict, economic development, banking and housing policies, and public-school governance.

I sought to develop a holistic perspective to understand the experiences and explicit actions of critical actors in Boston, what happened, and why. With each interview subject, I explored questions about specific issues during the period under study, the interviewee's actions, their experiences, and the outcome of the matter. I researched how decisions were discussed privately and publicly and played out in the community, the media, and the government.

While the interview subjects were offered complete confidentiality, all were willing to comment on the record. However, given that this study is primarily an oral history and sociological retrospective, with much of the data available in the public record, I have been mindful of and sensitive to the issues of personal harm when a policy or action may now seem misguided. I knew interview subjects might wish to prevaricate to protect their legacy or conceal errors in judgment or action.

The retrospective autoethnography I employed "constitutes an autobiographical sociology, whereby the sociologist probes one or more past personal experiences to identify and analyze something sociologically relevant."[48] The retrospective autoethnography methodology is alternatively called retrospective participant observation or autobiographical sociology, among other lexicons, in an emergent method of qualitative inquiry.[49] This alternative research approach of ethnographic interviewing and archival data is designed to provide "a different angle of vision on sociologically relevant topics."[50] Friedman's autobiographical sociology framework suggests three broad questions that I considered: "What happened to me, and why did it happen? In what ways was my experience like and different from others involved? What is the larger sociological significance of the experience?"[51] While I was not actively taking field notes during the period under study, I reviewed files and archival materials that placed me as a participant in many of the conversations and controversies.

Through archival research, I reviewed city documents, correspondence, and memos to and from city officials, census data, and newspaper and other media reports to develop a grounded theory approach to deepen my understanding of events and actions by key leaders and citizens during the period of this study. White's (1968–1994) administration's records were donated to the Boston Public Library and later transferred to the City of Boston Archives once they went into operation; Flynn (1984–1993) deposited all his papers and records in the City Archives; and the majority of the records of Menino (1994–2014) are in the City

Archives also, with some in possession of Boston University where he took a post to head up the Initiative on Cities following his retirement after twenty years as mayor. Other records were obtained through city departments and newspaper accounts.

Interviews for this qualitative study were recorded, transcribed, and analyzed to uncover themes in the approaches, issues, how officials made decisions, and the results of those decisions. The interviews were triangulated with archival data and interviews with several key informants to test reliability and attempt to deal with the problems of retrospective data accuracy.[52] Specific themes emerged regarding race relations and conflict and economic development policies pursued by each administration on the topics under study. I had expected the administrations of Flynn and Menino to be similar in many respects regarding these domains and differ significantly from the White era. However, the interview and archival data revealed significant differences between Flynn and Menino and similarities between White and Menino. Later research also compares both Walsh and Wu to Flynn.

## Significance of Research

*Sociological literature has offered a truncated historical perspective.*[53]

This book's inquiry into mayoral leadership and the policies and actions of Boston's governing regimes to respond to inequality and racial and ethnic conflict, including issues of public education governance, have not been extensively studied. Significant urban sociology and political theories have not used systematic historical analysis to understand the changing nature of immigration, race, ethnic relations, public schooling, and the economy. This study augments the research in this arena and charts new ground exploring how Boston's citizenry and governing regimes responded to events during this period and created a different city politically, economically, and racially.

These research questions are theoretically significant. Increasingly, scholars view comparative historical analysis as "part of a longstanding intellectual project oriented toward the explanation of substantially important outcomes."[54] As Stephan Thernstrom writes, "*Historical analysis of social phenomena is thus not a luxury for those interested in the past for its own sake. A study of the present that neglects the processes of change by which the present was created is necessarily superficial.*"[55] Historical sociology is central to understanding present-day Boston and constructing knowledge for future civic and political leaders. This study primarily focuses on the nine-and-one-half-year mayoralty of Flynn; it is the first book-length empirical study of this period in Boston's history.

Through interviews with a broad cross-section of Boston's past and present civic and government leaders, this book "gives voice to those individuals whose rights have often been ignored, or purposely subordinated, in the pursuit of expansion or profit and at the same time examine how those presumed to be in power understand their position and capacity in the development process."[56]

## 2 / Political, Social, and Economic History of Boston

*I look back to the sixties; we grew up in the sixties and came of age in the sixties—urban riots, decaying downtowns, white flight, exacerbated by busing. We grew up thinking that cities were dying, and boy, I wish I had seen how things would turn out because Boston didn't die.* (Dennis Kearney, 2013 candidate for mayor, interview)

This book examines how Boston's governing regimes responded to issues and shaped policy in race and ethnic relations, economic development and inequality, and public education. The following chapters analyze the governing regimes of the period under study in a historical context. This chapter provides some historical and political background.

## Historical Background

Boston's 350-year-plus history has shaped its political, economic, physical, social, and cultural characteristics. First settled in the 1630s as an English colony, the city became the financial center of New England. John Winthrop, an early settler and first governor of the Massachusetts Bay Colony, famously proclaimed Boston to be "The City upon a Hill" in 1630, referring to the Puritan community he envisioned settling there, with the church at the center of the "Godly Commonwealth."[1]

Boston became an independent municipality in 1822. The "Town of Boston" operated like other New England towns and had a seven-member board of selectmen. The significant change that occurred alongside incorporation in 1882 and a growing city was a governance structure led by a mayor, eight aldermen, and a school committee with one member elected from each ward. From 1822 to 1880, all of Boston's officials had been native-born Yankee Protestants, except for a few Irish politicians elected to office

850,000
801,444
800,000
750,000
697,197
700,000
641,071
650,000
617,594
600,000
574,283
550,000
589,141
562,994
500,000
450,000
400,000

1950   1960   1970   1980   1990   2000   2010

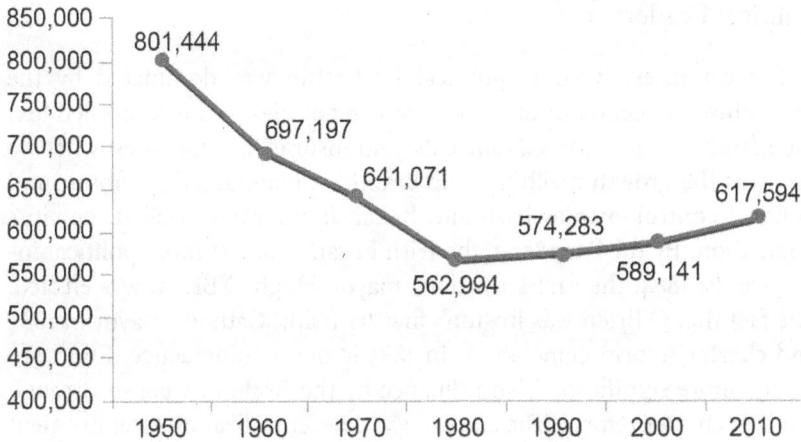

- Boston reached its population peak in 1950
- Boston's population, like many major cities, declined after 1950
- In recent decades, Boston's population has grown
- The 2010 Census marks the first time since 1970 that Boston's population has been over 600,000

CHART 1. Boston Population 1950–2010
Source: Boston Planning and Development Agency

toward the end of this period. Therefore, conflicts over the nature of city government from 1822 to 1880 involved Yankees versus other Yankees fighting along class lines.[2]

By the early eighteenth century, the city had become the economic center of New England. The city's physical development, which initially only consisted of the Shawmut Peninsula, grew to encompass the forty-seven square miles it occupies today. That expansion was possible by filling the harbor and wetlands and annexing neighboring towns.

The growing immigrant population in the middle of the nineteenth century—predominantly Irish, due to the 1845–1852 Great Irish Famine—led Boston to grow exponentially from about 15,000 during the mid-eighteenth-century revolutionary period to more than a quarter-million a century later, reaching its peak of 801,000 in 1950. From that population milestone, the size of the city decreased rapidly each decade until 1980 due to suburbanization and "White flight." In 1980, its population was 562,994, increasing slightly to 589,141 in 2000. Boston's population in 2020 stood at about 675,647 (see Chart 1).

## Political Leadership

For centuries, Boston's political leadership was dominated by the Brahmins—descendants of well-off British families—who controlled textile manufacturing, banks, railroads, and insurance companies: what we know as the growth machine. The Brahmins maintained economic and political control even as Irish and Italian immigrants swelled the city's population. By the late 1800s, the Irish began to assert more political influence. In 1884, the first Irish-born mayor, Hugh O'Brien, was elected. The fact that O'Brien was Boston's first Irish and Catholic mayor in 1884 and charter reform came about in 1885 is not a coincidence. Efforts to thwart more significant Irish influence by the Brahmins began through the 1885 charter reform. The council ward decentralization establishment was not working for the Brahmin class, as the ward-based council became a vehicle for the growing influence of Boston's immigrants throughout the city's wards. Nevertheless, the Irish were solidly in the majority by the early twentieth century. Irish political leaders John J. Fitzgerald (1905) and James Michael Curley (1914) were elected as mayors and were a more significant threat to the Brahmins.

As Doris Kearns-Goodwin points out in her biography *The Fitzgeralds and the Kennedys*, John Fitzgerald tried to employ progressive reform rhetoric. Still, he was "trained by the system of ward politics, his whole life pragmatically geared to satisfying the immediate needs of his special constituents; he could not suddenly change this orientation to a point of view that stressed efficiency, planning, and good government."[3] But he did and was successful.

Although they still controlled Boston's economy, the shift from a mercantile to an industrial and service base provided low-level jobs filled by Irish and Italian immigrants, some Jews, and a few Blacks. Boston's political culture is rooted in that early history.

In 1909, there was another effort to limit Irish influence. The state legislature wrestled significant power from the city, taking control of the police department, liquor licensing board, and tax policy. The Brahmin elites proposed giving the mayor complete executive authority, eliminating the aldermen and the common council in favor of a nine-member nonpartisan city council. The tide turned again, and in 1924, the city returned to a ward-based system ostensibly to respond to immigrant voters. The charter changed frequently to suit the growth machine. In 1949, it was altered to become a nine-member at-large city council, which stayed until the district representation campaign of 1981 described below. As noted later, Mayor Kevin White proposed a charter change in 1977 that would have moved to a form of district representation, among other changes, including a return to partisan elections, which the state legislature rejected in 1978.[4]

Curley was widely viewed as an effective ward boss and machine politician described by his critics as a "masterful and cynical exploiter of his own people's poverty; he enflamed the ethnocultural conflict of the city and turned Boston city politics into a three-ring circus."[5] James Connolly alternatively argues he was a "leading architect of ethnic progressivism." "The 'ethnic Progressivism' they formulated (Fitzgerald and Curley) cast the city's predominantly Yankee economic elite as selfish interests, greedily conspiring to deprive the city's blue-collar, immigrant majority—'the people'—of the social and political power they deserved. In a city where immigrants and their children were in the majority, this ethnic Progressivism became the framework through which many Bostonians came to understand their place in the larger community."[6]

Connolly continued,

Few individuals have defined the public life of a big city more than the legendary Curley, whose half-century-long political career included four terms as mayor, two terms in Congress, one term as governor, and two terms in prison. Like John F. Fitzgerald, Curley created a social narrative designed to define his constituency and mobilize it. But Curley's story was harsher, making cultural antagonism the defining feature of the city's public sphere. His depiction of a Boston long riven by ethnic hatred provided the framework within which Bostonians came to understand themselves and their city, fully eclipsing the more conciliatory vision promoted by a late-nineteenth-century Irish spokesman. Even at the end of the twentieth century, journalists, analysts, and most Bostonians imagine ethnic conflict as the essential fabric of Boston's social and political history, testimony to Curley's extraordinary ability to define the context in which he acted.[7]

Curley's campaign for a fifth term was unsuccessful when, after returning from prison, he told reporters, "I have accomplished more in one day than has been done in the five months of my absence." John Hynes, who had been acting mayor in his absence, was insulted and ran against him, winning and ending Curley's career.[8]

In 1949, the growth machine successfully dislodged Curley and created a new nine-member at-large city council system to replace the ward council districts in place since 1922. The reformers believed that wresting control of the city council from the ward bosses would put them in a better position to influence elected officials through campaign contributions and political organizations under their control, and it worked.

According to Cynthia Horan, a professor at the University of Toronto,

> The new-at-large system performed as hoped. Only one of the fourteen incumbents seeking election to the at-large council in 1951 succeeded; the pattern of ward representation changed. The former system of twenty-two wards had guaranteed all areas of the city a councilor, and, in particular, each of the city's fifteen central neighborhoods had a voice. Under the new at-large system of nine councilors in the 1950s, city councilors came from just nine wards and represented only seven neighborhoods. Moreover, the new at-large councilors tended to represent the reform voters. Indeed, only one of the nine wards on the council had consistently backed Curley in mayoral contests from 1937 to 1951; five had always supported other candidates. These reform wards controlled a majority of council seats throughout the 1950s. The new at-large system also tended to over-represent wealthier voters. Of the 36 councilors elected during the 1950s, fourteen resided in the city's wealthiest ward, which contained less than 5 percent of the population.[9]

Thus began the process whereby the growth machine emerged and undertook the economic transformation of Boston.[10] The results were dramatic: the demolition of the New York Streets area of the South End, the destruction of the West End, and the development of the Prudential Center. These were all part of the business-led pro-growth development politics of the 1950s and 1960s. From the 1950s and 1960s and into the 1970s and 1980s, neighborhood opposition emerged to the plans of Boston's business and government growth machine for a "New Boston," initially during Hynes's and Collins's tenure and gaining more power under the regime of White.

## The Growth Machine and Economic Transformation

> *I mean, Boston was still in a funk in 1971. Some would argue that we didn't recover from the Depression.* (Larry DiCara interview)

Boston did not die, but it was fundamentally scarred by the growth machine's efforts to set in motion an economic revival based on downtown development. The Brahmin upper class refused to invest in Boston, and only one significant downtown office building was constructed between 1929 and the early 1960s. The growth machine sought a way out of the economic stagnation and to control the city's development politics.

In 1959, a group of fourteen corporate leaders emerged, determined to keep the Irish politicians out of power and usher in an era of growth. The Boston Coordinating Committee, dubbed "The Vault," was led by the elite Yankee Ralph Lowell. Known as the Vault because members met secretly in the basement of the Boston Safe Deposit Bank, which Lowell led, the committee rallied behind Hynes's and Collins's growth machine urban renewal plans. The major daily newspapers and the Roman Catholic Church joined with the growth machine to transform the city and property relations.

Rev. W. Seavey Joyce, then Boston College's vice president of community relations, who later served as BC president from 1968 to 1972, was instrumental in starting the process. He expressed his goals for the city in an interview for the film *Mission Hill and the Miracle of Boston*: "In 1954, we needed some new building in Boston; we needed a skyline." As a first step, in 1954, he initiated the Boston College Citizens' Seminars as a vehicle "to bring together the Yankees who owned the city's economy and the Irish political leaders who ran the city."[11] The seminars at the First National Bank of Boston created the opportunity for a series of meetings (later described as "acrimonious") between the interest groups. From these sessions, Boston's growth machine emerged. Mayor John Hynes addressed the first gathering of the group, saying, "The only way that decay and blight may be uprooted is by a complete physical change in the affected neighborhood or area," referring to both the West End and the North End, which were poor and working-class immigrant neighborhoods at the time. These conversations launched the urban renewal era in Boston.[12] What followed was contentious public hearings, as Broadman captured in his documentary, with one woman proclaiming, "Urban renewal corrupted this town, turned people against people, the church against the people even. I'm sick of it—let's throw out the money changers."[13]

William Bulger, who grew up in public housing in South Boston and would serve as president of the Massachusetts Senate and later as president of the University of Massachusetts, recalls working as a bartender while a student at Boston College when they sponsored the Citizens Seminars:

> They formed the New Boston Committee to plan ways to improve the city they had left. We should look at the result of these seminars—the demolition of the West End, the building of the Central Artery, the elimination of Scollay Square—and judge the results. [Mayor James Michael] Curley was always distrustful of the New Boston Committee. To him, they were just another bunch of Goo-Goos. He battled with Jerome Rappaport, Hynes's assistant, one of the New Boston Committee's creators, and those eager to transform the city. Soon, a government of elected officials was replaced by a government of experts. To whom

does one appeal in the face of a bureaucracy's decision to raze an entire neighborhood? Such government action, clearly unjust, counterproductive, and unnecessary, would be imposed on the Boston citizenry to the loud applause of the unaffected proponents. The strong political leadership of the past was no longer in view. It all seemed to me so self-serving. But I was only a bartender.[14]

The various corporate-sponsored think tanks and organizations made Boston more friendly to private investment and corporate influence, including the postwar redevelopment plan and the creation of the Boston Redevelopment Authority (BRA) in 1957. The Boston Housing Authority, which later became the BRA, led the most extensive physical and economic transformation in the urban renewal of Boston's West End in the 1950s and 1960s, following the "slum clearance" demolition in the New York Streets section of the South End between 1955 and 1957.[15]

The BRA designated the city's planning agency and published several plans to lay the foundation for urban renewal and neighborhood demolition. The General Plan for Boston described the West End as an "obsolete neighborhood" and laid out the vision for the future "New Boston." Building upon the 1950 plan, the city's planning agency published the "1965–1975 General Plan for the City of Boston and the Regional Core" in 1964.[16] This plan, among other things, built upon the strategy to replace the West End with a more aggressive approach to urban renewal.

The growth machine overpowered the immigrant neighborhood of the West End, in large part due to the insular nature of their peer group culture and consequent lack of understanding of the forces at work to transform the neighborhood, as Herbert Gans describes in his classic portrait *Urban Villagers*.[17] Gans relates how, without the political power to stop the ultimate destruction of their community, the West End was cleared in less than eighteen months, much like the New York Streets section of the South End had been destroyed several years earlier.[18] The North End, Charlestown, and South Boston neighborhoods would not undergo similar "redevelopment," partly due to these communities' resistance and political power.[19] Roxbury would later experience urban renewal in the Washington Park section because of the support of the district's leading political figures, Otto and Muriel Snowden.

The Vault provided a forum where business elites could unify their urban renewal and redevelopment policy. The redevelopment team of city leaders was aligned with powerful business interests under the leadership of the Boston Coordinating Committee. They supported John Collins in his bid for mayor over South Boston's Irish Senate president, John Powers, who was close with and endorsed by US senator John F. Kennedy. Powers lost, and with Collins in the mayor's seat, he pushed the Vault's agenda, notably the "New Boston" downtown redevelopment.[20]

Their strategy was to remove poor and working-class residents from the central city and assist government leaders in the public arena to obtain the necessary support for their agenda. Resistance to the growth machine coalition policies intensified in Boston and other urban areas through the development of a "kind of militant community activism."[21]

## Economic Transformation

In the middle of the twentieth century, Boston was a troubled city "dying on the vine," as a *U.S. News & World Report* described.[22] Since the Depression, businesses refused to invest in Boston. Major manufacturing firms were abandoning Boston—some for the suburbs, but many for the South, particularly the textile and clothing industries. By the late 1940s, middle-class White residents fled to the suburbs, subsidized by government-sponsored highways and mortgages. The city's population saw some expansion due to the "Great Migration" of African Americans leaving the South. Still, by the 1950s, the population was shrinking, as was the city's tax base. Businesses and residents had been fleeing, and the economy was in disarray.

The Brookings Institution's study of the largest cities in the United States ranked Boston as a distressed city in decline. Racial turmoil erupted following the 1974 court-ordered desegregation of the Boston Public Schools. White flight, which had begun as early as the 1950s, accelerated, and Boston's neighborhoods faced disinvestment, arson, and a sharp increase in crime. The loss of manufacturing jobs contributed to the economic decline. Barry Bluestone wrote, "Nationwide, the proportion of employment in nondurable manufacturing has fallen by half between 1950 and 1990, from 14 percent to 7 percent. But in the Boston area, it has fallen by over three-fourths: from 21 percent to only 5 percent."[23]

However, between 1980 and 2010, Boston experienced significant immigration and substantial economic growth. This postindustrial period was distinguished by the increase in the professional and service industries and the redevelopment of parts of the city's downtown area and many inner-city neighborhoods. An analysis of the labor market transformations of this period shows that the loss of employment in manufacturing was replaced in the 1980s and 1990s by expanding jobs in the technology, finance, and service sectors, which were growing faster than the overall employment rate across the United States.[24] This industrial transformation led to a growing income divide in the New Boston and across the nation because of the disparity between the education and skills of many former industrial workers and those required by these growing sectors.[25] According to Peter Dorringer, director of the Institute on Employment Policy at Boston University, "The Boston economy reflects very sharply what we've come to think of as the two-tier economy, technical and managerial jobs, jobs connected with the financial and health sectors and high-wage businesses are growing, but are often taken by commuters, and also substantial growth in less-skilled jobs like restaurant and hotel work, building service work and health care, but these are 'low-wage dead-end jobs' that don't yield high incomes for people or the prospects for high incomes."[26]

In sum, Boston's economy was fueled by downtown growth in the 1980s, and the neighborhoods faced deterioration of services and disinvestment. The story of how civic, political, and community leaders responded to these issues, particularly in creating broad civic engagement and developing economic institutions, is told through the stories of key business and civic leaders in the following chapters.

## Changing Demographics and Immigration

Boston's population demographics changed significantly between 1980 and 2000, resulting in the city becoming a majority-minority city for the first time in 2000. The most significant growth was from new immigration. During this period, the percentage of Black/African Americans remained relatively unchanged, while there was a dramatic influx of Latinos

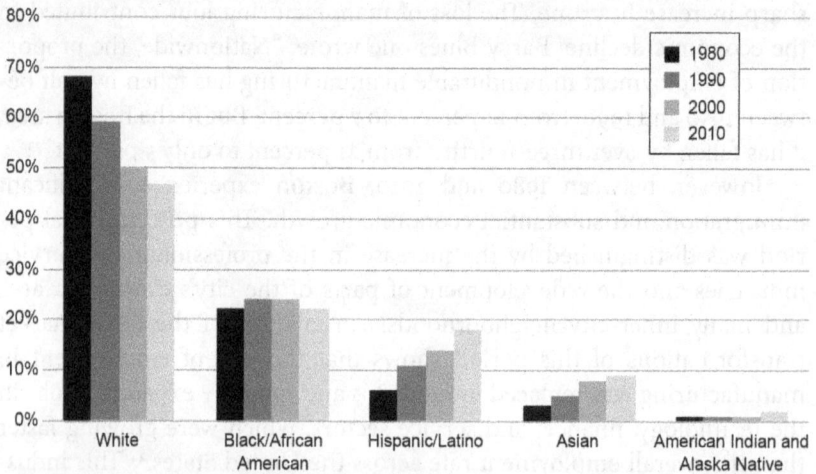

CHART 2. Boston Racial and Ethnic Population Breakdown, 1980–2010
Source: Boston Planning and Development Agency

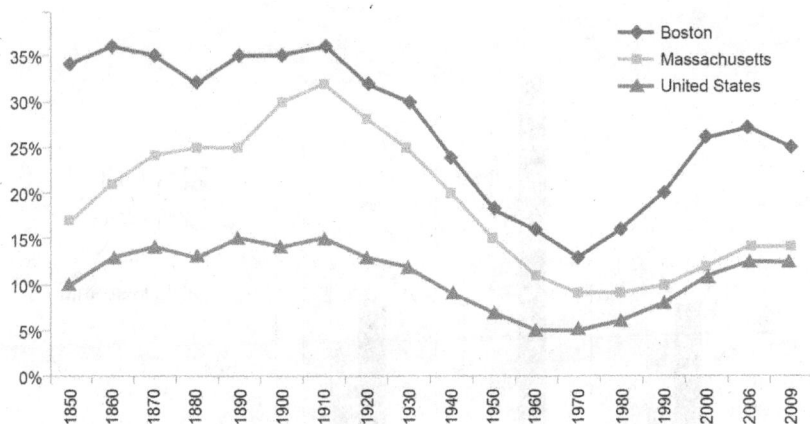

CHART 3. Proportion of Boston Foreign-Born Population, 1850–2009
Source: Boston Planning and Development Agency

and Asians, as displayed in Chart 2. Early immigration was mainly from Europe, but most immigrants were now coming to Boston from Asia and Latin America.

The composition of Boston's immigrant population was different during this period than at the turn of the last century, and the immigrant populations were at their highest levels since that time (Chart 3). From 1990 to 2007, 69 percent of Boston's foreign-born residents were from Latin America or Asia.[27]

As Chart 3 suggests, Boston has far exceeded Massachusetts as a whole and the United States regarding the percentage of foreign-born residents since 1850. Later chapters explore how city leaders responded to the social, political, economic, and cultural changes caused by the massive new immigration.

Poverty and slums have been issues in Boston since the first new immigrants arrived. Small groups from across Europe came to Boston through the late eighteenth century. Oscar Handlin wrote in his book *Boston Immigrants: 1790–1880*, "From 1835 to 1865 'the stream of emigration' continued to 'flow with unabated rapidity', little affected by conditions in America and by 1850, about 35,000 Irish were domiciled in the city; five years later there were more than 50,000."[28] Excluded from the merchant economy led by the Brahmins during the late-nineteenth-century industrialization, the uneducated immigrants were relegated to low-wage jobs as laborers and house servants. The transformation of many of these immigrants into middle-class homeowners is an American success story. But the other story is the migration of poor African Americans to

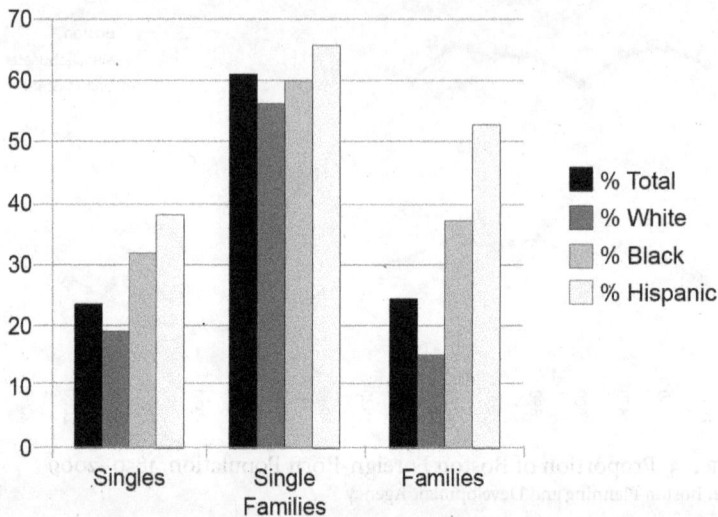

**CHART 4.** Boston Poverty Rates, 1980
Source: The Boston Foundation, 1989

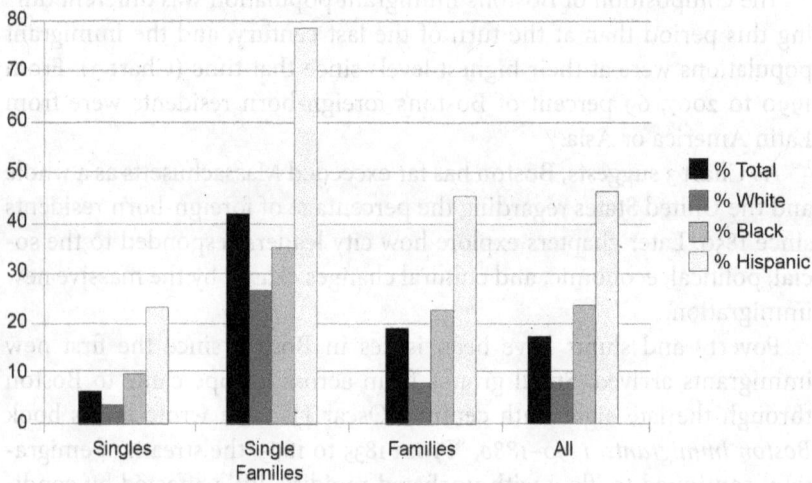

**CHART 5.** Boston Poverty Rates, 1989
Source: The Boston Foundation, 1989

Boston and cities across the country and the effects of race and poverty in such a transformation for this and other minority populations. "In 1984, the White poverty rate was 13 percent, while 29 percent of Blacks, 40 percent of Asians, and 50 percent of Latinos lived below the official poverty line," as Peter Medoff and Holly Sklar write in their 1994 book *Streets of Hope: The Fall and Rise of an Urban Neighborhood*.[29] Charts 4 and 5 show the poverty rates for select racial groups for 1980 and 1989. The data show that poverty was reduced in Boston by the end of the 1980s, though wide racial and ethnic disparities in poverty rates continued. The implications for poverty and income inequality between 1980 and 2000 are explored for their influences on civic life, urban politics, and policies.

## Growing Inequality

Gentrification of many Boston neighborhoods and growing inequality have also shaped Boston's physical and social fabric. While scholars differ on the definition of gentrification, it is defined here as economic and social process where the growth machine transforms urban areas, more often than not displacing current residents and businesses, in favor of wealthier inhabitants.[30]

Bostonians have experienced changes to their way of life resulting from immigration and demographic changes, as well as the process of cultural accommodation. The most significant challenge the city faced was probably persistent income inequality.

Table 1 shows that income inequality has grown nationally over the past five decades, with the top 20 percent increasing their income share from 43 percent in 1970 to 52 percent in 2020. At the same time, the bot-

TABLE 1. Share of Aggregate Income Received by Each Fifth and Top 5 Percent of All Households, 1970–2020

| Year | Number (thousands) | Shares of aggregate income | | | | | |
|------|-----|-----|-----|-----|-----|-----|-----|
| | | Lowest fifth | Second fifth | Third fifth | Fourth fifth | Highest fifth | Top 5 percent |
| 2020 | 129,200 | 3.0 | 8.2 | 14.0 | 22.6 | 52.2 | 23.0 |
| 2010 | 119,900 | 3.3 | 8.5 | 14.6 | 23.4 | 50.3 | 21.3 |
| 2000 | 108,200 | 3.6 | 8.9 | 14.8 | 23.0 | 49.8 | 22.1 |
| 1990 | 94,310 | 3.8 | 9.6 | 15.9 | 24.0 | 46.6 | 18.5 |
| 1980 | 82,370 | 4.2 | 10.2 | 16.8 | 24.7 | 44.1 | 16.5 |
| 1970 | 64,780 | 4.1 | 10.8 | 17.4 | 24.5 | 43.3 | 16.6 |

Source: US Census Bureau, Current Population Survey, 1968–2023

tom 20 percent of the income share decreased from 4.1 percent to 3 per-cent. In comparison, the top 5 percent of the population continues to earn a staggering seven times the income of the lowest fifth of the population in this country today.

Due to growing inequality and gentrification, Boston's class composition has fared even worse in income distribution over the past several decades. In 2009, the top 5 percent of Boston earners accounted for 25 percent of total annual income, while the bottom 20 percent earned just 2.2 percent of the yearly total.[31] This book explores the implications of growing income inequality and the responses of the governing regimes to this issue.

## The Governing Regimes

Political leadership has played a role in facilitating or impeding changes to Boston's urban way of life through implicit or explicit policies and gov-ernmental actions such as urban renewal, policies dealing with racial conflict, housing, and real estate development policies and practices in the context of national and international economic change. Alongside the changes in Boston's local culture, there have been leadership transitions during the period under study. From 1968 to 2024, there have been five governing regimes: the mayoralties of Kevin H. White from 1968 to 1983, Raymond L. Flynn from 1984 to 1993, Thomas M. Menino from 1993 to 2014, Martin Walsh from 2014 to 2021, and Michelle Wu from 2021 to the present. This modern era provides the framework for this study of Boston.

As described in later chapters, the policies and actions of each gov-erning regime, together with racial, immigration, and economic changes, have characterized a transformative period in Boston's history. This book provides an empirical window into the decision-making of each regime. It integrates the perspectives of political leaders, business leaders, civic leaders, and citizens. It explores how organized politics and emerging policies have affected widespread immigration and racial conflict, public education, and wholesale change in the city's economic base during this period. It shows that responses to the changes that occurred at the end of the twentieth century have transformed the city's economic, social, and political landscape.

The book examines some key questions raised before the public during this period. It explores how these questions were addressed and discusses the many civic actors' roles in the debates, controversies, and governance during this period in the city's history. This book chronicles and offers a sociological analysis of how politics and policymaking have changed and how Boston's transformed civic customs have created a new way of life in the twenty-first century. Theories about political power, governing regimes, and racial and ethnic conflict guide this exploration and provide insights into what happened and why.

The research's sociological significance lies in exploring the roles of the governing regimes through case study methodology and the oral history of participants during this era. This approach allows for a rethinking and expansion of conventional wisdom in analyzing current issues and problems in Boston. I hope that this may help in finding solutions.

# 3 / The New Boston and the 1983 Race for Mayor

*The night the results came in, I walked into the ballroom and saw all those folks out there celebrating, and I asked them if they knew what the election results were. It made me understand that we won something. We didn't get to be mayor, but something different happened in the city due to people coming together. I was a candidate. A whole lot of people felt that they were candidates, so they participated, and a lot of people took real ownership of the campaign.* (Mel King, candidate for mayor)

## Key Players and Electoral Politics in Boston

This chapter explores the context of Boston's 1983 mayoral election and the city's consequential governance transformation. As discussed in the previous chapter, the Irish had wrested the mayor's office from the Brahmins in the early twentieth century. A series of Irish mayors built patronage machines, the city's infrastructure, and later the skyline. The Fitzgerald and Curley regimes' Irish dominance of city politics ended in 1949 with Curley's defeat. The elections of Hynes (1949) and Collins (1959) culminated in the growth machine reasserting themselves. Then in 1967 came Kevin White, who narrowly beat anti-busing leader Louise Day Hicks to become elected Boston's fifty-first mayor.

## Kevin Hagan White

Kevin White, the product of a well-to-do Boston Irish political family, grew up in the lace curtain Irish district of West Roxbury. The Irish were often categorized as either "shanty Irish," those who were poor, or "lace curtain Irish," those more well-off. He ran for secretary of state in 1960 and was reelected twice.

White first ran for mayor in 1967 at age thirty-seven, on a platform primarily based on rejecting the urban renewal and development policies of his predecessors, Mayors Hynes and Collins. These policies ignited neighborhood opposition and led to the abandonment of many of the urban renewal plans. The community empowerment movement expanded to contest these policies and reform the political structure to include greater neighborhood representation.[1] White had seen the job as mayor as a stepping stone, commenting, "I was going down to go up," and "up" was the governor's office, which he ran for and lost in 1970.[2]

White served for sixteen years as mayor. During that time, the city underwent many crises, including school integration, the cleanup of Boston Harbor, and the city's public housing authorities being placed in federal or state court receivership; racial conflict and violence stemming from the 1974 federal school desegregation decree; and near financial collapse.

Sam Tyler, president of the Boston Municipal Research Bureau, spoke about the fiscal challenges Mayor White faced with the Tregor lawsuit in 1979 and Proposition 2½ in 1980 (a Massachusetts law limiting the property tax revenue a community could raise) and the crippling effects of these events on Boston's finances:

> Tregor was a defining moment for the city because Mr. Tregor owned an office building in Boston, and he sued the city because he felt disproportionally assessed. The courts ruled in his favor, which determined that the city owed $35 million in abatements. This decision came around the same time the city faced Proposition 2½, which also occurred during the White administration. That resulted in substantial reductions in property tax revenue. So, the combination of Proposition 2½ reducing the property tax revenue and this new burden of paying a significant increase of abatements forced the city to the only course of action it had, which was to seek home-rule petition authorization from the legislature to borrow to pay off these abatement costs.[3]

White weathered these fiscal storms mainly due to the economic growth period of the late 1970s, which enabled him to focus on commercial development downtown. Larry DiCara, a longtime city council member who ran unsuccessfully for mayor in 1983, wrote, "Mayor White had few options left, so he started selling city assets. All those public parking garages were in prime downtown spots. The lots were sold, the garages were knocked down, and new high-rise buildings took place. As a result of the financial crises brought about by the Tregor decision and Proposition 2½, he closed police and fire stations in the early 1980s."[4]

Growing resistance in the city's neighborhoods to White's policies favoring downtown growth while schools, parks, and local business districts deteriorated led neighborhood activists and organizations to call for greater political participation and a sharing of downtown prosperity.

Boston saw an upsurge in community and tenant organizing during White terms during the 1970s and 1980s. In the 1960s, opposition to the proposed I-93 highway through Boston's neighborhoods of Chinatown, the South End, Roxbury, and Jamaica Plain led to a grassroots multineighborhood coalition to stop the highway. The antihighway movement was successful in the 1970s after more than a decade of activism in stopping the highway expansion.[5] Similarly, East Boston residents fought against the airport's expansion; South End and Fenway community groups continued their fight against urban renewal, which began under Hynes and Collins and continued under White; tenants organized in multiple neighborhoods against skyrocketing rents and displacement. Local organizing emerged alongside the civil rights and antiwar movements in Boston and nationwide. By and large, Boston's neighborhoods were reacting to actions coming out of White's city hall. Jim Vrabel provides an essential chronicle of these battles and activism in his book, *A People's History of the New Boston.*[6]

Boston's civil rights leaders continued to fight for the desegregation of public schools and public housing, which led to many legal challenges. Most notable was *Morgan v. Hennigan*,[7] which led to Judge W. Arthur Garrity's school desegregation order in 1974, discussed in chapter 10. During his tenure, White dealt with many issues and community conflicts. Although he came to office as a reformer, he was controlled by the growth machine and downtown development interests and, at the same time, was unable to handle the implementation of the desegregation of schools or public housing.

In many respects, the opposition to the growth machine coalition of 1950–1980, racial segregation, and the emergence of Black politics in Boston during the same period led to the transformation that began in Boston with the 1983 election, what V. O. Key has termed a "critical election."[8]

According to Mel King, who finished third in the 1979 mayor's race, three stages led to the emergence of Black politics in the city: the service stage, during which Black residents were dependent upon White largesse; the organizing stage, which saw the assertion of Black power; and the institution-building stage, during which the community created organizations to both provide services and build neighborhoods through development.[9] This community activism coincided with growing opposition to the policies of the growth machine, and as John Mollenkopf writes, "First, though the neighborhood activism during the 1960s and 1970s did not halt the postindustrial transformation of US cities, it did undermine the local pro-growth coalitions, and neighborhood activism ended large-scale clearance projects."[10] With the emergence of tenants' rights organizations and feminist and gay and lesbian advocacy groups, progressive politics began to take shape in Boston.

As a result, several ballot initiatives emerged late in Mayor White's term. In 1977, a district representation ballot question was proposed to expand the engagement of the neighborhoods in the political process, especially the growing communities of color. In 1977, the initiative lost because some voters in predominately White neighborhoods, like Charlestown and South Boston, saw the measure as a way to elect more Blacks to the city council. Nevertheless, in 1981, district representation won. In 1983, two further initiatives received overwhelming support from Boston voters: "linkage," a measure to "tax" downtown development to benefit development in the neighborhoods (over White's veto), and a petition to create neighborhood councils to provide a greater voice for Boston residents in policies that impacted the city's neighborhoods.

Before the 1983 election, Kevin White had been mayor of Boston for sixteen years, first elected in 1967. He served four terms and, in many respects, came to be identified with Boston's skyline alongside the concurrent deterioration in Boston's neighborhoods, race relations, housing, and schools. In his last term, he was described as a "loner in love with his city," partly because he became so isolated from Boston's citizens and leading institutions. As University of Massachusetts historian James Green wrote, "While White tried, not too successfully, to avoid responsibility for the busing conflict, his housing and development policies continued to generate grassroots opposition, and the mayor could not escape responsibility for those policies. Indeed, during White's first three terms, Boston became a prime example of a city where neighborhood residents mobilized against pro-business development policies."[11]

After White's close reelection battle in 1975, most observers believed he had tired of the job. Although he won reelection handily in 1979, 1983 was different. White faced allegations of corruption (never proven; however, more than ten administration members faced corruption convictions) for fundraising and development decision irregularities. Larry DiCara, a city council member knowledgeable of the legal and development issues at the time, recounted, "Bill Weld, who was then the US attorney, basically forced Kevin [White] out. He may have even given a signal that if White did not run for reelection, he would stop this aggressive manhunt of trying to find some evidence that Kevin White was on the take."[12] Menino, a campaign operative in each of state senator and former Boston City Council member Joseph Timilty's unsuccessful campaigns against White, wrote about the perception of corruption: "White's vulnerability [was] thinking he was beatable because of the 'climate of corruption' in Kevin's administration with his fundraising techniques which included forced contributions from contractors and city employees, who paid in cash at a suite at the Parker House."[13]

To add insult to injury, the *Boston Globe*, on which White could usually rely for support, abandoned him. The *Globe* had endorsed White in his first bid for the office in 1967, but in an editorial in 1982 wrote, "The Kevin White of 1982, in contrast to the gleam in George McGovern's eye in 1972, proves Lord Acton's saying that 'Power tends to corrupt and absolute power tends to corrupt absolutely.' Of the half-dozen candidates now running, any of them would be preferable to Kevin White in 1982."[14]

Clarence Stone observed, "Politics in the form of the governing coalition shapes policy, and policy also shapes the regime."[15] Politics shaped Boston's development policy and opposition to that policy, which led to an election to succeed White that would be very different from those of the preceding years.

## Raymond Leo Flynn

Ray Flynn was the son of a longshoreman and a cleaning lady, raised a Roman Catholic in predominately Irish South Boston. He developed an early sense of social and economic justice from his family and his religious upbringing. A South Boston High School graduate, Flynn would attend Providence College on a basketball scholarship and later be named the most valuable player in the 1963 National Invitational Tournament. After a brief professional basketball career, Flynn worked in several fields, including as a high school teacher and a probation officer, before entering politics. He received a master's degree in education from Harvard University.

Flynn served the people of his city and state in the Massachusetts House of Representatives from 1971 until 1979 and on the Boston City Council from 1978 until 1984. From 1984 through 1993, Flynn served as the most popular mayor in the history of Boston. President Clinton appointed him as US ambassador to the Holy See in 1993. He used his talents to continue to improve the world he saw around him in South Boston, the city of Boston, the corridors of the Holy See, and around the world.

When Flynn entered the mayor's office, he did so with his family and "pockets of coalitions" in lockstep behind him. As a boy, he played sports in every neighborhood. He sold newspapers in the Boston Garden, Fenway Park, the Boston Arena, and Braves Field for years. Flynn had traveled the city as an elected official for over two decades in his old beat-up blue station wagon with rotting floorboards in the back seat.

As a kid growing up in South Boston, sports and competition drove Flynn and gave him purpose. From the age of twelve, Flynn had a singular focus on sports. He learned early the value of teamwork and how sports could impact young people's lives, from creating youth sports leagues to becoming a basketball, football, and baseball star in his own right. He understood how the city could impact a young person's life chances through quality education and a shot at a good-paying job.

Later, Flynn helped build the Boston Neighborhood Basketball League with Kenny Hudson, an NBA referee and general manager of the WILD radio station, serving Boston's Black community. Their efforts have been sustained to this day, wrote the *Boston Globe* in 2024. "For more than a half-century, the Boston Neighborhood Basketball League has brought peace to and love for the city"[16]

At a chance meeting in 1974, two days into busing, Flynn and Hudson talked about playing together on the Roxbury Moulton's basketball team when Flynn was the first White player on the club. Flynn recalls traveling with Jack Crump, the team's coach. When Crump picked him up at Broadway and Dorchester Avenue in South Boston with eleven Black players, Crump was asked why a Black team had a White player and responded, "Because he can shoot."

Hudson and Flynn discussed the teams playing in each other's neighborhoods without racial tensions. Flynn and Hudson convened a secret meeting with the leaders of sports teams in South Boston and Roxbury on the first Saturday after the schools opened in 1974. "Maybe the kids will listen to me more as Ray Flynn, the athlete, instead of Ray Flynn, the state representative," Flynn said. He and Hudson continued to engage sports leaders to find racial peace during busing.[17]

Flynn opposed busing, but as a moderate, both sides would criticize him—the virulent anti-busing movement in his neighborhood and the more liberal pro-busing supporters across the city. His deep sense of justice would shape his politics and journey from the legislature to the city council and the mayor's office, where he advocated for tenants, working families, and the poor.

Henry Allen, a leader in the school desegregation movement during busing, commented, "Flynn was an anti-busing activist in the 1970s as a state rep from South Boston. He was someone who really worked when he became mayor to heal divisions and reach out to the African-American and growing Latino communities."[18]

## Mayoral Candidate Ray Flynn—"Pockets of Coalitions"

Flynn spoke about playing sports and the issue of race:

I mean, I was drawn into politics with sports. I started a basketball program, which may seem insignificant, but I started it, and I started a softball program in South Boston. I ran into several brick walls. I learned you don't get anything done unless you're politically connected or have political instincts and motivation. To get things done, you have to know how to position politicians to make them feel that there's something in it for them, let them throw out the first ball, and put their name like the Moakley Club on the back of the shirts, you know, calling it something that is a political benefit to whomever. That was my introduction through sports, and sports is wholesome. It's clean, it's not, you know, vote for me because I'm going to be able to cut corners to get your development done, I'm helping your kids; I'm starting this program; I'm getting the playgrounds fixed, you're going to have a childcare program over here, guys can bring their kids down there, can play softball just coming back from Vietnam, you know all these different things led me into politics from sports.[19]

Flynn would tap into the network of sports organizations across the city, as Brian Wallace described in his book *A Remarkable Life*: "He organized a citywide basketball program called the Ray Flynn All-Boston Tournament. We had eight teams from most Boston sections, comprising the fifteen best basketball players from South Boston, East Boston, Brighton, Roxbury, West Roxbury, Charlestown, Dorchester, and Hyde Park. These were the cream of the crop with influence in their towns, and they wore the Ray Flynn shirts all summer. People paid attention when Ronnie Perry, Franny Costello, Russell Lee, Kevin Honan, Brian Honan, and 120 talented players wore the Ray Flynn jerseys. We had a remarkably successful tournament with the publicity you could not buy for six years. The players worked for us in the 1983 mayor's race."[20]

Flynn as a state legislator became known as the "jock legislator." In his first term, he quickly expanded his base from sports and neighborhood concerns to issues of concern to constituencies across the city and state.

While at Providence College, Flynn was an early champion in helping special needs children. He taught young kids at an orphanage in Providence how to play basketball and baseball. While in the Massachusetts House of Representatives in the early 1970s, he was a leading proponent in fighting for disabled and special needs kids. The result was the passage of the state's most important nationally recognized law to help special needs kids, Chapter 766. He remarked at the time, "Do you realize that there are 10,000 kids in this state who are not being schooled because they are both physically and emotionally handicapped?"[21]

Flynn remembers, "The coalitions were not the coalitions you might think they were. What were the coalitions? The coalition was me playing basketball at Roxbury Boys Club, where I knew half the kids in Roxbury. I was not a Southie pol to them; I was the first White kid to play on an all-Black semi-professional basketball team. I fought for disabled kids in this state when they were being ignored; I was not a Southie pro-life politician connected with the church, which was before any of that. There was no pro-life issue then; there was no busing issue."[22]

While serving in the state legislature, Flynn was elected to Boston City Council, drawing support from his hometown of South Boston, which formed the base to launch his mayoral campaign. As Mary Nee, a South Boston neighbor and family friend who would later join the Flynn administration, recalled, "The first mayoral campaign meeting was at the Boston Harbor Tennis Club. There was Brian Wallace, Jack McDonough, Peter Welsh, Jay Carney, Larry Dwyer, myself, and maybe half a dozen others. It was an extension of Ray Flynn's city council campaign team, which consisted of local homegrown folks, and that was the nucleus that started the campaign."[23]

Flynn formally announced his candidacy for mayor on April 27, 1983, in front of the West Broadway (D Street) public housing development in South Boston, pledging a "campaign of solutions."[24] Flynn would later reflect on the symbolism of the announcement at a distressed public housing development in South Boston:

> I announced my candidacy at the D Street project, and don't ever underestimate that announcement. What the hell did that announcement mean? I stood at the corner of D Street and Broadway, looking across the street; what did I see? I saw our police station closed. I looked over to my left; I saw our fire station had been deactivated. I looked up on the other side of the street; I saw the drug headquarters of Whitey Bulger, and I looked at the housing authority over my shoulder that the court had taken over for mismanagement and neglect. Nobody knew what the hell I was doing. I knew exactly what I was doing. Everything was there. People are still asking me why you announced it there. Even [campaign manager] Ray Dooley said don't announce it there. He wanted me to announce it in Parker House like everybody else did.[25]

According to campaign aide and later policy adviser Neil Sullivan, "The coolest decision was to announce for the office at the West Broadway housing development because it said this was about poor people, and this would be about poor people regardless of race, and race was the other major issue you had to deal with at the time."[26]

Flynn went on to tap into other coalitions, including the pro-life activists with whom he shared sentiments about abortion. He had previously

been visible on this issue, having cosponsored the Doyle-Flynn amendment as a state representative. This amendment barred public funding for
abortions, a position that won him as many friends as enemies. As Maria Karagianis, a reporter for the *Boston Globe*, wrote, "Because of stands
like these, Flynn has been unpopular among liberals, blacks, and feminist
groups he must win over to become mayor. Yet, in recent years, he has
tried to change and broaden his image (and has begun to succeed). He
has championed progressive issues like rent control and moved closer to
the black community. He has developed alliances with political figures
like State Representative Melvin H. King of Roxbury, a liberal black, and
former City Council member Rosemarie Sansone, a feminist."[27]

Flynn's support from the pro-life activists and his position on women's
right to choose gave many progressive women pause. At the same time,
many women rallied around Flynn and formed a core group of supporters. Much of Flynn's support from women came based upon their interactions with the candidate either as a state representative or city councilor.
As Mary Baker, an African American woman from Mattapan and Fair
Share leader, told Pierre Clavel,

> I supported Flynn. He helped us in our rodent control campaign
> when he was on the city council. Roslindale people wanted trees and
> got them immediately, but we couldn't control rodents. Flynn said
> that if you want power, get people to register to vote. When Flynn
> ran for mayor, we invited him here to discuss what he'd do for us.
> We wanted jobs, economic development, housing, equal jobs, and
> contracts on construction. There was much risk for me going against
> King, but the more ridiculous King got, the easier it was. He was ar-
> rogant. He wanted to hang onto the dashiki, but that era had passed.
> In the 1960s, you could get by with "Black is Beautiful," but this was
> the 1980s. Now, you have to have brains and ability.[28]

Another prominent leader and Flynn supporter was Nancy Snyder, the
Boston director of 9 TO 5, a working woman's advocacy group. Snyder
outlined her reasons for supporting Flynn:

> I decided to get involved in the campaign after Ray Flynn showed up
> at a State House hearing to advocate for a bill to address health and
> safety concerns of office automation, especially for working women.
> With other women in the campaign, we created the Women for Flynn
> committee and participated in mayoral candidate forums on issues
> affecting women. Women's right to choose was important to many
> progressive women working for Ray Flynn's candidacy. Most of the

potential impact of city government was in areas like jobs, training, housing, and human services. At the forums, Ray Flynn spoke to these issues and committed that health services currently provided to women by the city government, such as Boston City Hospital, would continue to be provided. It would have been easy for him to have missed these forums altogether. Still, for the women who supported him, this was validation and a rallying point to put their energy behind the Flynn campaign's social and economic justice priorities.[29]

Rosemarie Sansone led the state campaign for the Equal Rights Amendment and would win a seat on the city council in 1977, where she was Flynn's only consistent ally on renters' rights and other issues. She explained why she worked on Flynn's mayoral campaign: "I was involved in the mayor's race and did a lot with the people organizing Women for Flynn before the primary. But after the primary, when it looked like Ray Flynn was going to win, because of my connections to a more liberal community and the business community, I was the person many people could call because they didn't know anybody else. Hence, the city's business leaders called me to find out how they could help more and have some access."[30] Sansone and Treasurer George Russell would regularly communicate with members of the city's large corporations and with local boards of trade, neighborhood, and minority businesses, which had not been a priority of the White administration.

Sansone would go on to cochair the transition committee following the November election and reflected on Flynn's candidacy and priorities:

Housing always played a significant role in the campaign and a personal role in the candidate's life. Because he was from South Boston and because he always seemed very connected to public housing, where he had a great base of support from people in public housing, he probably always felt more comfortable talking to people in public housing across the city no matter what neighborhood. So, I think housing and poor people's issues were very, very important to him and very significant in the campaign and probably was one of the reasons that the people that were calling me, from the Vault and business community, felt they needed to call me because the issues that he's identified with were not necessarily issues that they cared about. To them, he appeared to be antibusiness. So, the downtown business leaders were concerned. He did have strong relationships with the neighborhood boards of trade in East Boston, Hyde Park, Mattapan, and Jamaica Plain, which were much more grassroots with community concerns. His downtown connections were not good when he got elected and not much better when he left office. They were not people he wanted to spend much time with; he wasn't necessarily hostile; it was not where his heart and soul were.[31]

When the Vault's head, John LaWare, proposed to Flynn that he create a formal business advisory committee, he was noncommittal, preferring to work through allies in the business community like Kevin Phelan and John Bok, two early supporters.

Marie Turley, a prominent Jamaica Plain activist, said she was involved in the Women for Flynn campaign effort and organized locally to carry out the nuts and bolts of the election. She joined the administration first in the Mayor's Office of Business and Cultural Development and, later, as the first female building commissioner in the city's history. As head of the Women's Commission, Turley spearheaded the development and dedication of the Women's Memorial on October 23, 2003. The sculptures at the Commonwealth Avenue Mall honor Abigail Adams, Lucy Stone, and Phillis Wheatley.[32]

Kristin McCormack, a Dorchester activist, worked as the director of the Dorchester Youth Council during that time. She explained, "The campaign was hysterical; it was a blast. It was like the little engine that could; we were always the underdog and deeply believed in what Ray Flynn stood for. It was around neighborhoods, grassroots empowerment, a little bit about tilting at windmills, and a little bit about populism. It was a very diverse group of people, which I liked. There were women from South Boston working alongside African American women and college-educated activists working with firefighters. It was a diverse campaign from a class and race perspective, which was great."[33]

Many Bostonians viewed Flynn's opposition to court-ordered school busing as a moderate and constructive force. Unlike many in his home district who identified with the racist anti-busing organizations, Flynn framed the issue as one based not upon race but class, a theme he would carry throughout his political career. The *Boston Globe* reported, "Flynn says he and his family were physically and verbally attacked because of his views and actions. A few years ago, Flynn helped prevent an attack on a black couple by a crowd of angry whites outside the State House. He was the only white politician to attend the funeral of Levi Hart, a 14-year-old black boy shot by a white policeman. Several years ago, he led a demonstration against the Ku Klux Klan when the organization tried to open a storefront in South Boston. And after voting for a city Human Rights Commission, he was called a 'nigger lover' in hate brochures anonymously distributed during the 1978 campaign."[34]

Flynn's populist framing of race and class issues led many progressive community and tenants' rights organizers to flock to his campaign. Leaders from groups organizing for decades, like the Massachusetts Fair Share and Massachusetts Tenant Organization, focused on affordable housing and rent control, linkage, and lowering utility rates. Other grassroots organizations were fighting airport expansion in East Boston alongside a broad cross-section of neighborhood leaders who populated the campaign. Neil Sullivan and Tom "Alex" Bledsoe were both Fair Share organizers who joined his city council staff to begin organizing for a run at the mayor's office. Tom Snyder, another Fair Share leader, who became Flynn's administrative services director, thought, "The theory was to try to find ways to unify ordinary working people across the divides of race or ethnic divisions in Boston. That's what Ray Flynn embodies."[35] Harry Grill, director of organizing for Boston Fair Share, would play an important role later in the administration's organizing efforts, such as the Boston Youth Campaign, the appointed school committee, and the Mandela secession referenda.

Fair Share is a grassroots social and economic justice organizing group founded in 1975 by Michael Ansara, a veteran of the antiwar movement and Students for a Democratic Society. In the populist organizing style of veteran community organizers like Saul Alinsky, the politics of both Fair Share and Flynn were aligned to replace divisive social issues with policies aimed at redistributing wealth to the poor and needy. Flynn initially didn't want to be associated with Fair Share, believing they might be too radical. Still, he said then, "But then I saw them fighting against the utility hikes, and I knew that Boston Edison had all of a sudden started charging my mother an extra $6 a month on her bill, so I joined with them on that issue and other things too."[36] Grill described Flynn's style in dealing with populist issues: "He was like a Fair Share leader."[37]

Flynn also drew on the network of leaders of the community schools and community health centers. Mayor White had created the community schools overseen by boards of neighborhood leaders, but later, in his final term, he tried unsuccessfully to close them. Because Flynn supported the community schools and health centers as a member of the Boston City Council, the local councils that ran these organizations now gave Flynn a natural network of additional support.

Other progressive allies included the Massachusetts Tenants Organization, which fought to save rent control in Boston. Tom Gallagher, who served in the state legislature in the 1980s and was one of its most left-wing members, recalled, "Ray Flynn had far and away the most concern for issues affecting poor people and the average working person. He has shown concern for the forgotten sector, the people in the neighborhoods, the public housing projects, and those perceived as not voting and, therefore, having no clout."[38] Michael Kane, a tenants' rights organizer and a King supporter, said of Flynn, "He had attracted all the good people in South Boston and had all those votes with him, kind of a Catholic left undercurrent. It was no accident that he had a photograph of Mother Teresa on the wall of his city council office. His moral vision was not that different from Berrigan's. [Daniel Berrigan, SJ, was an American Jesuit priest, antiwar activist, and Christian pacifist.] He was really strong on the right issues."[39]

Flynn also had strong support from organized labor. He received the first union endorsement in the campaign from Local 26 of the Hotel, Restaurant, Institutional Employees, and Bartenders Union on March 13, 1983. Flynn reflected on the endorsement fight:

> Mel King deserved the endorsement of Local 26. Most of the people were Black and Hispanic. Some people who were doing the catering were White mothers and single mothers. How did they swing my way? I was down there when they were picketing and demonstrating the building of new hotels going up nonunion under Kevin White. I showed up with coffee and two dozen doughnuts and gave them to the people on the picket line. After the third day, I met with the picketers and said, "I promise you one thing when I'm the mayor of Boston: no hotel will be built unless it's union." That was it.[40]

As *Boston Globe* columnist Robert Turner reported during the mayoral race, "Dominic Bozzotto, head of Local 26, said Flynn deserved the endorsement because he had supported the union at least as much as King. However, he added that the supposed prospects of the candidates played a role for some union executive board members. 'It's a shame, but I hear it often,' Bozzotto said. 'We've got to go with the possibility of winning. You hear that 'the only difference between Flynn and King is that Flynn can be elected mayor and King can't be.'"[41] The Boston Police Patrolmen's Association endorsed David Finnegan, former member of the Boston School Committee and the frontrunner, having run for mayor before, because they thought he could win, and the Boston Teachers Union endorsed Flynn because of his strong record on education. In a slap at King, the *Bay State Banner*, a weekly newspaper that served the Black community, endorsed Finnegan, thinking he could win and King could not.

While many progressives supported Flynn, many others were wary. Activists in the King campaign believed they had the moral high ground and were critical of the progressives who supported Flynn over King. As they wrote in *Radical America* after the election, "To our knowledge, the only leftists who supported Flynn were whites, predominantly white men at that, oriented to a social-democratic perspective and connected with unions or organizations committed to a 'populist' strategy. Even within this grouping, women active in local tenant organizing failed to rally strongly behind Flynn when the Boston Tenants' Organization endorsed him. Whatever the actual numbers, the more important question is what definition of 'left' or 'progressive' would support Flynn in the name of social change. The only logic that makes sense of this position expects social change to be led and defined by white men."[42]

Rosaria Salerno, a progressive activist, former Catholic nun, and King supporter who later would be elected as an at-large member of the Boston City Council in 1987, recalled, "In 1983, I was working very avidly for Mel. Flynn, who had the young left, had the young progressives with him rather than with Mel King, which was unbelievable for most of us to get our heads around before the victory. Why were they with Flynn? Why weren't they with King? But they were with Flynn. At a ward committee meeting before the preliminary, Flynn was the only candidate who said he would be with King if he didn't win the primary. King had articulated an outstanding agenda for the city, and I expected that I wouldn't be disappointed, that Flynn would marry that agenda and work on it."[43]

Those on the left of politics in Boston had considerable angst with the race between King and Flynn. The leading housing organization, the Massachusetts Tenants' Organization, and its leader, Lew Finfer, describe the process and rationale for their endorsement of Flynn, which was viewed by many as the most significant endorsement in the campaign up until that point:

> Community groups usually don't endorse candidates, but we said, "We're losing; we've got to show some strength." So, we developed a tenant ticket in 1981, and Flynn helped us accomplish much of what we did in '82 and '83. So, in '83, we made the difficult decision through a poll of our membership to endorse. It was very contentious. Most of our membership had experience with Flynn because Flynn was a champion for passing stronger housing laws and the city council's most prominent advocate. The vote was about 68 to 30, a pretty significant margin. Still, I think objectively, it was because we had more White members than people of color, and people's experience was that they'd seen Flynn fight for our cause.[44]

Flynn also drew heavily on his home base of South Boston; while predominantly Irish, there were many Polish and Lithuanian immigrants. His connection to the Irish community in South Boston and across the city, and indeed nationally, was well known. In the preliminary election, David Finnegan, in particular, drew support from the West Roxbury lace-curtain Irish, and Flynn won approval from the working-class and poor first-generation Irish. He also received support from members of groups such as Irish Northern Aid and the Ancient Order of Hibernians, two Irish organizations with roots in Boston. Father Sean McManus, pastor of the Mission Church in the late 1970s, said of Flynn, "He was always there when needed to stand up for equality, justice, and peace in Ireland. He spoke out fearlessly for justice for Catholics in the North of Ireland." These connections were well known to Boston's large Irish Catholic population and paid dividends in the election.

Flynn received no support from the major players of the growth machine in the preliminary election. He told me that Robert Beal, a major developer and member of the Vault, told him there was no way he would get elected. He relied on small campaign donations, and the running joke was that after a Flynn fundraiser, whatever was left over would be put on the bar to buy a round for the volunteers. In the final election, things began to change. The growth coalition was afraid of Flynn, but they were terrified of Mel King. The campaign began to see more significant generosity from those who had so heavily invested in the preliminary campaigns of David Finnegan, Larry DiCara, and Dennis Kearney.

## Melvin Herbert King

On March 28, 2023, Boston civil rights icon and state representative Mel King died at age ninety-four. King was a remarkable man in Boston's social, economic, political, and racial struggles for justice. He was a lifelong Bostonian, born in the South End, where he grew up. I worked with King and was fortunate to interview him for this book.

When his longtime friend King passed away, Flynn was proud to discuss what King did for the city. Kevin Cullen of the *Boston Globe* captured the special relationship between the two men when he wrote, "A Black guy from the South End, a White guy from South Boston, they bonded over basketball and maintained a lifelong friendship despite being political rivals in one of the city's most storied elections."[45] State Representative Byron Rushing spoke about King in his eulogy at his funeral April 11, 2023, "When we remember Mel, we need to understand that he was not ahead of his time. Mel was on time. He was only working in a city where most of its leadership was behind the time, a leadership that, for most of his life, never caught up." Rushing added, "King knew that while the arc of the moral universe may bend toward justice, it does not bend by itself."

King had a vastly different political trajectory from Flynn's. As an African American whose parents came from Barbados and Guyana, he grew up in the multiethnic South End of Boston. His father was a union organizer on the docks, and his mother was active in church and women's groups. King's career began as a teacher. A product of the Boston Public Schools, Claflin College in South Carolina, and Boston Teachers College, he would play many roles in his storied life. From youth worker to community organizer, he worked with youth and families at the United South End Settlements, where he became part of the settlement house movement and worked in the schools and on the streets of Boston. Like Flynn, he actively organized neighborhood youth in sports leagues to divert them from gangs.

King had firsthand experience with the impact of Boston's first urban renewal project. His family lived in the New York Streets area of the South End, which in the mid-1950s was the first section of Boston to face the bulldozers.[46] His family was an early victim of urban renewal. As the *Christian Science Monitor* reported, "King was in his teens, and city officials decided that a 24-acre area of the South End called New York Streets would face the wrecking ball. More than 800 families—including King's—would have to find someplace else to live. A prominent Boston newspaper had labeled the area 'Boston's Skid Row,' which King says 'was crazy. We called it home.' He describes it as a friendly, diverse community filled with working-class people. Still, it was torn down by September 1957."[47] Rushing remembered, "Mel never forgot and was always informed by the South End before gentrification. It informed and developed his ethics and his politics."

As a community organizer in Boston's neighborhoods of color, King saw firsthand the failures of the public schools. An ardent advocate for public education, he knew full well that the voices of parents and students from the communities of color were not being represented—they were ignored. He unsuccessfully sought a seat on the Boston School Committee thrice, in 1961, 1963, and 1965.[48] After failing to get elected to the school committee, he ran for state representative in 1973. He won, becoming one of the few African Americans serving in that legislative body, serving ten years from 1973 to 1983.

King ran for mayor in 1979, surprising many observers by coming in third with 17,490 votes, 15 percent of the vote, behind incumbent Kevin White and challenger Joseph Timilty. King beat fourth-place finisher David Finnegan by 184 votes.

While he did not win, he significantly affected important policies, including jobs for Boston residents, people of color, and women in the construction trades. He led the effort for district representation for the city council and school committee, which was approved by the voters in 1981 by a significant margin. Part of King's strategy for the 1983 mayoral race was to use the citywide charter reform referendum of 1981, which expanded the Boston City Council and Boston School Committee from being entirely at-large bodies to each having nine district representatives and four at-large members, expanding his base into neighborhoods that had not supported him in the past.

King was instrumental in changing city policy regarding community development under Mayor White. He led the fight to the site of what came to be known as Tent City. After more than four thousand people had occupied the site for a multiday period, the city temporarily abandoned its plan for a parking lot for Copley Place.

## Mayoral Candidate Mel King: "The Rainbow Coalition"

King built his 1983 campaign with solid support from the Black community, communities of color, and progressive activists, including leaders in the women's and gay and lesbian rights communities. His campaign was called the "Rainbow Coalition," a term later appropriated by Jesse Jackson's presidential campaigns in 1984 and 1988. King's work in the South End of Boston, fighting displacement, and across the city on racial conflict and education, coalesced a solid and loyal following.

He joined the campaign for mayor in 1983 in a field with eight other candidates. His campaign helped register more than 20,000 new voters in neighborhoods of color. He went from the preliminary election to the final with 47,848 votes, placing a close second by 270 votes to city councilor Ray Flynn with 48,118 votes.[49] King and Flynn were underdogs in the race against more well-financed candidates supported by the business community. King ran a campaign as a "transformative populist," placing the issue of racism front and center in his campaign. He garnered more than 90 percent of the Black vote and nearly 30 percent of White voters but lost to Flynn in a civil and progressive debate on the issues in the city. King and Flynn agreed on the vast majority of Bostonians' problems—principally that they were being left out of the economy in favor of downtown growth. They supported linkage; jobs for residents, people of color, and women; and greater neighborhood participation in city planning and decision-making.

As Jose Masso, a leader in Boston's Latino community and popular radio personality since 1975 with his WBUR show *¡Con Salsa!* explained, "Many leaders in the Latino community saw King as the leader of the 'progressives,' and we saw the future as a coalition representing the city's diversity."[50] Mossik Hacobian, another King supporter who lived in East Boston, ran a nonprofit community group called Urban Edge in Jamaica Plain. "Mel's was the first political campaign I got involved in," he said. "We were part of the Mel King Rainbow Coalition. It was a breakthrough for Mel to have a campaign office in East Boston. It was pretty bold then to have a Black politician in East Boston. Mel's candidacy was an opportunity to deal with the question of racism in Boston. So, it's not like I've ever been a real engaged political activist. It just seemed like a good thing to do to support. What he said was very inclusive about the Rainbow Coalition bringing everybody together. This whole injustice of the rich exploiting the poor seemed like Mel's campaign was dealing with that. It was refreshing to see that you could have a Black finalist in an election in a place as big as Boston."[51]

King's coalition included historically marginalized or ignored groups in Boston politics. As May Louie, a founding member of the Chinese Progressive Association, recalled, 1983 was her first electoral campaign, and she was part of the field apparatus of the King campaign:

> It was the first campaign in which the Asian activists were immersed. We learned to do all the traditional work. It was the first time in Boston that there was literature in Chinese in a political race. We wanted the community to vote in an informed manner for the interests of our community. We wanted to know where the candidates stand. Historically, there has been this internal tension within the community about traditional forces and the old guard with the rising young activist grassroots and grassroots right. Because the old guard is also the ward boss. So, we kept seeing the community shrink, and yeah, all of that was part of a lead-up. And the '83 mayor's race was the first time the activist sector was involved in a campaign. So, the ward bosses had been running the elections, and in '81, we passed district representation for the city council and school committee elections.[52]

Black business leaders were wary of King's radicalism. Some supported him reluctantly because they recognized the importance of electing Boston's first Black mayor, but they disagreed with his policy views, which they considered antibusiness. Flash Wiley, a prominent Black business leader in Boston, recalled a conversation he and other Black leaders had with King. "When Mel decided to run again in '83, he came to a group of us in the business community," he said. "Mel Miller, being one of the key opinion makers and publisher of Boston's newspaper serving the Black community, was there along with some other folks to talk about how he could get us on board. We told him, this may sound silly to you, but if you start looking like a mayor and look serious, put a coat and tie on, I think you'll get a lot more serious attention to what you're saying. Some of the things you say, many things you say, we can go along with, but we're business guys, so we don't go along with everything you say, but at least we know we'll have access."[53]

The King progressive activists saw themselves as the "true" progressives in the 1983 election. As they wrote in their analysis of the election for *Radical America*, "Though all white, we are a varied group. What drew us to such an extraordinary level of commitment and unanimity was the chance to be involved in a broad-based, multiracial coalition that seemed open to us as socialists, feminists, or lesbians. 'For once, I did not have to deny any part of my identity to work in a political campaign, let alone an election.' The campaign seemed to be a social movement with receptivity to radical ideas that allowed us to overcome long-standing skepticism about the usefulness of electoral politics."[54] King's campaign manager Pat Walker explained, "Mel saw the district representation campaign as the launching pad for the '83 race. We hoped to mobilize enough of the people traditionally sitting out during at-large elections and mobilize them for the district elections, bringing out a broader non–African American base to go after and a more energized African American base because people saw him as their representative."[55]

Despite the conflicts over ideology and political strategy, race did not appear to be an overarching issue in the October 11, 1983, preliminary election.

## The 1983 Preliminary Election for Mayor

After White's sixteen-year mayoralty, neighborhood organizations and residents strongly believed Boston needed a new direction. In May 1983, after White announced his decision not to seek reelection, nine candidates would compete for the top two spots on Boston's nonpartisan October 1983 preliminary election ballot. The candidates were city councilors Raymond L. Flynn and Frederick C. Langone; former city councilor Lawrence S. DiCara; former state representative Melvin H. King; former school committee president David I. Finnegan; Suffolk County sheriff Dennis J. Kearney; former Massachusetts Bay Transportation Authority (MBTA) general manager and deputy mayor under White, Robert R. Kiley; and two marginal contenders, Michael Gelber of the LaRouche movement and Eloise Linger of the Socialist Workers Party.

With the passage of the district representation charter change in 1981, this would be the first time since 1949 that city council and school committee candidates would be vying for district seats. The elite reformers, who sought in the late 1940s to dislodge Curley's Irish political machine and control city government on behalf of the growth machine, had made four significant changes to the governmental structure, which were challenged by the charter change. They had devised a new electoral system to wipe out ward politics, created the nine-member at-large city council, created the city's redevelopment apparatus, and altered the city's tax structure to attract private investment.[56]

The three previous mayors followed this path, but now the 1983 election would create a backdrop for the two progressive candidates, Flynn and King, to challenge Boston's growth machine. The other major candidates, Finnegan, DiCara, and Kearney, were willing to support the growth machine's interests and raised significant campaign funds from real estate, development, and banking interests.

The principal beneficiary of the growth machine's largesse was David Finnegan. He positioned himself as the alternative to Kevin White before White dropped out of the race with the campaign slogan, "Finnegan or him again." Finnegan inherited much of White's political machine and campaign contributors interested in continuing White's downtown development policies. A former member of the Boston School Committee and popular radio talk show host, Finnegan, from Dorchester, was the frontrunner in the 1983 race. He ran for mayor in 1979, finishing fourth behind White, Joe Timilty, and King.

Another contender backed by growth machine interests, Larry DiCara, had grown up in Dorchester and attended Boston Latin School and Harvard University. He was elected to the Boston City Council in 1971 at twenty-two. While DiCara supported the district representation campaign in 1977 and 1981, as a member of the Boston City Council and its president in 1978, he had long been positioning himself for a run at the mayor's office. He sought the mayor's office in 1979 before dropping out late in the race to take another shot in 1983. DiCara reflected on his campaign in his 2013 memoir, "For the first time since 1949, the best-educated candidate and the most progressive candidate did not win."[57] He was, of course, referring to himself, probably the only person who believed he was progressive. Not included in his memoir was campaign finance information related by one of his prominent supporters, Vin McCarthy, a gay activist and Boston lawyer who served as DiCara's campaign treasurer: "Larry DiCara got his campaign in trouble because Mario Nicosia, a major contributor, had bought up most of the South End real estate and proceeded to buy full-page newspaper ads, listing the ads as coming from the DiCara committee. That wasn't allowed under the law. I had to audit the campaign. We didn't find any direct involvement by the candidate, so he was able to stay in the race. I doubt Ray Flynn would have won the election if Larry had dropped out. The real establishment candidate was David Finnegan, who, best I can describe, was a 1983 version of John Collins and John B. Hynes."[58]

DiCara also had the support of, in the words of some King's supporters, "a small liberal gentry stratum of gays who supported Larry DiCara (an anti-union, pro-business liberal) in the preliminary."[59] The King campaign believed they had cornered the entire politicized lesbian and gay community, except for this small segment.

Dennis Kearney, the sitting Suffolk County sheriff during the mayoral election in 1983 and supporter of growth machine interests, served as a state representative from East Boston and Charlestown from 1975 to 1977. Kearney followed a path from Boston Latin School to Harvard University and was an adept politician with broad support from his East Boston roots and the Suffolk County sheriff's payroll.

Bob Kiley, a former member of White's administration and for a time the general manager of the MBTA, wasn't given much of a chance in the race. A New York native, he would position himself as the reformer outside the ethnic politics that had shaped contests for the mayor's office. City councilor Frederick C. Langone also lacked strong support, but the colorful twenty-two-year city council veteran from Boston's North End would make the race enjoyable.

"It was the first time that there was a mayor's forum in Chinatown," May Louie, a Chinatown activist, remarked. It was the first time the activist sector was involved in a campaign, as before, the ward bosses had been running the elections."[60] Pent-up demand for change, voter interest, and new voter registration soared. In contrast to the experiences in many other urban areas, turnout would reach an all-time high.

## Issues in the 1983 Race for Mayor

All those interviewed agreed that race relations were at the top of the list of concerns for the next mayor. However, when polled in August 1983, most Boston voters cited crime as issue number one for the new mayor.[61] Flynn grappled with rising crime as a campaign issue but then thought better of it. It wasn't his lane. Along with King, he was a champion for the tenants, poor and working-class residents. As his pollster, Allan Stern, recalled, he told Flynn, "People want authentic candidates. Crime is not your issue, but housing is. Whether or not it is important to voters, they know you are passionate on the issue—and that matters."[62]

Each candidate staked out their position on many problems facing Boston residents. The issues debated at the various neighborhood forums ranged from housing affordability and rent control, job creation, city services, and downtown-versus-neighborhood development to linkage and a policy to tax downtown development and use the funds to build affordable housing. The same poll found that more than 76 percent of the electorate supported linkage, and voters favored rent control by a two-to-one margin.[63] Those interviewed recalled a strong feeling in Boston's neighborhoods that in the later years of the White administration, they had been abandoned in favor of building Boston's downtown skyline and Faneuil Hall for tourists. Menino, recalling that contest in retrospect in 2014, questioned Flynn's and King's approach to development: "Mayoral candidates who were identified with White lost in the primary. The two finalists attacked 'the downtown interests' and, to my ear, sounded not just pro-neighborhood but anti-development, even anti-business. After sixteen years of Kevin White, 'development' versus 'the neighborhoods' was good politics, but was it good policy?"[64]

"There was only one thing that people talked about, and that is how you'd be different from White," DiCara said. "Kevin had outstayed his welcome."[65] Several of the preliminary election candidates interviewed reflected on the friendly tone of the race. As the sheriff and mayoral candidate Kearney recalled, "So, it was pretty friendly until about August when Bob Kiley decided to go negative on Ray [Flynn] and me, figuring that he had to knock us down for him to have a chance. But since Ray was polling better than me, he focused on Ray. Kiley attacked Ray, so it didn't get testy till September. At that point, the primary was just a couple of weeks away, but it was pretty friendly for most of the race. We were all out there doing our thing, and it wasn't that negative a race until the last couple of weeks."[66]

Kiley began an attack on Flynn on August 17, 1983, in a debate when he declared that Flynn was "on the wrong side of the police lines during the city's busing crisis." The issue resurfaced during one of the three televised debates of the preliminary race on September 14, 1983, when Kiley again challenged Flynn on his role in the busing crisis. Flynn shot back, "During the racial turmoil, I was out in the streets, talking to students and parents, white and black. I didn't see anyone else there behind me. In 1983, I was criticized for that. If we could return to 1974, we'd see who the peacemakers were."[67]

There were several other notable flare-ups during the campaign. Finnegan called out Flynn on what he called a divisive strategy for distributing different campaign materials in Black and White neighborhoods.[68] The final confrontation between Flynn and Finnegan was on the steps of city hall during a live newscast several days before the preliminary election. Frank Costello, Flynn's campaign press secretary, who later would assume that role in the new administration, recalled, "On the way to the press conference, Ray asked me, 'Why's he even calling me a chameleon? What is this chameleon?' I said, 'It's a lizard.' He says, 'A lizard?' I said, 'Actually, it changes color.' Flynn said he became angry with Finnegan Thursday night just before he confronted him on a WBZ-TV Channel 4 live newscast when his eleven-year-old daughter, Nancy, heard the radio ad and asked him what a chameleon is."[69] Setting the stage for the face-off, the Finnegan ad ran, "Do you know what a chameleon is? A chameleon is an animal that changes its color to fit its place. Can you think of any politicians like that? Well, take Ray Flynn, for instance. He's been for the ERA, and in another place, he's been against it. He was for capital punishment, then moved a little and came out against it. He's been for and against Ed King. For and against Ronald Reagan. For and against hiring more cops. He even distributed two different brochures in one neighborhood."[70]

Flynn responded on live TV,

David Finnegan, here in Boston, is the candidate of the rich. Many people are poor, who are looking for housing, who want to walk the streets in safety, who can't find jobs, and whose children can't get educated. David Finnegan is taking all the money from the downtown interests, which has been fundamentally wrong in this city for the longest time. This will not be a campaign for the rich and David Finnegan representing their interests. Ray Flynn is going to fight that every step of the way. David, I will tell you that the building behind us is not for sale. That building belongs to the people of this city, the people that our parents brought to this country to fight for integrity and honesty in government. It's not for sale, David. I'm not going to allow it to be for sale, and I'm going to fight it every single step of the way.[71]

Each candidate had a different take on the face-off. Finnegan's press secretary, Listo Fisher, said of Flynn, "He's falling apart; he's falling apart." Peter G. Meade, a member of the White administration and Finnegan adviser (and later the BRA director under Mayor Menino), shook Finnegan's hand and said, "Congratulations, I think you just won the election." Flynn's press secretary, Francis Costello, said the Finnegan ads represented a "desperation tactic from a candidate groping through innuendo to find a spot in the preliminary election." After the interview, Finnegan said that he thought Flynn "lost his cool." Flynn disputed, saying, "I just tried to state my position. What he was stating was something I wouldn't sit still for."[72]

Brian Wallace, a longtime friend of Flynn's from South Boston, described the two candidates' different approaches: "I spoke to a friend who told me he and his wife were at the Falmouth Yacht Club on July 4, 1983, when Finnegan and his entourage came in. They all had been drinking heavily, and they kept introducing Finnegan as the next mayor of Boston. I told my wife, 'Ray Flynn just hit his thirteenth barbeque in West Roxbury. I knew then that Finnegan would not win.'"[73]

While Flynn and Finnegan were jousting on City Hall Plaza, King was with Jesse Jackson and eight hundred supporters in the South End's Concord Baptist Church, declaring that his Rainbow Coalition had already changed Boston. King introduced Jackson at the endorsement rally as a "country preacher" and provided him with a copy of his book, *Chain of Change*. The large crowd was holding "Mel King for Mayor" signs in English, Chinese, and Spanish, chanting, "Win, Mel, win," and "Run, Jesse, run," encouraging Jackson's 1984 run for the presidency. Jackson did run, garnering more than three million votes, winning five primaries and 18 percent of the vote total.[74]

During the preliminary in the 1983 mayoral race, most candidates were reluctant to use the word "racism" in forums and events. The major candidates in that election responded to the question of whether Boston is a racist city with the following: DiCara: "Boston's not a racist city. The city certainly has racial problems. The problems are cultural; they are historic." Finnegan: "No, nobody can deny there are racial problems, racial disharmony. It's probably the one scar on the fabric of an otherwise progressive city." Flynn: "I think there are significant problems relative to racial relations, like many American cities. However, I think the real problem is economic discrimination." King: "Yes. There's an incredibly high level of racism in the city of Boston. I think it's important that we begin with the term racism because if we don't, we are not going to come to the kind of solutions to the problem that Boston requires." Kearney: "I think there are problems of racism in Boston, but no more so than in the population at large in the country."[75]

So, except for King and Kearney, the candidates did not want to label the city racist. The final two candidates, King and Flynn, took different approaches, which are evident in their remarks. As discussed earlier, King followed the transformative populist approach, and Flynn followed the redistributive populist approach.[76]

The common political wisdom was that Finnegan would be one of the two finalists. Finnegan had secured broad support from several factions, including growth machine and downtown business interests. As a result of his presumed frontrunner status, the political wise guys jumped on board with Finnegan when White declined to seek reelection. The biggest surprise to the old guard was that King had a chance. As DiCara put it, "I don't think anybody started to figure that Mel would be in the final because the Black community traditionally has had lower turnouts in preliminary elections. Mel did extraordinarily well among Black people and young and educated people; when he ran in '79, he'd got 17,000 votes. When he ran in '83, he got 48,000."[77]

The political wisdom was turned on its head when Flynn and King were the top vote-getters in the preliminary election on October 11, 1983. Flynn received 48,118 votes, outpacing King's 47,848 by 270 votes. Each gained support from 28 percent of the electorate and won eleven of the city's twenty-two wards, thus propelling them into the final. Many believed the chameleon incident helped Flynn pass Finnegan to face King in the runoff. And resulted in a sharp and durable realignment away from the growth machine politics of the previous three administrations. Fifty-six percent of the electorate in the preliminary election supported either King or Flynn over the more traditional growth machine-backed candidates.

A key dynamic in the election was the number of new voters. Registrations increased by over 20,000 in the Black community, and voter registration went from 48 percent the previous year to 83 percent in 1983.[78] By September 1983, Boston saw some 40,000 new voter registrations, with the majority in predominantly Black voting wards.

More than 169,039 residents went to the polls on October 15, 1983, far exceeding all Boston's municipal elections since 1949, when the population was one-third larger: this turnout vaulted King and Flynn into the final election in November.[79]

The strongest reaction to the election results came from *Boston Globe* cartoonist Paul Szep in his depiction of Dame Boston (symbolizing the Vault, Boston's corporate leaders) fainting and being rescued by King in a dashiki and Flynn in a scally cap. It was now clear to the growth machine and their allies that one of two progressive populist candidates would soon be mayor of Boston. The son of a longshoreman and cleaning lady from South Boston would face off in the final election against an African American South End political activist.

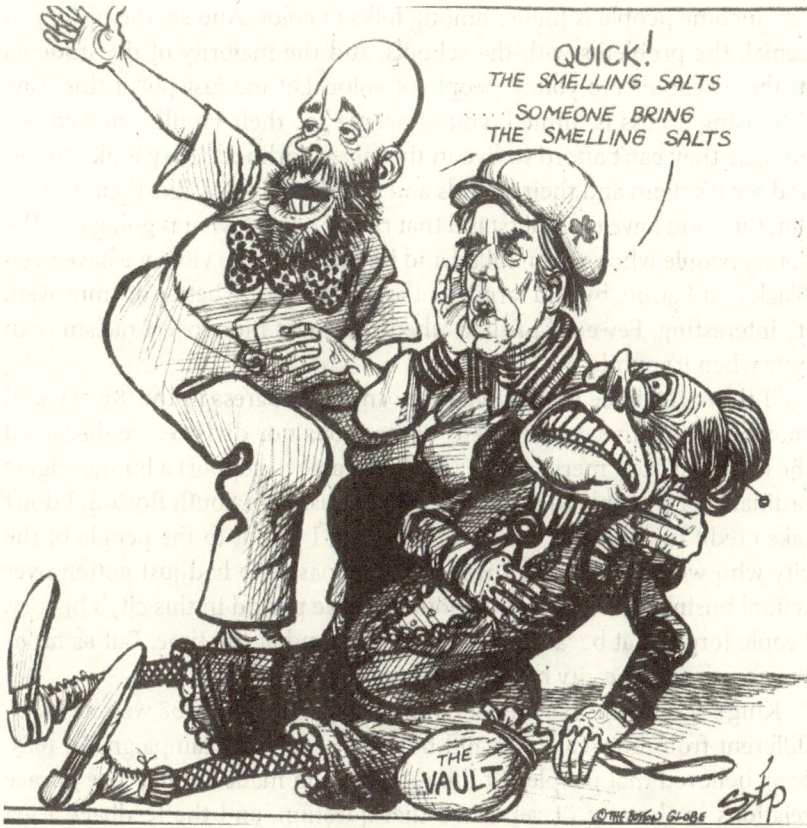

King and Flynn exchanged these words at a debate after the preliminary election: "Given that there are reports that the business community is afraid of the two of us, what do you think is wrong with them?" asked Mel King. "I think they just went astray somewhere," answered Ray Flynn.[80]

## Final Election November 15, 1983

On the surface, with a White candidate from Irish South Boston and a Black candidate from the integrated South End, race certainly would be an issue in the final campaign. Both men recalled in 2008 their somewhat different perspectives on race as a campaign issue. "Race is *always* a strong word, either an issue or related," King said. "The proportion of low-income people is higher among folks of color. And so, the history of denial, the problems with the schools, and the majority of the students in these schools are young people of color. Let me just put it this way: if housing access is limited, young people see their families moved out because they can't afford to live in this neighborhood. They look around and see it's them and their friends and people who look like them moved out, then you have to understand that race is part of what is going on. The young people who've been killed and impacted by the violence have been Black and Latino, by and large. You ask if things are better or improved; it's interesting. Fewer of us died when there was more overt racism than now when it's subtle."[81]

"I think the issue of race made enormous progress in the '83 mayoral campaign," Flynn said. "It wasn't contentious nor divisive; we discussed the issues on their merits. As mayor, I was able to support a human rights ordinance. I was able to integrate public housing in South Boston. I don't take credit for it. I give credit to Mel King. I give it to the people of the city who were tired of the division of the past. We had just gotten over school busing, the most contentious, divisive period in this city's history. People forget that because they weren't around at the time. But as far as I'm concerned, the city has come a long way."[82]

King's and Flynn's recollections and perspectives in 2008 weren't much different from how each felt and how they ran their campaigns in 1983. King believed that people felt the 1983 election made a difference in race relations in the city. "I get asked that question, and the feedback I get from people I meet around the city is that they say yes," King said. "The kind of campaign we ran made a difference in the city, and they thought it brought the city closer together. They felt that given the city's racial climate and polarization, they had more access to different parts of the city than before. That was one of the significant aspects of having a coalition of a cross-section of folks where the issue was access for all, including race, gender, and age. The night the results came in, I walked into the ballroom and saw all those folks out there celebrating, and I asked them if they knew what the election results were. It made me understand that we won something. We didn't get to be mayor, but something different happened in the city due to people coming together."[83]

Flynn won the mayor's race, beating King 65 percent to 35 percent on November 15, 1983, in a turnout of over 201,118, or 70 percent of the electorate. This election saw the largest turnout in Boston's history since the 1949 election when the city's population exceeded 801,000, versus the 563,000 of 1980.

TABLE 2. Final Election for Mayor of Boston, Voter Turnout and Population

| Year | Votes Cast | Percentage Registered Voters who voted | Boston Population± |
|------|-----------|-----------------------------------------|---------------------|
| 1949 | 300501 | 74% | 766386—Hynes (W) Curley (L) |
| 1967 | 195624 | 68% | 616326 (1965)—White |
| 1971 | 189534 | 64% | 616326 (1965) White |
| 1975 | 159363 | 62% | 637986 (1975) White |
| 1979 | 147743 | 61% | 637986 (1975) White |
| **1983** | **201118** | **70%** | **562994 (1980)—Flynn** |
| 1987 | 98591 | 40% | 601095 (1985) Flynn |
| 1991 | 89885 | 39% | 601095 (1985) Flynn |
| 1993* | 118317 | 51% | 574283 (1990)—Menino |
| 1997 | 67798 | 28% | 555860 Menino |
| 2001 | 88871 | 36% | 602360 Menino |
| 2005 | 97160 | 36% | 609690 Menino |
| 2009 | 111190 | 31% | 645169 Menino |
| 2013 | 142007 | 38% | 653103—Walsh |
| 2017 | 109034 | 28% | 688276 Walsh |
| 2021 | 144380 | 33% | 654283—Wu |

.Source: City of Boston Election Department

Flynn became the first mayor elected from South Boston. In 1914, South Boston's Thomas Kenny, with the support of both the Irish-dominated Democratic Party machine and the Yankee Republicans, was beaten by James Michael Curley, and Curley carried South Boston with 53.4 percent of the vote.

Based upon the intensity and extent of electoral engagement, the 1983 mayoral election was a critical election in Boston history, one that was to begin the process of realigning priorities and bringing new optimism to the city. As Flynn and his supporters knew, however, his tenure as mayor would not be without its challenges, especially around issues of race relations after defeating the first African American finalist in the city's history.

## How Did Flynn Win?

Many factors led to Flynn's victory. He had been running for mayor since his election as an at-large member of the Boston City Council in 1977 and had a record of having worked on issues across the city. While he maintained a strong base in his home neighborhood of South Boston, his focus on issues impacting poor and working-class residents resonated in many neighborhoods across the city. Flynn had a broad-based campaign staff led by Ray Dooley, whom Flynn would hire to broaden the campaign's appeal. Dooley had been a member of Students for a Democratic Society and aide to progressive state representative Tom Gallagher from Brighton. The campaign organizers tapped into the "pockets of coalitions" from housing organizations, pro-life groups, labor, sports leagues, Irish leaders, women, community groups, and neighborhood activists. Flynn built a team that could transcend traditional politics in Boston. Peter Dreier recounts, "Flynn needed to get liberal activists on his side, knowing that he couldn't be elected mayor with only the working-class Whites from South Boston, Charlestown, and Dorchester. So he cultivated the community organizers and leaders from groups like Massachusetts Fair Share, the Massachusetts Tenants Organization, liberal unions like Service Employees International Union (SEIU) and the hotel workers, and others who had been through the battles of the previous decade around institutional expansion, income inequality, tenants' rights, tax reform, gentrification, and other issues."[84] Others shared similar memories, as a then-Roxbury resident and King supporter Flash Wiley remembered: "Ray Flynn asked if he could come to speak to the African American community in Boston because he was planning on running for mayor, and he wanted to talk, find out what our needs were, and get a sense of us. So, Nixon went to China, and Flynn came to Roxbury."[85] McCarthy, a liberal partner in the large Boston law firm of Hale and Dorr who supported DiCara's campaign, also recalled, "Even during his campaign, when he was running against Mel King in the final, Ray had no reason to expect to receive significant votes in the Black community. Still, he went to every candidate night in the Black community, shook every hand he could, and was very gracious. Of course, that paid off immediately after the election because people felt safe with Ray as mayor. Ray became the mayor of the Black people, the gay people, and the wealthy people had to put up with him; that's the best way you can say it."[86]

"If you have confidence in yourself and you believe in yourself," as Flynn reflected, "you want to meet as many people as you possibly can and express to them who you are. Beacon Hill, Roxbury, Bay Village, South Boston, it doesn't matter, gays, Blacks, Jews, Brahmin Yankees, Irish Catholic. It doesn't matter."[87]

While Flynn campaigners attributed the victory to the ragtag coalition of poor Whites and poor Blacks, a lot of labor, and having run a fierce campaign, DiCara offered a different conclusion: "The question was who would be the two finalists, and most of us knew, but we wouldn't have said that publicly at the time; we knew that if one of the finalists was Mel King, then the other person would be mayor. Most of us thought Finnegan would be in the final."[88]

Ken Wade, Roxbury coordinator for King's campaign and a South End activist, said at the time, "The mayoral election in '83 was a turning point in the city's history. Both candidates who reached the final election symbolized Boston's desire to get beyond the past."[89] Wade remembered that Flynn and King had strong records on the issues: "Given the things that Ray ran on and that Mel ran on, it seemed we had two candidates that were very similar regarding where they were on the issues. It suggested that the city had turned the corner. Kevin White served sixteen years, and in 1983, there was a lot of concern that there wasn't a lot of focus on the neighborhoods. Ray and Mel thought the community needed to be more involved in the development decisions that affected their communities. They had robust, affordable housing platforms. They believed that the schools needed attention. There were many similarities."[90] *Boston Globe* columnist David Nyhan summed up the sense of the city when he described the preliminary election:

It couldn't have been closer. A few votes separated Ray Flynn, a craggy-faced Irish battler from South Boston, Rocky with Shamrocks, and Mel King, a brawny, bald, bearded black activist who brought his dashiki from the streets to the State House. They spent barely $200,000 each, besting three rivals who spent a combined $2 million. Flynn and King ran mirror-image campaigns on ground-floor economic issues: housing, jobs for the underclass, and dignity for the poor. They had virtually no TV ads except for a few at the end. They retailed their way into the final on unrelenting evocations of the aspirations of the dispossessed. They rose together on the hopes of the poor, the near-poor, and a working class that felt left behind in Kevin White's glitzy downtown. Neighborhood people, trying to keep their block from sliding into urban desolation, took a stand for Flynn or King. This pair is virtually interchangeable on racial harmony, jobs for the poor, strict controls on condo conversions, and better public housing in a town where one-tenth of the people live in mainly substandard public projects. The chosen alternatives are the tireless populism of Flynn, the Joe Sixpack of the field, or the dignified determination of the impassive and imposing King. Flynn came out of Southie battling abortion and busing and molted into a little-guy hero on rent control. Like King, he became a symbol of change. Empowerment of the poor and working class was their twinned theme.[91]

Others felt that Flynn won because of the issue of race coupled with the King campaign organization's failures. As Nyhan commented, "King's runoff campaign was a sociological triumph but a political disaster. His quixotic self-imposed $150,000 campaign spending cap deprived him of any serious radio and television ads. Some ill-conceived remarks about anti-Semitism and Fidel Castro backfired. He got 29 percent in the preliminary but only 35 percent in the final."[92] The *Boston Globe* poll two weeks before the final election reported,

> Since King's nomination three weeks ago, there has been considerable political speculation that some voters would not consider his candidacy because he is black. That perception appears to be supported by the polling data. For instance, a third of those sampled did not "strongly disagree" with the following statement when read to them: "If a black person is elected mayor of Boston, it would be bad for the city." Among the 65 percent of those polled who strongly disagreed with the statement, King led Flynn by 52 to 37 percent. But Flynn held a commanding lead of 73 to 10 percent among the 32 percent who agreed with the statement or expressed only mild disagreement. Irwin Harrison, the president of Research Analysis Corp., explained that the question was designed to test resistance to a black candidacy. "Anyone who did not strongly disagree with the statement is at least partially receptive to such arguments," Harrison said. As evidence of that phenomenon, Harrison noted that, even among those who expressed mild disagreement with the statement, Flynn held a 67 to 12 percent margin over King. The issue's sentiment appears to have changed since the question was asked during a poll conducted for the *Globe* in August. Then, only 51 percent "strongly disagreed" with the statement, compared with 65 percent last week. The survey also disclosed that King's politics are unsettling to some voters. More than a third of those sampled said they believe King "is too much of a radical." Only 6 percent said that of Flynn, who holds positions similar to King on many economic issues facing the city.[93]

In assessing why King lost, King's campaign chair, J. D. Nelson, offered, "Both candidates conducted a good, high-class race. Many people did not see real differences between Mel King and Ray Flynn. Many people have indicated it was a different choice, so we were unsuccessful in showing some real differences. You have to say that if people perceived no differences, they went with their natural inclinations. That is, they voted for their own."[94]

# 4 /  Community Organizing as Political Governance

*Not all those Flynn hired were community organizers when they arrived, but broadly defined, they were expected to play that role and help organize to achieve the administration's policy objectives. Decentralizing power and impact was both an internal and external objective of organizing.* (John Riordan, director of neighborhood services, interview)

When Flynn assumed the mayor's office, he did so with his family and many "pockets of coalitions." To broaden the scope of his governance, Flynn populated his administration with diverse leaders from Boston neighborhoods; activists and community organizers; African American, Latino, Asian, and LGBTQ+ leaders; labor organizations; and newcomers from the influx of Bostonians. He even appointed supporters of his rivals and offered his 1983 opponent, Mel King, and members of his Rainbow Coalition positions in the administration. This inclusive approach, akin to that described by Doris Kearns Goodwin in her renowned book *Team of Rivals: The Political Genius of Abraham Lincoln,* brought together people from all the coalitions that propelled him to victory, including those from opposing campaigns who were politically astute. He even hired unsuccessful city council and school committee candidates, recognizing their political skills, sense, and constituencies as assets to expand the new administration's reach. The young political and neighborhood activists and the established city leaders in the neighborhoods all found a place in the Flynn administration.

Constructing the governing regime was no easy task. It involved assembling an administration that could effectively represent the city's diverse interests and address the inherited issues. This was an early test for Flynn, as factions began to form almost immediately over significant policy initiatives.

Many of the newly appointed community and political activists in the Flynn administration were unfamiliar with running a city government.

As Jerry Rubin, a community activist who had worked on the campaign and would later join the administration to work on housing policy, noted, "Governing is more complicated than campaigning. One of the things I'm very proud of with the administration is that we governed pretty close to how we campaigned." This observation reflects the learning curve and the administration's commitment to staying faithful to their campaign promises.[1]

Flynn was acutely aware of his role as the city's new leader. In his first term—and for much of his nearly ten years as mayor—he was omnipresent, arriving at every fire, every incident of racial violence, and every community meeting. When the first snowstorm hit the city soon after he was sworn in, Flynn quickly rode a snowplow (which made the evening news and the morning papers), not only to demonstrate his hands-on approach to governing, but also to show that the city's working-class neighborhoods would be his priority for city services. Under White, city snowplows appeared in wealthier neighborhoods before moving to less-affluent areas. This was part of an articulated strategy to change the dynamic between city hall and the neighborhoods of Boston, and the new mayor recognized this as one of the most significant issues he would face coming into city hall in 1984. "Well, the obvious one was the alienation of the neighborhoods," he explained. "People felt betrayed, and their voice wasn't being heard. Yes, political operatives in the neighborhoods were answerable to city hall and Mayor White. But the people didn't feel that way. And I always felt that good policies are good politics; the more people you could bring in, the less people would feel alienated."[2]

Neil Sullivan, who would first assume the title of director of the Mayor's Office of Neighborhood Services and later policy adviser, remembered that the concerns of the business community were heightened when Flynn appointed his campaign manager and former Students for a Democratic Society leader, Ray Dooley, as director of administrative services. As such, Dooley was the city's chief financial and administrative officer, overseeing the government's treasurer, auditor, budget, labor relations, and personnel functions. Governance—even financial matters—took a leftist turn under Flynn.

Flynn was very conscious of the role women like Rosemarie Sansone and the Women for Flynn had played in his campaign and would play in the administration. He appointed many women to top posts as heads of departments ranging from business and cultural development, health and hospitals, the housing authority, capital planning, constituent services, and economic development, to public facilities, jobs and community services, budget, rent equity, the emergency shelter commission, and as his chief of staff. He appointed the first Latina, Carmen Pola, as his director of constituent services and the first woman as deputy superintendent to head the Boston Police Department's newly created sexual assault unit. Most of these women would continue to play significant roles throughout Flynn's tenure.

Another challenge would include hiring the conservative neighborhood political leaders and the band of progressive activists recruited for the campaign and living up to his promise of creating a diverse city administration. As King supporter and business leader Flash Wiley noted, "Well, the first thing he did was make two historic appointments. He appointed the top two financial guys in the city, Black guys who had been Mel King's supporters. So, George Russell became the city's treasurer, and Leon Stamps became the city's auditor."[3] "I think it's pretty clear that the Flynn administration worked very hard to change the perception of the city to do more to get more people of color involved in significant roles within the administration, and that hadn't happened under Kevin White," King supporter Ken Wade said. "He paid that attention to broadening ties with folks in the community."[4] Flynn reached out to King personally the day after the election, saying he would welcome him and his supporters, offering him a position in the administration. "There were overtures made about whether there would be any interest, and at that point, I didn't have any interest in working for city government at that time," Wade recalled. "I was content to be the outside advocate continuing to push things from that perspective."[5] Wade explained why no substantial number of King's political activists joined the administration: "I think it might have been a combination of loyalty to Mel, even though Mel didn't send that signal," he said. "There were still some issues there that they couldn't figure out how to work out. I think that it might have been many of the activists thinking back then that a better role would be to be on the outside, you know, continuing to push the issues and the agenda that way."[6]

Others directly assessed why King's supporters hadn't joined the administration. "Ray Dooley didn't want to work with us afterward," King's campaign manager, Pat Walker, recalled. "I think he didn't think he needed us. I'm unsure why, but we met with him and Neil Sullivan. I said, 'Well, here you are. You guys have the power. How can we work together?' And it was like a bunch of platitudes, and well, let's get together, and we could do this postelection analysis and this and that. I pursued that for about a year, but Dooley was clearly in control and wanted to minimize his exposure on the left. He was more concerned with the right side, the more traditional Irish working-class base."[7]

Another King campaign organizer, Egelston Square Latino activist Pablo Calderon, offered a different point of view, describing Flynn's approach this way: "Once Ray Flynn was elected, he made it his number-one priority to come out to all of us, organizing for Mel to sit down and say, 'Hey, I want to work with you guys; I want you to become part of my administration. This is what the city needs.' So, he didn't see it as a threat; he reached out to us to see how we could incorporate some of the Latino leaders in his administration, and then he started hiring people, Carmen Pola, constituent services; Felix Arroyo, education adviser; David Cortiella, head of the housing authority; and Jovita Fontanez, election commissioner. I could give you a list of about thirty Latino people he appointed. He opened many opportunities for us, and we knew he was genuine."[8]

John Connolly, Flynn's development adviser, believed Flynn "was trying to get enough players inside the tent so that he could communicate satisfactorily with all the players outside the tent. That's what he was looking for, and that's what he got. He got Neil Sullivan out there talking to everybody a quarter of an inch left of the center. Stephen Coyle and other people were doing the development work. I mean, people were spread out all over the place."[9]

Peter Dreier, who worked with Flynn on the city council and was an early supporter of Flynn's mayoral campaign, became his housing adviser. He recalled efforts to organize the "leftist" faction in Flynn's new administration to coalesce the progressive activists. "I organized a meeting at my apartment, probably during the first six months of the Flynn administration," he said. "I invited people to strategize how we could effectively build bridges between the progressive 'insiders' like ourselves and the progressive 'outsiders' who were doing the organizing work that many of us had been doing before we went to city hall. We didn't want to be divisive within the Flynn administration, but we did want to share ideas about how to get our progressive policy ideas implemented. We knew that Flynn shared many of these policy ideas, but he was also under pressure from others within the administration to avoid looking like he was abandoning his 'base.' Nothing real came out of that meeting because people were nervous that we'd look like we were creating a 'faction' within the administration if the word got out. In the end, we each did our own thing to influence the mayor and connect with the activist groups in the community who appreciated Flynn's progressive policies but thought he wasn't radical enough. I don't know. I didn't want to cast any aspersions, but I felt isolated."[10]

So, in the early days, there was a concerted strategy by most of the new team of leaders in city hall to avoid political divisions by focusing on getting the entire team to follow the lead of their new mayor. "We went after racial violence, municipal finances, and city services," Sullivan said. "We organized neighborhood cleanups, using what we knew about community organizing to make the neighborhoods look better immediately. We saw neighborhood services as an ongoing campaign. Mayor Flynn rode on a snowplow to greet the first big storm. No administration had ever been as ready for a snowstorm. We wanted these to be the areas where we would stake Ray Flynn's claim to leadership as the new mayor of Boston during his first few months in office."

And when it came to racial violence, Flynn followed through on his promise to respond to incidents, personally visiting victims of racial violence. "Mayor Flynn was on the scene for every racial incident that first year—to bring the noise, attention, and focus," Sullivan recalled. "Our number-one priority was ending the racial violence that had persisted for almost a decade, people getting hurt just because they were the wrong color. We went after it, and we got it done. We didn't eliminate racism, but we did end racial violence."[11]

Jim Jordan, a reporter with the Black newspaper *Bay State Banner* who became a press aide to Flynn during his first term and later became director of strategic planning for the Boston Police Department, summarized Flynn's approach this way: "He took the power of the mayor's office and focused on civil rights."[12]

The mayor's leadership style and governance philosophy were crucial for the changed public discourse on race relations and the tangible results of dealing with the issue. Flynn viewed his role in governing Boston this way. "In a city, you don't govern; what you do is your guide," he said. "You try to bring out the best in people. If you can bring out the best in people and help people see the most hopeful part of their lives, I might be able to say something that will help your children and your family. I think that's how you guide and govern the city."[13]

And his philosophy was also evident in the approach he and his administration took to the issues of the day, including race relations. He appeared at nearly every racial incident and promoted racial harmony at every opportunity. From the first Martin Luther King Jr. celebration of his administration at Faneuil Hall in January 1984, Flynn recounted a speech given by eleven-year-old Robert Rodney at a city-sponsored event. The event was held at the city's Parkman House, the second significant community event since Flynn took office. Using the Parkman House for community events was a divergence from the practice of White, who used the facility, located on exclusive Beacon Street, for private events. Flynn recalled what happened after the young boy gave the speech. "He got himself so worked up after he delivered this Martin Luther King speech, 'I Have a Dream,'" he said. "There was this awkward moment where he didn't know what to do. So, he turned around, walked over to me, and hugged me, like a mother would do with a scared child. And of all these people, there were many Black people on that stage that he could have walked over and hugged. But what he decided to do was come walking over, and he hugged me. I've thought of that a hundred times, 'Why me, and why not his teacher?' Well, that, to me, was one of the most meaningful symbols of the moment. I knew right then and there that I didn't need to read an editorial, I didn't need to look at the election results, and I knew I had made it in Boston. I knew that I was his mayor."[14]

While consciously emphasizing racial harmony, Flynn's governing philosophy also focused on class issues in the city. As a progressive leader, he promoted broader social and economic justice themes. In his inaugural speech, he said, "The hopes that unite us are greater than the fears that divide us."[15] He sought to translate that mantra into both policy and politics. He often spoke about the effects of poverty. He championed the cause of people without housing in Boston and later nationally as leader of the US Conference of Mayors' Committee on Hunger and Homelessness.

Flynn shared a similar philosophy with the four-time mayor, James Michael Curley, who said, "Government was not created to save money and to cut debt, but to take care of people. That's my theory of government."[16]

In summarizing his political philosophy, he discussed the three pictures that adorned the walls of his large office in city hall that overlooked Faneuil Hall. "St. Francis house: we helped them build that St. Francis homeless shelter, and they invited me down for breakfast one morning, and the homeless people were all there," he said. "And they presented me with a picture, and it's a Dorothy Day picture. And it's entitled 'Christ in the Bread Line.' Now I had that: if you walked in my door, if you walked in the mayor's office, immediately to the left. There were no political pictures except one of Hubert Humphrey on the wall. But I never had pictures of myself. I had a picture of a young Black fellow who gave this Martin Luther King address over at Faneuil Hall, mesmerizing the place. That's my politics right there in that picture."[17]

## Community Empowerment—Neighborhood Councils and Planning

In his inaugural address at the Wang Center on the first day of the new administration, Flynn made a promise he kept throughout his tenure. "Ours is to be a time of rebirth in Boston's neighborhoods," he said. "A new generation of neighborhood leaders will begin the process of decentralizing the delivery of services. Our theory of government will be trickle-up, not trickle-down. Let the word go forth that starting today, there will be only one interest group with special influence in city government—you, the people in the neighborhoods of Boston."[18]

He sent a clear signal of a change in how the city government would respond to the neighborhoods. Flynn was determined to chart a new course for the city. Through creating constituent and neighborhood services offices, meetings were held across Boston, beginning within the first month of the new administration. During the first community meeting held in Mission Hill, the administration outlined its purpose: "Tonight's meeting is a step toward including the community in solving neighborhood problems. It's something residents feel hasn't been provided in some time by the city government," the Office of Neighborhood Services director said.[19]

Neighborhood councils were endorsed overwhelmingly in a 1983 referendum, which asked, "Shall the City of Boston establish democratically selected neighborhood councils in each neighborhood that could approve, initiate, or veto new development in their neighborhoods?" Thus, the neighborhood councils were initiated in the first year of Flynn's administration as vehicles to improve connections between city hall and neighborhood leaders. The administration quickly established and supported existing neighborhood cleanups, crime watches, development planning groups, and youth programs.

The implementation of neighborhood councils was controversial. While there was broad support for them across Boston, during the initial neighborhood meetings convened by Flynn, many established neighborhood groups—particularly those in the wealthier areas, such as the Beacon Hill Civic Association and the Neighborhood Association of the Back Bay—opposed the formation of yet another group that would, in their view, diminish their power. In Hyde Park, a primarily White middle-class area, city councilor Menino opposed the creation of a neighborhood council, believing it would undercut the role of the district city councilors. In neighborhoods such as Roxbury and Jamaica Plain, while there was strong support for neighborhood councils, neighborhood activists wanted the councils elected and armed with veto power over development, something Flynn was unwilling to cede, as both he and King agreed during the mayoral campaign.

In the 1980s, Flynn established seven neighborhood councils and ten Planning and Zoning Advisory Committees (PZACs). Each group assumed the arduous task of creating a rezoning plan for their neighborhood, the first time it had been undertaken since 1964. Officials wanted it to be a bottom-up approach to creating new zoning in the city instead of a top-to-bottom approach. People wanted to plan for the future of their neighborhood. Bernie Doherty, chair of the Jamaica Plain zoning committee, said, "It comes down to a quality-of-life issue, but more so, we are seeking to strike a balance. We are not looking to discourage commercial or residential development. Still, we are seeking balance and equity."[20] Doherty emphasized that the zoning committee was a forum for "neighborhood businesses, organizations, and residents. There were no developers or their lawyers on the committee."[21]

As Flynn was implementing neighborhood councils, a new group led by community activists, including many of King's Rainbow Coalition members, formed the Coalition for Community Control of Development to press Flynn on veto power. Neighborhood engagement and decision-making were contested endeavors. Leaders from the campaign of Mel King proposed a home rule petition that would expand the number of neighborhood councils, provide veto power, require staffing resources, and expand membership in the zoning board and commissions. The coalition's main goal was to institutionalize neighborhood councils, for which, as implemented to date, members had been initially appointed by the mayor.

Nowhere was this issue more prominent than in Roxbury, which had seen decades of disinvestment and abandonment. The new Boston Redevelopment Authority (BRA) director, Steve Coyle, created a plan for significant development and investment in the neighborhood. The draft plan had yet to be adequately discussed with neighborhood and political leaders. When a draft of the BRA Dudley Square redevelopment plan was leaked to the *Boston Herald,* the headline read, "BRA Proposes $750 Million Roxbury Plan." Some suggested that the Neighborhood Development and Employment Agency released it to the press because they thought the BRA was operating on their "turf." The elected officials, Neighborhood Council, and the Greater Roxbury Neighborhood Authority were furious and demanded control over all neighborhood development with veto power. "The veto power was a huge deal because they were asking to become a development authority like the BRA, and you just couldn't have it if they wanted to be assured that nothing would happen unless they agreed or had sufficient input," Muhammad Ali-Salaam, BRA staffer leading the Dudley planning effort, explained. "That would be fine, but there was no way we would give them veto power."

A lawsuit was filed and later withdrawn, and the planning process Steve Coyle initiated would completely rezone Roxbury over twelve thousand parcels with thirty-nine thousand neighborhood residents. Hundreds of meetings were held with the neighborhood leaders, organizations, and businesses. According to Ali-Salaam, "Many didn't trust the BRA, which had screwed up for years, and thought this was another Model Cities or BBURG program that wouldn't solve the problem, but rather take the focus away from the real problems. The mayor wanted something done," he added, "the right thing done!" [22]

BRA director Stephen Coyle convened a meeting for the Roxbury community with King, attended by more than a hundred community activists concerned about the BRA's proposed development strategy for the neighborhood. Coyle recalled significant opposition to whatever the BRA was doing for the first year. He brought Mel King and a hundred people, leaders of Roxbury, together. "What if I were mayor?" King said at the meeting. "What if Mel King is the mayor, and he sent this Black dude into Southie saying he's going to put all this development in there? So, we have a White Irish mayor sending a White Irish guy in here. That's why we're angry." [23]

As Coyle recalled, he had a different view of those political dynamics. "Look, I don't know anything about that," he said. "My family was originally from Southie. My first nine brothers and sisters were born in Southie. When the family was evicted by the predecessor at the BRA to build a project, they were homeless for almost a year. I don't have any love for governments or the BRA. My relatives would laugh if they knew I was running the BRA. The test will be, whether you like it or not, we will try to develop because development and jobs are needed. The way it's been done for the last thirty years or longer, that's not how Ray Flynn will do it. There are going to be projects here. People come and work on those projects. There's going to be housing built. You're going to build it." [24] So he laid out the alternative vision.

Ali-Salaam talked about the work Coyle, he, and the talented BRA staff had undertaken: "We had hoped to be part of the healing process. I was grateful to be part of the solution—the healing process started with Ray and his administration and continues today." [25]

## Safe Neighborhoods Campaign

The band of young city activists brought into Flynn's administration populated the ranks of the major city departments and were enthusiastically changing the face of city service delivery, grappling with issues of violence, and responding to the myriad unmet needs in the city ignored by the previous administration. There was a high expectation that Flynn would deliver and do better for the neighborhoods. The challenges were complex, as Ted Landsmark recalled. "While working in the Flynn administration, one of my jobs was to reduce the violence rate, particularly the murder rate, in the city," he said. "And I was young and naive then, so when the mayor came to me and said, 'Can you do this?' I said, 'Oh sure,' and thought, 'What am I thinking? I don't know how to reduce the murder rate.' Well, one of the things we knew was that if we had the right kinds of street workers, out in neighborhoods, during the right hours—that is to say, at night and particularly on weekends—they would be able to work with the young people who are most prone to get involved with violent activity. And we created this group of street workers."[26]

Increasing youth outreach and street workers, creating the Safe Neighborhoods Campaign, and engaging the Black ministers were critical components of the strategy that had Flynn out there personally in response to every incident of racial violence and trouble in Boston. At the same time, the late 1980s saw an increased prevalence of crack cocaine, rising gang violence, and a high homicide rate. The strategy did work, however, by reducing dramatically the number of youth homicides in the city, going in one year to zero. Homicides in Boston went from 152 in 1990 to 36 in 1996. The strategy was addressing the neighborhoods' security and safety concerns. The personal leadership of Flynn and his team, along with scores of community partners, was reflected in the Boston Globe poll: "A remarkable 43 percent of respondents said they have personally met Flynn; the number climbed to 46 percent among people of color."[27]

## Office of Neighborhood Services

The Office of Neighborhood Services was created by Flynn when he took office to connect city service departments to neighborhood councils and organizations. As director John Riordan, who had previously worked in Dorchester organizing conversations on racial divisions, recalled, Flynn made it clear to his department heads and the administration that he would "bring the neighborhoods into city hall and bring city hall to the neighborhoods, which was both symbolic but sustentative."[28] With coordinators in all of Boston's neighborhoods and liaisons to particular constituencies and linguistic minority residents, the administration had a broad network to respond to and address constituent and neighborhood concerns. Flynn hired many of the neighborhood activists who have been leaders of local grassroots organizations in their neighborhoods. The hiring of community organizers to key positions had unintended consequences. Flynn would say he had hired all the neighborhood activists, and there were few left outside the government you could call upon.

While not everyone was always satisfied, the office received high marks with coordinators in every neighborhood and a twenty-four-hour constituent hotline for any problem, large or small. The office drew plaudits as a successful link to city hall. Bill Walczak, a resident of Savin Hill in Dorchester who led the Codman Square Health Center, commented, "The office's neighborhood liaisons are a constant presence at community meetings and produce prompt action on resident complaints," echoing the remarks of activists from the North End to Jamaica Plain. "He's been successful at bringing home the bacon for city hall initiatives; now is the time to allow the nonprofits to play a larger role," Katherine Mainzer, director of Citizens for Safety, a coalition of community groups, added. "He's a popular mayor. He can afford to let the leash go a little."[29]

In keeping with his governing style, Flynn expected his department heads to meet regularly with neighborhood leaders on their areas of expertise and play an active role and presence in their neighborhoods. Riordan explained, "Not all those Flynn hired were community organizers when they arrived, but broadly defined, they were expected to play that role and become actively involved in their neighborhood."[30] And as Peter Dreier noted, "Ray Flynn thought like a community organizer. Every battle for a policy was a campaign."[31]

Flynn would meet regularly with the ONS staff to review the pressing neighborhood and constituent issues they were hearing and how the administration responded to them. Problems ranging from housing and business development to abandoned cars to vacant lots, neighborhood cleanups, neighborhood celebrations, public safety, health, parks, and essential services were everyday agenda items. The office would field tens of thousands of calls yearly. He was clear with his department heads that he expected them to be "out in the neighborhoods . . . not just behind their desks in city hall."[32] They knew they needed to be responsive to Flynn's neighborhood team.

Boston was changing, racially and ethnically, in significant ways between 1980 and 2000. Flynn responded by appointing the ONS liaisons to contact the new immigrant communities. Under White, little city halls served in considerable measure as his political army. He also had representatives working with the Hispanic, gay, and lesbian communities. As Ann Maguire, a Mel King supporter, Flynn's first liaison to the gay and lesbian community, recalled, "Flynn gave me an open book to help people in the community, whether it is discrimination, housing, partner rights or representing him on the AIDS Task Force, we got it done. He never once told me you can't do this; you can't do that."[33] Flynn continued those efforts but expanded the staff, hiring community leaders to liaise with the Asian, Vietnamese, Cambodian, Haitian, and Cape Verdean communities, growing fast in Boston's neighborhoods. About the Cape Verdean liaison appointment, Adalberto Teixeira—who hosted a Cape Verdean radio show and had worked in Roxbury before joining the administration—Flynn said, "Diversity is what makes Boston great. There are strong values in the Cape Verdean community that should be connected to all levels of government. Someone at the other end of the phone will share those values and provide access to city services for a growing population in Boston."[34]

The number of Cambodian and Vietnamese refugees making Boston their home rapidly increased. Mayor Flynn's appointment of liaisons to those communities was attuned to issues of the new immigrant communities. "The murder of a third of the Cambodian population under the brutal Pol Pot regime remains a recent memory," he said. "We need to break down the barriers of deep distrust so that people realize that the government can be an ally instead of an adversary." Flynn hired Vun Kim Sous as the Cambodian liaison, who helped the city broker an affordable housing project from overcrowded apartments on Carol Avenue in Brighton. "He has enormous compassion for Cambodian refugees who seek to live freely here in Boston," Flynn said of Kim Sous on his appointment. "Having experienced the difficulty of living in a new country and learning a new language and culture, Sous knows what is necessary to make the transition easier."[35] He also hired Van Lan Troung as his Vietnamese liaison, who would respond to the growing influx of refugees, particularly in Dorchester.

ONS staff worked with the diversity that was Boston's strength, including the Native American community in Boston when Flynn's office intervened to keep the Boston Indian Council, now called the North American Indian Center of Boston, open, and the Arab American community when they proposed installing a plaque honoring Kahlil Gibran in the mayor's fifth-floor office area. The mayor's office took on diplomacy in negotiating the so-called sausage wars—the conflict between the street vendors surrounding Fenway Park and the local businesses and the Red Sox; the author was dubbed "Henry Kissinger of the Sausage Wars" by the Boston Herald in 1988.[36]

In addition to the liaisons serving Boston's newcomers, in 1987, Flynn launched the first Immigrant Rights Unit to help immigrants with health care, job training, educational resources, and legal services. The unit was established when federal authorities were cracking down on illegal immigrants, such as Irish, Haitian, and Central American refugees. "As a city, we promise there will be a community of compassionate, open-hearted people waiting to welcome you, to help you gain the resources and tools to make good lives for yourselves and your families—out of the shadows of fear," Flynn said. "I believe that the right to health care is a human right, and city health services will be made available to immigrants, most of whom do not have health insurance, through Boston City Hospital and the twenty-five neighborhood health centers." Frank Costello, Flynn's Irish American adviser, said, "We think this is the first-of-its-kind program for a city in this country to address the needs of its immigrant population."[37]

Menino continued the Office of Neighborhood Services despite trying to have it eliminated under Flynn while chair of the city council Ways and Means Committee. He backed off after an uproar from neighborhood groups across the city. Walsh and Wu have also maintained the office's functions.

# 5 / Confronting the Housing Crisis and Landlords

> *Business groups always complain that government policies to make the private sector more responsible to consumers, workers, communities, and the environment will "kill jobs" and hurt the "business climate." Very often, they are bluffing, but the media and politicians don't know that or are afraid of a backlash from the business community. My metaphor has always been that you want to choke the private sector and squeeze them just to the point where they can still breathe but not to the point where they are dead. I saw my role as trying to help figure out where that point was where they could still breathe, and they were complaining that "You're killing me," but they were still alive, and they were not going to die.* (Peter Dreier, mayor's housing adviser, interview)

When I interviewed city councilor and senior administration official Rosemarie Sansone, she spoke about the importance of housing to the mayor. "Housing always played a significant role in the campaign and a personal role in Ray Flynn's life," she said. "Housing and poor people's issues were very important to him." This chapter looks at the story behind the policies Flynn fought for to respond to the growing housing crisis—housing affordability, including building new housing and rehabilitating the more than four thousand vacant public housing units across the city, rent control, and regulating condominium conversions. Flynn expected to force banks, developers, and landlords to help remedy the situation, referring to redlining and blockbusting and the "devastating economic and social chaos such practices had in Boston's neighborhoods in the 1970s when racial tensions were especially high."[1]

This chapter focuses on housing affordability, development, and regulation. Redlining, blockbusting, and discrimination in mortgage lending follow in chapter 6. Chapter 7 discusses development policies, including linkage and inclusionary housing, and minority and resident jobs and training initiatives are also explored in the chapter. These policies framed a comprehensive response to Boston's poverty, housing costs, and economy and are highlighted in the oral history of many participants.

## Boston's Rising Housing Costs and Affordability Crisis

Flynn staked his mayoralty on addressing the city's housing crisis. His experiences with poor and working-class families' housing insecurity across Boston's neighborhoods made a lasting impression. The destruction of the New York Streets section of the South End, the clearance of the West End, the abandonment of the city's poorest residents in public housing, and his predecessor's focus on the glitz of downtown at the expense of the neighborhoods shaped Flynn's thinking. As a state representative and city councilor, he was often the lone voice on housing issues. He teamed with State Representative Mel King, who fought hard to preserve their city for families like their own. The headwinds from the growth machine and its allies were fierce. Into that storm, they reached across every neighborhood. To the surprise of many and the horror of others, King and Flynn beat the pundits and the downtown interests, and together they reached the final in the mayoral election of 1983. At the end of Election Day, it was clear that Boston's housing affordability crisis during the 1970s and into the 1980s would be a top priority for the mayor and his administration.

Most emblematic of the housing crisis was a decision by the Kevin White administration in October 1974 to abruptly advertise and solicit proposals for an eighteen-story luxury high-rise housing development on the site of what had become known as Tent City.[2] Tent City began by occupying the city-owned parking lots, led by the Community Assembly for a United South End, on the weekend of April 27, 1968. Despite Mayor White's calls for the protesters to vacate the site, they stayed for four days, and twenty-three people faced arrest. In the demonstration was Rev. Dr. Martin Luther King Sr., father of the civil rights leader, who told demonstrators, "We are with you," along with mothers from across the South End. One of the mothers who joined the demonstration with her two children, Jovita Fontanez, standing outside a shack built on the vacant city land by Puerto Rican teenagers where signs read in Spanish, "Viva la causa parate bra Puerto Rico," and "I am willing to be arrested." Fontanez would later become a senior official in Flynn's administration. Another parking lot owned by White's fire commissioner, William J. Fitzgerald, sat vacant for nearly two decades. The community did not back down despite the calls to end the demonstration and vacate the site.[3] Finally, when Flynn came into office, he promised King and the people of the South End that the site would become affordable housing.

White had campaigned on rent regulation and, early in his administration, attempted to address the issue through rent control, which he later tried to eliminate under pressure from the Greater Boston Real Estate Board. According to a report commissioned by the White administration in 1969, rents for the poor, elderly, and Blacks rose 23 percent annually in Boston.[4] Increasingly, Boston's poor, working-class, and minority families were forced out of the city. By 1990, Boston was one of the costliest cities in the nation. The rapid pace of development drove the increase in the city's housing costs and created a critical housing shortage.[5]

The lack of housing affordability and an increase in the in-migration of poor southern Blacks contributed to the persistence of poverty and housing segregation. "The big issue was the city's rising housing costs," Flynn's housing adviser Peter Dreier explained. "Boston was a city of renters; about three-quarters of the people in Boston rented their homes. Boston had substantial price increases, and working-class families were being pushed out, or their kids couldn't afford to buy homes in their neighborhoods. So, there were all these efforts to gentrify the city, and then Kevin White tried to do away with rent control. The guy who had once said, 'When landlords raise rents, Kevin White raises hell,' was now turning his back on that, so there were fewer protections."[6]

A report prepared for White by his thirty-member Linkage between Downtown Development and Neighborhood Housing Advisory Committee in October 1983 highlighted the problems the city faced:

> This rapid growth in downtown development indicates that Boston is a prosperous city. A look at the demographic and housing statistics for Boston tells another story:
>
> - Boston's population had the fifth lowest median household income of the country's thirty (30) largest cities.
> - The share of persons in poverty status in Boston was twice that of the metropolitan area.
> - More than twenty percent (20%) of Boston residents in 1980 were in "poverty status," a five percent (5%) increase from 1970.
> - According to the Department of Housing and Urban Development guidelines, fifty-eight percent (58%) of households in Boston were of low and moderate income in 1980.
> - The rental housing stock, upon which seventy percent (70%) of Boston households rely, is aged and increasingly troubled.

Housing affordability was a significant problem, particularly for Boston's tenants. In 1980, almost 40 percent of Boston's renters were paying rent that amounted to over 30 percent of their income. This rent burden, especially for lower-income renters, indicates an "affordability gap" as property owners with an aging, inefficient housing stock cannot find tenants with the means to pay for it.[7]

As rents continued to escalate throughout the 1980s and the number of units converted to condominiums increased, the affordable housing crisis accelerated, exacerbating poverty in the city. Older adults were hit particularly hard. Michael Taylor from South Boston, who had run unsuccessfully for the newly created district city council seat in 1983, came to work as the commissioner of elderly affairs for Flynn. Taylor spoke about the issues confronting elderly residents of Boston. "Under the White administration, the elderly commission got stale and was used politically," he said. "Housing was the central issue, but it was not the focus of the city's agenda. There were about ninety-five thousand residents over sixty-five, and a big problem was the conversion of rooming houses into condominiums and the high rents that the elderly were paying. Single-room occupancy housing was converted, so three or four units were taken off the market to make way for one condo unit. So, rent control and condo conversions were the issues in every neighborhood. We, along with the mayor and his administration, focused on protecting the elderly and all tenants."[8]

The era of downtown development, following the urban renewal debacle in the West End and the pitched battles in the South End, Charlestown, Roxbury, the North End, and South Boston (though the latter three neighborhoods were mainly able to hold off the incursions of the Boston Redevelopment Authority urban planners), put tremendous pressure on the city housing stock. Working-class families were increasingly being priced out of their neighborhoods. This was a significant issue in the 1983 mayoral and city council elections. King and Flynn ran on a platform of supporting rent control and leveraging the benefits of downtown development to build affordable housing in Boston's neighborhoods. Now, after Flynn had won with widespread support from housing activists, he needed to deliver on his promises.

During Flynn's first term in office, he made considerable progress in creating affordable housing, immediately eliminating the practice of selling city-owned land to the highest bidder—whether part of the tragedy of urban renewal or vacant for some other reason. The vacant land was then available to address the community's priorities for housing, open space, and other uses. Two city agencies—the Boston Redevelopment Authority (BRA) and the Neighborhood Development and Employment Agency (NDEA), later the Public Facilities Department (PFD)—would be responsible for implementing the plan for city-owned properties. The Boston Housing Authority would be responsible for recapturing the more than four thousand vacant public housing units and transforming distressed developments such as Columbia Point into viable communities.

Affordable housing production in Boston benefited from both linkage and Flynn's focus on getting units in the ground. As Chart 6 indicates, housing starts rapidly accelerated beginning in 1984, continued through 1987, and then leveled off until 1998. Flynn's focus, in part, was the goals he had set in his 1986 State of the City address when he announced an intent to build thirty-four hundred new housing units for that year. To achieve this, Flynn convened weekly meetings of all the agencies that played any role in housing development. The BRA, the Public Facilities and Inspectional Services Departments, and the Office of Neighborhood Services were involved. Chaired by his development adviser, John Connolly, department heads were required to report weekly on permitting new housing starts. Flynn would direct his departments to improve their performance to meet his goals or expedite the housing production process if they fell short. "When I went to work for the city in 1986, Ray Flynn had identified the most significant dynamic: no longer are we doing business for the benefit of the big boys, the developers," David Williams, a reporter with WBUR radio who joined the Public Facilities Department, remembered. "We are here for the people in the neighborhoods. The most exciting part of what I did was to be part of shaping his plan to convert the

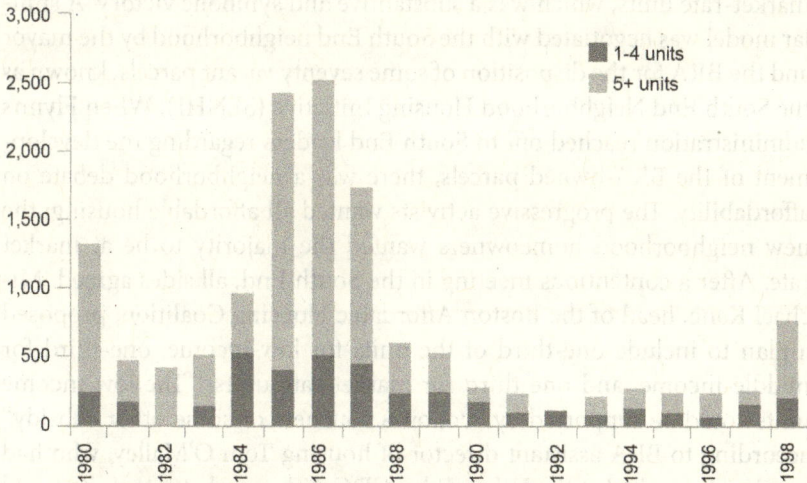

CHART 6. Housing Production in Boston, 1980–1998
Source: Boston Planning and Development Agency

abandoned property into affordable houses. The decisions on land disposition were made based on who could deliver economic justice. Flynn was
there to make sure it happened."[9]

Housing starts goals set for both 1986 and 1987 exceeded expectations. In 1986, the plan was for 3,400 new housing units to start in Boston, and the city got 3,715; in 1987, Flynn called for 4,000 new units,
and the city saw 4,064 new permits issued. "The goals were valuable as
'internal marching orders' for city departments," Melvyn Colon of the
Dudley Street Neighborhood Initiative said. "The goals have sped up
the disposition of city land and broke down some of the backlogs for
building permits and variances."[10] Nearly 20,000 housing units created
during Flynn's term in office, while not eliminating the shortage, had
a meaningful impact. Chart 6 shows that during the first years of the
Flynn administration, a record number of housing starts occurred, with
more than half publicly assisted and three-quarters affordable to working families. The chart shows housing starts fell off during the 1990 recession and from a significant withdrawal of federal support from the
Department of Housing and Urban Development during the Reagan administration, reducing annual housing funding between 1981 and 1986
for low-income housing assistance from $33 billion to under $10 billion.
Federal funds for job training decreased from $11.5 billion to $2.4 billion
during that period.[11]

Many signature housing projects during the period under study were
successful. Tent City and its 273 units are a mix of low-, moderate-, and
market-rate units, which was a substantive and symbolic victory. A similar model was negotiated with the South End neighborhood by the mayor
and the BRA for the disposition of some seventy vacant parcels, known as
the South End Neighborhood Housing Initiative (SENHI). When Flynn's
administration reached out to South End leaders regarding the development of the BRA-owned parcels, there was a neighborhood debate on
affordability. The progressive activists wanted all affordable housing; the
new neighborhood homeowners wanted the majority to be at market
rate. After a contentious meeting in the South End, all sides agreed. Michael Kane, head of the Boston Affordable Housing Coalition, proposed
a plan to include one-third of the units for low-income, one-third for
middle-income, and one-third for market-rate units. "The low-income
units could be supported by Section 8 vouchers or some other subsidy,"
according to BRA assistant director of housing Tom O'Malley, who had
previously worked at the Urban Edge CDC. "The market rate units could
stand independently; the moderate rate units were the hardest to finance,
which is why linkage was so important. While some in the neighborhood

wanted the formula applied project by project, we knew that would be difficult and agreed that the entire portfolio would seek to meet those targets."[12]

The factions in the South End had been through decades of struggle with the White administration and the BRA, and the neighborhood was suspicious of any city proposal. One example was when Flynn proposed the Tree of Life project, a hundred-unit transitional housing residence for women. There was significant objection to the proposal and the decision-making when the administration exempted the project from the community decision-making process, saying that the site was an exception to the mayor's general pledge of community involvement in decisions about land use. Facilities for certain groups, like the homeless and the mentally ill, were considered "special-need" sites. The mayor had made a decision based on a clear social need. Kip Tiernan, the founder of Rosie's Place, a homeless shelter for women in the South End, responded, "I think Ray Flynn is one of the most caring guys who came down the pike. The proposal was presented as a fait accomplii—'This is what we will do.' He has succeeded in further factionalizing the community."[13] In response to the neighborhood concerns, the city looked to include supportive housing in smaller projects throughout the neighborhood.

There would be other projects that would encounter community opposition. Following successful affordable housing developments in the Charlestown Navy Yard, South Boston's Andrew Square, and Back of the Hill in Mission Hill by the Bricklayers Union, Tom McIntyre, union president, and Bill Rawn, his architect, proposed affordable brick rowhouses for a vacant city lot on Centre Street in Jamaica Plain. Teachers at the local elementary school used the dirt lot for parking, and the neighbors feared they would end up on crowded streets if the cars were displaced. After the proposal won approval from the Jamaica Plain Neighborhood Council, after intense lobbying by housing advocates, with ongoing local opposition from the abutters, the project was abandoned.

Chinatown, too, had long faced the pressures of being squeezed between the adult entertainment district and New England Medical Center (now Tufts University Hospital) with a scarce supply of affordable housing. Between 1980 and 1988, only seventy units of affordable housing were built there. A high priority of the mayor was to increase housing production, and the Oak Terrace project brought another sixty units of affordable family housing to Chinatown. "Regarding affordable housing, no line is drawn in the city," Flynn's Chinatown coordinator, Yon Lee, said. "Everybody is working for affordable housing in this town. It is the best thing that has happened in Chinatown in a long time." As the BRA's

O'Malley said about the project at the time, "It is the number-one priority for the BRA to get into the ground."[14]

The BRA oversaw the redevelopment of the Charlestown Navy Yard. According to Ted Chandler, a member of the BRA staff, "While developers eyed the Navy Yard for luxury housing development, Steve Coyle insisted that new housing be accessible to low- and moderate-income families as well. Working with the Bricklayers Union, they built award-winning family affordable housing on the waterfront."[15]

While Flynn had many housing victories, constructing a large-scale affordable housing project in the former West End—which had been razed in the 1960s by Boston's urban renewal bulldozer—was probably the most symbolic. As chapter 7 discusses, the West End housing development was personal for BRA director Steve Coyle:

> Who will ever know the fight we had with Jerry Rappaport to keep that land . . . or the battle I had with my board, or the number of times Jerry got to the City Council to pressure me, or the number of times members of the administration tried to get me to change course. The West End fight was for all the people of Boston who were driven from their homes, my family, my relatives, and the thousands I never knew. It was a fight that had significant meaning to those swept away. The only person at city hall who knew about my family being evicted was Ray Flynn; not even my staff knew. He understood that I would have died first before giving up that fight, so he never bothered me; we had just one discussion, and I explained about my parents, my aunt Annie, and how her daughter Jackie was assaulted in the Maverick project after the family moved there. Sometimes you need somebody on the team who doesn't give a crap about what people think; we shared that trait. Once, when we were in San Francisco, Ray asked me what I thought would have happened if my family had stayed in Southie. I said I didn't know.

He paused, then said with his huge laugh, "You'd have gone to Stanford; it's in the cards."[16] As Flynn said about Lowell Square, the Rappaport challenge, and the West End, "I wanted to restore some justice for the people of the old West End who had their homes and neighborhood taken from them."[17]

The connection between linkage and affordable housing was symbiotic. The BRA reported that more than $58.2 million had been awarded to various affordable housing projects between 1985 and 1999. The response to the urgent need to rebuild the city's supply of affordable housing became integrated with a broader community development strategy, including upgrading neighborhood business districts, promoting open space and urban gardens, and increasing homeownership opportunities. The success story of the Dudley Street Neighborhood Initiative (DSNI) is recounted in chapter 7 as a partnership between the DSNI, the BRA, and the PFD. When neighborhoods wanted to see more homeownership, the city went into gear. Pat McGuigan, who directed PFD's housing division, recounts a conversation with Flynn. "Ya know, Pat," Flynn told him, "I am going to go to heaven, but the neighborhood could go to hell."[18] That comment emphasized the multifaceted approach needed to strengthen community development in partnership with neighborhood leaders through neighborhood councils and other neighborhood planning and zoning groups. Flynn was reflecting on neighborhood concerns he often heard about the best mix of housing options in each neighborhood.

The city would contract with the neighborhood organizations to clearly define roles, responsibilities, and agreed-upon outcomes. From 1987 through 1989, for example, construction began on more than four thousand housing units in the minority neighborhoods of Roxbury, Dorchester, and Mission Hill, according to the city's Public Facilities Department. "The use of linkage funds, community development block grant funds, all city assets, and other public and private financing vehicles were key to the housing success story," McGuigan recounted.[19]

Those who followed Flynn in the mayor's office made a significant impact. While he set a high standard, Tom Menino, Marty Walsh, and Michelle Wu each pursued aggressive housing agendas, understanding that housing is probably the most crucial issue in the city. As described earlier, Menino was slower to exert his influence to prioritize affordable housing, resulting in hundreds of luxury units being developed and significant affordable opportunities lost.

## A New Housing Policy for the People—Rent Control and Condo Conversion Protections

The cumulative effect of this political and economic shift in Boston was evident in the deterioration of Boston's neighborhoods, mainly their housing stock. The most controversial housing policy in Boston was rent control. Rent control was implemented in 1968 due to significant pressures in the rental housing market. The *Boston Globe* reported, "In Boston, rents have gone up 34 percent since 1959, increasing more than in any other major city except San Francisco."[20] The Boston rent control effort began due to protests by elderly Allston and Brighton residents who argued that students drove up housing prices by 30 percent to 100 percent annually, and they were forced out of apartments they had lived in for many years. Boston started by devising an interim local rent plan, which was controversial and challenged by the real estate industry.

Throughout 1969, the city council and mayor grappled with implementing a more comprehensive rent control strategy. Following a state Supreme Judicial Court ruling, Chapter 842 of the Acts of 1970 was adopted, giving Boston (and other large cities of more than fifty thousand) the power to regulate rents. The rent control enabling law overcame the lobbying of the real estate industry. It passed due to the effective lobbying of the housing community groups and the efforts of Governor Francis Sargent and South Boston state senator John Joseph Moakley, who rescued the legislation from the jaws of defeat. Boston enacted a home rule petition in 1972 and created the Rent Equity Board. White appointed the five-member rent board to oversee the process of rent increases and evictions. An estimated 140,000 rental units, about 60 percent of the city's rental housing stock, were covered under the law.[21]

White, originally a solid public supporter of rent control, had sought to strengthen the effectiveness of the law in the early 1970s. In a 1975 reelection ad, White claimed, "When landlords raise rents, Kevin White raises hell." Not everyone agreed with rent control; several small landlords and businesspeople opposed it. "The worst thing Kevin White ever did is put in rent control. . . . It destroyed Jamaica Plain," Ed Burke, owner of Doyles Café in Jamaica Plain, said.[22] However, after his narrow 1975 reelection victory and bowing to the real estate industry pressure, White approved vacancy decontrol, effectively gutting Boston's strict rent control provisions. As a result, within several years, an estimated forty thousand units were decontrolled. Over the objections of tenants' groups and several city council members, including Flynn, White sought to continue vacancy decontrol in 1979. Members of White's administration faced indictments for falsifying rent records and bribery, resulting in thousands of dollars in illegal costs to tenants.[23] His new attitude about rent control dates back as early as 1976, when he said in an unguarded comment to reporters, "Rent control stinks."[24] Housing became a significant issue in the 1983 campaign to succeed White.

Candidates Flynn and King were strongly pro-tenant and supported reinstituting vigorous rent control. Candidates with real estate industry backing opposed rent control. According to records from the Massachusetts Tenants Organization, DiCara supported rent control measures proposed by tenant advocacy groups in 1972 and 1975. In 1979 and 1981, he opposed "stronger rent control proposals and an eviction ban during condominium conversions," the Boston Globe reported.[25] He was courting the real estate industry for his 1979 mayoral run and was rewarded with the second-highest political contributions from the industry in 1979 and 1980. He would ultimately drop out of the 1979 mayor's race but be re-elected to the city council as the highest vote-getter. He would leave the city council in 1981 to position himself for his 1983 run at the mayor's office.[26] Both 1983 mayoral candidates Finnegan and Kearney voiced support for the weakened regulations at the time, which White had gutted, but did not support Flynn's or King's call for a return to full rent control.

Once elected, Flynn launched an effort to restore strong rent control in Boston. Six months into his administration, on June 26, 1984, he asked the city council to end vacancy decontrol and reinstate complete rent control and control condominium conversions, rapidly accelerating by 1984. "This has nothing to do with being liberal or conservative and everything to do with wanting to help poor and moderate-income people," Flynn said about his proposal. "A vote against it will further exacerbate the housing problem in Boston."[27] The proposal would have expanded coverage to eighty-five thousand units, half the city's housing stock, and exempted two- and three-family homes. The vacancy rate at the time was only 3 percent. During White's tenure, the city had lost more than eighteen thousand units, primarily due to condominium conversions, which became part of the next wave in the gentrification of Boston.[28]

Most city council members opposed Flynn's proposal, owing more allegiance to the real estate industry than tenants or the mayor. The real estate lobby actively opposed the legislation. "The real estate board cleverly elected Tom Hines as their president, thinking he had connections to Flynn or back channels to Flynn," Peter Dreier, Flynn's point man on the rent control legislation, recounted. "He called me up the first week I was there and wanted to take me out for lunch, and I had a policy that I would not let anybody pay for my lunch. So, we met at the Bostonian Hotel for breakfast. I had never been there before, so it's a good symbol of our naiveté and inexperience. I get there, and, you know, I was a poor college professor at the time, and suddenly, I'm eating this fourteen-dollar omelet. He said, 'Look, can we work this out [rent control]?' I said, 'What are you looking for?' We could not give him what he was looking for: a really weak law. I had enough bravado to say, 'Look, we're going to win,' and I tried to pretend I was incredibly self-confident; 'we're going to win this, so if you want to negotiate, fine, but, you know, we're going to win so what can you give us?'"

"He knew I was bluffing," Dreier added, "because he talked to all the council members and learned that Jerry Rappaport was working hard behind the scenes. He [Rappaport] gave Flynn a lot of money after Mel King was in the run-off, but Flynn gave it back. It showed me how he operated. He was giving out cash. Jerry Rappaport was giving out cash to the council members. I saw him give Flynn an envelope with cash in it, and Flynn gave it back; good for him. The first test of Flynn's populism was rent control, and we won maybe 60 percent of what we wanted. So, one problem was the community groups like City Life that supported Mel didn't want to help Flynn get rent control passed. There was still that anger."[29]

The rent control battle demonstrated the uncertainty the progressive flank in the administration had, considering the tremendous influence of the real estate lobby and growth machine in influencing city policy. Jerome Rappaport, a staffer to Mayor Hynes and who later would epitomize the growth machine by facilitating the destruction of the West End, would now stop Flynn's rent control efforts. He would later challenge his proposed linkage ordinances. The city council watered down Flynn's bill. "The city's real estate interests have spent at least $182,000 to defeat rent control and condominium conversion legislation brought before the Boston City Council this year," the Massachusetts Tenants' Organization charged. "Seven of 10 councilors who received real estate money voted 'against tenants.' Michael Rotenberg, president of the Rental Housing Association of the Greater Boston Real Estate Board, responded, 'You do not buy a councilor's vote by a political contribution. At the very best, it gives you opportunity and access.' Rotenberg said it is difficult to make a connection between a contribution and a councilor's position on rent control, noting that district councilor Bruce C. Bolling (Roxbury) received more real estate interest money than district councilor Thomas M. Menino (Hyde Park–Roslindale) yet Bolling backed Flynn's plan, and Menino did not."[30]

John Logan and Harvey Molotch suggest that the growth machine "must influence government decisions to maximize returns from their holdings, and they must also make campaign contributions (or bribes) to public officials."[31] In Boston, that approach worked despite Rappaport claiming, "You can't buy people's souls with a contribution."[32]

The Boston City Council, with the lead from the real estate industry, rejected Flynn's housing package and sent him a weakened bill, which the Massachusetts Tenants' Organization (MTO) called "voodoo rent control." The MTO asked Flynn to veto the measure. Flynn realized that the city council was poised to block his plan and would need to reach a compromise to salvage most of his housing plan.[33] In the negotiated compromise with the city council, the new law would limit rent increases in some sixty-five thousand rental housing units and prohibit evictions of low-income and elderly tenants for condominium conversions.

The defeat was when Flynn, his staff, and progressive supporters real-ized that, while he may have won control of the mayor's office, the real estate industry controlled the city council. There was a mixed sense of the results of Flynn's first major defeat. Finfer, head of the MTO at the time, said that the new housing law was "a significant step forward," though at the same time citing Boston's severe housing shortage and booming real estate market. "Many tenants still need to be covered; the 12.5 percent rent-increase ceiling, twice the inflation rate, is too high, and a strong enforcement agency is needed," he said. Even the weakened measure was adamantly opposed by the real estate industry leaders, concerned about their bottom line, who were able to muscle enough votes in the city coun-cil to defeat Flynn's measure.

Finfer reflected on the loss, wondering whether Flynn and his staff had done all they could to enact the law and reflecting on the nature of his re-lationships with Flynn's cadre of progressive activists who had joined the administration. "It was also interesting learning about our colleagues and friends," he said. "Many of them went to work for Flynn, but there was this point when rent control was lost, and they held this press event with District 1 city councilor Travaglini. We had worked on Travaglini because he was the swing vote. We had massive meetings in the North End with all the Italian ladies who were getting pushed out, and they were pushing him. So, we thought we'd win. We knew Jerry Rappaport called up and put the squeeze on him [Travaglini], and he was willing to be squeezed, and we lost. Then I felt like, where are my friends? So, it was a painful les-son because I felt like, why aren't they dealing with this, or why aren't they talking with us about this? They're just moving on and trying to make it look better than it was. So, that was a lesson."[34]

Others agreed, including John McDonough, a state representative and housing activist. "Flynn didn't push as hard because he probably believed that he couldn't win, and he didn't want to lose in a fight because that makes you look weak," he said. "Then the city council feels like they con-trol you and don't have to pay attention to you. So, instead of pushing for rent control, I think the focus of attention for groups like City Life was to expand affordable housing with some subsidies and government controls."[35]

The theme of conflict between Flynn's goals and his ability to imple-ment them to the standards held by some of his earliest supporters would repeat itself throughout the administration's early years. "Flynn also knew he would look weak if he lost it because all the *Globe* and the *Herald* people were testing him to see whether he could be a mayor who could get things done," Dreier recalled. "In retrospect, it was the worst of all possible worlds. My first test was rent control, and I lost it. I learned a lot from that experience: Flynn won on a pro–rent control platform; it was one of his big issues. It was one of the defining things in the campaign; he would bring back strong rent control, and everybody who worked on the campaign knew that was what he said. Once he got elected, there were voices in the administration that spoke to him, 'Okay, you got elected; you do not have to follow up on that.' So, I thought, okay, we won; now we use the political army that got him elected to mobilize to get this legislation through a pretty hostile city council. A few of Flynn's advisers and department heads did not believe in rent control and would not spend time using their ties to neighborhood residents or city council members to help Flynn pass this prominent issue. It was challenging to navigate, and I felt like I was walking on a tightrope without a net below. Ultimately, we won about 60 percent of what we wanted, which was still disappointing. We had to spin it a victory, and it was hard to do that."[36]

Flynn put the best face on the early defeat. "It showed a commitment to the poor and elderly that eviction will not be tolerated in our city," he said, noting his refusal to give up. He refiled legislation to strengthen rent control and regulate condominium conversions—a rapidly escalating part of the housing crisis.[37]

## New Rent Control and Condo Regulations Implemented

Flynn knew that expanding rent control and controlling condo conversions would help slow, if not stop, the dramatic economic changes in Boston's neighborhoods. The evidence of gentrification and displacement was abundantly clear, and the city needed strong controls and aggressive, affordable housing production and protections. Flynn's rent control proposal was rejected in June 1984 by the city council by a seven-to-six margin. Flynn had personally lobbied the city council, and the bill's defeat meant the extension of rent controls from twenty thousand units to eighty-five thousand units, representing half the city's housing stock, would not go into effect. Instead, a rent increase cap of 15 percent was instituted, and the council imposed limited condominium conversion protections for low- to moderate-income, elderly, and handicapped tenants. The initial city council swing votes were councilors Bolling, Travaglini, and Menino. Activists convinced Bolling to support the measure, putting pressure on Travaglini and future mayor Menino. Despite the Massachusetts Tenants Organization (MTO) organizing in Travaglini's district, MTO claimed that influential developer Jerome Rappaport had swayed him. Travaglini proposed exempting owner-occupied apartment buildings of six units or fewer from rent control. Flynn agreed, and Travaglini still voted "no." In Menino's case, he hid behind an amendment requiring annual rental unit inspections. As a result, a *Boston Globe* editorial called his statement to a Hyde Park audience that he would not accept Flynn's compromise proposal because it came at the last minute "the most disingenuous statement of the debate."[38]

Condominium conversion policies requiring a permit from the Rent Equity Board to remove units from the market were defeated. In a dramatic speech, Bolling called upon his colleagues to be "men and women and vote for the future of Boston."[39] Kelly's version was adopted, requiring a waiting period for low- to moderate-income, elderly, and handicapped tenants before they could be evicted for condo conversion. Later, in 1985, the council enacted an ordinance regulating investor conversions. Flynn called the measure a "victory for Boston residents. With the cooperation of the council, we now have a policy that places our housing emphasis to a great extent on shelter for people and not a shelter for taxes." Frank Doyle, Flynn's council liaison, said, "The council saved a potential 1,500 rental units from being converted into condos for which eviction packages had already been prepared. Seventy-five percent of condo conversions in the past two years were for investment purposes and not for home ownership."[40]

The Massachusetts Supreme Judicial Court (SJC) found unanimously that the ordinance went beyond state-enabling legislation. Flynn reacted to the SJC decision, saying, "The challenge of the amendment was an example of the Real Estate Board's 'social irresponsibility.'" He called it the "Greedy Boston Real Estate Board."[41]

Between the early 1970s and 1983, Boston lost 18,000 rental units through abandonment and condominium conversion. By 1987, three years after Flynn took office, more than 31,556 units had been converted to condominiums representing 12.2 percent of the housing stock, with working-class neighborhoods such as South Boston, East Boston, and Roslindale bearing the brunt of the conversions. "The most alarming thing in the 1987 figures is the number of three-deckers converted to condos," Constance Doty, head of the Rent Equity Board, observed. "Thirteen percent of all condos added by master deeds last year were in three-deckers. This points to a change in the condo market. It is not just a downtown phenomenon."[42] Finally, in 1988, the city council passed a neighborhood stabilization ordinance in a nine-to-four vote that required a removal permit before converting rental housing units to condos. "Today's vote is a big victory for stability in Boston," Flynn said. "Now the sons and daughters of long-time Boston residents can live in the neighborhoods where they grew up."[43] "Condominium conversions have helped make the Boston real estate market one of the nation's most active," the *New York Times* reported. "Since 1980, property values have surged, and condominium conversion has outpaced new construction. From 1980 to 1987, 21,500 apartments were converted into condominiums, while 16,250 new housing units were created. The Rental Housing Association of Boston vigorously opposed the plan, as they did in 1985. Dana Pope, the association president, said, 'The city is putting the problem of affordable housing on the back of the rental housing industry.'" According to the *Times,* "Boston's new permit system covers 73,000 apartment units that are or were under rent control out of a total of 122,350 private rental units in the city. It also covers 20,000 of the 26,650 subsidized apartments here."[44]

John Riordan, Flynn's chief of staff who mobilized community support, noted that the neighborhood stabilization ordinance "slowed the conversion process and evictions; however, there was a rapid transformation of condo conversion in Boston."[45] Some believe the pace of the conversions caught the administration off guard, and the conversions significantly reduced the existing affordable housing stock. By the time the administration put stronger regulations into effect—after three attempts—there was little that could be done to change the economic dynamic. "Rooming houses were rapidly lost due to conversions, over 90 percent in ten years," Doty observed. "The legislation continued condo conversions due to the wave of investor-owned conversions. The unintended consequence for neighborhoods like Councilor Kelly represented, who opposed Flynn's original legislation, was that gentrification was rampant while he was trying to protect his hometown. A 1990 study by economist Paul Harrington showed that more than 40 percent of the residents of South Boston had lived there for less than five years. Affordable housing in Boston's neighborhoods became an endangered species."[46]

Rooming houses have disappeared at an alarming rate. They once provided affordable homes for many who would otherwise be homeless. One example is the South End, where in 1965, there were 965 licensed lodging houses and, by 1983, only thirty-seven.[47] Single and elderly residents were forced out, in many cases, by luxury condominium conversions, leaving many of the former residents homeless.

Chart 7 documents the rapid acceleration of condominium conversions, escalating yearly from 1985 to 2013.

Rent control, opposed by organized real estate groups and absentee landlords, influenced most of the city councilors. Kelly was the key opposition leader who collected significant campaign contributions from real estate. "Councilor Kelly accepted nearly $5,000 in contributions last year

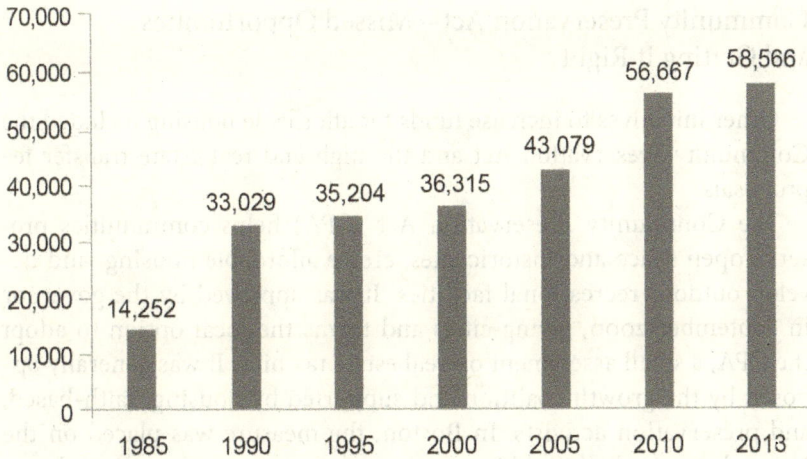

CHART 7. Residential Condominium Conversion in Boston, 1985–2013
Source: City of Boston Assessing Department

from real estate interests," MTO said, "but Kelly denied that the money had influenced his position against expansion of rent control."[48]

Some questioned the role played by the future mayor, Menino, and whether others could have been persuaded to change their vote. But according to Flynn, he had tried to reach a compromise and left it all on the floor. Years later, those in Flynn's South Boston neighborhood, who had largely followed the lead of Kelly—whom many saw as beholden to the real estate interests and who opposed the legislation—had come to realize that Flynn's efforts would have potentially saved their neighborhood from massive gentrification in the face of the condo influx.

"Print the names of the councilors who voted for the Kelly package," Finfer said following the vote on the housing package. "They voted for absentee landlords and against the tenants. The vote demonstrates the power of money and the influence of the real estate and banking industries. The mayor should be commended for what he is doing. However, the city council has consistently rejected any attempts to preserve the city's housing stock with more substantial rent control or condo conversion control laws. I am satisfied that Flynn worked hard to promote strong controls and came close to victory. You can always do more."[49]

The Boston Globe would editorialize, "The vote rejecting Mayor Flynn's plan for expanded rent control and a tighter rein on condominium conversions means that the trends which make Boston increasingly a city for only the wealthy and the poor will continue."[50]

## Community Preservation Act—Missed Opportunities and Getting It Right

Other initiatives to increase funds for affordable housing included the Community Preservation Act and the high-end real estate transfer fee proposals.

The Community Preservation Act (CPA) helps communities preserve open space and historic sites, create affordable housing, and develop outdoor recreational facilities. It was approved by the governor in September 2000, giving cities and towns the local option to adopt the CPA, a small assessment on real estate tax bills. It was generally opposed by the growth coalition and supported by housing, faith-based, and preservation activists. In Boston, the measure was placed on the November 2001 ballot, asking voters to approve a 2 percent surcharge on real property. The proposal, if adopted, would have provided $28 million, $14 million from Boston taxpayers, and a $14 million match from the state. Mayor Menino held off endorsing the CPA plan until the Friday before the election to signal to the growth coalition that his support was, shall we say, not all in. Advocates characterized Menino's reluctance as more of a sign of ego in that it was not his idea. The housing and faith-based groups that led the CPA campaign even went as far as hiring Menino's pollster to try and get him on board with his political organization sooner to help pass the legislation, according to housing activist Lew Finfer, who was involved in the organizing.[51] The measure lost, with 43 percent opposed and 32 percent in favor. Joan Vennochi of the *Globe* summarized, "Voters rejected the ballot question, which the business community paid big money to defeat because it called for a property tax surcharge. The mayor, the leader of the city, wasn't sure where he stood until last Friday. He favors affordable housing but also favors developers' contributions."[52]

Menino never reintroduced the CPA in fifteen years, leaving upward of $300 million on the table.[53] After Menino left office, with the city council's approval in a twelve-to-one vote, Walsh placed the CPA on the November 2016 ballot, asking voters to approve a 1 percent surcharge. It would raise approximately $20 million annually and cost taxpayers, on average, twenty-eight dollars more a year. The measure passed with 74 percent of the vote. "It's a big statement of who we are as a city," Walsh said after the vote. "With all the anger and rhetoric of the presidential campaign, people were willing to pay a little more to help others who didn't have it."[54] The CPA campaign organizers praised Walsh for his leadership in securing the housing and preservation funds.

In December 2019, Walsh and the city council also proposed a 2 percent transfer tax on high-dollar real estate sales in Boston, which would have raised approximately $100 million for city housing programs. The real estate industry lobbied aggressively to oppose the measure, and it died. Mayor Michelle Wu refiled the bill, including a tax relief provision for seniors who own homes. As of 2024, the proposal is awaiting legislative action and, if passed, could support thousands of affordable housing units, including a continuation of the rent subsidy pilot program, which, at the urging of Mel King, Walsh initiated and increased supportive housing for people experiencing homelessness.

# 6 / Redlining, Blockbusting, and Fighting Bank Discrimination

*"I can be your best friend, or I can be your worst enemy. I want a billion dollars," said Mayor Flynn to the assembled bankers. The bankers privately lamented, "Who is this punk telling us a billion dollars? These people think we are going to cave in to blackmail. We will never cave in to blackmail. We will never do that; they are just wrong. What do you think we have to do to close this deal?"* (Mayor Ray Flynn to the bankers and the bankers response)

Boston was undergoing a demographic shift, a common trend in urban areas after World War II. The influx of Blacks and immigrants into the city, while creating fear in many neighborhoods, also showcased the resilience of these communities. Bob Consalvo, a Hyde Park community leader and Flynn's education adviser, recalled, "There was that them-and-us thing. You had blockbusting in Hyde Park down by Ross Field. That was traumatic for Hyde Park. People were nervous about minorities moving into their neighborhoods. That did much damage to Hyde Park, blockbusting by the real estate industry and the banks."[1]

Some have characterized the rapid racial and ethnic change in Boston as a tragedy for the city, as great as the destruction of the West End. "The neighborhood was changing almost before our eyes; blacks were moving in in droves," a young White woman, a lifelong resident of Wells Avenue in Codman Square, remembered. "It was pretty scary. Like everyone else, my father was deathly afraid of his property value going down and for his safety. It was a frightening time."[2]

The disinvestment and level of housing abandonment throughout Boston's neighborhoods was rapidly increasing—the practice by banks of "redlining" certain areas of the city was well established in Boston. The bank policy dates to the government's Home Owners Loan Corporation (HOLC), initiated as part of Roosevelt's New Deal. HOLC mapped 239 cities, using red to identify neighborhoods considered "hazardous" and "dangerous" where banks had stopped issuing mortgages altogether or charged exorbitant fees and interest rates. A new and ominous real estate and banking term was coined—"redlining."[3] The practice was wide-spread in Boston. "We formed the Jamaica Plain anti-redlining commit-tee to encourage banks that had the deposits of the people living in the neighborhood to lend back to those who had made the deposits," Michael Reiskind, a Jamaica Plain activist and head of the local historical soci-ety, remembered. "Local housing or community reinvestment by banks is a federal law, but it started in Jamaica Plain. The Jamaica Plain leader of that committee became head of the state committee, Massachusetts Urban Reinvestment Advisory Group, MURAG."[4] In a *Boston Globe* spe-cial report in 1983, "Changing the Heart of the City," reporters Daniel Golden and David Mehegan reported, "Out of MURAG's and other, similar groups' agitations, Congress in 1978 passed the Community Reinvestment Act, which was followed by a state law requiring banks to meet the credit needs of poor and middle-income areas in their commu-nities. Since passed, the banks have become more amenable to making loans in city neighborhoods,"[5] until they weren't, as the Federal Reserve Report in 1998 demonstrated.[6]

In the Roxbury, Mattapan, and Dorchester neighborhoods, where redlining was compounded with dramatic racial change and housing abandonment, local banks formed the Boston Banks Urban Renewal Group (BBURG). Developed, in part, with the push of the White admin-istration, "BBURG was seen as a response to the assassination of Mar-tin Luther King Jr. In 1968, the requirements of the Housing Act of 1968 forbid discrimination in making home mortgages available."[7] With the growing unrest in Black communities across the nation following King's assassination in Memphis, the Black United Front, led by Mel King and Chuck Turner, convened a meeting of five thousand African Americans at Franklin Park's White Stadium. They issued twenty-one demands for greater community control. The banks and the politicians took no-tice.[8] The implementation of BBURG, launched in 1968 by twenty-two banks and other savings, loan institutions, and cooperatives, was what then-mayor White called "a major new urban program for Boston which teams private capital and expertise, governmental coordination and plan-ning, and self-directed economic development by the poor and provides greatly expanded home ownership in the inner city."[9] On the surface, this was an effort to expand Black homeownership, but it caused a significant upheaval in the targeted neighborhoods.

"When I first got to Dorchester, Columbia Road had this code word that was the dividing line in 1970 between the Black and White com-munities," Lew Finfer, veteran community organizer, recalled. "Everyone was very conscious about what streets were starting to get integrated. The

Boston Bankers Urban Renewal Group (BBURG) pushed many people out of their homes and created distrust. BBURG hurt race relations because it led to all this deterioration. Over one thousand homes were foreclosed, and many became abandoned houses."[10]

The program is best described as reverse redlining, where a geographic area was prioritized for mortgage lending. As city councilor Tom Atkins said, "I had heard of redlining—the practice of denying mortgage loans in predominantly minority areas—but never before had I encountered it in this variation where federally insured money was provided to people of color only on the condition that they buy where the bankers told them to."[11] Some argue that eradicating the Jewish neighborhood in Mattapan was merely the unintended consequence of good intentions, while others claim it was a prearranged scheme. Whether conscious or unintentional, the program led to blockbusting in the BBURG-defined area between 1968 and 1970, transforming the fifty-year Jewish settlement of 90,000 in favor of 120,000 Black residents who moved into the area.[12]

Peter Canellos summarized the results of the BBURG program in a 1988 *Globe* article: "With the encouragement of Mayor Kevin White, a group of Boston banks had launched a $27 million minority-housing program that wiped away old Jewish Mattapan and added 'redlining' and 'blockbusting' to the Boston vocabulary. The program's racial turmoil presaged the busing crisis six years later."[13]

The policies and process were documented in *The Death of an American Jewish Community* (1992), the urban sociological study by Hillel Levine and Lawrence Harmon. "Codman Square became the dividing line between Jewish and Catholic communities in Dorchester. There was much hostility between the groups," according to Bill Walczak, head of the Codman Square Health Center. In his autobiography *In Search of History*,[14] Theodore White discusses fighting through Catholic kids to get to the Codman Square branch library. "I was told by a longtime resident that during the 1930s, in the era of anti-Semitic broadcasts by Fr. Coughlin, a Catholic priest with a nationwide audience, Catholic youths would cross Washington Street on Friday evenings to find Jewish boys to beat up, something they called a 'Jew hunt,'" Walczak remembers.[15]

"Starting in the 1960s, Jewish residents became replaced by Blacks, mainly coming from the southern US. In this transition, arson erupted, and there were hundreds of fires each year. Though most of this was the result of redlining decisions by government and insurance companies and blockbusting by real estate agents, this was not widely known at the time and complicated negative and racist views toward Blacks. I remember an incident in the mid-1970s on Templeton Street, now Monsignor

Lydon Way, where a Black family that moved into a three-decker was fire-bombed out the night they moved in. The saga of the Debnam family, which moved onto Centre Street, was documented in Anthony Lukas's book *Common Ground*,"[16] Walczak recounted.[17]

Kristin McCormack, who lived on Meeting House Hill in Dorchester, remembers a firebombing on Melbourne Street that was racially moti-vated. "Some White neighborhoods were quickly changing, and many people didn't like that."[18]

Janice Bernstein, a Mattapan resident and leader of the Mattapan Or-ganization, disagrees that BBURG had good intentions and was an acci-dent. "Both speak of 'unintended consequences.' They mapped us out, and they killed us," she said. She and her husband recalled becoming aware of the program "when real estate agents showed up on our doorstep in 1968 announcing that twenty-five hundred Black families were about to move into the area. They would say, 'Your neighbor across the street is selling to Blacks. Maybe you would be interested in selling.'"[19] Some blocks had 90 percent ownership turnover within a year.[20]

Because of real estate and banking policies, the White administration did not know what was happening in the neighborhoods. "I didn't know the neighborhood was dying," White told Levine and Harmon. "I wouldn't have let that happen. The Jewish community was not making noise. Such swift change, and they were not making noise. I missed this completely like you would a child off to the side in a large family."[21] The result was rapid and escalating foreclosures and housing abandonment. "In a few years, the Jewish population of Mattapan plummeted from about 90,000 to barely 1,500—an abrupt shift accompanied by fierce social conflict."[22] The impacts of the policies were still felt years later. "Even now, twenty years later, the decay is unabated," Canellos said. "Many three-deckers have been torn down, and others boarded up and abandoned. Most stores that closed in the late sixties have never been reopened." As housing activ-ist Finfer told Canellos: "'Well over 1,000 of the 2,500 mortgages handed out were foreclosed.' He said he blames the banks, real estate agents, and federal inspectors, 'The banks never exhibited a willingness to help fami-lies keep their houses. Instead, they instituted "fast foreclosures" and got paid through federal mortgage insurance.'"[23]

The devastation lasted for decades, as noted by BRA project manager in Grove Hall Muhammad Ali-Salaam, who recalled Flynn's reaction viewing aerial photographs of Blue Hill Avenue. "I was with the mayor in the BRA offices when he stepped into the conference room, wallpapered with aerial photographs of Blue Hill Avenue, which told the story of dev-astation," he said. "The mayor looked at the pictures and said, 'What the hell is this, Hiroshima?' I said, 'No, Mr. Mayor, this is Roxbury. This is Blue Hill Avenue.' He said, 'You are kidding. We have to do something about this.'"[24]

During the White era, Boston's housing crisis had worsened. Thousands of public housing units had been abandoned, and arson for profit was on the rise. Arson was a significant issue in many low-income neighborhoods of Boston. In one such area, Symphony Road in the city's Fenway section, arson became a crisis. The work of the community, led by future city councilor David Scondras, resulted in the indictment of thirty-three people, including three lawyers, two retired fire captains, and a lieutenant in the state fire marshal's office for conspiracy to commit arson for profit. The community group Symphony Tenants Organizing Project (STOP) has been organizing for years to improve housing conditions for the neighborhood's low- to moderate-income residents. Through their efforts, they stumbled into the arson-for-profit conspiracy. Scondras called to tell me he had just found a dead dog on his front steps with a note, "You're next." STOP tried to enlist the White administration to little avail. "What the White administration failed to do was build a working relationship with STOP—the Fenway community action group that had insisted for the past year that arsonists were active in the Fenway," Ken Hartnett wrote in the *Boston Globe*. "Part of the reason may have been a history of antagonism with some of STOP's leaders, including David Scondras, who contributed to Joseph Timilty's position paper on the city's economic condition in the 1975 campaign; part of the reason may have been bureaucratic inflexibility, and a conservative unease at dealing with community organizers who neither dress, talk or behave in a middle-class manner; and part of the reason may have been STOP's skepticism toward City Hall."[25]

Neighborhood leaders had always been suspicious about the source of the fires, which had hit more than thirty buildings on Symphony Road and neighboring Westland Avenue during the late 1970s. Five persons had died in the fires. Frank Bellotti, the state attorney general, prioritized this investigation. "This is a civil rights case," the head of the investigation in the attorney general's office said. "It concerns poor and underprivileged people being burned out of their homes and their neighborhoods being scared. Do you know why we wanted to get involved? It was because Boston was being blighted. People said the tenants were doing it, but it was the god-damned landlords."[26]

Other neighborhoods of Boston were not spared. In 1981, Roxbury's Highland Park neighborhood was dubbed "The Arson Capital of the Nation." Abandonment and increased speculation drove arson here and in the Dudley Street area. As Dudley area community activist Bob Haas said, "They were burning down very quickly. What could make so many houses burn down when so many people needed housing?"[27] As Flynn laid out in a 1984 op-ed in the *Globe*, "'Escape arson' is when building owners become overextended; 'insurance profit arson' involves absentee owners burning to collect the benefits; 'gentrification arson' occurs to facilitate the removal of tenants to raise rents or convert to condominiums; and 'redevelopment arson' takes place in areas targeted for significant improvements. Buildings that do not fit into these plans but might otherwise be saved for affordable housing are often burned to facilitate land clearance. Arson not only kills people; it also kills neighborhoods."[28] Each of these "types" of arson was destroying lives and homes in the neighborhoods, turning vibrant communities into wastelands.

In his study of arson in Boston, James Brady, director of Boston's Arson Strike Force, wrote about how he developed a sociology of arson at the time, using demography and urban economics: "It demonstrates that arson is a consequence of economic decisions undertaken by the banking, real estate, and insurance industries and the racketeering operations of organized crime syndicates. I argue that routine profit-making practices of banks, real estate agents, and insurance companies lead to abandonment, gentrification, and neighborhood decline, destabilizing urban communities and providing the context and motivation for several varieties of arson."[29]

Concerns about affordable housing, poverty, and racial conflict dominated the 1983 mayoral election and set the stage for change after Kevin White's departure. As Flynn entered office and faced these inherited elements of an urban crisis, he was determined to implement policies to achieve some semblance of economic justice for Boston's neighborhoods and their poor and working-class residents. The administration responded immediately to the most urgent crises, including creating the Arson Prevention Commission, organizing government agencies, and appointing neighborhood anti-arson organizers, activists, and researchers to respond to the crisis in the city.

## Flynn and the Community Fight the Banks and Win

During the Flynn administration, the role of banks in neighborhoods emerged as a significant issue, and the response of the administration and community organizations took center stage. Banks continued their redlining practices established years earlier, and the Boston Bankers Urban Renewal Group's actions in Mattapan were not forgotten. As discussed previously, housing affordability in Boston was a significant problem. "By 1987, the Boston area had the largest gap between earnings and house prices of any of the nation's fifty largest metropolitan areas. Other banking practices, however, gave a distinctly racial dimension to Boston's housing affordability problem: in low- and moderate-income white neighborhoods, readily available bank credit fueled the speculative frenzy of gentrification and condominium conversion that reduced the ability of long-time residents to afford to continue living in their neighborhoods," according to Jim Campen, professor of economics at the University of Massachusetts–Boston.[30]

Flynn would take many steps to get the banks to respond to Boston's neighborhoods. These included implementing a linked-deposit ordinance, which would measure the level of bank investment and guide where the city deposited its funds. He called upon banks to divest holdings in South Africa; attempted to restrict condominium conversions; accelerated the production of affordable housing, particularly on city-owned land; and, most importantly, fought to get the banks to create a mortgage lending fund in direct response to their discriminatory lending practices, as documented by the Federal Reserve Bank of Boston's 1989 report, and the Boston Redevelopment Authority's study released later that year.

In 1988, the Federal Reserve Bank of Boston had been secretly preparing a report on mortgage lending in Boston's neighborhoods. A copy of the report was leaked to the media. On January 11, 1989, the *Boston Globe* led with the front-page headline, "Inequities Are Cited in Hub Mortgages: Preliminary Fed Finding Is 'Racial Bias.'" The study, "Expanding the Potential of the Community Reinvestment Act: The Case for Affordable Housing in Boston," analyzed mortgage figures in sixteen neighborhoods for 1985 and drew upon statistics from five years, 1981–1985, to factor in demand variables, such as median purchase and rental prices, housing mix, historical turnover rates, and physical condition of the neighborhoods. The report found,

> Even after considering the variation in demand, "lending bias appears to be a significant factor, explaining why fewer than expected one- to four-family mortgage loans are made by banks and thrifts in minority neighborhoods in Boston," the study says. One set of figures shows that if race were not a factor in lending mortgages for one- to four-family houses, there would be a 113.4 percent increase in mortgages in Mattapan/Franklin Park and a 109.4 percent increase in Roxbury. The same table indicates that mortgage lending would decrease 62.8

percent in West Roxbury, 44.9 percent in South Boston, 39.7 percent in Charlestown, 37.4 percent in Roslindale, and 32.4 percent in Hyde Park. "Thus, long after the passage of the CRA, banks and thrifts continue to compete more aggressively in white neighborhoods in Boston and leave the minority neighborhoods to the mortgage companies," the study says. "Boston has become a city with significant unmet credit needs for affordable housing and continues as a city with significant racial lending bias."[31]

There was an immediate and loud community outcry, and Flynn and his administration immediately stepped up to respond to the report's findings. Peter Dreier, Flynn's point man on housing issues, was mentioned by one person interviewed as responsible for leaking the Fed study to the *Boston Globe*, which Dreier denied. Dreier recalled his conversation with Flynn. "I told the mayor that I was going to hire this academic researcher from Minnesota to come in here and do a study of redlining, and if so, we can get a lot more money into these poor neighborhoods you want to help," he said. "He wanted to know how this would help poor Black folks in Roxbury, Dorchester, and White folks in South Boston and East Boston. I said it would, although I was not telling the whole truth because redlining is primarily about racial discrimination in mortgage lending, and the remedy is to target more conventional loans and bank branches into neighborhoods that have suffered from blockbusting and redlining. He was right to be wary about how his detractors might exploit its potential divisive politics."[32]

The Fed study led to Flynn directing his BRA director, Stephen Coyle, and his housing director, Peter Dreier, to conduct their study of mortgage lending and work with the community organizations to develop an action plan. The BRA board initially rejected funding the study, but the day following the release of the Boston Fed study, Flynn wrote a memo to BRA chairman Robert Farrell. "I am deeply disturbed by recently published reports that Boston banks may discriminate based on race and geography in their lending practices in Boston's neighborhoods. Many Boston residents remember the devastating impact that such practices, known as 'redlining,' had in Boston's neighborhoods during the 1970s. They created economic and social chaos. We cannot tolerate discriminatory practices by banks or other financial institutions in Boston's neighborhoods. The very fabric of our neighborhoods is at stake. My administration has worked hard to develop affordable housing for Boston residents in every city neighborhood. I would be agitated to learn that some of Boston's lending institutions may be working at cross-purposes with this goal."[33]

The BRA board, which had been protecting the banks, then reversed its decision to conduct its analysis under pressure from Flynn.

So, Dreier got the BRA board to hire Charles Finn to conduct its study of mortgage lending despite several of the BRA board members' having opposed the study. There was disagreement within the administration, as Dreier explained, saying there were some administration officials who thought, "You are going to piss off the bankers. You are going to need them for other things." Dreier described the context: "This was national news; there was a big story about this in the *New York Times*. So, Flynn was now in the middle of this swirling controversy and was on the right side, although some folks inside city hall disagreed. Once it reached that point, they could not stop it because now it had a life of its own."[34]

A group of community advocates formed the Community Investment Coalition (CIC) to press the banks to respond to the findings of the Fed report and, later, the one conducted for the BRA. Lew Finfer, one of the coalition's lead organizers, talked about the strategy to pressure the banks to respond. "The coalition organized demonstrations at the Bank of Boston and BayBanks and successfully challenged the banks for not meeting their Community Reinvestment Act (CRA) responsibilities."[35]

There were disagreements between coalition members. "At some point, it would be how militant to be, but then, surprisingly, Gus Newport, the head of DSNI, wanted to make a deal," Finfer said. "We were focused on an affordable mortgage program, but things were written into the proposal around housing financing, banking services, and branches, which was good. Still, our priority was a new mortgage program enabling people to buy homes."[36]

There were other disagreements, as reported by the *Boston Globe*: "The rift developed when the Massachusetts Association of Community Development Corporations, which develops nonprofit housing statewide, declined to join the newly formed Boston-based Community Investment Coalition. The community coalition comprises the Greater Roxbury Neighborhood Authority, Dudley Street Neighborhood Initiative, Massachusetts Affordable Housing Alliance Home Buyers Union, and Hotel and Restaurant Workers Union Local 26. The association, which has 49-member community development corporations statewide, decided it could not endorse the coalition's plan to prioritize Roxbury, Mattapan, and Dorchester's credit needs."[37]

Dreier recalled clandestinely coordinating with members of the Community Investment Coalition. "I am about to issue a report on behalf of Flynn demanding one billion dollars over the next years in loans, philanthropy, and new branches," he told Lew Finfer. "Why don't you ask for two billion?"[38]

"We formed that coalition to press the banks for change," Roxbury community activist Ken Wade remembered. "We reached an unprecedented agreement. While the studies were done on home mortgages, we had to have a broader understanding with the banks than just mortgages. We had to do something more comprehensively. It had to deal with economic development, housing, and mortgage lending. So, we crafted a three-part program, and the city and community worked in tandem on that. The city weighing in, in the way that they did, it was no question, helped create additional leverage to push things in the right direction. The banks could have just cut a deal with the city, but they did not."[39]

The heat on the banks continued when the Greater Roxbury Neighborhood Authority (GRNA) released its study in August 1989, threatening to file a federal lawsuit against the discriminating banks. The GRNA study's findings were like that of the Fed study:

- The most mortgage money received by residents of a high-income Black tract was almost seven times less than the least amount granted in a high-income white tract.
- A predominantly white, middle-income tract in East Boston received ten times more mortgages than a primarily Black, high-income tract in North Dorchester.
- A white tract in North Dorchester received nearly four times more mortgage money than a Black tract with a higher median income in the same neighborhood.
- White South Boston and East Boston tracts received six times and eight times more mortgages, respectively, than Black Roxbury tracts with higher median incomes and median house values.[40]

The Community Investment Coalition (CIC) followed suit, releasing a "Community Reinvestment Plan" for $2.1 billion in bank investment over ten years. The plan included calls for rehabilitating eighty-eight hundred rental and cooperative housing units and financing thirty-four hundred new units. It also called for opening fifteen branch offices and fifteen automatic teller machines in Roxbury, Mattapan, Dorchester, Jamaica Plain, and the South End.[41] The issue upon which the city and the CIC agreed was the need to supply below-market mortgage loans. However, on that point, the bankers continued to balk.

In the fall of 1989, Flynn signed an executive order establishing a linked-deposit program to guide the investment of city resources in Boston banks. The *Boston Globe* reported at the time, "To encourage lenders to correct lending patterns inequities, Mayor Flynn said the city would begin steering its financial deposits to banks, showing a commitment to meeting the credit needs of minority neighborhoods. The mayor said he would sign an executive order creating a 'linked-deposit' program. The city treasurer must evaluate a bank's performance on home mortgages, small business loans, and other services before selecting it for municipal deposits."[42]

Flynn was working hard to get in front of the mortgage lending crisis. Late that year, following the original draft report leaked earlier to the media, the Boston Federal Reserve Bank released the final report. "Geographic Patterns of Mortgage Lending in Boston, 1982–1987"[43] was based on a statistical analysis of about forty-eight thousand real estate transactions in Boston's neighborhoods. Unlike previous Boston lending studies, it included data on loans made by private mortgage companies and banks outside the metropolitan area. The study found that lenders granted 24 percent fewer home loans in Boston's Black neighborhoods than in White neighborhoods. The discrepancy existed even after discounting other factors in Black neighborhoods, such as lower incomes, less wealth, lower-valued housing units, and less housing development.[44]

Flynn's response was swift, and he then met with the leaders of the major banks at the city-owned Parkman House. Dreier remembers Flynn saying to the bankers,

> "I can be your best friend, or I can be your worst enemy. I want a billion dollars," and they said, "Who is this punk telling us a billion dollars?" I doubt any of these bank CEOs had ever been talked to like that by a public official. However, they were also afraid of Flynn because they knew he was popular, would get reelected, and that some powerful Boston folks who sat on the banking committee in Congress, like Barney Frank and Joe Kennedy, would go after them, too. Flynn continued, "You got to do it together; I do not want one bank coming out alone." He told them to get their act together and develop an industry-wide plan that reflected his [Flynn's] and the community's proposal.[45]

City officials and the CIC were both concerned that the bankers would make an end run and announce a plan unilaterally. The banks had held three community forums and were trying to figure out how to proceed with a plan without committing to below-market-rate mortgages to low-income Black families. A Flynn development adviser, Bart Mitchell, worked with the bankers he characterized as "scared to death by the Community Reinvestment Act, thinking that they had a lot of vulnerability." He recalled speaking with a leading banker: "These people think we will cave in to blackmail. We will never cave in to blackmail. We will never do that; they are just wrong. What do you think we have to do to close this deal?" He added, "They had no sense of irony whatsoever!"[46] The stage was set for the showdown in late 1989.

Flynn proposed a Boston Neighborhood Reinvestment Plan to broker a deal with all three sides, attempting to compromise between the CIC proposal of $2.1 billion and the Massachusetts Bankers Association plan released without financial commitments. The Flynn plan called for $150 million in equity investment in affordable housing, the construction and financing at flexible terms of three thousand units of affordable housing, $500 million in discounted mortgages for first-time home buyers, $75 million in neighborhood economic development, and ten new branch banks in minority and underserved neighborhoods.[47]

Flynn's plan expanded the focus beyond Boston's minority neighborhoods to include South Boston and Charlestown, as well as Roxbury and Dorchester. This speaks to the ongoing role played by race in all aspects of city governance. Flynn had always looked at economic issues in purely class terms. Still, issues of race could not be avoided, and proposing legislation to benefit only minority neighborhoods would potentially provoke a racially biased response from Flynn's base constituency. Flynn's expanded plan partly responded to the situation described by councilors and city officials who said, "Flynn is facing backlash from residents of white neighborhoods who say that below-market mortgages are a form of affirmative action that will enable low-income people of color to purchase homes in white areas."[48]

Several factors clouded the negotiating environment. First, there were disagreements between several factions in the community on the issue of below-market mortgage loans. Second, from October 1989 through January 1990, the Stuart incident reignited racial problems in the city and would cloud the final negotiations. In this incident, Stuart's White pregnant wife and unborn child were murdered in Mission Hill. Stuart claimed it was a Black perpetrator and was later found to have murdered his wife and child himself. (The implications of the Stuart incident are explored in chapter 9.) Third, Flynn and Coyle delayed the release of the BRA study by University of Minnesota economist Charles Finn, hoping to maximize its impact on negotiations, but the delay fueled the controversy further.

Finally released late in 1989, Finn's study showed that "Boston's white neighborhoods received home loans at nearly three times the rate of Black neighborhoods of comparable income from 1981 through 1987."[49]

The bankers acknowledged that the release of the Finn BRA study had forced them to continue negotiations with the city to reach broad support, including the issue of below-market loans to the minority community. The bankers were going to announce a plan without city and community backing in late December. Still, the head of the Massachusetts Bankers Association said at the time that the BRA study "had thrown everything into confusion."[50] Flynn pressed the bankers on several fronts as the negotiations entered early 1990. In addition to below-market mortgages, Flynn had issued an executive order creating the linked deposit plan described earlier.

Not all agreed with the mayor's tactics. As Menino, head of the city council Ways and Means Committee and Flynn's successor several years later, said at the time, "Many bankers felt betrayed by the public release of the study as they believed they were making a good-faith effort to produce a reinvestment plan while coping with substantial operating losses," he said. "The mayor is taking a major political risk by taking on the banks now. Several banks are in serious trouble. I have always found that the banks are responsive to the needs of the city. For this to happen at this crucial time is a tough call by the administration. I question nailing the banks at this stage of a financial crisis."[51]

Flynn and his team pressed on and announced an agreement on January 10, 1990, between the banks, the city, and the Community Investment Coalition that included a "$400 million reinvestment plan for the city's minority neighborhoods and low- to moderate-income homebuyers that includes at least $30 million for below-market mortgages. The breakthrough on the reinvestment plan came after most of the city's largest banks agreed to provide mortgages at least one point below standard, resolving an issue that had threatened to negate months of talks."[52]

Despite this victory, some compromise was necessary that troubled some members of the Black community. However, Bruce Marks, executive director of the Union Neighborhood Assistance Corporation, which implemented much of the mortgage lending, attributed much of the turnaround to the city's linked-deposit program. Under an executive order signed by Mayor Flynn in 1989, the city increased its deposits in banks with favorable compliance ratings while freezing or removing deposits from banks that refused to comply. Marks said, "I think you have seen that it used to be a paper tiger, but now it has teeth and is becoming the junkyard dog. Boston Safe Deposit had one of the worst records before; now, they are one of the best. Shawmut used to be one of the worst, and now they are one of the best. The next one we must stick our fangs into is US Trust."[53]

After the deal was struck, the Community Investment Coalition expressed frustration with the slow progress in implementing the one-billion-dollar plan. The coalition's Diane Strother said, "It infuriates me. It doesn't look any better than it did before. They need to get on the ball and develop something to benefit us." Coalition member Willie Jones added about the banker's delay, "When it comes to creating excuses, these guys are professionals at why they can't give you money." Speaking for Flynn, Tom Snyder said, "Are they producing tangible results for neighborhood residents? No. The mayor feels the banks have a compelling legal obligation to write mortgages for working and needy families, and we are still waiting."[54] The pressure from Flynn and the community groups eventually led to the plan's implementation.

Finfer told me, "Since its beginning in 1991, over twenty-six thousand people in Boston have received these affordable mortgages; over 60 percent of the mortgage holders are people of color. The program has a significantly lower foreclosure rate than other bank mortgage products because people take a first-time homebuyer or postownership class and are motivated buyers starting their American dream of homeownership."[55]

The issue of fair lending practices, however, continued in subsequent years. Despite institutionalizing the linked-deposit program under the Menino administration, a 2002 report by the Massachusetts Community and Banking Council (MCBC) by Jim Campen of UMass–Boston concluded that "African Americans were denied loans three times as often as white applicants were in 2001." The report also showed that minority borrowers received fewer home purchase loans than in any year during the 1990s. "Although blacks make up 24.5 percent of Boston's population,

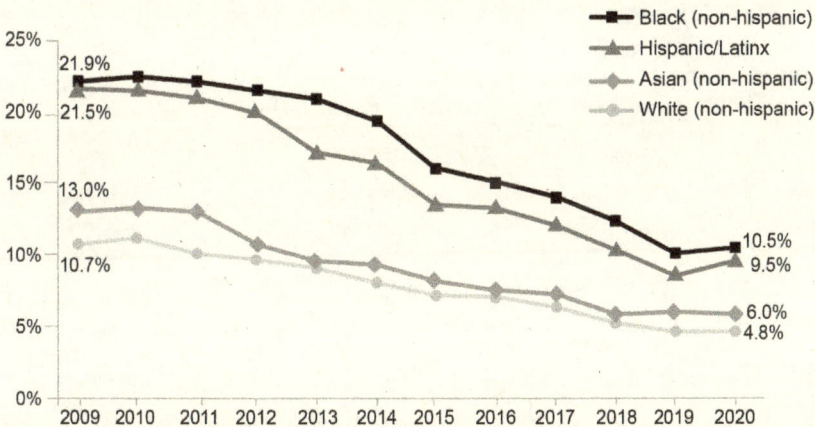

CHART 8. Mortgage Denial Rates by Race and Ethnicity, 2009–2020
Source: Boston Planning and Development Agency

they received only 11.5 percent of loans issued," the report said. "While up from 10.8 percent in 2000, it still was lower than in any year in the 1990s and below the 20.8 percent peak in 1994. Blacks received 708 home loans in 2001, the least since 1992." Campen concluded, "Race continues to be an issue. It is a bigger issue now than in 1990."[56]

In 1989, Menino mused, criticizing Flynn's approach to the banks, "I have always found that the banks are responsive to the needs of the city."[57] Yet, years after Menino became mayor, as Campen noted, racial disparity in lending became a more significant issue than before he became mayor. Still again, between 2009 and 2020, Blacks were denied mortgages at twice as high a rate as Whites, as Chart 8 shows.[58] The city needs a more strategic and focused agenda to reverse this troubling trend.

Chapters 8, 9, and 10 explore how Mayors White, Flynn, and Menino handled the contentious and vital issue of race relations and conflict.

# 7 / Challenging the Growth Machine: A New "Social Contract"

*Millionaires don't need mayors; poor people do.* (Mayor Ray Flynn interview)
*Ray Flynn had a social contract theory that the city moves ahead, that every-*
*body moves ahead together.* (Stephen Coyle, BRA director, interview)

The Ray Flynn administration's primary policy focus directly responded to the growth machine's total control of the city's development process. This control, which had been established over the prior decades, was a significant challenge that Flynn aimed to address. His administration inherited a city grappling with increasing poverty and housing costs and an economic development agenda that neglected the city's neighborhoods.

One of the key initiatives of the Flynn administration was managing Boston's downtown growth, a strategy that underscored his commitment to social and economic justice. Flynn frequently reiterated that his administration's development policies would reflect his vision, where economic growth would be inextricably linked to economic justice, job creation, and affordable housing for the poor and working-class residents of Boston's neighborhoods.

As previously discussed, Boston's economy had undergone significant transformations after World War II, first due to deindustrialization and federal highway and housing policies and later due to urban renewal. The growth machine coalition that took root in Boston following the defeat of the Irish populist mayor James Michael Curley in 1949 was firmly entrenched throughout the administrations of Mayors Hynes, Collins, and White. The cumulative effect of these profound political and economic shifts in Boston was evident in the deterioration of Boston's neighborhoods, mainly the housing stock and the parks, playgrounds, and infrastructure.

## Resisting Urban Removal

The South End was the primary urban renewal target in the waning days of Mayor Collins's administration, but neighborhood opposition slowed the process. Led by community activists such as Mel King, whose family was displaced in the New York Streets urban renewal process of 1955, the Community Assembly for a United South End (CAUSE) challenged the continuation of urban renewal. The taking over of the Boston Redevelopment Authority's site office in the South End in April 1968 was followed by the occupation of the South End urban renewal parcel that came to be known as Tent City.[1]

Although Kevin White promised a new approach to growth in the city, he changed course when elected mayor. White's growth machine coalition was like that of Mayors Hynes and Collins before him. The downtown area experienced rapid economic growth promoted by real estate and business leaders. According to a senior White administration official who reflected the administration's general thinking, "There was $100 million spent on urban renewal in one square mile in the South End," the official said. "Finally, it improved the neighborhood, and it had a tendency to displace people. So there was a cry for subsidized housing, which made the neighborhood less attractive again. You have to be prepared to accept a certain amount of displacement. Boston's family income is 25 percent below the metropolitan area. It even fell in the 1970s, despite gentrification. Can a city prosper over time if 20 percent of its population is below the poverty line? Can a public school system survive if half its students come from poor homes where the parents do not put a premium on learning?"[2]

As Harry Spence, the Boston Housing Authority (BHA) receiver, suggested, "There has been a sense at some level in City Hall over the last fifteen years that there are just too many poor people in this city and too much subsidized housing, and if they just let public housing slide, the poor will go away. Besides being a peculiarly malicious policy, it won't work—poor people *can't* go away."[3] They let public housing slide, and the courts put the housing authority into receivership.

Economists estimated that from 1960 to 1976, Boston increased its office capacity by 17 million square feet or nearly 40 percent. From 1979 to 1982, the city absorbed $1.5 billion in private development capital. Another $2.7 billion in projects were underway and scheduled to be completed by 1986, with an annual construction rate of 2.2 million square feet. Projections for 1987 to 1992 indicated that office construction in Boston would occur at a rate of 1.9 to 2.4 million square feet per year.[4] As James

Jennings and Mel King wrote in their book *From Access to Power: Black Politics in Boston*, "During his tenure, Mayor White performed his political-managerial responsibilities superbly; he adopted and implemented policies that favored the powerful and wealthy and hurt the poor. His major accomplishment was developing an atmosphere considered positive by big business interests; most of the mayor's more important actions were taken at the expense of those at the lower end of the socioeconomic ladder."[5]

The growth rate in the downtown commercial and housing markets continued to price working-class families out of the housing market. Resistance to the White administration's growth machine coalition policies and distrust of the Boston Redevelopment Authority led to a new level of political discourse in the city and at the ballot box.

Flynn implemented redistributive policies, using his power and the bully pulpit to force developers to do what they would not have done out of generosity—making a profit while supporting his social, economic, and political agenda. This strategy of employing the progressive cities theory tactics used in several other cities was not without its detractors, both within and outside the administration.[6] The most prominent of these redistributive policies was linkage. According to several city officials, Flynn used linkage to fight poverty, build affordable homes, and slow the process of poor people being pushed out of the city.

## Linkage: Sharing the Benefits of Downtown Growth with the Neighborhoods

Flynn campaigned in 1983 on a platform of economic and social justice. In 1983, White, bowing to the real estate lobby, resisted implementing linkage programs. Local activists, led by Mass Fair Share and the Massachusetts Tenants' Organization, had organized a ballot initiative supporting linkage. The city council, led by councilor Bruce Bolling, who had authored the original linkage law, approved the ballot initiative. Over White's veto, the question appeared on the ballot in the November 1983 election, asking voters, "Shall the City of Boston require developers to rehabilitate, develop, or partially fund one unit of low- to medium-cost housing for each unit of luxury housing created, or for every 1000 square feet of office or hotel space which is placed on the market?"[7] The measure was approved overwhelmingly.

In response to the inevitable, White appointed a commission to study the issue, led by Bolling and White's longtime ally Edward McCormack, the Massachusetts attorney general and a man White helped enrich as a developer in the waning days of his term.[8] The commission initially recommended a $2.50-per-square-foot exaction for projects over fifty thousand square feet. The proposal drew a harsh response from activists, and the commission later agreed to a five-dollar-per-square-foot exaction for projects over one hundred thousand square feet (with the first one hundred thousand square feet to be exempt) to be paid over twelve years. Two committee members, Albert Wallis, Greater Boston Legal Services attorney, and Emily Achtenburg, a housing planner and consultant, were the lone dissenters against the weak measure that the committee and White supported.[9] Councilor Flynn opposed White's plan, and during the campaign he made it clear that the proposal would not help the city address the housing crisis. Once in office, Flynn aggressively defended linkage against developer challenges and moved quickly to expand the exaction on projects. While housing activists and Flynn opposed the initial commission proposal, Bolling believed it was a way to move the issue forward.[10] The Greater Boston Real Estate Board actively opposed the measure following its approval by the city council.

Linkage was a hot-button issue in Boston. The city's neighborhoods were deteriorating while the downtown was booming with the new construction of luxury office towers. There was a particular crisis in the availability of affordable housing. Housing pressures were escalating, and White had all but eliminated rent control. There was not a coordinated city response to the housing crisis. A poll in the summer of 1983 found that an overwhelming majority, 76 percent of voters, supported linkage whereby downtown commercial real estate projects would contribute funds for housing in Boston's neighborhoods.[11] White knew that linkage was inevitable, and after he declined to run for reelection in May 1983, the issue dominated the mayoral forums and debates. Of the nine candidates running for mayor, all except David Finnegan endorsed some version of linkage. Later, even Finnegan backpedaled, saying he would negotiate linkage with developers while calling linkage "a tax of dubious constitutionality."[12]

In the preliminary mayoral election on October 11, 1983, Mel King and Ray Flynn—the two most vigorous proponents of linkage—finished in the top two spots. White announced three days after that election that he would support linkage. Flynn called the commission's proposal "an important first step; however, the formula for payment of the linkage fee set by the advisory committee would generate approximately $2.5 million per year, rather than the $5.5 million per year which our formula would have generated." Bolling and McCormack, committee cochairs, termed the committee's recommendation "a compromise report," but "one that will ensure that there will be some tangible spinoff with downtown development that will enhance housing development at the neighborhood level."[13] So, in the closing days of White's mayoralty, the Boston Zoning Commission approved a watered-down version of the linkage measure, which was the most palatable to the development community and still likely to face a court challenge.

Councilor Bruce Bolling, the cochair of the linkage committee and author of the original legislation that the city council adopted and White vetoed in early 1983, is often not credited for his crucial role in forging the compromise to initiate the linkage policy later modified by Flynn and other mayors who followed.

When Flynn assumed office in 1984, the linkage was a unifying policy in his diverse administration. While his advocacy for strong rent control prompted behind-the-scenes divisions inside the administration, linkage would be a vehicle for Flynn to implement his aggressive, affordable housing agenda. The development team and the neighborhood activist members of the administration saw linkage as a critical resource during dwindling federal dollars to cities.

The administration's efforts were put on hold when real estate interests, led by controversial developer of the West End urban renewal project Jerome Rappaport, challenged the linkage law in court in June 1985, claiming that the law biased the city zoning process in favor of developers who could make a higher payment. Flynn and Coyle aggressively battled the Rappaport challenge. Linkage was essential to Flynn's ability to unite Boston's neighborhoods and respond to the downtown-neighborhood disparities, issues that were a cornerstone of his campaign in 1983. On April 4, 1986, Massachusetts Superior Court Judge Mel Greenberg struck down linkage provisions in the Boston zoning code, calling linkage an "illegal tax." Flynn vowed to appeal the decision, saying he would fight to go to the Legislature if necessary to preserve linkage as "an honest and equitable way to reach out to those who have been left behind amid unprecedented growth."[14]

Flynn would aggressively take on the fight. He could not stand by and potentially lose $35 million to $40 million from thirteen proposed projects.[15] "Economic growth must mean economic justice for those who have not shared in Boston's prosperity," Flynn said in response to the lawsuit. "My administration is about helping people who have been left behind."[16] Coyle led the city's challenge to the court decision. Like Flynn, Coyle saw linkage as part of the "social contract" between the various interests in the city. Coyle recalled discussing linkage with Flynn, who said, "What you are suggesting is we let downtown development occur responsibly because it was six billion dollars if and only if, at the same time, we are investing in affordable housing projects." "So, I took the mission of Ray's social contract, thinking that you must convert development into an enterprise for the community. It is jobs; the dollars for linkage meant you had achieved minority and community hiring goals, and we did in record numbers. Having downtown development as it happened from 1977 until when Ray came in, if you put up a million-square-foot building, lots of people will work, and nothing went out to the neighborhoods, you created a further distancing from the emerging downtown and the emerging economy in the community. If you put a hundred affordable housing projects in the ground across the communities, built by people in the communities, it is just a different world. So, Ray had a social contract theory that the city moves ahead that everybody moves ahead together."[17]

Not all development community members supported Rappaport's challenge, at least publicly. Donald Chiofaro, the developer of International Place, a project scheduled to pay $8 million in linkage fees, said he had no problem with linkage. "I build office buildings downtown, and the better downtown and the city work, the better my investment works," he said. "Linkage funds will help create housing and job training to improve the city."[18] Coyle was also adept at "convincing" members of the development community, particularly those with projects pending approval, to support the mayor's agenda. "Rappaport, the controversial developer who tore down the West End, had rallied the development community against linkage," Coyle said. "As BRA director, you must know your actions have political outcomes and consequences. It is not a game of Monopoly. I knew that certain developers who were in the pipeline had force; they were new. Don Chiofaro, Roz Gorin, Ed Sidman, and Ronnie Druker were new people; they were not the old Boston. Let us promote this new group of developers and get them to back linkage so there would be at least two factions within the real estate community: those who would coalesce with Jerry Rappaport's and block linkage saying, 'It is a tax, it is illegal,' and the others saying, 'Hey, it is part of the social contract, it is what you pay to grow. The BRA is going to meter approval so we could get ourselves in the ground and leased before we get flooded,' which was the equation."[19]

In 1985, Flynn proposed to increase the linkage fee, fearing that the payment's current value needed to be revised to accelerate the building of much-needed affordable housing. He also added a fee for job training. Meeting resistance on three sides—community activists, the development community, and the city council—he sought to compromise. Community activists believed that he needed to raise the formula higher. Members of the Boston Linkage Action Coalition, an organization of tenants' groups and Mass Fair Share, from which many Flynn staffers had hailed, wanted Flynn to increase the linkage payment to ten dollars per square foot. They also wanted to force developers to pay it before construction, eliminate the exemption for projects under one hundred thousand square feet, and force developers of luxury housing projects to pay linkage. On the other side, many members of the growth machine shared prominent business-man and developer (and Vault member) Robert Beal's point of view: "When the original formula was put in place, most of us said, fine, it is like a mosquito bite. It may itch a little, but it is not overwhelming. But do not do it to the point where you get a case of malaria."[20] Then-head of the Greater Boston Real Estate Board, J. Thomas Marquis, said, "The concern is that the door is open now. First, we had linkage. Now, we have extended linkage. What happens when we have extended-extended link-age? At what point does the market turn around? At what point do you kill the golden goose?"[21]

In early 1986, the BRA approved the mayor's changes to linkage. These changes would increase the resources available by shortening the pay-ment period required of developers and adding job training provisions requiring contributions to a job training trust fund. The changes to the zoning code were now law in Boston. Still, Flynn filed a home rule pe-tition to avoid further challenges, which the Massachusetts legislature approved and resulted in Chapter 371 of the Acts of 1987 legislative autho-rization for Boston's linkage program.

Later that year, on August 21, 1986, the Massachusetts Supreme Judicial Court overturned the April 1986 Superior Court ruling against linkage. "This legal victory will allow the people of our neighborhoods to share the benefits of Boston's booming downtown economy," Flynn said. "It will mean job and housing opportunities which otherwise would not have been possible." Janice Fine, spokeswoman for the Linkage Action Coali-tion, said at the time, "As far as we are concerned, it is neighborhoods one and Rappaport zero. To prevent future litigation, we want to ensure the city shores up the ordinance." At the time of the ruling, the BRA es-timated that the city would begin reaping nearly $40 million in linkage payments starting in 1987.[22]

As of 1986, in addition to Boston and San Francisco, linkage exaction policies and housing trust funds had been initiated or considered in Santa Monica, Miami, New York City, Denver, Chicago, Hartford, Honolulu, Minneapolis, Seattle, Oakland, Cambridge (MA), Toronto, and London, among others.[23] The ruling would allow the administration to continue aggressively pushing for affordable housing in Boston. In his 1986 State of the City address, Flynn established a goal of breaking ground on thirty-four hundred new or rehabilitated housing units that year and expanding the linkage to parcel-to-parcel linkage.

## Parcel-to-Parcel Linkage and Eminent Domain Authority to the Community

Flynn's first-in-the-nation proposal linked a desirable downtown parcel to Parcel 18, a vacant site in Roxbury. It required minority developer partners representing at least 30 percent of the development team with project equity—and it got it. Groups representing Black, Asian, and Hispanic investors were partners in developing both parcels.

Flynn and Coyle argued the city's reasoning before the BRA board, where Flynn appeared in person. "Based on data showing that four city-owned garages sold to developers in 1983 spurred $800 million worth of development projects, but none of the developers were people of color and that while the government has tried to improve the status of people of color, poverty remains in minority communities,"[24] Coyle explained about parcel-to-parcel linkage. "It is about capital formation in the communities of color," he said. In his September 25, 1986, resolution to the BRA board—setting the framework for the parcel-to-parcel linkage program connecting the development of the Kingston-Bedford garage in the downtown Chinatown section of Boston with the vacant Parcel 18 in Roxbury—Coyle wrote, "Over $7 billion was invested in Boston in the last nine years. In addition, the city has approved $3 billion in private downtown development projects since mid-1984; employment growth has followed quickly behind the capital investment." Coyle documented that poverty was increasing and employment for people of color was at its lowest in the downtown economy, with only 16 percent of minority resident workers employed downtown. Even more striking, Coyle concluded, "There has not been a single minority developer engaged in the private development of large commercial projects in Boston."[25]

A particular focus had been the city disposition process for surplus parking garages. Of the five municipal parking facilities sold by White in Boston in the early 1980s, generating an estimated $843 million, none had gone to minority developers or had provided minority developer equity.[26] Flynn's and Coyle's goal was to change that equation, provide opportunities for wealth creation in communities of color, and develop a parcel in Roxbury that might not otherwise elicit development interest. "The plan, which joins public land with mostly private financing, will help build a neighborhood economy in Roxbury," Coyle said. "There are now 9,000 jobs in Roxbury, and this development would add another 3,500. Meaningful social progress will occur in Boston if people of color can access the development economy. We are talking about people of color owning $100 million worth of this project. It will change Boston."[27]

The goal was to create wealth in the minority community and use public land to create community equity. Coyle engineered the Parcel 18 deal. "It is the greatest idea since sliced bread," he said. "I can also tell you it is the riskiest development undertaking in the city's history."[28] Risky or not, the mayor and Coyle, with an agreement from Governor Michael Dukakis, undertook the venture, and it paid off for the neighborhood, the city, and minority equity investors.

The so-called MassPort Model emerged later from the leadership of Duane Jackson, a member of the MassPort Board. This model also required minority equity investors to develop MassPort projects, like the Omni Hotel, in 2022.[29] The MassPort Model arrived on the development scene thirty-three years after Parcel 18—the Flynn/Coyle model—and has been effectively used for city- and state-supported development projects.

"It may be the best chance for Roxbury to come back to life on several fronts. Until now, people of color could not get into the economic mainstream," Marvin Gilmore, chair of the Parcel 18+ task force, said. "There was nothing on that site before this. Now, there will be something there. It is bound to benefit the community."[30] Gilmore cofounded Unity Bank and Trust Company in Roxbury in the late 1960s, the first Black-owned and -operated commercial bank in Boston, and was president and CEO of Community Development Corporation of Boston for forty-two years.

With linkage in place, the BRA continued to approve the large-scale projects proposed by developers for downtown, some of which were proposed under the White administration. This "managed growth" approach would yield construction jobs and expand the city's service economy. Late in 1984, the BRA reviewed and scaled back ten major development projects while requiring that developers make best-faith efforts to comply with the Boston Jobs for Boston Residents policy and hire 50 percent Boston residents, 25 percent people of color, and 10 percent women.

In announcing the completion of the review of the ten projects, Coyle estimated they would add up to $1.3 billion in new investment in the city. "Creating Boston Jobs for Boston Residents through balanced growth remains a significant commitment of my administration," Flynn said. "The real significance is what these projects mean regarding jobs—25,000 permanent jobs and 12,000 construction jobs. Frankly, until today, development in Boston has only been beneficial to a small number of people. Our neighborhoods lagged behind downtown because our people still needed to receive their share of Boston's new jobs. I intend to build an economic life in this city that includes all its citizens. We are inaugurating a new development policy for our city. We are beginning an era in Boston when downtown development will translate into jobs and economic benefits for the people of all our city's neighborhoods. The paradox of prosperity in our downtown and poverty in our neighborhoods can now be addressed."[31]

"To its credit, the Flynn administration has also demonstrated that it is possible for the city, which for too long handed developers a blank check, to gain from downtown development," the *Boston Globe* editorialized.[32]

Chart 9 highlights the development of downtown office space between 1980 and 1998. During Flynn's tenure, 1984–1993, downtown developments provided significant resources for affordable housing projects in Boston's neighborhoods through linkage, construction, and permanent jobs for Boston residents.

Linkage became firmly entrenched in Boston during the Flynn administration. In 1989, a *Boston Globe* story called linkage part of the landscape in Boston. "Six years later, after amendments to city zoning laws, court challenges, and modifications, linkage is no longer a political buzzword," reporter Peggy Hernandez wrote. "While many developers and institutions engaged in expansion projects resent the program, they accept that linkage payments are part of the negotiating process to obtain

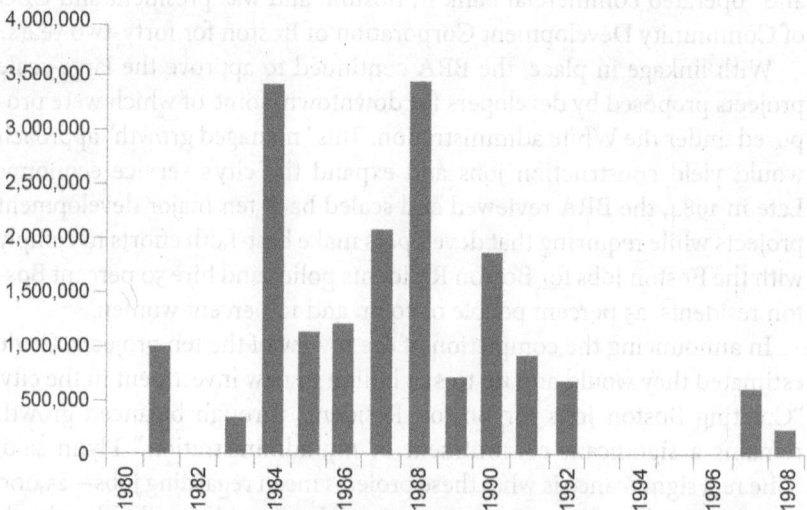

CHART 9. Office Space Construction in Boston, 1980–1998
Source: Boston Planning and Development Agency

city building and zoning permits. 'If you step back and look from 1983 to 1989, you see linkage has gone from theory to projects, concept to reality,' Coyle said. 'It has become a real force for housing in Boston. Everyone should take a measure of satisfaction in what's been done and resolve to do more.' Linkage has 'been almost a lifesaver for Roxbury,' said Ken Wade, chairman of the Roxbury Neighborhood Council. 'The level of affordable housing in this community would not be accomplished had it not been for linkage.' Added Tom McIntyre, vice president of the Bricklayers Nonprofit Housing and Development Corp., which has built linkage projects in Mission Hill, South Boston, and Charlestown, 'Affordable housing is a big mosaic, and you could not get to the batter's box without linkage. It is seed money that community groups need to solidify a whole development project with mortgage lenders.'"33

According to Tom O'Brien, BRA director under Menino, Flynn implemented the program around linkage, which was a significant change. "Now, it has become institutionalized," he said. "It is set in Boston and will never go away. It is the law of the land."34

"In terms of linkage, that is something that Flynn developed," Marie Kennedy, a city planner and King supporter, said. "I think it is something he can legitimately claim. It was developed in other cities initially proposed by Bruce Bolling and backed by Mel King."35

For Flynn, linkage was more than a housing and training fund; it symbolized his values and a way to promote economic justice and racial harmony. "Linkage becomes the concept that speaks to the race issue indirectly, even as it speaks to the development issue," Neil Sullivan said. "Stop fighting across the races; somebody else is getting rich while you are attacking each other. Change it up. Change the culture. Change the climate. We were following a time-honored community organizing maxim. It is not the issue; the enemy moves the people to action. We consciously tried to displace the other race as the enemy and substitute the corporations, developers, and rich people for it. Flynn loved it because that was how he felt. It always comes back to the primacy of Ray Flynn. We had to be authentic to who he was."36

Linkage and the Boston Residents Jobs Program were vehicles that moved beyond the symbolism to produce thousands of low- to moderate-housing units and training and job opportunities for neighborhood residents. The data compiled by the BRA in its 2003 report, "The Boston Economy," best makes the point: "Since the inception of the linkage program through June 2000, $58.2 million has been awarded to various affordable housing projects. Through 1999, this funding allowed the construction or renovation of 5,979 housing units in 89 projects in the city's neighborhoods. Affordable housing units for low- and moderate-income residents comprise 80 percent (4,812 units) of this total."[37] A later report by the Neighborhood Housing Trust notes its success: "From its inception in 1986 through December 31, 2012, the Neighborhood Housing Trust has committed $133,804,969 in linkage funds. These funds have helped create or preserve 10,176 affordable housing units in 193 development projects throughout the City of Boston."[38]

After Flynn left office in 1993, pressure mounted for Menino to continue and expand linkage. Menino convened a group of developers and housing activists who recommended increasing the linkage fees. Menino was reluctant to raise the formula, fearing pushback from the growth machine. He was also engaged in a battle with the state legislature. According to the Neighborhood Housing Trust, which administers the linkage funds, the Massachusetts legislature finally approved a home rule petition in December 2001 that increased the affordable housing linkage fee to $7.18 per square foot and the job training linkage fee to $1.44 per square foot, nearly a decade after Menino took office.

Provisions in the law required an additional increase in 2006, and at that time, the affordable housing linkage fee was increased to $7.87 per square foot and the employment linkage fee to $1.57 per square foot.[39] Critics contend that this increase did not match inflation and that fewer funds were available than when Flynn expanded the linkage law in 1986.

Mayor Walsh led an effort to increase linkage in 2018 and 2021, and Mayor Wu achieved a further increase in 2021. Linkage funds to build affordable housing in Boston accounted for more than $227 million since 1986.

## Community Development Corporations: "The Secret Weapon"

The myriad community development corporations (CDCs) in every Boston neighborhood were essential partners in producing neighborhood housing and rebuilding neighborhoods. CDCs emerged in the 1960s and 1970s mainly from tenant organizing in the fight against urban renewal, neighborhood associations, and politics. State legislation sponsored by Mel King gave CDCs a boost in the mid-1970s. As the head of the city's Public Facilities Department (PFD), Lisa Chapnick, said, "CDCs are the city's secret weapon. When we do business with a CDC, we know what they want is what the administration wants—the preservation of affordable housing for the long term. The CDCs are the primary weapon when the city declares war on abandoned buildings. The next frontier is land. We are challenging the CDCs to tackle many of the city's 700 to 750 vacant buildable lots."[40] CDCs have been responsible for thousands of affordable housing units in Boston. The city provided political and financial support, investing significantly in their success in supporting operations, technical assistance, capacity building, housing subsidies, and land.

## City Grants Neighborhood Eminent Domain Power

Like all his politics, Flynn's neighborhood development approach was rooted in neighborhood residents taking charge. An extraordinary example was the efforts by a local neighborhood group, the Dudley Street Neighborhood Initiative (DSNI), which—after several years of organizing to clean up vacant lots, reduce crime, and rid their neighborhood of drugs—petitioned the Boston Redevelopment Authority for the power of eminent domain to assemble enough vacant property to build affordable housing.

"This is a wonderful community where many different kinds and generations of residents and other stakeholders have come together to control what happens here for the benefit of the residents. We've been able to halt the devastation, establish community institutions like the land trust, and find innovative solutions together," said May Louie of DSNI. The 'devastation' to which Louie refers was caused by a combination of arson during the 1970s and 1980s, and illegal dumping of waste materials, including lead, that continued into the 1990s.[41]

Unheard of in cities across America, then and today, DSNI sought the power wielded by the government, including Boston, to clear urban areas of poor people and develop the land for the well-to-do.[42] "The power of eminent domain is a power that can be abused, as the painful experience in Boston's West End reminds us. However, Boston is also a place where eminent domain has been used creatively. Consider the experience of the Dudley Street Neighborhood Initiative, which has enabled a low-income community in Roxbury to reclaim its future. The community confronted a serious problem. Absentee owners held decaying properties that stood in the way of redevelopment plans. The initiative lobbied the city to give it the power of eminent domain. The result of this public/private partnership has been a widely acknowledged improvement in the neighborhood."[43]

Flynn reflected on the strength of the Dudley Street area, saying, "You could walk into the area, and you would think you were walking through the United Nations. Long-term residents were there when James Michael Curley was the mayor of Boston, and then we have people who just arrived from Cape Verde and everything in between. Dudley represents not only the greatest of Boston in its diversity, but I think it's the future of

America as well. Any time you can get a neighborhood organization to work closely and cooperate with the city government, that's a real win-win situation. That's not only great policy, it's also great politics."[44]

Flynn turned city land over to community groups and CDCs and, in the case of DSNI, bucked his own BRA board and granted eminent domain power, previously used to displace residents through urban renewal, to the neighborhood organization. The BRA board was poised to deny approval of eminent domain power to DSNI because its chair, Robert Farrell, questioned the legality until Flynn intervened. Flynn summoned the BRA board to his office and read them the riot act. Farrell subsequently resigned after nearly twenty years on the board.

This challenge to the status quo marked Flynn's break from the past, where neighborhoods were ignored. He showed respect and confidence in the people in the community to solve the problems that the government, for too long, had walked away from facing. In supporting the eminent domain authority for DSNI, Flynn said, "I saw an opportunity for the neighborhood to take control, to have power, to make decisions that affect their neighborhood and their life."[45]

Managed development in Boston had many benefits for the city and its neighborhoods. Affordable housing was rapidly produced, public housing improved, maintenance increased, vacancies decreased, and parks, police stations, playgrounds, City Hospital, and Faneuil Hall were renovated. With each administration policy, from the Boston Residents Jobs Policy to providing summer jobs for youth, the focus was on employment and the economic and quality-of-life benefits for Bostonians.

## Boston Residents Jobs Policy: "The Best Social Program We Got Going Is a Job" (Ray Flynn)

The Boston Residents Jobs Policy (BRJP) required developers to hire 50 percent of Boston residents, 25 percent of people of color, and 10 percent of women on all city-assisted development projects. Soon after taking office, the mayor issued an executive order extending the policy to private construction projects requiring city approval. White and the development community opposed linkage and the BRJP, essential for addressing rising housing costs and access to jobs, particularly in low-income neighborhoods. "I can think of no initiative that's more healing for the city than getting jobs for poor Whites and Blacks, for all the working people of Boston," Flynn said of the jobs program at the time.[46]

The BRJP has had an erratic history. The initial impetus for the policy in Boston was Chuck Turner's efforts in the 1970s. Turner led the Third

World Jobs Clearinghouse and was later elected to the city council, advocating for more jobs for people of color in the construction industry. In the mid-1970s, Turner led picket lines protesting the lack of people of color working on rebuilding Boston State College, where he often hit a roadblock.

In 1979, King used his platform to follow Turner's lead and push the hiring agenda for minority jobs. Then-mayor Kevin White, who had not pursued a jobs agenda for Boston residents, abruptly issued an executive order creating the program late in the 1979 preliminary election, in which he was a candidate. His order was never implemented due to a lawsuit by several contractors and unions challenging the policy's constitutionality. Initially, the challenge prevailed at the state's Supreme Judicial Court but was overturned by the US Supreme Court in February 1983. During this period, Turner reevaluated his strategy when thousands of White construction workers started demonstrating against Mayor White's jobs policy. The policy they formulated led to a city ordinance approved by outgoing mayor White the day before the October 1983 preliminary mayoral election. It required 50 percent of Boston residents, 25 percent of people of color, and 10 percent of women on all city-funded construction projects. It was viewed as a way to forge a consensus on a divisive issue. King and Flynn actively supported the policy during the 1983 election.

When Flynn took office, he expanded the policy to include private construction projects that required city approval. "The approach—which was to convert race issues into class issues to provide opportunities for poor and working-class blacks and whites—has become the centerpiece of Mayor Flynn's political rhetoric and a key tenet of his municipal level economic program," the *Boston Globe* reported. Gathered at the signing event were Chuck Turner, the activist behind the original plan; head of the bricklayer's union, Tom McIntyre; developer Don Chiofaro, who built International Place; and those who fought for years for the policy alongside those who opposed who had an interest in unifying behind the new and expanded policy.[47]

Flynn saw the jobs program implementation and linkage as his "social contract" with Boston's neighborhood residents. Flynn thought he could make the policy work partly through his close relationship with the unions. "This is what trade unions used to be," he said, adding, "For years, people in the neighborhoods have subsidized the development of the downtown area. Their property tax dollars were used to pay for the police and other city services in the downtown area. There is substantial growth, and I want to ensure the people in the neighborhood will benefit from it. In a city with many needy residents looking for employment opportunities, it is important to let those people get the jobs."[48]

As the first year unfolded, the residents' job policy resulted in Boston residents holding 42 percent of the construction jobs, people of color at 32 percent, and women at 4 percent. As the program progressed, the numbers became uneven. Some saw the policy requirements for contractors only to use "best efforts" and a lack of enforcement as barriers. In contrast, others pointed to unions' reluctance to create more opportunities, and still others cited a lack of training and apprenticeship programs as a barrier. Compared to other state vocational schools, the city's Humphrey Occupational Resource Center has consistently failed to train Boston kids for occupations in the construction industry. "Trade unions have made a solid effort to admit more people of color and women but have found that applicants from Boston often do not meet the minimum qualifications," Ted Landsmark, director of the Mayor's Office of Jobs and Community Services, said. "Our kids have not been as competitive as the graduates of the other regional technical schools. If we had a functioning Humphrey Center with a feeder system out of the middle schools, we would have many more Boston residents and people of color working these union jobs."[49]

There had been a real or imagined fear that if the city were overly aggressive, there could be another challenge to the policy, as happened in the late 1970s when Worcester, Fall River, and Quincy faced challenges overturning similar programs.[50]

King criticized Flynn for not implementing the residents' jobs program faster in the first year of his tenure. Responding to criticism by King of Flynn's efforts to enforce the Boston Jobs Ordinance, "Paul Grogan, director of the Neighborhood Development and Employment Agency, which monitors compliance with the Ordinance, said Flynn's administration has taken a harder line than Mayor Kevin H. White's administration, under which Grogan also served." He went on to say that "under White last year 35% of those employed on the projects were residents, 27% were people of color and 4% were women. In comparison, under Flynn this summer, 44% of the jobs went to residents, 32% to people of color, and 4% to women."[51]

The BRJP proceeded haphazardly, with the numbers fluctuating yearly. The Menino and Walsh administrations were criticized for what advocates believed was ineffective monitoring and compliance enforcement. Chart 10 demonstrates that the job numbers were not meeting the goals.

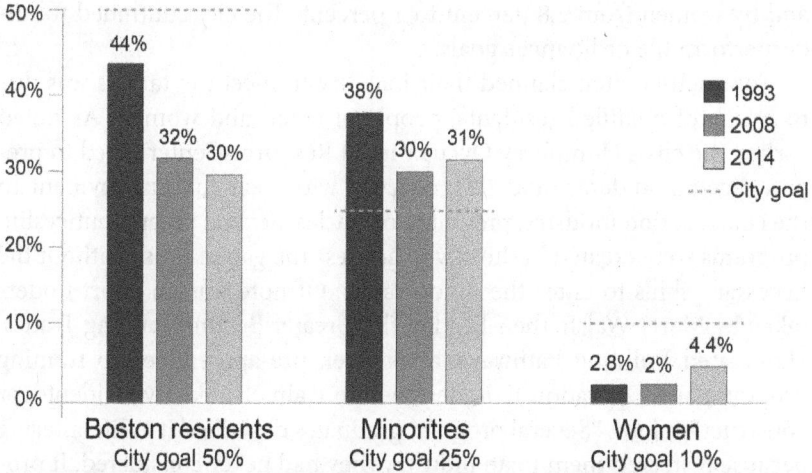

CHART 10. Boston Residents Jobs Program: Work Hours, Residents, Minorities, and Women, 1993, 2008, and 2014
Source: City of Boston Residents Jobs Program

After nearly twenty years of the program, during the Menino administration, the original leader of the policy initiative, Boston city councilor Turner, became so frustrated that he said, "I think that it has failed. As I look at these numbers, I think we cannot allow these projects to go on with these kinds of percentages."[52] In an interview, King shared his frustration. "Even in the case of the police station being built in the heart of Roxbury, we were not getting the jobs," he said.[53] City councilor Tito Jackson was more upbeat at the dedication of the Bruce Bolling Municipal Building in Dudley Square in 2015 when he praised the late councilor Bruce Bolling, the first African American to serve as city council president. "For the redevelopment of the Ferdinand building, more than 45% of the jobs went to Boston residents, more than 48% of the positions went to people of color, and nearly 10% went to women," he said. "That is one of the most important pieces of legislation that Councilor Bolling led and passed. I refer to it regularly for what it says and means for the city."[54]

Progress in meeting the requirements of the BRJP has been uneven since its inception. During Flynn's tenure, some progress was being made, primarily due to his commitment to the program as described and his relationships with the unions. Since Flynn left office, the numbers have dipped. Between 1993 and 2008, work done by residents went from 44 percent to 32 percent, by people of color from 38 percent to 30 percent, and by women from 2.8 percent to 2 percent. The city continued to underperform the ordinance's goals.[55]

Contractors often claimed their inability to meet the targets was due to a lack of qualified residents, people of color, and women. As noted earlier, the city's Humphrey Occupational Resource Center failed to prepare Boston students, and this, coupled with near-full employment in the construction industry, presented obstacles. Several preapprenticeship programs were created in the city to address the gap in those without the necessary skills to enter the union ranks. Of note was an effort undertaken by Marty Walsh, then-head of the Greater Boston Building Trades. He created Building Pathways, a six-week pre-apprenticeship training program, and Operation Exit, designed to train at-risk city residents for construction jobs. "Several program graduates described it as life-altering because it steered them to an industry they had never considered. It provided steady employment and significantly better pay and benefits than most blue-collar jobs," as reported in the *Boston Globe.*[56]

In 2017, Walsh expanded the three-decade-running Boston Residents Jobs Program to increase the requirements for residents from 50 percent to 51 percent, the number of people of color from 25 percent to 40 percent, and the number of women from 10 percent to 12 percent of the work hours by trade on both publicly funded and private projects in Boston.[57] While BRJP advocates applauded this move, the developers, construction companies, and unions knew it still only required so-called best-faith efforts, the same as ever. As WGBH put it, the policy was "all bark, no bite."[58]

Enter the Wu administration. For the first time since the BRJP was initiated in 1983 and later revised in 1985 by Flynn to include private projects requiring city approval, the Boston Employment Commission fined a contractor not for failing to meet the goals but rather for not filing timely reports.[59] This may have sent a long-overdue signal that the city was serious about sharing prosperity with its residents and compliance with the jobs policy.

So, in evaluating the program, it is clear that the hiring goals generally needed to be met. They ebbed and flowed depending upon the leadership of the city administration in office at the time. One must concede, however, that the BRJP accomplished something that would not have been achieved otherwise: It put thousands of Boston residents, people of color, and women to work in the city's booming economy. It was also long overdue to make the city's vocational technology school work and prepare Boston residents, people of color, and women for opportunities in the then-robust economy.

## Reimagining Blue-Collar Jobs

The agency charged by Mayor Flynn to focus on blue-collar jobs was the Economic Development and Industrial Corporation (EDIC). The state legislature created EDIC in 1971 as a quasipublic entity that leads local economic development activities at industrial and manufacturing properties in Boston, including the Raymond L. Flynn Marine Park (formerly known as the Boston Marine Industrial Park). EDIC owns the two-hundred-acre park on the South Boston waterfront, home to nearly two hundred businesses and many maritime-related industries, a working dry dock, and deep port access for container vessels. EDIC also owns a small industrial park in Dorchester, Alsen Mapes, and parcels of land at the Crosstown Industrial Park (Melnea Cass and Mass Avenues), which, at the time, were home to Morgan Memorial Goodwill, Strideright, and Digital Equipment Corporation. EDIC had several tools available to promote economic development, including an industrial development bonding authority (Boston Industrial Development Finance Authority), a loan program for small businesses (Boston Local Development Corporation), and a technical training center located in the industrial park (Boston Technical Center).

EDIC supported the city's existing industrial economy through its industrial parks and loan programs and targeted new growth companies in biomedical research, health care and life sciences, environmental engineering, and advanced manufacturing sectors. Looking to integrate technology with career pathways in Boston's emerging new economy, the agency developed demand-driven strategies to capture health care and clean energy jobs that provided promising careers for Boston residents. The Greater Boston Chamber of Commerce and Associated Industries of Massachusetts (AIM), representing 3,000 companies, joined with EDIC to implement the strategy outlined in their report, "Growth in the '90s: Prospects for Strategic Economic Development in Boston." John Gould, AIM CEO, called the effort "one of the most positive and thoughtful action plans I have seen for economic development in the city."[60]

In 1990, EDIC merged with the Mayor's Office of Jobs and Community Services, melding education and training programs as well as the neighborhood jobs trust and the residents' jobs program. The goal was to connect industry with a trained workforce and draw upon the vast network of community-based agencies to provide education and training services to Boston residents. EDIC was self-supporting, earning rental income from its industrial park tenants who were paying below-market rates to create and retain jobs in the city. These funds supported the agency's related mission and activities including a small business loan program in collaboration with several community development corporations financed through the Boston Local Development Corporation.

The agency focused on the city's industrial economy and neighborhood businesses and linked residents through job training and education. The agency pushed the state to surplus the Boston State Hospital site for mixed-use development. The disposition had been held up for years by then–state representative Angelo Scaccia, who pushed for the deinstitutionalizing impacts of closing the state mental health facility. The site would ultimately become home to hundreds of mixed-income housing units, Mass Audubon's Boston Nature Center, a wildlife sanctuary, and the MassBiologics Manufacturing Facility.

The Crosstown Industrial Park had been home to Digital Equipment Company's manufacturing facility. Supported by generous tax incentives to locate on the Roxbury Parcel, Digital announced in December 1992 that it would close the facility and lay off 190 workers, many from Boston neighborhoods. "There is a national problem of corporations profiting at the expense of workers and neighborhoods. Digital rung up profits in the 1980s with tax incentives, and now the community is left high and dry," Flynn said, and he filed a complaint with the attorney general's office about the tax breaks that Digital received and walking away from their corporate responsibility to the community.[61]

## The Seaport: A Gleaming Disappointment

Flynn's commitment to the working waterfront stemmed from his deep family ties to the port. Like many of his neighbors in South Boston, his father was a longshoreman. (He, too, worked as a union longshoreman while in college.) Throughout the EDIC's existence, there has been pressure to transform the waterfront site to look less like an industrial working waterfront and more like its new neighbor, the Seaport District, home to multiple office towers for the biomedical industry and luxury condominiums for the wealthy.

A special Boston Globe Spotlight report, "A Brand New Boston, Even Whiter Than the Old," highlighted the growth of the Seaport District and the exclusion of people of color and average Bostonians from the multi-billion-dollar equation. As reported,

> Start with a swath of nearly 1,000 acres, where rotting railroad piers and asphalt parking lots had lain fallow for generations. Invest more than $18 billion in public money to create some of America's most valuable property. One of the city's whitest neighborhoods was born.

How white? This white: Lenders have issued only three residential mortgages to Black buyers in the Seaport's main census tracts, out of 660 in the past decade. According to recent US census estimates, the population is 3 percent Black and 89 percent white, with a median household income of nearly \$133,000, the highest of any Boston ZIP code. It is also an example of how the city's Black residents and businesses missed out on the considerable wealth created by the building boom. This is a city in which Blacks are almost a quarter of the population, and their tax dollars were part of what helped jump-start the new Seaport. "It is a brand-new neighborhood, and it's not diverse," said Darryl Settles, an African-American real estate developer and restaurateur. "I don't know one person of color that has made any money from the development of the Seaport. Not one."[62]

Bostonians of all races have been priced out of the new neighborhood. "The Seaport is this glaring area that lacks diversity found elsewhere in the city; I'm not defending the Seaport," said Walsh. "There are some Black people that feel that they just haven't been part of it." The Seaport's whiteness is not the result of overt prejudice but rather a symptom that indicates Boston has not addressed systemic issues involving race.[63]

In response to an article by columnist Shirley Leung in the *Boston Globe* in 2021, I wrote,

> The Seaport is a "gleaming disappointment" for the city. The Seaport District was Boston's last golden opportunity to share the city's prosperity with all its residents. It never happened. As Leung notes, "The city's newest neighborhood is also among its whitest." Promoting a white enclave with tax breaks and free rent would seem unimaginable in a time of racial reckoning. How many Roxbury, Dorchester, or Mattapan businesses are awarded free rent and tax breaks? Low- and moderate-income residents and businesses help finance these giveaways through their taxes.[64]

Boston's newest mayor, Michelle Wu, said about the Seaport, "To me, the Seaport looks like a playground for the rich. It is the result of a broken system; developers get away with a handshake."[65] "Nine percent of the about 5,800 new units in the Seaport were designated for people with moderate incomes. A two-bedroom apartment in the Seaport can rent for more than \$5,000 a month and cost more than \$2 million to buy."[66] This is not the affordable housing and the diverse and inclusive neighborhood the city planners promised.

## The Endless Reorganization of the City Development Agencies

During the 1983 mayoral campaign, Flynn proposed abolishing the BRA in favor of a new Department of Planning and Development. Rather than eliminating the BRA, his approach focused on engaging community residents in the planning and rezoning of their neighborhoods through neighborhood councils and planning and zoning committees. Shared decision-making in housing and development projects was put in place. BRA director Steve Coyle explained, "We engaged everybody we could about building Boston; development was different than having it jammed down people's throats as had often been the practice of other administrations."[67] Empowerment was achieved by including and granting eminent domain power to a community group and initiating the first significant minority equity development partnership in the city, as noted earlier.

After Flynn left office, Menino initially proposed to create a super-agency run out of the fifth-floor mayoral office suite reporting directly to him but settled on administrative changes merging the boards of the EDIC and the BRA without making significant structural changes to either agency. Mayor Walsh changed the name of the development agencies to the Boston Planning and Development Agency (BPDA) after a $670,000 rebranding effort, maintaining the independent legal structure of each. Like Menino, Walsh did not make fundamental changes while tinkering around the edges. Mayor Wu proposed to abolish the existing city development agencies.[68] Her initial effort sparked opposition from the BPDA board, with member Ted Landsmark saying, "We have a request to accept immediate changes without clarification as to what those immediate changes are."[69] Following a BPDA board meeting where the proposal was tabled, Wu returned to the drawing board.

Much of Wu's campaign to dismantle the BPDA stems from her critique of her predecessors Menino and Walsh. Joan Vennochi wrote that, according to Wu, "The BPDA focus on building buildings rather than the community has held back the talent of its staff and deepened disparities in our city. Growth wasn't harnessed to benefit all our communities. Not planning for affordability and transit meant that housing prices soared and traffic snarled."[70] Others have tried, but no one has accomplished the overhaul Wu proposed. It is a test of her capacity to govern and implement the changes she believed were necessary. In April 2024, Wu achieved, in part, her goal of creating a city planning department and transferring the functions of the BRA and EDIC—that is, the BPDA—to this new department. On March 27, 2024, the city council approved the creation of the new department by a vote of 8-2 with two abstentions. "Some members derided the vote as rushed and undemocratic."[71] On April 2, 2024, symbolically in the West End neighborhood, Wu signed the new ordinance, which created the city planning department into law. "Today, we mark a long-overdue new chapter in Boston's growth—grounded in affordability, resiliency, and equity. This ordinance is the biggest step Boston has taken in 70 years to finally begin untangling a system of development rooted in an outdated ideology that left scars in our communities. I look forward to the work ahead with all of our residents to engage with this new Planning Department and shape Boston's future."[72]

Gregory Maynard, executive director of the nonprofit Boston Policy Institute, said, "Nothing they're doing is going to change how planning and development works. . . . They're just moving deck chairs. It's really important to remember that nothing that the council passed affects the legal powers or responsibilities of the BPDA."

Rodney Singleton, a community activist and Roxbury resident for over sixty years, opposes the ordinance because he said it falls short of policies Wu included in a 2019 white paper, which proposed ending the existing BPDA and separating planning powers from development.

Before the official change creating the city planning agency, four neighborhood organizations across the city wrote an open letter to Mayor Wu about the development reform efforts, stating in part,

> The amount of friction and distrust between the city autocracy and normal everyday citizens has never been higher. A reform effort like Squares and Streets, which replaces neighborhood zoning and favors instead bureaucratic centralized authoritarian rulemaking, is broadly viewed as a step backward. It didn't have to be this way, but this is where your people and the BRA have brought us. Mayor Wu, 2024 can herald a new dawn for you. You're halfway through your mayoral term, but stormy skies greet you right now. What also greets you is a massive block of residents who supported you during your campaign and sincerely want your campaign platform—true reforms, more growth, more equity—to become reality. But Boston is badly off-track right now. Please work with us, your constituents, and previous campaign supporters to right the boat and put Boston back on a track of trust and cooperation. It might take a little humility, but the benefits will be legion. Please make these corrections so that we can feel great about supporting you again.[73]

Wu believed that the restructuring had undergone a multiyear process; she went further than her predecessors and created a new city planning department, ceding budgetary oversight to the city council for the first time. Some think she went too far, and others not far enough. The creation and launch of the new city Planning Department began in July 2024 while still awaiting State Legislative approval for disassembling the BPDA. Mayor Wu referred in an interview to the overall city strategy to address the most important challenges residents face by "rebuilding the social and physical infrastructure of the city which needs to be done right over a period of time. BPDA and the City Planning Department are really about building the infrastructure to help our families and to plan for our future together; analyze the tradeoffs that are involved so they can codify that into the rules for growth."[74]

Beyond the polemic, in the final analysis, the mayor is the key decision-maker on what gets approved and built in Boston, and all the rearranging of agencies doesn't change that fact.

# 8 / Boston's Racial Politics: Ending Racial Violence

*Mayor Flynn was on the scene for every racial incident—to bring the noise, attention, and focus. Our number-one priority was ending the racial violence that had persisted for almost a decade, people getting hurt just because they were the wrong color. We went after it, and we got it done. We did not eliminate racism, but we did end racial violence.* (Neil Sullivan, policy advisor, interview)

## Racial Conflict in Boston

Boston has a long history of struggle around racial issues. The city was active in the abolitionist movement and a stop on the Underground Railroad. Leaders such as William Lloyd Garrison (editor of the abolitionist newspaper *The Liberator*), Frederick Douglass, and W. E. B. Du Bois visited frequently. The number of Black residents in Boston remained small until the period between 1940 and 1960, when the population tripled to 63,165, according to J. Anthony Lukas, author of the Pulitzer Prize–winning *Common Ground*.[1] Lukas characterized Boston's race relations as relatively harmonious during that era, although Black residents were generally confined in the mid-twentieth century to three areas: The Hill, an area near Franklin Park; Crosstown, an area of the South End near Massachusetts and Columbus Avenues; and Intown, a neighborhood of Lower Roxbury.[2]

Boston's racial conflict, never far below the surface, erupted openly with the school desegregation order and busing students between White South Boston and Black Roxbury. Busing was not the beginning of the conflict. Although Flynn inherited the remnants of busing's racial turmoil when he became mayor, many other incidents defined Boston in the eyes of the nation. The 1975 police shooting of an unarmed Black man, a maintenance worker at Boston City Hospital, was detailed in Lawrence O'Donnell's book *Deadly Force: The True Story of How a Badge Can Become a License to Kill*.[3] A federal court awarded the family a monetary

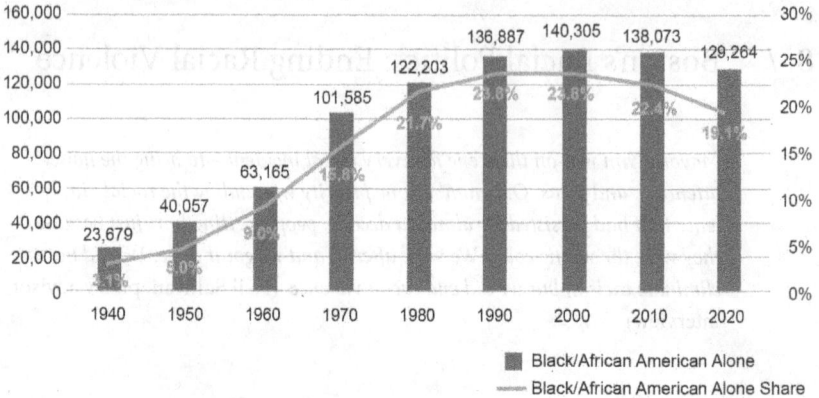

CHART 11. Black Population in Boston, 1940–2020
Source: Boston Planning and Development Agency

judgment that Mayor White and his police commissioner, Joseph Jordan, refused to pay. When Flynn took office, he delivered the check to the Bowden family. "One of the more mean-spirited and unexplainable episodes in this city's recent history has come to a moving and a very classy end with Mayor Flynn's quiet delivery of a check for $843,498 to the widow of a black man shot by two white police officers nine years ago," the *Boston Globe* opined.[4] In 1976, a group of White anti-busing protesters attacked Black attorney Ted Landsmark with an American flag while he was walking on City Hall Plaza. Pulitzer Prize–winning photographer Stanley Forman captured the incident, and the photo, viewed in newspapers around the globe, became known as "The Soiling of Old Glory." In 1979, a 15-year-old Black football player was shot and paralyzed during a football game in White Charlestown. Two White Charlestown youths were convicted of the shooting. In 1979, Flynn, then a city councilor, confronted a mob of teenagers brandishing a White power sign and chasing a young Black couple on the Boston Common. Flynn and State Senator Joe Timilty rescued the couple from their pursuers.[5] In 1980, a fourteen-year-old Black youth, Levi Hart, was shot by a White police officer. Flynn was the only White politician to attend his funeral. In 1982, in Savin Hill, five White teenagers chased William Atkinson, a thirty-year-old African American man who was a nursing home maintenance worker, onto the MBTA tracks. An oncoming train struck and killed him. The list, unfortunately, could go on.

By the 1970s, race relations had deteriorated, and the Black population had become marginalized and even more segregated. Landsmark, the civil rights leader attacked on City Hall Plaza in 1976—the year of the bicentennial—who later became a senior city official in the Flynn and Menino administrations, remarked, "Something was happening somewhere in the political and cultural structure of the city, such that the housing authority, the police department, the fire department, and the school department were all under federal court orders to integrate and open themselves up," he said. "What I also realized was that if you look below the level of public agencies, that, going around Boston, there were no Black people selling suits downstairs in Filene's Basement, and oddly enough, if you went into most bars in Boston—unlike New York—there were no people of color who were waiters and waitresses. No Black bus drivers or African Americans were working in construction—in most areas where people might earn a living as a working-class person in Boston. There was no access, so what was going on in the schools represented the first step of a pattern of exclusion of groups of people, African Americans, from access to the economic resources they needed to have a decent life in the city. That had been going on for some time, and this is the thing that a lot of my African American friends do not like to hear: there was a lot of complicity with that in the Black community."[6]

"What I hear all the time when I visit other cities or when other people visit Boston is that you do not see the minority population," Kearney said, reflecting on the issue of race in the city. "I walk around Boston; most days, I do not see Black people, whereas if I were in DC or New York, I would not just see Black minorities. You know it, and you see it. It is different in downtown Boston."[7]

Bridgit Brown, a forty-five-year-old resident of Dorchester, echoed Kearney. "To be a Black person in Boston is often to be the only one," she said. "The only one in the office, the only one in the leadership position. It is lonely. You are aware of the racism. You are aware of the subtleties. It is like the air we breathe if you are Black."[8]

A *Boston Globe* Spotlight team investigated racism in Boston in a seven-part series published beginning in December 2017. The team examined issues ranging from the city's image to sports, universities, development, and power. The series begins thus: "Google the phrase 'most racist city,' and Boston pops up more than any other place, time and time again. A national survey commissioned by the *Globe* this fall showed that among eight major cities, Black people ranked Boston the least welcoming to people of color. More than half—54 percent—rated Boston as unwelcoming."[9]

Busing in the mid-1970s is most often blamed, but issues of race and racism are much deeper in the fabric of Boston's neighborhoods. It was not just a 1974 court order; policies and practices of the growth machine and many political leaders have contributed to the problems of racism and racial and economic disparities in the city. "Race relations because of busing, the Ted Landsmark incident, Boston was always looked at nationally as having serious race relations issues," said Rosemarie Sansone. "There were some parts of Boston that Black people could not walk into: Charlestown, the North End, South Boston. Flynn broke down some of these barriers because of what he did. He was very visible, the police department was visible, and things began to change; get better. He played a significant role in healing the city."[10]

"Race relations were not great before busing," Dorchester Codman Square community leader Bill Walczak said. "Hostility in Codman Square between Blacks and Whites got worse after the busing decision in 1974. Groups of White and Black youths would tangle at night, and there were shootings and even a racial murder. The sound of gunfire at night frightened many families, driving them out of the city. There were efforts to bring people together, and Codman Square had interracial groups that formed. Creating a peaceful neighborhood required more."[11]

"People were nervous about minorities moving into their neighborhoods," Hyde Park resident and Flynn administration official Bob Consalvo added. "Blockbusting did much damage to Hyde Park; many people felt it. White people felt that their community was changing and did not like it. That is usual racial stuff. You had the violence at the time with the Whites and Blacks and the Ted Landsmark kinds of incidents with the kid getting beat up and dying; they pulled him out of the car during the busing period. So all of that was there, and it just disrupted everybody. It was like an underlying current of distrust and upset; people were upset that their lives were changing."[12]

Some of what was happening could be explained by the racial blockbusting disrupting several Boston neighborhoods, as discussed in chapter 6. Other factors included Boston undergoing significant racial succession between 1960 and 1980. The Great Migration—the rapid migration of African Americans from the rural South to northern cities like Boston, New York, and Chicago—coupled with federal and state housing and transportation policies and private investment decisions helped facilitate this change. During White's sixteen-year mayoralty, Black and White neighborhood residents both experienced changes, and racial divisions and conflict were commonplace. TV news commentator Jon Keller called race the "killer virus of Boston politics."[13] This chapter explores what the three top city leaders between 1980 and 2000 did—and did not do—to address issues of racial conflict in Boston during this period. Later, chapter 13 takes a brief look at the issue under Mayors Walsh and Wu. We begin here with a look at the mayoralty of White, whose policies set the stage for examining that era.

## Kevin White and Race

> *One of Boston's thorniest problems continues to be the exploitation of racial animosities by demagogues. By and large, they have been able to operate without a direct challenge from the city's highest government leader. Action and results have been sadly lacking.* (Boston Globe editorial, 1980)[14]

Throughout his sixteen-year tenure, Mayor White was initially viewed favorably for handling race relations and conflict in the city. He began his first term at the height of the civil rights movement, when racial strife exploded in cities across America. In June 1967, outgoing mayor John Collins faced a challenge with the takeover by angry mothers of the Grove Hall Welfare office, a test he failed miserably since riots followed for several days.[15]

"When Collins was mayor in June of 1967, the welfare rights mothers protested," Hubie Jones, head of the Roxbury Multi-Service Center, said. "We had a riot for four days; I mean a real riot, four days. At the time before the thing erupted, the mothers for adequate welfare, who created a sit-in, asked Collins to come out and talk to them. He says no, 'I conduct city business at city hall.' So, they say, 'Oh really,' and so the damn thing escalates. At that moment, you knew that, as powerful a man as Collins was—and he was a powerful man—he probably had made a tragic mistake, and this was not going to be fun running the city anymore. He suddenly decides to leave."[16]

Following Collins, White—who had faced school committee president Louise Day Hicks from South Boston in the 1967 mayoral election final—was swept into office, many believed as a repudiation of Hicks's you-know-where-I-stand brand of demagoguery. Hicks was a leader of a school committee embroiled in a battle with the Massachusetts Board of Education over desegregating the Boston Public Schools following the passage of the Racial Imbalance Act of 1965, which outlawed segregation in public schools.[17]

White is credited by many for being attuned to racial issues in the city early in his tenure. His handling of the aftermath of the assassination of Dr. Martin Luther King in April 1968 and his deft management of the James Brown concert held in Boston the day following King's assassination have been widely cited. While sporadic unrest occurred in several areas of Boston, this was nothing compared to the riots in more than 160 cities nationwide. White worked closely with leadership in the Black community—particularly city councilor Tom Atkins, the first African American elected to the city council since the 1949 charter change—to ease the tension.[18]

White had national ambitions, and by 1970, according to those interviewed, he was ready to move up. He was soundly defeated when he unsuccessfully ran for governor against Republican Francis Sargent, even losing the city of Boston. As he told reporter Lawrence Harmon, "You know where my mind was in 1970? I was going to be an interplanetary leader. The next step is the governorship."[19] By all accounts, his failed bid to be George McGovern's running mate in 1972 and the busing crisis in 1974 took their toll on White and his interest in the mayor's job. He ran for reelection in 1971, handily defeating Hicks. In 1975, he narrowly defeated State Senator Joseph Timilty, whom he again beat in 1979. White was not the same man as when he came to office in 1968. His efforts during his first two terms in office earned him the support of more than 80 percent of the Black electorate in the mayoral races of 1967, 1971, and 1975.[20] After the 1975 election, White's focus turned to building the world-class city he envisioned, while racial violence and race relations were relegated to lower on the list of the mayor's priorities.

White, who had faced significant racial turmoil in the city during his first three terms, was viewed by many as a strong leader in race relations. In his 1980 inaugural address, heading into his fourth and final term, he claimed to place a high priority on responding to racial violence. "First, to combat racial violence, we will govern with no tolerance for racial intolerance, posturing, politicking, and temper tantrums, which have permeated and distorted our aims in the past and will be given no license or legitimacy in this city," he said in his inaugural address. "Simply stated, racism in any and all of its ugly manifestations will not be condoned, and it will be confronted directly and aggressively by this government."[21]

By the end of the summer of 1980, the *Boston Globe* was editorializing about White's leadership failures in addressing racial conflict. In one editorial, "Mayor White: Sounds of Silence," the newspaper wrote, "By his criteria, the beginning of Kevin White's fourth term as mayor of Boston has been something of a failure. In his inaugural address last January, White declared that curbing racial violence was a top priority of his administration. Eight months later, an epidemic of street violence wracks the city, much of it with a racial tinge that is without local precedent."[22] Just over a month later, in another editorial, the *Globe* asked, "Where is Mayor White?" stating, "One of Boston's thorniest problems continues to be the exploitation of racial animosities by demagogues. By and large, they have been able to operate without a direct challenge from the city's highest government leader. Action and results have been sadly lacking."[23]

White would appoint several commissions, including the Committee on Violence and the Boston Committee, whose members included the mayor, Roman Catholic cardinal Humberto Medeiros, First National Bank chairman Richard Hill, and William Davis Taylor, chairman of Affiliated Publications, owner of the *Boston Globe*. In considerable measure, the sixteen-year mayoralty of White was defined as much by race relations as it was by the burgeoning skyline and Faneuil Hall marketplace. Racial conflict was thrust onto center stage with the 1974 federal court busing decree and would never leave. White's handling of the attack on Ted Landsmark in April 1976 on City Hall Plaza was widely criticized, as was his management of various racial attacks and incidents of improper police behavior, most notably the James Bowden case. Then, in 1979, high school football player Daryl Williams was shot and paralyzed by a sniper while he scrimmaged with his team in the predominantly White Charlestown neighborhood.

White's relationship with leadership in the Black community was an enigma. White used fear as a tool to keep Black leaders' support. "Fear was described as one of White's most important political resources by every Black elected official in Boston—one stated that fear of political and economic reprisals is what helped to maintain the paternalistic relationship between some Black leaders and city hall," James Jennings and Mel King wrote. "Since the economic foundations of Blacks in Boston are so dependent on white power structures, Black leaders were not willing to participate in political activities that might be viewed as threatening by the Kevin White machine."[24]

Hubie Jones explained how White responded to a group of Black leaders concerned about racial violence during busing at a meeting at Freedom House in Grove Hall. "So, Kevin White had a tough time. It all broke apart during desegregation, even with his allies," Jones said. "He went to a Freedom House meeting, and the Black community jumped all over him because he was not providing enough safety for the kids. He picked up his coat and said, 'I am not taking this crap from you people. You do not know what I am up against. Goodbye!' and he storms out of Freedom House. So there was this schism between Black leadership that had worked with him, and he lost his grip on the Black community."[25] As Ira Jackson, White's chief of staff, recalls, "It was very tough for Kevin White to face angry, frightened Black parents because he had promised them that their children would be safe, and they were not. He had to admit that he had failed, and he asked for their forgiveness, but he was not able to deliver on the first and most important obligation that any leader has, which is to keep his community safe."[26]

Many believed White was at a loss dealing with race issues in the city. The *Boston Globe* wrote in 1983, examining White's four terms in office, "According to observers, he often seemed insensitive. Once, during the 1975 campaign against State Senator Joseph Timilty, when a reporter asked him why he had not worked harder to hire more Blacks to high positions in city government, he responded, "Well, I have an answer for you. Vote for someone else.""[27]

## Raymond Flynn and Race

*Flynn summarized his commitment to improving race relations in Boston, calling his desire to unite the city "the single most important goal of my life." (Joan Vennochi 1984)[28]*

Flynn grew up in the predominantly White South Boston neighborhood, attending South Boston High School, where his skills on the basketball court led to a scholarship at Providence College. When he returned to South Boston, he played briefly for the Boston Celtics before pursuing a life in politics. While a state representative, he became known as a leader in the anti-busing opposition to the 1974 federal court decision. "Nobody understood the people of South Boston during the busing," Flynn explained. "They wanted to lump them together and call them racist. They were not racist; they were just concerned people, concerned parents like we all are about our children. From my perspective, it had nothing to do with disliking Black people for me. Why would I be playing on an all-Black basketball team in Roxbury? Why would I be hitchhiking to Harlem to play on the Harlem playgrounds against Black kids? Because what, I do not like Blacks? No, I love basketball and wanted to play against the best. They were the very best, and I wanted to go out and beat them."[29]

A 1983 poll released on the cusp of Flynn's inaugural indicated that the city's racial climate was as bad as ever. Flynn knew he had to take bold and decisive action. "He [Flynn] has restored to the city some of the credibility lost under the previous administration, especially regarding race," according to African American city councilor Bruce Bolling. "He is setting a high tone on race relations. [Police Commissioner] Roache is particularly strong on race. These are significant signals, and Boston needs that right now. He is doing well."[30]

"Flynn was very committed to convincing people that it was an administration that was going to be open to the needs of the Black community," Nancy Snyder, Flynn's chief of staff, explained. "As a result, mainly because he was from South Boston, he worked very hard, again, both symbolically and with content around reaching out to leadership in the Black community, making appointments from the Black community, being very present in the Black community, and working on issues that were important to the Black community. Race relations were vital to his legacy, and he did not shy away from challenging race-related matters. He embraced them and was meticulous and thoughtful about whom he needed to have in the room. One of the reasons he trusted Mickey Roache was because Mickey was also from Southie, but Mickey was excellent on race issues and had many relationships. He also carefully picked those who worked on these issues."[31]

The chief executive of another major city saw the issue in the same way as Flynn. "Generating a new attitude and spirit is one of the most significant contributions a mayor can make to a city. It is also one of the most difficult things to accomplish," San Francisco mayor Dianne Feinstein commented. "If Ray Flynn has given Boston a new feeling of forward movement, he has already come a long way."[32]

Everyone did not embrace Flynn's role as a racial healer. Many in Flynn's hometown of South Boston were openly hostile, frequently calling him a "nigger lover." He was often referred to derisively as "Sugar Ray" (apparently after Black boxers Sugar Ray Robinson and Sugar Ray Leonard). Flynn would fall back on using sports to address issues of racial conflict, and the results often paid off. At the site of racial tension in Dorchester's Wainwright Park, Flynn organized a celebrity basketball game, pitting neighborhood kids against a team that included the mayor himself and Celtics players Dave Cowens and Mal Graham.[33]

Flynn summarized his commitment to improving race relations in Boston by calling his desire to unite the city "the single most important goal of my life."[34] Several of those interviewed thought that Flynn placed such a high priority on race relations because of the perception many people had of his role as an anti-busing leader. He tried hard to change the image of himself and the city from that associated with the turbulent busing period and focus on what was important to him: helping all poor and working-class people by ending racial conflict and providing jobs, housing, and economic opportunity. "The issue was that White people needed to understand the causes of these problems and change their attitudes, and maybe it was a White guy that needed to lead the charge on this," Bill Walczak said.[35] As Vin McCarthy, a prominent Boston lawyer and leader in the LGBTQ community, observed, "Ray Flynn healed the incredible scar tissue throughout the city over the busing crisis, as simple as that. One could not have expected the guy coming out of South Boston who had been on one side of the busing issue, who had been a spokesperson for the South Boston–impacted people, would be the instrument to bring the healing because it just embarrassed people of the city. I mean, they were just, you know, sick of it, and by the time it got through and the city was a joke in the rest of the country, being called the Mississippi of the North, people wanted it to end."[36]

Flynn sent a clear signal to the city and the police department with his first actions concerning race relations in Boston. Following the Bowden incident, a top aide began to negotiate a termination of the contract with Police Commissioner Jordan, seeking to replace him. The mayor spoke about the qualifications he would look for in a new commissioner: "Honesty is something I am deeply concerned about, and I think the first requirement would be honesty, then sensitivity to the diversity of the city's population, then professionalism and competence."[37]

Early in his first term, Flynn contacted boyhood friend and South Boston neighbor Francis "Mickey" Roache, who was head of the Boston Police Department's Community Disorders Unit (CDU). Roache recalled, "This is a big one because the mayor, first of all, says, 'What can I do to help the CDU?' Because he sensed what was going on. Mayor Flynn, before he was mayor—I had never seen an elected official show up as he did on every racial incident that was an issue in any community. That is startling."[38]

From a city hall policy perspective, there was a need and an opportunity—in the ensuing months before a new police commissioner would be named—to respond aggressively to every racial incident in the city. "It is where we learned the art of the crackdown," Neil Sullivan explained. "We cracked down on racial violence, and we cracked down on gang leaders nine years later. The latter was a federal crackdown, direct indictment, and prosecution of gang leaders. In the case of racial violence, we had the right tool, a state civil rights law that Mickey [Roache] had successfully pursued, that allowed additional sentencing if a racial epithet was used during an assault and battery incident."[39]

Flynn, holding a series of community forums to solicit recommendations on the qualifications for the new police commissioner, heard loud and clear that what was needed was a person who could respond to the pressing issues of racial conflict in the city. Following Commissioner Jordan's resignation on February 1, 1985, he appointed Roache as acting police commissioner, becoming permanent on March 13, 1985.[40] Roache had a track record as head of the CDU to continue the department's aggressive assault on racial violence and strong relationships with religious and community leaders. "His appointment is indicative of the high priority the administration has toward molding a department that takes seriously the need to protect all citizens despite color or class," said Rev. Charles Stith, a prominent African American religious leader of the Union United Methodist Church. "Mickey's credentials are outstanding in reflecting real sensitivity to the major public safety issue in Boston—racial violence,"[41] stated Martin Walsh, regional director of the US Department of Justice's Community Relations Service during busing. Walsh added, "By making good on the court judgment [referring to paying the Bowden judgment] and naming a new police commissioner, Flynn helped establish his concern for the city's minority communities."[42]

As David Nyhan of the *Globe* wrote in 1987, "Flynn spends a lot of time and energy on racial matters. Virtually every victim of racial animosity in this city gets a visit, a call, or some signal of personal concern from the mayor. And the cops, the fire department, moreover, the city's other agencies respond promptly to the mayor's concern."[43]

The successful partnership with the Boston Ministerial Alliance became a national model for reducing youth violence. The Safe Neighborhoods Campaign to reduce youth violence in Boston showed positive results. Headed by Ted Landsmark, the fifty-point plan relied heavily on the city infrastructure of community schools, health centers, neighborhood coordinators and liaisons, and public safety agencies—the police and other emergency personnel. Key to the initiative's success was the partnership with the Black ministers and community agencies and leaders. Regular events were held in the city's public housing developments; youth workers were deployed to areas of concern, and summer jobs were a central part of the strategy. The local media later dubbed the effort "The Boston Miracle."

As the *New York Times* offered in assessing Flynn's performance after winning his third term in office in 1991, "In his first two terms, Mr. Flynn was widely credited for easing racial tension from a conflict over court-ordered school busing in the mid-1970s. Although he had opposed the busing himself at the time, Mr. Flynn, as Mayor, made a concerted effort to reach out to Boston's Black population, opening predominantly white housing projects to Blacks. He restored many of the city's neglected neighborhood parks. He increased the number of Blacks, Hispanics, and Asians on the city payroll to 22 percent from 6 percent. People of color make up 35 percent of Boston's population."[44]

## Thomas Menino and Race

> *Mayor Menino asked to name the best thing he had done for Boston, "My Number 1 thing is bringing racial harmony to the city." Referring to the bitter battles in the 1970s over school busing, he added, "We do not have the nonsense that we used to have because I do not tolerate it."* (Katherine Seelye 2012)[45]

When Thomas Menino became acting mayor on July 12, 1993, race relations in Boston were far from settled. Menino's predecessor, Ray Flynn, played an active, almost obsessive role in working to bring racial harmony to the city. Menino did not follow a similar path, characterized by many as a more cautious politician. While the acting mayor and a candidate for the full-time job, Menino, according to Peter Canellos of the *Boston Globe,* would need to be prepared: "The threat of a racial blow-up in this still-desegregating city is omnipresent. Flynn had devoted much of his administration to easing the threat, but it still sits like a raven on the shoulder of whoever leads Boston."[46] Canellos described the night acting Menino received a phone call about racial violence in Charlestown:

> For Menino, Tuesday's phone call led to a night of monitoring police activities following the stabbings and melee involving groups of whites and Hispanics in Charlestown's Bunker Hill housing development while debating whether to make an appearance on the scene as Flynn no doubt would have. For Menino's mayoral rival, state Rep. James T. Brett, news of the Charlestown incident conjured up memories of similar incidents in his native Dorchester, after which Brett stepped in to quell tensions. Unlike Flynn, who came out of the crucible of South Boston, where racial issues were played out in the open and politicians made stark choices, Brett and Menino had generally stood above the fray, acting as healers and facilitators when conflicts broke out in Dorchester or Hyde Park, which Menino represented on the City Council. City Councilor Charles Yancey (Mattapan) suggests that for this reason, neither candidate is well prepared to be mayor. The mayor, Yancey said, must be an overpowering moral force against racial violence. "Incidents of intolerance must be challenged incessantly by the next mayor. That will set the tone. The next mayor will be the person who sets the tone of the whole city."[47]

Menino did recognize the undercurrent of racial conflict when, in 1994, he responded to Hyde Park neighbors' complaints about Black youth in the neighborhood." He said. "They say crime, but they mean race. It is the most crucial issue we face as a city. If I have not done anything else when I leave office, I hope I have helped us learn to live together as a city."[48]

When he was running for city council in 1983, Menino believed racial conflict in the city was an issue in the mayor's race, and he shared his thoughts in his Boston University office. "The mayoral election of 1983, race was a big issue," he recalled. "It divided the city. It was an uncomfortable city for people of color. Flynn did a decent job of bringing people together. There were still many people left behind. The city's minorities back then were just African Americans. Now, there are Cape Verdeans, Dominicans, and El Salvadorians. We have a much different minority population. Latinos are the fastest-growing group, making up 17 percent of our city's population. How do you integrate them into the mainstream of Boston? That is a challenge. That is a real challenge. We are going to be a prosperous city if we create opportunities."[49]

As mayor, Menino would have to deal with the ongoing integration of public housing, particularly in South Boston. While his friend and ally Kelly opposed the integration of the city's public housing developments, Menino distanced himself from Kelly. "I cannot speak for any other politician, but the city is more diverse than ever; it is changing, and we must learn to live with it," he said. "We are doing better than when I took office and will keep improving."[50]

Howard Husock, a documentary filmmaker who directed a film on Menino's first city council campaign in 1983, recalled that Menino viewed diversity issues in familial rather than racial terms. "Because he relates to other people's families, the idea of racial hatred does not occur to him," he said. "He relates to the two-income families moving into the neighborhood. If the neighborhood were going to change, he would not fight that; he understood that would have been absurd."[51]

Menino explained his approach to dealing with racial issues in the city, commenting on the Stuart incident. "I always believed you got to be out there, but we overreacted instantly over that [the Stuart incident]," he said. "I am not criticizing anybody for it. I always try to be moderate and be as honest as possible to the public and not call it racial; it was racial, but I would not do it. I would not divide the city. You know the mayor is the titular head of the city. Whatever he says, people believe. I may have been wrong, but they believed it."[52]

Menino believed that calling an incident racially motivated would divide the city and seemed to distance himself from the approach of his immediate predecessor, Flynn. He recalled the reaction early in his first term when he described a firebombing in West Roxbury as racially motivated, aimed at terrorizing a Black family from buying a house there. "Those are serious accusations to make, and if they are true," Menino said, "we will not tolerate this; we will not tolerate such horrendous acts. We will prosecute as far as possible."[53]

The following day, the mayor and the police department began to soften their response and back off their initial statement describing the incident as a hate crime. Menino was there when the community gathered for a service several days later. "The city is working with the Black family to help them find a new home, and the mayor walked away from reporters who asked him if his public comments may have fueled speculation that the fire was racially motivated. 'My statements did not influence the situation; this is the community's night. This community was hurt, and now they are trying to stand strong together,' Menino said."[54]

Menino said that "he got killed" on calling the West Roxbury fire racially motivated. "When I became mayor, they built a new house in West Roxbury," he recalled. "A Black family bought it. It was firebombed. I knew it was a firebomb. The fire department knew it was a firebomb. The neighborhood said no, no, no, it was an accidental fire. I got my head kicked in. Monsignor Helmick from St. Theresa's Church was the only person who stood up for me. He stood up and said, 'The mayor's right. This is a racial incident.' We took it very seriously."[55]

During Menino's mayoralty, from 1993 through 2014, several racially motivated incidents received widespread attention. In reviewing the period from 1993 through 2000, the question of racial harmony is very much contested. Menino was not particularly visible on racial violence and conflict issues during his twenty-year tenure, often leaving other city officials to respond.

Many believed that Menino had an easier time dealing with race issues as an Italian American than his predecessor, Flynn, an anti-busing leader from South Boston. "Flynn brought the racial baggage of South Boston to the city, and it clouded his ability to develop a coherent racial consensus," Rev. Eugene Rivers, a Menino ally, commented at the time. "As an Italian American, Menino brings a different sensibility not shaped by the same polarization that characterized the Irish in Boston."[56]

In 1994, his first year as mayor, Menino said, "This is an issue people do not want to confront. The groups that are changing are not Italian and Irish anymore; they are coming from depressed areas. If we do not face that challenge, we will have a society of haves and have-nots."[57]

Menino faced several other high-profile race-related incidents during his tenure, including several lawsuits. First, the case of Rev. Accelyne Williams, the seventy-five-year-old minister who died in a botched police drug raid at his home on March 25, 1994, just a couple of months into Menino's first term. The Boston Police Department concluded in a report on its investigation that "the death of Rev. Accelyne Williams was a tragic accident."[58]

Initially, while conceding the raid was a mistake, Commissioner Evans did not apologize to the Williams family. "This is a tragic incident, and we deeply regret the incident," he said at the time. "It is too early in the investigation [to issue an apology]. If an apology is necessary, we will make that." Menino said only that he had extended sympathies to the families of the victim, adding, "I have asked the police commissioner for a full report. I hope to have it on my desk as soon as possible."[59]

Menino later discussed the incident and if there were any specific racial incidents he recalled during his tenure as mayor. "Just a couple of times, like when we raided the wrong apartment with the minister," he said. "[Police Commissioner] Paul Evans calls me on a Friday afternoon, and he asks me, 'What kind of a day are you having?' I told him, 'I am having a great day. I am ready for the weekend.' He says, 'After I talk to you, Mayor, you are going to have a shitty day.' So he explained to me what happened. He says, 'What do we do?' I say, 'Be honest about it. Let us tell people exactly what happened.' I told him to get on the phone and call all the so-called Black leaders. I will make some phone calls. I went to the NAACP dinner that night; I explained it and apologized for it. If you look at the incident, what saved us is that we apologized. Nobody ever apologized for mistakes like that before," Menino said, referring to Flynn and the Carol Stuart case, in which Flynn was criticized for purportedly not issuing an apology—a notion that was incorrect."[60]

Many credited Menino and Evans for their handling of the Williams incident. By apologizing, they helped diffuse the anger in the Black community. Menino and the Boston Police Department were heavily criticized for how they handled several other high-profile incidents. When fellow officers beat Black detective Michael Cox during an incident in Dorchester, several investigations were launched by the police, the state district attorney, and the US Attorney's office. Cox also filed a civil suit against the officers and, later, the city.[61] As Brian McGrory wrote for the *Boston Globe* about the city's handling of the Cox case,

> The quiet rustling coming from the city government is the sound of
> Mayor Thomas M. Menino and Commissioner Paul Evans seeking
> cover from controversy, protecting themselves at the expense of the
> city. Four years after Cox was beaten unconscious by his brethren cops,
> city leaders have barely acknowledged a problem and, consequently,

have done virtually nothing in search of a solution. Finally, yesterday, Evans expressed publicly what he has long alluded to in private: a strong desire to settle the civil rights suit brought by Cox against the city. "I do not dispute the fact that Michael is a damned good cop who suffered injuries," he said. Menino told a gathering of *Globe* editors and reporters that the Cox case "was an occasion we would never be proud of. It is not a happy or good day for the Boston Police Department."[62]

McGrory went on to report that Menino was rejecting the settlement with Sergeant Cox: "In the four years since, the injustice has spread from the scene of the crime to the corridors of power all across this city, where the police commissioner, the mayor, and various state and federal prosecutors have proven themselves either inept at reining in the Police Department or indifferent toward the brutality that sometimes comes out of it."[63]

The Cox case was detailed in Dick Lehr's book *The Fence: A Police Cover-Up along Boston's Racial Divide,* in which Lehr wrote,

> Mike Cox filed a federal civil rights lawsuit against his police colleagues and department. He knew he was stepping way out of line. "I have accused them of things which I don't necessarily know anybody else in the police department has ever done before." The claims could cost them their jobs and monetary damages, and "it could send them to jail." Taking legal action may have brought some satisfaction, but Mike now wrestled with the fear factor. For Mike, it went like this: He'd become a troublemaker, and the quickest way for those troubles to end "was by me not being on this earth or being killed." That was the way Mike Cox's year ended—believing his life was at risk. It wasn't the unfounded fear of the outsider. Mike was one of them. He'd been a cop for six years and knew the score. He understood completely that his lawsuit meant that he was locked in combat against the police culture, and by taking it on, he had become the enemy.[64]

The "blue wall of silence" prevailed, and no officers were ever charged with the beating of Michael Cox. After balking, Menino and Evans agreed to settle the civil rights lawsuit. Reverend Rivers, one of Menino's staunchest allies, would call for an independent commission to investigate the racial incidents in the Boston Police Department, a call the mayor and commissioner would reject. Rivers pointed to several incidents that he believed were racially motivated. "Placing of a noose over the motorcycle of Lieutenant Valimore Williams, a black commander, last month; a lawsuit filed by officers alleging they were passed over for promotion because they are white; and the 1995 beating of Sergeant Michael Cox, a black officer, by fellow officers who mistook him for a suspect. Things are tight. The racial climate is tense."[65]

Menino had asserted, "I never really had a bad racial thing when I was a mayor, not really, no." However, he had said at the time of these incidents, "Is there racial tension in the police department? All society, everywhere, has racial tension. I do not think it is the degree that people are trying to make it."[66] (The new mayor, Michelle Wu, appointed Michael Cox as her police commissioner in 2022.)

## Same Problem: Different Approaches

A comparison of Flynn's and Menino's approaches to racial conflict reveals a need for a solid and consistent focus and public discourse to avoid slippage. While Menino made statements about racial conflict in the city, and it was clear that he had solid personal opposition to discrimination of any kind, the evidence suggests that he chose a different path than his predecessor. Understandably, his style and approach differed from that of Flynn, who came to the mayor's office during ongoing racial conflict and had something to prove as a South Boston resident and an opponent of busing. In contrast, Menino did not face the same constraints as a city councilor from Hyde Park and someone who inherited the mayor's office at a time of relative racial stability.

Even with these discernible differences, Menino's tenure can be characterized as a reluctance to pursue aggressive policies to address the worsening tensions in the city. The *Boston Globe* editorialized in 2000 about the "prosecution gap" under the Menino administration. "A tough response to bias crimes defined the administration of Mayor Raymond Flynn, who sought to heal a city fractured by racially motivated attacks on people of color," the paper wrote. "In today's multiracial city, however, the perpetrator is just as likely to be a member of a racial minority as white."[67]

Menino was also criticized for dismantling the fifteen-year-old Minority and Women Business Enterprise (MWBE) development program, created under executive order by Flynn in 1987. The program was based upon legislation drafted by councilor Bolling to require 15 percent of city contracts to minorities, with 30 percent in neighborhoods with large minority populations and 5 percent awarded to women businesses. "Significantly, the order sets a new and higher standard for making sure that Boston residents share in the benefits of economic growth," Flynn said at the signing. Bolling said he was relieved that this has finally come to fruition. "This is an issue that I have been pushing for since I have been in the city council."[68]

The city often struggled to meet the executive order requirements and was constantly threatened by a legal challenge. When it was contested by an Everett construction company and other cities were facing similar legal challenges, Menino pulled the plug on the program.[69] Minority business leaders pleaded with Menino not to abandon the program and to put up a fight and await a ruling in a similar case to the one that Denver, Colorado, was facing. Despite Denver's success in defeating a federal court challenge, which the US Supreme Court declined to review, Menino eliminated the program over their opposition simply saying, "It is unfortunate that in cities across the country, programs similar to Boston's MWBE program are being struck down."[70] The Boston Globe went on to editorialize, "When faced with challenges to the city's affirmative action programs, the Menino administration has blinked. Its actions threaten a retreat from diversity and a return to the clubby world of contractors, banks and bonding firms."[71]

During his tenure, he faced criticisms about his relationship with the Black community. A confidential memo written to the Black Ministerial Alliance accused Menino of "Planning to water down the city's affirmative action programs, attempting to cut minority neighborhoods out of the federal empowerment zone grant, failing to keep promises to revitalize Blue Hill Avenue, and engaging in 'trickery and deceit' in removing former school Superintendent Lois Harrison Jones." Menino responded, saying, "I think we have done a good job serving that community, and we are going to do a better job." Rev. Charles Stith asked critically, "Is there a vision emanating from City Hall that translates into the African American community becoming part of the mainstream economic life of the city?"[72]

Discrimination was an issue that Menino said he cared about deeply. When Menino was asked what issue was personal to him, he cited racism, but he may have been responding more to his experience with ethnic prejudice. "Racism, I will not tolerate it; that is the interesting thing about my life," he said. "I was in the first grade. I will always remember this. It is only a little thing, but I will always remember it. My name is M-E-N-I-N-O, unlike the 'Manino' on the mushroom jar. The first-grade teacher told me that my parents did not know how to spell my name and that the Italians could not spell. So she changes the spelling. I went through the first grade with my name spelled wrong. That is a little thing. It has always stayed with me, and I will never tolerate people being discriminated against."[73]

Menino did achieve some notable successes during his tenure. The Boston Police Department reduced gang violence in Boston, the issue that replaced racial violence as a top city priority. Working with the Ten

Point Coalition, a group of ministers in the Black community and the police worked closely to address the needs of disconnected young people and combat growing youth violence. The critical elements of the strategy included collaboration with community partners, strict enforcement of laws, and targeted interventions with juvenile offenders. Menino knew youth violence was escalating in the city. He knew he could not solve the problem alone. A paper by Jackson and Winship in 1996 comparing Flynn and Menino on race relations noted that "Menino reached out to the Ten Point Ministers by having 'get to know each other dinners' at his home in Hyde Park. Ray Hammond, Gene Rivers, Bruce Wall, and others would join the mayor and his wife, Angela, who would make a big pot of spaghetti for them. They would sit around the dinner table and talk politics, education, religion, and what was happening in the city."[74]

Menino also prioritized the assimilation of new immigrants, expanding the efforts initiated by Flynn, as described in chapter 4. In 1998, he created the Office of New Bostonians to help ease the assimilation of new immigrants to the city. He also responded to discrimination against LGBTQ citizens of Boston. Ann Maguire—Flynn's liaison to the gay and lesbian community and Menino's head of human services in his first term—recounted the mayor's response to the US Supreme Court decision that allowed the South Boston Allied War Veterans to exclude gay and lesbian marchers from the annual St. Patrick's Day Parade in South Boston.[75] "When Tom Menino was elected, he was getting tremendous pressure to march in the St. Patrick's Day parade," she said. "After he became mayor, we had this new organizational structure cabinet. The mayor and the six chiefs would go out, and we would sit there and answer questions. I was chief of health and human services. Charlestown High School was the first place we went. It was packed, standing room only; people were asking questions. One of the guys raises his hand, and he asks, 'How come you are not marching in the St. Patrick's Day Parade?' The mayor said, 'You know you have to stand up for what you believe, and if you start doing stuff against what you said you believe in, no one will ever believe you. So I want you to know my word out there. It is good that I will not march in that parade.' Do you know what happened? Everybody in the place clapped. People knew your word's importance and that he would stick to it. Menino was under tremendous pressure when he was elected to march in the St. Patrick's Parade in Boston. Do you know what he did? He never did it."[76]

"Time heals all wounds," Dennis Kearney said. "Ray Flynn had it tougher. However, I give Tom Menino equal marks; even though he has not had it as challenging, he has affirmatively held the line and has done a

great job on racial relations. On a whole bunch of things, like not marching in the South Boston St. Patrick's Day parade because gays were excluded, that was heroic."[77]

What is surprising is that much of the increase in hate crimes in the
late 1980s to early 1990s was attributed to the fact that police only began
recording attacks against gays and lesbians around 1990. This may account, in part, for the rise in the incidents highlighted in chapter 9.

In assessing the approach to race relations and racial conflict by the
regimes of White, Flynn, and Menino, the evidence shows significant differences in governing practice, style, and outcomes. Each regime had to
confront racial conflict during their time in office, and the approaches
each took were based less on personalities and more on governing priorities and philosophy. Government communalism suggests that for the city
and its people to protect those citizens who face racial discrimination,
hard work is required of political, business, and civic leaders to develop a
more tolerant and accepting city. The evidence demonstrates that much
work remains to be done in this regard in Boston. "Boston had found a
way to discuss racial issues with less acrimony, and Boston had become a
more complex city demographically, both culturally and racially, thanks
to immigration," Neil Sullivan said. "Menino did not carry the burdens of
the past as Flynn did—which was good. We transitioned from a ground-
breaker to a gardener. Gardening is a more peaceful activity but cannot
happen until the ground is broken."[78]

# 9 / Civil Rights and Wrongs: The Search for Racial Justice

> *What was going on in Boston went far beyond busing and blockbusting. I was looking at all these incidents of assault and vandalism, and much to my surprise, I realized that we had no idea what the racial problem was or how serious it was. There was a pattern of racial crimes in specific neighborhoods not being addressed. They were victimized because of their race. The race problem had moved out of the schools and into the streets and neighborhoods of the city.* (Police Commissioner Mickey Roache, interview)

Out of the turmoil in the schools and the neighborhoods of Boston, the Boston Police Department's Community Disorders Unit (CDU) was born on April 7, 1978. It would be the first such unit in the country to address racially motivated hate crimes specifically. That year, 607 racial incidents were reported. The charge for the CDU then, as it is today, is for district personnel to refer incidents to the CDU if elements of bias or hate motivation are detected at the initial reporting stage. These cases are then screened and investigated by the CDU to determine whether bias against the victim based on race, ethnic/national origin, religion, and, later, sexual orientation was considered as a factor in the incident. After screening and investigation, all cases are classified into one of three groups: *hate crimes* include those cases that CDU determined to be hate crimes, *miscellaneous* consists of those cases that have indicators of hate crimes but not enough to be conclusive, and non–hate crimes include those cases that are determined not to be hate crimes.[1]

Between 1978, when the CDU was formed, and 2000, Boston saw, on average, more than 266 incidents of race-motivated hate crimes each year. The CDU closely monitored the integration of public housing in Boston during the period since the CDU's creation through 2000. Racially motivated hate crimes declined in the mid-1980s and then rose significantly at the end of the century.

Looking at the racial incidents of the early 1990s, Michael Rezendes reported for the *Boston Globe,* "Citywide, the number of reported civil rights violations decreased from 273 in 1990 to 218 in 1991. Police officials said that among the few increases in reported civil rights violations were

| Year | Racial Incidents |
|------|------------------|
| 1978 | 607 |
| 1979 | 482 |
| 1980 | 338 |
| 1981 | 207 |
| 1982 | 223 |
| 1983 | 174 |
| 1984 | 177 |
| 1985 | 183 |
| 1986 | 157 |
| 1987 | 158 |
| 1988 | 152 |
| 1989 | 202 |
| 1990 | 273 |
| 1991 | 218 |
| 1992 | 252 |
| 1993 | 276 |
| 1994 | 259 |
| 1995 | 242 |
| 1996 | 233 |
| 1997 | 276 |
| 1998 | 407 |
| 1999 | 342 |
| 2000 | 302 |

MAYOR WHITE (1978–1983), MAYOR FLYNN (1984–1993), MAYOR MENINO (1994–2000)

**Administration**
- Mayor White
- Mayor Flynn
- Mayor Menino

CHART 12. Racially Motivated Crimes in Boston, 1978–2000
Source: City of Boston Police Department

rises at two predominantly white South Boston public housing developments, where the number of minority residents has gone up over the last
four years. At the West Broadway development, the number of reported
civil rights abuses rose from 11 in 1990 to 34 last year. During the same
period at the Old Colony development, the number of alleged civil rights
assaults increased from 15 to 20."[2]

Menino also faced a class action lawsuit in 1996 brought by public
housing tenants who claimed that they were the targets of racial violence
in several public housing developments in South Boston and Charlestown. The US Department of Justice suit claimed that the plaintiffs, who
are Haitian, Hispanic, Trinidadian, Nigerian, St. Thomian, Black, Black
African American, and Hispanic, alleged that they, their families, and
their visitors were repeatedly subject to racial violence, harassment, and
intimidation because of their race, color, and national origin by White
tenants and others during named plaintiffs' tenancies at two predominantly White BHA developments—Old Colony in South Boston and
Bunker Hill in Charlestown. This alleged harassment includes racially
motivated physical violence, threats of physical violence, destruction of
property, racist graffiti, and racist name-calling, and the BHA failed to
investigate or respond to their complaints adequately.[3]

The case was ultimately settled between the City of Boston and the
US Department of Housing and Urban Development through an agreement with the city and the BHA denying the allegations and agreeing
to a settlement of one million dollars for the plaintiffs and five hundred
thousand dollars in attorney fees.

## Dismantling the Bulwark Against Racial Violence

In 2000, the *Boston Globe* published a special report, "As Reported Hate
Crimes in Boston Surge, Prosecutions Drop." Reporter Judy Rakowsky
argued that the CDU, the first in the nation, "is a shell of what it used to
be, undercut by political pressure from heavily voting South Boston."[4] Rakowsky added, "Records show that despite a sharp rise in hate crimes in
recent years, the CDU is locking up a shrinking proportion of offenders.
Reported hate crimes in Boston have jumped 57 percent, from 276 in 1993
to 433 in 1999,[5] nearly the highest level since the state's hate crime statute
was enacted in 1980. While the number of complaints has spiked, the
percentage that resulted in criminal charges being brought dropped from
21 percent in 1993 to 9 percent last year, a reduction of 56 percent."[6] She
reported that Kelly, a close ally of Menino and an outspoken critic of the
CDU, acknowledged much of the responsibility. "The squad definitely has

a lower profile. 'Let sleeping dogs lie.' I relayed my concerns to a number of people in authority in the police department, and maybe behind the scenes, District Attorney Ralph Martin played a role."[7]

Councilor Bruce Bolling noted, "There is no question that the CDU has been important in helping this city turn the corner on race relations. It has investigated cases of concern to the minority community and has allowed certain incidents to get the light of day. They made some tough but necessary calls that helped the city overcome the traumatizing desegregation period."[8]

Sergeant William Johnston commanded the CDU through much of Flynn's term after taking over from Roache in 1985 when he was appointed commissioner. Rakowsky interviewed Johnston, who wrote to Commissioner Paul Evans in a March 14, 1996, memo about the CDU under Menino. "It is rather embarrassing that the unit for which we have been held in such high esteem, for which we are a national model and which we can thank for clearing our reputation as the most racist city, has become the department's black sheep," he wrote. "CDU detectives have been put aside, largely ignored by Police Department supervisors, and treated as if they had done something wrong."[9]

The political power of South Boston was cited as the principal cause for the dismantling of the CDU by Johnston and others. The local *South Boston Tribune* called the CDU "Caucasian Detainee Unit." The CDU was a constant topic in the *Tribune* from 1993 to 1997, during the neighborhood's integration of public housing developments. As Rakowsky reported,

> In June of 1994, John Ciccone, director of the militantly anti-busing South Boston Information Center, praised the legal maneuvering of Steve Lynch, who was elected state representative that year before becoming a state senator (and later a member of Congress). 'Attorney Steve Lynch has once again come to the rescue and will represent' free of charge sixteen Old Colony residents served with civil injunctions based on CDU investigations to stay away from hate-crime victims, Ciccone wrote in his column. Ciccone warned the CDU to back off, writing in May 1994 that the squad 'is just getting themselves in deeper and deeper.' He called for disciplinary action and the transfer of every detective on the squad. 'The pressure is on the CDU, and it will continue to mount,' Ciccone wrote. 'Their contempt for South Boston will be their downfall,' he said in a column that announced a June meeting with top police officials to air complaints about [the] CDU. 'They are in a battle that they

will not win.' By June 30, Ciccone's mood had brightened, and he gave an upbeat account of what had happened at the meeting eight days earlier with Superintendent Boyle and Captain Tom Crowley of the South Boston police district. Ciccone said Boyle had assured him, Kelly, and other Southie leaders that he would investigate all their complaints.[10]

As Johnston described it, "White politicians had used the integration of the South Boston projects as an excuse to play out their bigotry. They did not complain when Whites moved in from other parts of the city or Asians. They did not complain until Blacks moved in. And then they said it was unfair because the city was taking away housing from neighborhood people."[11]

While city hall was incredulous and Commissioner Evans and District Attorney Ralph Martin disputed the story and its findings, the *Globe*'s editor, Matthew Storin, defended its accuracy, as did Rakowsky and deputy managing editor Ben Bradlee Jr. "This was a carefully documented story about the decline of a once nationally recognized detective unit that served as a bulwark against racism in Boston," Bradlee wrote. "The article showed how the Police Department neutered the Community Disorders Unit under pressure from South Boston leaders and how the prosecution of hate crimes in the city in recent years has fallen sharply, even as the number of reported incidents has spiked up."[12] The *Globe*'s ombudsman, Jack Thomas, questioned the story's accuracy. However, the statements that deserve the most weight are those of Sergeant William Johnston, who had commanded the CDU and had communicated his concerns to the police commissioner, as the story reported.[13]

Commenting on the Rakowsky report at the time were Police Commissioners Roache and Bratton, as well as Flynn. Roache, who was the CDU's first commander and served as police commissioner from 1985 to 1993, said that the unit has always been a target. "The people in the CDU need protection so nobody can get at them," said Roache. "You do not abandon the people who make a difference." William Bratton, who succeeded Roache as commissioner before leaving to take the same job in New York, said, "The CDU sent a powerful message at a time in Boston when the White community was getting out of hand expressing itself in violent acts. The people may still have their racist attitudes, but you certainly can control the behavior." Moreover, Flynn said holding press conferences to announce its annual reports was necessary. "There was a real need to send a clear message that the city would be governed by one set of rules and laws."[14]

Jim Jordan shared his thoughts on the Boston Police Department's civil rights and hate crime enforcement. "The true thing is that later, there was a victory that the Boston police districts were much more tuned into enforcing civil rights laws," he said, suggesting that it was not a lack of enforcement but rather a central part of the police work.[15]

After Rakowsky's story, city councilor Stephen Murphy, who headed the council's public safety committee, offered to call a hearing at the urging of councilors Chuck Turner, Charles Yancey, and Mickey Roache. "I am not convinced a weakened CDU is a bad thing," Murphy said, adding he thought the squad had been selectively prosecuting White youths in South Boston. Menino's only comments were that any personnel or policy changes at the Community Disorders Unit did not mean hate crimes were a lower priority. "Nothing matters more to me than race relations," he said, noting that "maybe they don't have any grounds for prosecution." When asked why the change from when Flynn held press conferences to announce the CDU's annual report, Menino said, "We are not into glamour and limelight."[16] What Johnston said the CDU was into, however, was dealing with the pain that racial incidents cause. "A broken window is not a major crime," he added, "but in a racial case, a broken window is not a broken window once you put your head inside and see what happens to that family."[17]

The CDU was an essential part of reducing racial violence in the city. While there was still overt racism, as many have described, the hate crimes began to subside once the integration of the White public housing developments had reached a critical stage. The racial incidents continued to decline after that.

## "Stop and Frisk": Targeting Youth of Color

Following the reelection of 1987, Flynn entered his second term in office, facing significant issues, including the completion of the South Boston public housing integration and rising violence in some Boston neighborhoods due to gang wars and the scourge of crack cocaine, which plagued cities across America. The number of murders annually in Boston (proxied for the overall level of violence in the city) had increased dramatically, from 75 in 1987 to 95 in 1988 and 152 in 1990. The administration was looking for a strategy to respond to what had become a youth gang problem.

In 1988, the Boston Police Department created the City-Wide Anti-Crime Unit and began to use the tool of direct indictment through the Armed Career Criminal Act. "We sat down with US Attorney Wayne

Budd and developed a strategy on the real violent offenders, [and passed] the Armed Career Criminal Act, which gave a three-year mandatory off to jail, and they went," Police Commissioner Mickey Roache said. Following the murder on August 19, 1988, of twelve-year-old Darlene Tiffany Moore, who was shot while sitting on a mailbox by suspected gang members on Humbolt Avenue in Roxbury, the "stop-and-frisk" policy was instituted. "In 1988, Humboldt Avenue was the focal point of Roxbury's drug trade—'heroin alley,' some called it. Burned-out homes, empty lots, and broken-down cars scarred the stretch along the broad avenue near Homestead Street. The dominant street culture revolved around cash, clothes, and cocaine. Rampant drug use—especially crack—was behind a frightening rise in crime."[18] Suspects could be randomly searched, and the police were beginning to get hold of the gangs. The new policy, while promoted by the police department and many community leaders, had its detractors in city hall and the community. The implications for race relations were a concern for Neil Sullivan. "First, 'stop-and-frisk' had clear racial overtones because Black youth were searched and White youth were not," he said. "In general, Black and White people had a different sense of what was happening. At the time, we were demographically a Black and White city. In the following decades, race was no longer just a Black and White issue, as cultural diversity became just as visible as race."[19]

The stop-and-frisk policy elicited widespread anger and criticism from Black elected officials, who believed it created a double standard based on race. "The stop-and-search practice was infuriating, not only because we believed it amounted to a dangerous infringement of civil rights but also because it divided leadership in the Black community," State Senator Bill Owens said, criticizing Flynn.[20]

Many in the African American community, led by the Interfaith Ministerial Alliance, did not oppose the stop-and-frisk policy until the aftermath of the Stuart incident in 1990. "Ironically, there was a press conference about two weeks before the Charles Stuart affair, and Black community leadership stood behind Flynn," Black civic leader Hubie Jones, dean emeritus of the Boston University School of Social Work, recalled. "So, we were going to keep our community safe; people were terrified. Tiffany Moore, a little twelve-year-old girl, got shot on a mailbox; violent youth stormed into Morningside Baptist Church; and the leaders stood behind the mayor and Mickey Roache on stop and frisk. Charles Stuart happens, and these same people were now on the mayor's case about going into Mission Hill, ravaging Mission Hill, looking for the so-called Black perpetrator."[21]

## "The Cruel Hoax on Boston": The Murderous Furrier

Immediately on the heels of the stop-and-frisk controversy, on October 23, 1989, race relations in Boston took a turn for the worse. Carol Stuart, a pregnant White woman and an attorney who lived in the suburbs with her husband, Charles—a furrier on fashionable Newbury Street—was returning from childbirth class at the Brigham and Women's Hospital on Mission Hill. Charles claimed he was carjacked and "a Black man" shot both Carol and him. Carol died along with her unborn baby. Charles was seriously injured, and he later identified a Black suspect in a police lineup, Willie Bennett, as the shooter.

As author Dart Adams said in an interview for the HBO documentary *Murder in Boston: Roots, Rampage & Reckoning*, at that moment, "We all fit the description, we knew what was about to happen, we knew the hell that was about to descend upon us."[22] And it did. As Ron Bell, Mission Hill resident, said, it "was open season on Black people."[23] Sullivan added, "Police leadership implemented stop-and-frisk; it was the beginning of our losing control of the police—our ability to direct police work."[24]

However, statements made to police on January 3, 1990, by Charles's brother, Mathew Stuart, identified Charles as the shooter. On January 4, 1990, after issuing an arrest warrant, the police reported that Charles Stuart committed suicide by jumping off the Mystic Tobin Bridge. Sources have suggested and otherwise implied that unidentified individuals may have "facilitated his fall." Whatever the cause, when it became clear that he had been the perpetrator and not a hooded Black man, the issue of race reached a crescendo in Boston. "When he hit the water, it was a holy-shit moment for the entire region. We just got duped by the guy in believing the very worst of what we are," said *Boston Globe* editor Brian McGrory.[25] "It was a reckoning for this city," added journalist Howard Bryant.[26]

The response to the shooting by the mayor and police department was widely criticized after it was learned that the perpetrator was not Black after all. "Because Mayor Flynn said, 'Call out all available detectives,' some viewed him as overreacting to the moment, and we own that one," Sullivan said. "It is incredible what that moment meant. He was reacting to the fact that, after a year of horrifying and unprecedented violence among Black teenagers, the Carol Stuart murder had the effect of misleading White people to think that 'even White people' are getting shot and killed now in the streets of Boston. Of course, this was not true and never became true—but less than a decade after the city was plagued with

White-on-Black and Black-on-White violence, it is easy to see why White residents felt that way, even if they did not say it out loud."[27]

Commissioner Roache disputed the actual impact of the police response. "Mayor Flynn announced that all resources in this department would be available to do everything possible, but people got the impression that there would be an army," he said. "What do we have, about fourteen or fifteen detectives citywide? We did not put an army out there."[28]

Additionally, the Boston Police opposed the Suffolk County district attorney's decision to arrest suspect Willie Bennett on unrelated longstanding minor charges. "No, you have got to be kidding me," Roache responded. "They were like traffic things, other things that had been around for ages. Unfortunately, they fabricated it. Then they lied to the grand jury. Then they finally got it right, but we got killed for it."[29]

The mayor, media, police, and the public bought into Charles Stuart's hoax. The police have been criticized for shoddy police work for not following up on leads that might have pointed to Chuck Stuart's involvement, including the fact that, as the *Globe* reported, several police officers were not convinced Stuart wasn't involved. They were removed from the case. "At least 33 people knew Chuck was responsible for Carol's death before Matthew went to the authorities. Eleven of them knew the truth by the day of Carol's funeral—two months before Chuck picked Willie Bennett out of a police lineup."[30]

Michelle Caruso, investigative reporter from the *Boston Herald*, claims she believed Charles was likely involved but said, "If the *Herald* were to do a story questioning Chuck Stuart's integrity and honor, and we turned out to be wrong, we would have been destroyed."[31]

All those interviewed agreed this situation was challenging, given the city's racial history. "We had a press conference, and Senator Ted Kennedy stood up and said, 'This is your mayor, this is my mayor, he's going to keep this city together, he's going to keep this community together, and I'm with him 100 percent,' and that is what we did. Nothing happened," Flynn recalled. "When you think about it, I was in Los Angeles after Rodney King, with Mayor Tom Bradley and the race riots. We never had anything like that. We never had a racial incident of profound significance that I am aware of in the ten years we were in city hall."[32] Frank Doyle, city director of intergovernmental relations, described the overall climate that framed the incident. "Flynn had been cultivating community capital. He had amassed a lot of credibility when things got tough; he had a wellspring of goodwill and trust he could tap into because people believed he was trying to do the right thing and had been doing it for years."[33] "There were sorrowful moments around the Stuart case, harrowing times when

Flynn had worked so hard on bringing the city together, and I think he was devastated by the whole Stuart thing," Kristin McCormack, who directed the jobs and community services office, said. "He took the race stuff very personally; he was very serious about it."[34]

Some in the Black community disagreed with Flynn's assessment. As Hubie Jones, said, "I think he lost some currency with the Black community, but he got reelected big time."[35] Civil rights activist Ken Wade added, "It sets some things back a little bit, at least in terms of the way that the police handled the search for the perpetrator. Then to have it end up as it did. The Mission Hill community, in particular, felt besieged. It was another one of those situations where they felt a rush to judgment. That did cause some consternation. I do not think it threw things back to where they were in 1983—just a setback, as is bound to happen in any city. You have to have two steps forward and a step back now and then, so I do not think that necessarily puts the city back on a different path."[36] At Muhammad's Mosque No. 11 in Grove Hall, Minister Don Muhammad said, "Flynn enjoys deep support among average Black residents." He disputed assertations that the Stuart affair cut into the allegiance of Black voters. "I don't think his support ever diminished from its high point. I'm not talking about political people or people described as Black leaders. I'm talking about rank-and-file people who have supported this man because he has responded to issues that this community needs to be concerned with."[37]

In exploring the impact of the Stuart incident on the progress of race relations in Boston, Sullivan suggested, "It would be wrong to say that it undid the gains, but setback would be the word. It suddenly divided us along racial lines again, Black and White. The gang violence had been building, the homicides were piling up, and crack cocaine was real and affecting everything, but White people were never the victims until it seemed to happen that night. There is collateral damage to progressive change, and there is collateral benefit to bad moments. The collateral benefit was that we do not know everything and do not have youth violence under control. However, we eventually got control of it, from the Safe Neighborhoods campaign to the Boston Miracle."[38]

In the aftermath of the Stuart case, some Black leaders wanted an apology from Flynn for what they considered the police overreaction. Louis Elisa, head of the Boston chapter of the National Association for the Advancement of Colored People (NAACP), called the Stuart case a watershed event. "The mayor owed an apology not just to Mission Hill but to every Black person in the city of Boston who was traumatized and victimized by political hysteria," he said. "Every White person was looking at every member of the Black community as a possible killer."[39]

Mayor Flynn apologized to the Bennett family, telling Mrs. Bennett, "What has taken place has been very unfortunate." He said on January 5, 1990, "Everybody owes an apology to the Mission Hill neighborhood . . . to the black community, and they [the Stuarts] all owe an apology to the people of the city. We should all stand in line waiting for that apology."[40] Hubie Jones shared his thoughts on this moment: "Flynn did a decent job of apologizing for the actions of the police caught up in believing Stuart's lie. Unity in Boston had been placed at great risk."[41]

The Mission Hill neighborhood felt, on the one hand, besieged and, on the other, misunderstood, characterized as a "symbol for everything bad about urban America—too many guns, uncontrollable poverty and streets that drug dealers have usurped."[42] In the aftermath of the Stuart incident, the residents of Mission Hill painted a different picture, saying the portrayal was unfair, simplistic, and inaccurate. Many residents said it is one of the city's most diverse, caring, and close-knit neighborhoods. "The neighborhood has been degraded by people who never bother to go beyond the easy stereotypes," said Maria Sanchez, a longtime resident of the neighborhood. Added Kenny Reeves, "I am a young Black man that lives in a housing development in Mission Hill. I am not a drug dealer. I help counsel some of the kids in the area, and there are other kids like me."[43]

On December 20, 2023, thirty-four years after the cataclysmic events, Mayor Michelle Wu issued a public apology on behalf of the city to the families of Bennett and Alan Swanson, the two Black men wrongfully arrested in connection with the Stuart murder, saying, "What was done to you was unjust, unfair, racist, and wrong and this apology is long over-due. To every Black resident—I am sorry not only for the abuse our city enacted but for the beliefs and the bias that brought them to bear."[44] Wu was just four years old and living in Chicago at the time of the tragic Stuart murders. While Boston still has a well-deserved reputation concerning racial conflict, the progress of racial healing Flynn championed both before and after the Stuart case has made a significant difference in the racial climate of the city today.

The Stuart incident divided the city. Most White *and* Black Bostonians believed the police and media accounts about a Black perpetrator that Charles Stuart had told them. When his story unraveled, the mayors apologized—Flynn in 1990, Wu in 2023—as did the police commissioner in 2023. Only the media haven't apologized. Based upon two years of research, the *Boston Globe* did an eight-series high-tech print and online investigative report and a nine-episode Podcast released December 1, 2023, thirty-four years after the incident. *Nightmare in*

*Mission Hill: The Untold Story of the Charles and Carol Stuart Shooting* contained an epilogue titled "Media Sins," where reporter Adrian Walker said his editor Greg Moore "remains proud that issues of race and class figured prominently in the *Globe*'s coverage from the beginning. He said he has no regrets." Another reporter on the story, Renee Graham, felt differently, Walker added: "What really got her—all these years later—is the lack of any accountability for what we got wrong."[45] No apology yet from the *Boston Globe* or the *Boston Herald*. Don't expect one. And that is a sin.

Jim Jordan, director of strategic planning at the Boston Police Department, observed, "When the Stuart thing broke, it was the issue that swallowed everybody. It showed the magnitude of the problem of racial violence. We had a press conference in front of the headquarters, and thirty news organizations were there. With Stuart, everything was magnified, and because of race, it indeed showed one thing: race was still an important matter to be dealt with all the time in the city."[46]

## The Challenge to Improve Race Relations in Boston

Finally, the *Boston Globe* assessed Flynn's record in responding to Boston's communities of color, suggesting, "Despite the disaffection expressed by King and most of the minority elected officials in the city, a statistical analysis shows that Flynn has made progress in integrating public housing developments, hiring nonwhites for city jobs and encouraging private developers to give jobs to minorities."[47] The Stuart incident took its toll on the perceptions of race relations, as shown in a *Globe* poll conducted in August 1991, almost two years after the incident, with 46 percent of residents believing race relations were worse and 45 percent believing they were better or about the same. The poll also rated Flynn's response to the Stuart incident with 43 percent believing he did an excellent to average job with 42 percent characterizing his response as below average. "The minority community and the people of the city of Boston have been hurt by what they feel has been a very unfair portrayal of this community and this city," Flynn suggested. "I don't know if words will ever make up for that injustice."[48]

Consalvo, Flynn's education adviser, summarized the mayor's focus on race relations when he recalled what he told the mayor: "I'm sick of race; everything you do, you are talking about race, and it is driving me crazy, and many people in the city crazy. Flynn said, 'It is the most important issue, and I've got to keep doing it.' He was serious about it and may have had many other quirks, but he could pull it off by the strength of his personality. It did not solve the problem; look at what happened with the Stuart incident."[49]

As he prepared to depart for the Vatican in the summer of 1993, most observers gave Flynn high marks on improving race relations during his near-decade tenure as mayor. *Globe* reporter Peter Canellos wrote, "During the busing crisis and well into the '70s, Boston's neighborhoods loomed in the national imagination as war zones, peopled by grotesque extremists of many stripes. Then came Flynn, with his mild manner, emphasis on fairness, and devotion to simple values. He represented the best of Boston, and most leaders agreed. Flynn appointed more minority officials, built much affordable housing in distressed minority neighborhoods, and spoke out early in his tenure against racial violence."[50] "Boston has had an awful national image for race relations," said media and political strategist Joyce Ferriabough. "Racism is not gone, but there is a better feeling in the city. Flynn has tried hard to create a level playing field. There have been some blots, like the Stuart case, but improving race relations is part of his legacy."[51] The *Boston Globe* wrote in its investigation of the Stuart case, "Flynn really was trying. He started showing up personally at the scene of every act of racial violence. He fought racist redlining practices by banks, created jobs for people of color, and, in the late 1980s, desegregated the city's public housing complexes. He appointed a new police commissioner— Mickey Roache—who had made a name for himself running the Police Department's civil rights office. Flynn staffed his administration with a cadre of progressive activists—including Landsmark, the Black lawyer attacked with the flag in the famous photograph."[52] As Consalvo said, "he was serious about it."

Mel King contradicted the positive assessment, but he put some blame on members and leaders of the minority community: "I've always said that one of the mistakes people constantly make is to say that race relations have improved simply because whites and blacks aren't throwing bricks at one another."[53] King went on to criticize Black and Hispanic leaders for their inability to agree on a wide range of issues, from the Police Department's stop-and-frisk policy to Flynn's school committee referendum campaign. "Fighting racism in a house divided is draining, and we are a house divided."[54]

In conclusion, dealing with racial conflict and race relations was a contested undertaking for Flynn, with many observers giving him high marks, but a small number of activists in the Black community criticized his approach and the fact that violence and poverty were not eradicated in their community.

## Mandela and the Secession Effort: Community Control or Black Nationalism

Efforts to empower Boston's neighborhoods of color were sometimes fraught with difficulties. Several African American activists believed that creating a conflict with the city administration would provide the best hope for improving opportunities for their community. In 1986, some proposed that sections of Roxbury, Mattapan, Jamaica Plain, and Dorchester secede from Boston and that they create an independent city to be known as Mandela. The political expression by Blacks in Boston to gain control over development in their communities and the Mandela effort discussed below was a form of nationalism.[55]

In the summer of 1986, a "self-proclaimed small group of intellectuals, carpetbaggers, with no constituency in the community,"[56] proposed to carve out 25 percent of Boston's land area and 22 percent of the city's population, more than 90 percent minority, into a new city. Arguing that for Boston's Black community to succeed economically, they would have to "control their land," the organizing effort would follow the path of the Black Nationalist movement advocated earlier by one-time Roxbury resident Malcolm X. Early in his career, Malcolm X followed Nation of Islam leader Elijah Muhammad's teachings that White society enslaved and kept African Americans from achieving political, economic, and social success. Like the later Mandela effort in Boston, Black Nationalists fought for a state of their own, separate from one inhabited and governed by White people.

The two principals in the effort, Andrew Jones and Curtis Davis, formed the Greater Roxbury Incorporation Project (GRIP). They obtained five thousand signatures to put the nonbinding measure on the municipal ballot on November 4, 1986. "Our community is at a crossroads," Jones said. "We have to decide whether to fight for political access within Boston and what that will get us or whether to establish our own community."[57] Some leaders in the Black community weren't too enamored by the Jones and Davis effort. One prominent leader, Joyce Ferriabough, the longtime Black media and political strategist, confronted Jones after hearing him grumbling about Flynn's "plantation politics." "How do you want your ass kicking?" she asked. "Over easy or well done?"[58]

After working for nearly three years into his first term to transform racial relations in the city, Flynn believed that progress was being made through economic development, increasing jobs for people of color in construction and city hall, integrating public housing, and policing and community empowerment strategies. However, the level of progress remained a significant concern to many residents of the predominantly Black neighborhoods of Roxbury, Mattapan, and Dorchester, and the Mandela effort of 1986 seemed to some to offer an opportunity to effect radical change.

Flynn and many in the city's Black, corporate, and religious communities were concerned. They believed the proposal was divisive and would turn back Boston's progress. They formed the "One Boston" organization to lead the effort to oppose the secession proposal. Rev. Charles Stith chaired the opposition and brought in Joyce Ferriabough to lead the effort, and Flynn dispatched political aide Harry Grill to organize against it. "The referendum's fate would be decided not during a discussion at the Harvard faculty club but in a political campaign in the streets of Boston."[59] Stith would write in the Boston Globe, "The appointments of Doris Bunte to head the housing authority, Laval Wilson as superintendent of schools, George Russell as city treasurer, and Leon Stamps as city auditor is evidence of the climate of inclusion now prevailing in the city and the political clout of the minority community."[60] Kevin Phelan, a business leader who raised money to help defeat the effort, said, "Too much progress is being made in the city. Why would you contribute to divisiveness when harmony seems to be the rule today?"[61]

In a two-part series for the Boston Globe in 1987, Charles Kenney wrote, "Flynn took the Mandela proposal very personally. He told some of his department heads that it was the worst thing to confront the city since the busing crisis. He saw it as a grave threat to his efforts to unite Boston, an idea that had been the central theme of his campaign for mayor. In thousands of speeches and discussions throughout the city during more than a year of campaigning, Flynn repeatedly said that his intention, if elected mayor, was to bring the city together. For him to have done anything but strenuously oppose Mandela would have seemed wildly out of character."[62]

The Black community was divided on the Mandela secession question and many other issues. Five of the nine members of the elected Black leadership supported the ballot initiative, and leaders of the prominent Black churches vigorously opposed it. "However, it was all becoming a part of the web," Hubie Jones recalled. "With this Mandela thing—let us take this part of his city under our control—and it took off for a while until the mayor realized, 'Whoa, this could be trouble,' and he got the city's power structure to shut it down."[63]

With assistance from the city budget, assessing, and treasury departments, John Riordan, Flynn's chief of staff, prepared a memo detailing the secession proposal's financial implications. The memo laid bare the economic facts. "Because Mandela is an overwhelmingly residential area, much of its tax burden would be shifted from commercial and industrial to residential property, resulting in a staggering 61 percent increase in residential property taxes and a 44 percent increase in commercial and industrial property taxes," he wrote. "Mandela would have costs of $456 million in its first year and revenues of only $320 million, leaving the new community with a whopping deficit of $136 million."[64] For Ray Dooley, director of administrative services and Flynn's campaign manager, the financial message would be an important rallying cry to defeat the proposal. While the Mandela referendum organizers challenged the analysis, they did not offer a sound economic alternative.

The secession plan was placed on the Boston municipal ballot in 1986 and again in 1988. Both times, it was defeated, though the margin of opposition narrowed from three to one in 1986 to less than two to one in 1988. "The strategy was to canvas the city and read to voters what they were voting to approve or disapprove on the ballot," Flynn pollster Allan Stern said.[65] The referendum language read,

### VOTES CAST ON QUESTION TO FORM
### A NEW CITY OF THE COMMONWEALTH
### TO BE CALLED MANDELA
### STATE ELECTION, NOVEMBER 4, 1986

#### QUESTION 9
#### This Question Is Nonbinding

#### SUMMARY

Shall the Representative from this district be instructed to vote in favor of legislation forming the following wards and precincts of the City of Boston into a new city of the Commonwealth: ward 4, precincts 8 and 9; ward 9; ward 10, precincts 5, 6, and 7; ward 11; ward 12; ward 13, precincts 1, 2, 3, and 5; ward 14; ward 15, precincts 1, 2, 3, 5, and 7; ward 17, precincts 1, 2, 3, 4, 5, 6, 7, and 10; ward 18, precincts 1, 2, 3, 4, 5, 6, and 21; ward 19, precinct 7?

In the 3rd, 5th, 6th, 7th, 9th, 12th, 13th, 14th, 15th, and 17th
Suffolk Representative Districts

When potential voters read this, they were undoubtedly more confused than ever—thirty-five thousand voted no, which led to the question's defeat in every ward of the city.

Although the measure was defeated in both referenda, it highlighted the continuing debate on race relations and equality as unfinished business in the city, revealing divisions that had not been seen since busing in 1974. As *Boston Globe* columnist Robert Jordan noted, "Mayor Flynn won because the 3-1 vote against secession allows him to continue working toward his goal of bringing the Black community into the city's economic mainstream. If the non-binding referendum had passed, Boston's racial problems would have escalated."[66] In response to the secession effort, Flynn called for unity and a common purpose, "a united house standing tall."

As *New York Times* columnist Matthew Wald wrote, "While in other cities, this might be dismissed as a rhetorical flourish, Mr. Flynn, who wrote the speech himself, was alluding to a history of racial discord and a proposal last summer to carve out 12.5 square miles of Boston, including all its predominantly Black areas, as a new city to be called 'Mandela.' The vote implied that racial separation here was better than it might have seemed during the school busing crises that shook the city a decade ago. Boston has often been described as two cities, though the traditional division has not been between the races but between the colleges and universities and the work-a-day city."[67]

In 1989, GRIP organizer Andrew Jones, not giving up after the second defeat at the polls, sought to have the legislature approve a ballot question for the voters that would authorize a charter commission to study the issues of creating an independent city. The measure was not adopted. State Representative Byron Rushing supported the ballot measure and introduced the charter commission legislation at the State House. "The desire to break off from the city should not be considered a criticism of the mayor [Flynn]," he said. "It is criticism of many mayors. It is a criticism of the disenfranchisement and powerlessness of this community. You cannot say the state of municipal services in Roxbury can be blamed on one administration. It's blamed on a series of administrations that did not have this community as its priority."[68]

"The suppression of racial violence led to a peaceful period among the races," Neil Sullivan noted. "The Mandela secession movement to separate Roxbury, much of Dorchester, and Mattapan from the rest of the city kept the focus on race. Still, it was a political discussion over how best to serve the Black community. That proved to be something of a wrestling match. There were plenty of small blows, but no one was trying to take anyone else out. Then violence, 'stop and frisk,' and the Stuart murder unleashed anger across racial lines. Regarding race relations, this was the great slippage we would have to recover as quickly as possible."[69]

Rev. Joseph E. Washington, the senior adviser on equal rights to Flynn and pastor of the Wesley United Methodist Church in Dorchester, said, "Boston is slowly, surely, and inevitably opening up to people of color and women. Politically, the establishment understands that for this city to work, it has to change its image. City's leaders are trying to include rather than exclude."[70]

Although defeated, it again highlighted the continuing debate on race relations and equality as unfinished business in the city, revealing divisions that have not been seen since busing in 1974.

## Integration of Public Housing: Equity and Access

Flynn was a longtime champion of public housing and its residents. He announced his candidacy for mayor in the D Street public housing project on April 27, 1983, noting that public housing was "taken over by the court because of mismanagement and neglect," which was not unique to South Boston. At his announcement, "gesturing across West Broadway, Flynn pointed to a fire station that lost one of its companies and a police station that has been downgraded to a substation."[71]

In February 1975, Paul G. Garrity, chief judge of the Housing Court of the City of Boston, heard *Armando Perez et al. v. Boston Housing Authority*,[72] a class action suit brought by tenants living in apartments owned and operated by the Boston Housing Authority (BHA). Garrity ordered the BHA to present a plan of remedies, which he then found inadequate. Garrity judged that the BHA had essentially abandoned its low-income tenants. After several efforts failed, the court decided that the BHA could not carry out the essential functions of a public housing authority, including financial planning, housing maintenance, and systematically filling vacancies. Garrity ordered the receivership in February 1980 and appointed Lewis "Harry" Spence as the receiver.[73]

The BHA was founded in 1935 to administer the local response to the Housing Acts of 1934, 1937, and 1949. BHA tenants faced unsafe and unsanitary living conditions, leading to the 1980 receivership. They were looking to the new mayor for action. The BHA was home to approximately 10 percent of the city's population.

Immediately upon taking office, Flynn faced the integration of the Bunker Hill housing development in Charlestown, resulting from several Black families reaching the top of the long waiting list. When tenants learned of the planned move-in of several Black families, a community meeting was organized, and Flynn called upon the CDU's director, Sergeant Mickey Roache for a plan. Roache put together a public safety and media plan for the mayor, who then convened a meeting in Charlestown at the housing development.

"It will take some meetings with you and some other key people to convince the media that these are five ordinary families moving into a better housing situation; that is all it was," Roache told Flynn. "They were eligible. That is the key."[74] Frank Costello, Flynn's press secretary, met with journalists at major news outlets to urge them not to sensationalize the matter and to show sensitivity to the new families moving in and the rest of the neighborhood.[75]

Frank Jones, head of the Boston Committee—a group created by Mayor White to focus on race issues in the city—attended a community meeting with tenant leaders and Father Jim Conway, pastor at the local parish. At the meeting, the police department superintendent stood up and said, "Hey, listen, I talked to my detectives, OK, and they said there is no way Blacks are going to move in here because if they do, they are going to be mowed down with machine guns on the street."[76] Flynn would not accept this. He convened multiple small meetings with the tenant, community, and religious leaders to explain the plan and enlist their support. "The low-key planning was crucial to this," Flynn said then. "It shows to me there is no problem too difficult to resolve. Change has to begin somewhere, and the first step is always the most difficult, given the city's tragic history. The broader issue is that people are coming together with a positive, potent message. The people in Charlestown are pleased to be involved in this part of Boston's history. It's not perfect and has a long way to go, but it is encouraging."[77]

The move went smoothly, but the controversy about integrating public housing in Boston would continue. In 1984, the everyday life of the Bunker Hill project, virtually all White and Irish Catholic for forty years, changed, and that change simultaneously brought both continuing dissension and progress.

In October 1984, Judge Garrity held a hearing on the mayor's request to return control of the housing authority's management to the city administration. Before receivership, the BHA was governed by a five-member board, with four appointees made by the mayor and one by the governor. Flynn had proposed that the city would assume direct management of the BHA and the mayor would appoint an advisory committee, including housing experts and a tenant representative. At the hearing on October 18, 1984, at which Garrity was considering the request of the city to end the court receivership of the BHA, Garrity expressed concern because Flynn was expected to appoint as administrator Doris Bunte, an African American state representative from Boston. Bunte had previously been a member of the BHA board and had been fired by Mayor Kevin White for failing to comply with his wishes.[78] As Flynn requested, Judge Garrity returned control of the housing authority to the city in October 1984 when he found the receivership successful enough to end it. Flynn appointed

Bunte as administrator, the first housing authority director in the United States who raised a family in public housing.

Commenting on the appointment of Bunte—a public housing tenant—a *Boston Globe* editorial opined, "The selection of Bunte is one of great boldness."[79] At her announcement ceremony, Bunte identified three priorities for the BHA: maintenance, maintenance, and maintenance. She also made steady progress building on the efforts of Spence, the receiver, in stabilizing public housing, home to the city's poorest population. Following his established practices, Flynn appointed longtime aide Larry Dwyer as his liaison to work alongside Bunte to assist her in turning the housing authority around and rehabilitating the estimated four thousand vacancies in developments across the city.

In the fall of 1987, as Flynn was in the final week of his first campaign for reelection against city councilor Joseph Tierney, the US Department of Housing and Urban Development (HUD) issued a report on racial discrimination in assigning minority tenants in two South Boston housing developments. It was about to withhold critical federal funds. The report criticized the city's efforts to integrate the all-White Mary Ellen Mc-Cormack and Old Colony public housing developments in South Boston, "for failing to exercise an option in the agency's tenant selection process that allows them to give preference to people of color on the waiting lists for Charlestown and South Boston at any time."[80] In an interview with the Quincy *Patriot Ledger* a week before the election, Flynn announced his intention to integrate the South Boston housing developments. The next day, the *Boston Globe* reported, "Flynn pledged to move black tenants into the South Boston projects even if he encountered political opposition in the neighborhood where he makes his home. When asked how he would handle possible disruptions caused by black families moving into predominantly white projects in South Boston, where the city met with much resistance during school desegregation, Flynn responded, 'Well, I will do what I did in Charlestown. I'll appeal to the good people of South Boston.'"[81]

He chose the *Patriot Ledger* to leak the story because he knew it was the primary news vehicle for South Boston residents, who had long abandoned the *Boston Globe* because of its support for court-ordered busing and how they felt treated by the *Globe* in 1974. Following a *Globe* column on June 16, 2009, in which columnist Adrian Walker wrote, "Flynn announced his housing project integration plan in the *Patriot Ledger* of Quincy as if he wanted to hide it from his constituents,"[82] Flynn responded in a June 20, 2009, letter to the editor: "Nothing could be further from the truth. I announced that I would integrate public housing in South Boston days before the final election in the 1987 mayor's race. I stood before my friends and neighbors and stated my intentions because I did not want to come to them with the plan after the election. I said that public housing integration was required by law and that it was morally the right thing to do. This very public announcement cost me the vote in my neighborhood, and it made the peaceful integration of South Boston public housing possible."[83]

Flynn defeated challenger Tierney resoundingly on November 3, 1987, with 67.23 percent of the vote, garnering more than 90 percent of the vote in the Black community. (Flynn received 70.6 percent of the total vote in the September 22 preliminary.) It was the highest ever in the city, besting John Hynes's 66.9 percent victory over James Michael Curley in 1951; in 2001, Menino received 76 percent of the vote in the final election. Flynn lost South Boston's two wards by about four hundred votes out of ten thousand cast. Neighbors reacted to the election: "He was not responsible for forced busing, and we are just getting over that, but he is to blame for this forced housing and all the problems that will start all over again," said a forty-two-year-old plumber. A thirty-one-year-old woman who lived in the West Broadway housing project said, "'As long as they do not move me out, I do not care who they move in next to me.' She voted for Flynn without reservation."[84] Flynn reflected on the situation during an interview, comparing the integration of public housing with the desegregation of the schools:

> Well, it was two different things. Housing integration was more difficult in many respects because people were expecting the worst. I was warned—[federal court] Judge Joe Tauro and I talked about this—and Judge Tauro said, "This is going to be hell; Boston is going to turn into an inferno." And I said, "No it's not, because we're in control. Who do you think I have working in these neighborhoods? Who do you think is somebody who doesn't know these people? They are them." I had these people working in the neighborhoods like you and all these other people; what the hell were you there for? You knew everybody, and you had credibility, trust, and confidence. You were there because you had a track record of credibility established with the people. They trusted you, and that's what it was all about. We had trusted people in all the neighborhoods, and they knew that city hall wouldn't screw them because that's not who we were.[85]

Police Commissioner Mickey Roache said, "Integration was one of Mayor Flynn's greatest achievements."[86] Sargent Bill Johnston, head of the CDU, commented, "Race has become the overriding issue with the mayor and the police department. Not just in the BHA but all over the city."[87] However, not everyone agreed. "Housing segregation was also a problem; public housing segregation was deliberate," Judith Kurland, appointed by Flynn to head Boston City Hospital, observed:

Ray Flynn had plans about housing. He came from South Boston, which strongly links public housing and political leadership. If you look at the city's leadership, especially the leadership that came out of South Boston, many of those people came out of public housing. The ability of families in South Boston to stay in public housing for generations made for a different kind of culture about public housing. Much like a European model, a different type of support for public housing is a good one. The culture and the political support for public housing were extraordinary, and Ray Flynn became part of that. However, I always look at people with phenomenal political capital, where they used it, and where they will expend it. He had phenomenal political capital; look at how easily he got reelected. He did not use it around issues of race; he gets and takes much credit for the desegregation of the South Boston housing projects. Nevertheless, I know what the HUD regional office told him; he had to do it. He is saying to wait until after the election. That isn't leadership; that is accommodation for something that would happen.[88]

Flynn challenged Kurland's account:

No one believed for one minute that we would not level with them, be honest, and do what was in their best interest. Now, they may disagree with us, and as I said to the people before the housing integration, I wanted to let you know you may disagree with us. You like this town, and you like the way things are going. You don't want any change, and you don't want any uncertainty in your life. I understand that. I perfectly agree with you, and I'm just telling you this. I have a different decision to make. I have a law; I'm facing the law. And I have to do what is morally right. I have the law and my conscience and can't ignore either. Now I can do what they did in busing, ignore the law, and ignore what is morally right, and say, "That asshole judge, it's all his fault." But that's not what we chose to do; that would've been the easiest thing. Then I went over to St. Monica's, I gave myself a death wish and told them what I would do, and I had every politician in town knocking the hell out of me. I knew I would lose South Boston; I may lose half the city. Nonetheless, how could I possibly integrate public housing without telling these people before the election? What was I going to do? Say, "Vote for me because I'm your neighbor and friend. Do you remember me playing Little League? I used to coach your kid, and we were all buddies here." And then say to them after the election, "Oh, thanks very much for that overwhelming vote. I got 89 percent of the vote here; I won every single ward and precinct in Boston, as I did in the previous election, but now I have something to tell you. I perhaps should have told you yesterday, but I wanted you to vote first. And what I want to tell you is we're integrating housing." Then there would have been trouble for all the right reasons. They would have said, "You lying son-of-a-bitch."[89]

The St. Monica's meeting took a toll on Flynn. He recalls leaving the meeting, going to the pizza shop across the street, and watching his neighbors file out of the church. He knew they thought he had let them down, but he had to do the right thing, the moral thing. In tears, he left the pizza parlor without eating.

Following the meeting before the November 4, 1997, election, supporters of his opponent, Joseph Tierney, were spreading misinformation on the implications of the integration plan. Rumors were circulating that White tenants would be moved out of the developments to make way for Black tenants. Flynn was upset by the misinformation and dispatched Dwyer from South Boston to meet with the tenants. Dwyer challenged the disinformation effort. "Unfortunately, misinformation is out there, calling this forced housing," he said. "It is nothing of the sort. It has been upsetting to some residents." Dwyer and BHA officials explained the future policy to the tenants. "We have told them they will not be moved out of their units. Some people are trying to strike fear in their neighbors, and we will not allow it to happen. We will not allow the residents to be used as political pawns."[90]

While Flynn went on to lose Wards Six and Seven in the election in his home neighborhood while winning the other twenty wards citywide, his neighbors had rejected his plan to integrate public housing, but he said if he did it over again, he would do the same thing. Commenting on Flynn's action, Joyce Ferriabough asserted, "The mayor did the right thing. If he is not about assuring the constitutional rights of all citizens, he is in the wrong job."[91]

The BHA developed plans to integrate public housing in South Boston in response to the HUD report in October 1987. While initially the BHA administrator Doris Bunte, appointed in 1984, and Flynn criticized the HUD report as based upon old information, on November 18, 1987, HUD accepted BHA's voluntary compliance plan and proceeded with the integration of both the Mary Ellen McCormack and Old Colony housing developments in South Boston. Dwyer said that the previous mayor and BHA "were guilty as hell" in avoiding integration. "Our bottom line, now, when people come to the top of the list, they go where they go."[92]

Community meetings were held, and Police Commissioner Roache and the Community Disorders Unit drew up a public safety plan as was done two years earlier for the Bunker Hill housing development in Charlestown. Dwyer recalled the very low-key outreach he and other community leaders made in the neighborhood, saying, "We met with tenants and even reached out to Whitey Bulger's gang to let them know that if they jeopardized the plan, we would be back in school desegregation days with 350 federal marshals patrolling the streets. That wouldn't be good for anyone, they were told."[93] BHA administrator Bunte said she expected that "Black families will begin reaching the top of the waiting list for the two projects early next year."[94]

The NAACP, led by the Lawyers Committee for Civil Rights, filed a lawsuit against the BHA and HUD despite the BHA's agreement to proceed with the integration plan to which HUD agreed. The NAACP lawsuit over denying minorities the right to housing in the White developments when they came to the top of the list set up a conflict between the parties. Bunte tried, unsuccessfully, to convince the Lawyers Committee to drop the suit and join their efforts to implement the BHA-HUD plan. Bunte said, "The suit is unnecessary and the timing unfortunate because the city has already agreed to take remedial action."[95] The Lawyers Committee for Civil Rights refused. "Doris Bunte and other tenant activists, while not arguing with the philosophical idea of integration, fear that the self-righteous attention given the issue will obscure the more mundane and complicated task of removing the stigma from public developments by making them all equally decent places to live." Bunte emphasized saying, 'My priorities are maintenance, maintenance, maintenance.'"[96]

Hubie Jones, said, "You now have a housing authority, in a wholly different position than before receivership, that is being managed in a way to make sure that facilities are maintained, that tenants are listened to, and that renovations are going on. South Boston and integration is an aberration that has got to be dealt with, and it will be, but it cannot be seen as a direct analog to what previously existed."[97]

While the integration implementation proceeded, several events further highlighted the racial conflict engendered by the plan in South Boston. Flynn had announced at the above-mentioned St. Monica's meeting his intent to proceed with the integration. In the intervening period, a group of religious leaders—the Combined Religious Community of twenty clergy—organized the South Boston Prayer Service for Racial Harmony in May 1988. City councilor James Kelly of South Boston, an ardent foe of the integration plan, wrote to Cardinal Bernard Law asking him to move or cancel the prayer service scheduled for St. Monica's Church in South Boston. "Publicity surrounding this service has, unfortunately, focused on its location in a way which could lead to the erroneous impression that racial discrimination is a problem of geography, which it is not," he wrote. The cardinal declined to cancel or move the service. "Racial discrimination is a problem of the human heart," he said.[98] Also rejecting his call to cancel the ecumenical worship service was the St. Monica's pastor, Rev. Alfred Puccini.

The prayer service held on May 22, 1988, was attended by over six hundred people from South Boston and across the city, led by Catholic, Baptist, and Muslim clergy. Commenting on the prayer service, Rev. Charles Stith, pastor of the Union Methodist Church and an influential Black leader, said it "represented a statement that a profound spirit is sweeping the city. People are prepared to have the city characterized differently." "Everyone knows that we cannot let the past happen again," city councilor Rosaria Salerno said. "People are ready to set a different tone. So we have already taken the sting out of what happened ten years ago."[99]

Flynn, who attended the service, was in the same church where he was baptized and had informed his neighbors less than a year earlier that the housing developments would be integrated. Although Flynn was jeered by some of the reportedly hundred people who gathered outside St. Monica's to object to the integration plan, one sixty-year-old resident of the Old Colony development said, "This has always been a white town, and it should stay that way."[100] Flynn went on to praise the service. "There is a real feeling of coming together, of unity in the city," he said. "Today was one of the most important days in the history of Boston. People were not there because they had to be there but because they wanted to be there."[101] Flynn later said, "I knew that the media would bring out the worst of the neighborhood from a small number of residents' points of view."[102]

"I believe today's service to be a watershed moment for this city to end racial stereotyping and a beginning for racial harmony," said Bishop John Borders III, pastor of the Morningstar Baptist Church in Mattapan. Minister Don Muhammad of the Nation of Islam in Roxbury ended the worship service, urging those in attendance to carry the message of peace and nonviolence into their daily lives. "The issue is not [B]lack or white," he said, "but whether you are wrong or right."[103]

The integration mainly proceeded peacefully. There were some incidents, however, and as the CDU reported, many of these were connected to racially motivated hate crimes. The NAACP and the BHA had reached agreement in August 1988, with Dwyer saying, "We have virtually settled every major issue in the suit." NAACP lawyer Barbara R. Arnwine added, "I think it's fair to say the agreement is much fairer now as it stands."[104] The case finally ended on October 4, 1989, with a consent decree approved by Federal District Court Judge Joseph Tauro, who wrote in his decision memorandum, "I want to close these remarks by making clear my firm feeling that the tone which made possible the substantive and symbolic achievement we recognize today had to come from the top. Dr. Benjamin Hooks, the executive director of NAACP, and Ray Flynn, the mayor of Boston, provided the patience and guidance that enabled those on the front lines of negotiation to hammer out and finalize this consent decree. I commend Dr. Hooks and Mayor Flynn for their critically important leadership."[105]

Doris Bunte, who led the BHA from 1984 when the authority came out of receivership, left her position in 1992. Bunte received wide praise for improving maintenance and reducing the number of vacant units. Flynn appointed David Cortiella as her successor to oversee the progress of integration and the increase in the number of livable units in the housing developments. "Cortiella was forced to resign in 1994, primarily because of poor conditions in the elderly developments," the *Boston Globe* reported. Cortiella was the administration's highest-ranking Latino and a Flynn holdover, and Latino activists widely criticized his departure.[106] Menino, who appointed several people to the post after Cortiella, including Joe Feaster as acting head and Sandra Enriquez—named administrator in 1996 after a long search—finally landed on Bill McGonagle in 2009. McGonagle served as executive assistant to Bunte and deputy administrator under Cortiella and Enriquez. He grew up in the Mary Ellen McCormack housing development in South Boston, and many credit his leadership at the BHA as an essential ingredient of the successful integration of the housing developments. In 1994, with a surge in public safety concerns in BHA developments, the Boston police and the municipal police merged forces, going from twenty-one to eighty-seven public safety officers, according to McGonagle. "It would give the BHA enough bodies to make a real impact upon drugs and crime," he said.[107] The *Boston Globe* editorialized in 1995 about McGonagle, "Throughout the desegregation efforts in South Boston and Charlestown, McGonagle urged calm, deflected the misinformation campaigns of local racists, accompanied incoming minority tenants to their units, and stayed with them to ensure their comfort and safety," the paper wrote. "He faced threats from reactionaries, who are suspected of spraying his car with bullets outside his home. Due largely to his efforts, the McCormack project is 37% minority today."[108]

McGonagle, who retired after forty years at the BHA, first starting as a custodian and rising to administrator, would reflect on his tenure. "It was always the small moments that showed me that change was possible," he said. "It was a hot summer day, and the children in the development—Black and White, maybe five or six years old—were playing together in a kiddie pool in the courtyard," remembering the divisive early days of integration at Old Colony in Southie. "It was clear to me that those kids were going to grow up together, and at the end of the day, they would be neighbors and friends."[109]

Minister Don Muhammad of the Nation of Islam offered, "The mayor is to be commended for the continued integration of housing projects in South Boston and for increasing the number of people of color on the city's payroll. I think blacks are walking in South Boston now because some efforts were made to get people into housing there."[110]

# 10 / "Death at an Early Age": Public Education Debates

*I took Jonathan Kozol's seminar at Yale, which discussed what was happening in the Boston Public Schools. We would listen to recordings of what was said about Black kids enrolled in the Boston Public Schools. There were, at that time, elected school committee members who would, in a public meeting, call all the Black kids monkeys and describe them in the most disparaging of terms. Those resource allocation disparities were not accidental.* (Ted Landsmark, director of Safe Neighborhoods, interview)

## Public Education in Boston

Public education in Boston has long been a contested undertaking. The city is the birthplace of public education in America—home to the first public school, the Boston Latin School (1635); the first public elementary school, the Mather School (1639); the first public high school, English High School (1821); and Horace Mann School for the Deaf & Hard of Hearing, the first public day school for deaf students (1869). Like all of Boston, the school system was governed initially by the Brahmin elites and later by the Irish newcomers. Boston's first school committee originated in October 1789. The committee consisted of twenty-one members elected annually: nine selectmen plus members who would represent each of the city's twelve wards. Since 1909, the school committee has consisted of five at-large members until the change to district representation in 1983, as outlined earlier.

This chapter explores race, segregation, public school governance, and performance issues. It discusses school desegregation efforts and the lingering aftermath of the 1974 court-ordered desegregation of public schools. Every person interviewed as part of this study—really anyone alive in the city during the busing crisis of the mid-1970s—has an opinion about or laments the negative impact the period has had on Boston, its schools, neighborhoods, and reputation fifty years later.

Beginning in the middle of the twentieth century—soon after the Supreme Court outlawed school segregation in *Brown v. Board of Education* in 1954—scholars and journalists began paying much attention to public education, particularly racial segregation issues. Their books and studies focused primarily on equality, including the racial achievement gap, test scores, the impacts of segregation, violence, school dropout rates, college access, enrollment, school funding, and graduation rates.[1]

A particularly widely reviewed study was commissioned by the National Center for Educational Statistics to study educational equality in the United States. It was one of the most extensive studies in history, with more than 650,000 students in the sample. The 1966 study was a massive report of over seven hundred pages titled *Equality of Educational Opportunity* (otherwise known as the Coleman Report), which fueled debates about "school effects."[2] The report is commonly presented as evidence that family background is determinant and school funding has a negligible effect on student achievement. They are among the report's key findings and subsequent research, although many of Coleman's conclusions are widely disputed.

When educational researchers have written about urban education, the dominant discourse from the mid-twentieth and twenty-first centuries has been about inequality of opportunity and disparities in achievement based on race, class, and ethnicity, and the extent to which variations in school funding and neighborhood conditions compound these inequalities. These have become central issues in discussing schools' missions and how they serve the public.[3] This discourse complements the earlier notions that cities are disorganized and problematic places that need schools to prepare the next generation's workforce, assimilate immigrants into the mainstream culture, and provide opportunities for Americans to escape poverty through education.[4]

The rise of the various urban and educational schools of thought has generally followed such events as periods of industrialization and immigration; the political activism that emerged in the 1960s; the economic decline of cities, the urban budgetary crisis, and postmodernity; and the economic transformation of urban areas, which today centers on issues of race and class.[5]

The Progressive Era reformers of the late 1880s to the early 1900s pushed for significant changes in the management of Boston schools. The reform era was a movement toward centralization and professionalism, as well as expansion of the high school, creation of the kindergarten, and replacement of the decentralized, patronage-based school boards.[6] Boston schools followed the historical centralization/decentralization path that other districts experienced from the Progressive Era until the 1960s.

Repeated attempts were made to remove all control of school governance from Boston's electorate to take politics out of public education; proposals emerged in 1944 and 1970 to abolish the elected school committee.[7] Not until 1991—following two decades of debate over school performance characterized by charges of a failing system as well as governance controversies—did Flynn propose and the Boston City Council, state legislature, and a Republican governor approve a home rule petition for the appointment of school committee members by the mayor. Minority elected officials opposed the proposal, but the governor ultimately signed it. The governance change required a referendum after five years, which in 1996 was overwhelmingly approved by Boston's voters.[8] The discourse on race and power that emerged during the implementation of the mayor-appointed school committee and has continued since is explored in this chapter. Boston's Black political leadership contested the governance change, though Black ministers and the leadership of the White business community broadly supported it. This controversy over school governance is an essential window into local politics since Boston was a city that had undergone the racial and political turmoil associated with school desegregation in the 1970s.

## Busing in Boston

The desegregation of America's public schools remains a contentious and unfulfilled social endeavor. The use of busing to achieve that goal— which took root in the 1960s and 1970s—has been particularly controversial, particularly in northern and midwestern cities.

The dominant ideas of the school desegregation movement took shape first in response to the Supreme Court decision in *Plessy v. Ferguson* (1896),[9] which held that "separate but equal" facilities (in this case, railroad passenger accommodations) met the constitutional test of the equal protection clause of the US Constitution. *Plessy*, therefore, reinforced the long-standing practice of maintaining segregated educational facilities, although several jurisdictions had long abandoned the practice.

Not until the US Supreme Court decision in *Brown v. Board of Education of Topeka, Kansas*—when on May 17, 1954, Chief Justice Earl Warren issued the conclusion of the unanimous court—were racially segregated schools outlawed. "We conclude that in public education, the doctrine of 'separate but equal' has no place," the court said. "Separate educational facilities are inherently unequal. Therefore, we hold that the plaintiffs and others similarly situated for whom the actions have been brought are, by reason of the segregation complained of, deprived of the equal protection of the laws guaranteed by the Fourteenth Amendment."[10]

While de jure segregation "in the field of public education" was out-lawed in 1954, the court did not prescribe a remedy to transform the education system in more than twenty states where educational segregation was allowed. Following *Brown* a year later, the court was concerned that there was no progress in dismantling segregated schools. In 1955, in what is known as *Brown II*,[11] the court further elaborated on its ruling, requiring desegregation to proceed with "all deliberate speed." *Brown v. Board of Education* did not overturn *Plessy*, and in other societal domains, segregation continued. For more than a decade, school boards resisted desegregation. Not until President Lyndon Johnson signed the Civil Rights Act of 1964 into law on July 2, 1964, was the separate-but-equal doctrine of *Plessy v. Ferguson* overturned.

The Civil Rights Act paved the way for more aggressive federal intervention to implement its and *Brown's* provisions. In 1971, in the case of *Swann v. Charlotte-Mecklenburg Board of Education*,[12] the Supreme Court ruled that busing was an allowable tool to achieve desegregation if it did not endanger the health or safety of children or significantly influence the educational process. Thus, the busing era was born by providing federal district courts with one legal framework to achieve desegregation.[13]

Like other large metropolitan areas, Boston underwent a dramatic demographic shift following World War II, fueled by the rapid migration of African Americans from the rural South to northern and midwestern cities, the Great Migration. The US Commission on Civil Rights found that "Boston's Black population increased substantially between 1960 and 1970. Their numbers rose from 63,165 to 104,707. The Black population increased by 65.8 percent when Boston's total population declined by 8.1 percent."[14] Black migration, coupled with federal highway and housing policies that facilitated White flight and suburbanization, led to increasing housing and school segregation. In April 1965, Massachusetts state commissioner of education Owen Kiernan issued a report on racial imbalance in Massachusetts to address the issue. Known as the Kiernan Commission, the authors of the report "Because It Is Right Educationally" identified fifty-five racially imbalanced schools in the state, forty-five of which were in Boston.[15] The outcome of the commission's findings was that on August 18, 1965, the Massachusetts legislature adopted the Massachusetts Racial Imbalance Act, making Massachusetts the first state to pass such a law. The historic law defined racial imbalance as a school with more than 50 percent non-White students. The state required the Boston School Committee to address the imbalance in its school system without prescribing specific methodologies.[16]

The Boston school district had been plagued by inequalities between White and Black segregated schools, described by Jonathan Kozol in his

1967 book *Death at an Early Age*, in which he chronicled the plight of students attending a segregated and overcrowded ghetto school in the Roxbury neighborhood.[17] As a teacher later fired for reading students a passage from a poem by Langston Hughes, Kozol experienced firsthand the injustice of segregated education in Boston.

Minority parents, to little avail, have long sought remedies from the all-White Boston School Committee. They'd marched on the school committee and city hall to fight desegregation,[18] and later a "Stay Out for Freedom" day saw more than eight thousand students walk out of school and attend Freedom Workshops.[19]

So when the state passed the Racial Imbalance Act in 1965, many liberal reformers thought change was in sight. The all-White school committee both resisted and ignored the state law. The leaders of Boston's Black community were not prepared to wait any longer for action from the school committee, and in June 1963, three thousand Black students boycotted the schools.[20] Boston's de facto segregation and the unwillingness of political leaders to address it led the NAACP to file suit on March 15, 1972, on behalf of fifteen Black parents and forty-three children. The case came to be known as *Morgan v. Hennigan*.[21]

After hearing the case for more than two years, the storm erupted on June 21, 1974, when Federal District Court Judge W. Arthur Garrity Jr. issued his ruling concluding that the Boston School Committee and the school department *"had knowingly carried out a systematic program of segregation affecting all of the city's students, teachers and school facilities, and had intentionally brought about or maintained a dual school system."*[22] The ruling would require, in Phase I, that students from two of Boston's poorest neighborhoods, White South Boston and Black Roxbury, be bused to schools across town. Michael Patrick MacDonald, author of *All Souls* and a South Boston resident who grew up in the impoverished Lower End, recalled, "There could have been many things done. Still, it is bizarre, to say the least, that in the first year of busing in Boston in 1974, Phase I of the plan was only to involve Roxbury, the poor Black neighborhood of Boston, and South Boston, a neighborhood that we later found out held the highest concentration of White poverty in America. So pitting those two neighborhoods against each other was a terrible idea, and of course, violence broke out, and the riots in South Boston would happen at the end of my street, something that excited the kids in the neighborhood."[23]

Busing in Boston and nationally followed the civil rights era when blatant patterns of racism and inequality were becoming more apparent. In Boston, increasing housing segregation, resulting from city and federal policies, and the rapid in-migration of African Americans and

Hispanics—coupled with what Judge Garrity found was intentional racial discrimination in assigning children to schools—created the perfect storm. Ruth Batson, Boston civil rights leader at the forefront of the organizing efforts for educational equity in the schools, said, "We were not pushing for desegregation because of the brotherhood-of-man concept. Where there were white students, that's where the money went. We felt if we moved our students to where they were spending the money, we would benefit. We certainly didn't think that just putting Black and White kids together meant that Black kids would improve."[24]

There is near-unanimous agreement that busing has harmed education in Boston. US Department of Justice official Martin Walsh, describing Boston's school desegregation ordeal, termed it, "an exorcism, following which the resolution of other stubborn civil rights problems became possible."[25]

At the time of Judge Garrity's decision, White was in his second term, having been reelected in 1971 with the overwhelming support of Boston's Black community. The final election was a rematch against his 1967 opponent, Louise Day Hicks, who had left the school committee and was elected a member of the Boston City Council. Flynn reflected on his experience during busing. "You had the politics, Mayor White—he did not know what to do," Flynn said. "His administration had no idea what to do. The business community was paralyzed, completely paralyzed. The Catholic Church did not know what to do; they made all the wrong statements at the wrong time to the wrong people. Cardinal Medeiros had no idea what this was all about. He comments, 'Catholic church schools will not be used as havens to people avoiding attending integrated schools.' That was never the issue; it was a real putdown to people. It was unnecessary and insensitive, and he did not have to say it, but he did. Then, in the appearance on City Hall Plaza, Ted Kennedy thought that he would go over there and speak to the anti-busing people. I was not there; they were not my people, just completely off the mark. I talked to Eddie Martin, a key Kennedy aide, and said, 'Eddie, what is this?' He said, 'Ray, a huge mistake.' It was the end of his presidential ambitions."[26]

Ira Jackson, White's chief of staff, recounted, "Kevin White was contemptuous of the scheme that Judge Garrity imposed, but did Kevin White ever once say, 'I won't enforce it'? No. Now, was he a profile in courage? No. And I don't recall any other elected officials being profiles in courage during busing. They all headed for the hills." Lyda Peters, a friend of Ruth Batson's, recalled her saying, "Not one politician, including the mayor of this city, ever said this is the right thing to do."[27]

Menino, a Hyde Park High School monitor during busing, recalled the impact of busing on Boston. "Boston was a city that was divided," he said. "It was a city in crisis. I was in the corridors of Hyde Park High during busing. I know what it was like. Kids were throwing rocks at priests. People stood in the middle of Cleary Square praying and saying the Rosary."[28]

Dennis Kearney remembers the busing period during which he was a state representative whose district included East Boston and Charlestown, two neighborhoods not impacted in Phase I of Garrity's order, as he makes clear.

> It was just Southie in '74, but Charlestown and Eastie were in '75, September of '75. When I took office in 1975 and all of '75, right through the reelection, the dominant issue was busing. That was everything. My focus was not on statewide or state matters. It was busing, and the problems spun off in my legislative district. East Boston and Charlestown were all White. The busing decree ripped at the fabric of the community and family that existed. Some people in Eastie never left Eastie and never came to Boston, and people from Charlestown were the same. You know their communities and schools; their connection was central to their identity. Then you have the government telling them, well, no longer, those schools that are such a connection to your community and your family are your schools. We are going to send you to other parts of the city, and we're going to bring kids from different parts of the city into your schools. My view of the world is that the busing order didn't recognize that connection and the degree to which it ripped that sense of neighborhood, and that was what offended, that is what people were reacting to, and then, of course, on top of that, it was a racial issue as well because they were being hit over the head and told you could no longer go to your local school. All those neighborhood community-oriented institutions and family connections that are important to you do not matter anymore.[29]

The institutions of family, church, and school are essential to Bostonians. It was not that White children in the city's schools were getting a good-quality education. "The South Boston High School was all White, Dorchester High School was nearly all Black, and Hyde Park High School was integrated," Larry DiCara argued. "In all three schools, facilities were horrible, and the children's ambitions were not much better. So, one thing I figured out early on in this fantasy world that poor White people lived in was that if you went to Charlestown High, Southie High, Eastie High, and all the kids were White, the educational environment you would find was absolute bullshit, and I figured that out early on, which is not what people wanted to hear, by the way."[30]

MacDonald agreed. "For the most part, the busing plan in the seventies put up more walls than Southie had ever had before and caused the dropout rate to surge," he said. "The percentage of kids from Southie High who went on to college was only 10 percent before busing. Busing was only taking poor people and sending them to each other's shitty schools."[31]

Left out of the equation in busing were many Asian and Latino students who faced similar concerns and threats because of busing and the attendant racism. As May Louie, a Chinatown resident and member of the Chinese Progressive Association, explained,

> In the Asian American and Latino communities, the kids were part of the busing because they were part of the mix of how to do the numbers, but they were not protected in the court order because the court order was Black and White. Thus, in '75, when busing hit the elementary school level, Chinese immigrant children were bused to South Boston, and their school buses were stoned. So, the kids were throwing up. I mean, these are the babies, right, and they don't speak English, they don't know what's going on, and so some of us who are English speakers help form a Chinese Parents Association. We worked with some immigrant parents and helped them articulate their demands to ensure their children would be safe. So the women quickly ceased sending their children into situations where they were emotionally traumatized and physically endangered. They organized a 90 percent–effective boycott of the schools to force attention to the issues. They won some of the demands, which included Chinese bilingual transitional aides and bilingual bus monitors.[32]

Clara Garcia, executive director of Inquilinos Boricuas en Acción (IBA)—a community development corporation started in the South End neighborhood of Boston in 1968 to address displacement of low-income families due to urban development—recalled that busing was not an issue initially for the families in Villa Victoria because the children attended mostly the local Blackstone Elementary School. In subsequent phases, Latino kids were bused to Charlestown, and they frequently experienced conflict with White teenagers. A big problem with the schools was that many of these kids were placed in Chapter 766 classrooms because they were English-language learners, although Chapter 766 was not designed for that purpose. She described the city's relationship with IBA: "I had a great relationship with Mayor Flynn. Whenever we needed him, he always made himself available."[33]

Many had questioned White's abandonment of two institutions serving the city's poor and people of color—public schools and public housing—wondering if this was not part of an actual strategy. The *Boston Globe* noted in its examination of White's four terms in office, "He was praised and pilloried for his role in busing. While some charge that he walked away from the problem, his staff points to the more than 250 'coffee klatches' he held with families around the city to ease tensions. The fact that he was beholden to a Federal judge for the operation of the city schools was, some suggest, his fault and his nemesis."[34]

As a state representative from South Boston, Flynn opposed busing like most of his neighborhood. He recalled the impact of the decision by the federal court. "After busing, the city never recovered, and the schools never recovered," he said. "The great economic ladder to climb out of poverty, people like us, was public schools. I am the only mayor of Boston who graduated from public schools. White didn't, Menino certainly did not, and I do not know where Hynes went; I think he went to BC High. You know, you never had the identification and association with schools by the mayor."[35]

As Menino wrote in his 2014 book, *Mayor for a New America*, "Busing was intended to end school segregation, but it promoted re-segregation with only a brief stop at integration. Schools that were 40 percent minority in 1979 were nearly 90 percent minority two decades later. The 1980 census revealed that a third of the White and Black families with children under eighteen had fled the city. Eight thousand fewer people lived in South Boston and thirteen thousand fewer in Roxbury. Support for Garrity's plan among [B]lacks had fallen to 14 percent. Busing left Boston's schools segregated by race and class."[36] The fight was necessary. As Ruth Batson summarized, "When we fight about education, we're fighting for our lives. We're fighting for what that education will give us; we're fighting for a job, we're fighting to eat, we're fighting to pay our medical bills, we're fighting for a lot of things. So, this is a total fight with us."[37]

The storied history of the Boston Public Schools would take a book, and one has been written: *Reforming Boston Schools, 1930–2006: Overcoming Corruption and Racial Segregation* by Joseph Cronin (2008). Cronin was the first Massachusetts secretary of education and observed the Boston schools for over forty years. Many still argue that the court decision paralyzed the school system for decades.

## Governance of the Boston Public Schools

Governance of the public schools in Boston (and nationally) has a contested history. During the Progressive Era (1880–1920), reformers were intent on taking the politics out of public education, and they pushed for changes in governance structures across America. In Boston, the effort led by the Brahmin and the elite business class sought to take school governance out of the hands of the Irish political machine led by Mayor James Michael Curley and other ethnic politicians. The school board was changed from a ward representation system to an at-large system of five school committee members, where it remained until the charter reform of 1981 was enacted. In 1984, the first year of the charter change, the school committee (and city council) each comprised thirteen members: four at-large representatives and nine district representatives. Many hoped this would provide greater responsiveness to parents and children and better reflect the diversity of the city's changing population.

When Flynn was elected mayor in 1983, so was a new school committee. The new committee replaced the five-member at-large committee and had four people of color from the thirteen-member body. In 1977, John D. O'Bryant became the first Black politician to serve on the Boston School Committee since 1900, and in 1981, Dr. Jean McGuire became the first Black woman elected to an at-large seat on the Boston School Committee.

When he entered the mayor's office, the school's school assignment plan was still in court-ordered receivership from the 1974 order. In the first week of his administration, Flynn visited several schools. In February 1984, he met with the State Board of Education, saying he was prepared to lead on education. "I hope to see public education returned to the city shortly," Flynn told the board. "We have to build up confidence that we are, in fact, serious about moving public education forward."[38]

"I think Ray Flynn's view was that the White administration had ducked some of the essential city services, education, and housing, some of the most important institutions and services a city provides," Nancy Snyder, Flynn's chief of staff, recalled. "Part of his statement in the first year was not only are we going to accept these things out of receivership, but we are also going to embrace them, we are going to lead them, we are going to make them better because that is what a city does, that is what a mayor does. You know you do not hide from complex challenges; you tackle them, and coming out of receivership, Flynn would accept responsibility for the schools."[39]

There needed to be an agreement in the administration on how much of a priority the issue should be and how much political capital to expend on the school department. "Why are you bothering with the schools?" Bob Consalvo remembers telling the mayor. "You could be a great mayor if you just left them alone and did all the other things that you were doing.

He said, 'Bobby, if I do not do something for those kids, I cannot live with myself.'"[40]

Snyder talked about Flynn's frustration with the progress in the public schools: "Flynn realized he had no power over the school issues and needed to do something about that. That is what drove the whole appointed school committee debate. He was incredibly frustrated around schools because he did not have the necessary leverage to make the changes he had to make if you were going to make progress around schools. He understood his restraints, having lived through the whole education problem. He believed that education was the key to transforming people's lives. In his view, the elected school committee and the superintendent were all about the school system for adults and not the school system for kids. He found that incredibly frustrating and had no political leverage."[41]

In 1989, Flynn appointed an eleven-member Advisory Committee on School Reform, chaired by Hubie Jones, the Boston University School of Social Work dean and a leading activist in the Black community. "Ray Flynn asked me to chair his school reform panel," Jones recalled. "I knew what the deal was. I agreed. The deal was that he wanted an appointed school committee. He had become upset with the elected school committee regarding what they were not doing. Okay, and so he got that. I took many hits in the Black community for taking democracy away, taking our vote away. For the folks of color on the school committee, this was leverage they had for whatever they wanted to do, so they had different power than the school committees under Hicks and that crowd, but that was still leverage. That was political currency. They were not doing their job. It was better to have the mayor, based on what we had with White, to have an engaged school committee, and a mayor engaged with the school committee and trying to get the schools to improve. It was going to be controlled by the mayor. Period!"[42]

Jones and the advisory committee released its report on May 1, 1989, proposing a seven-member school committee to be appointed by the mayor. In response to that report, Flynn said, "Whatever political capital is necessary to put on the line to do it, I will go out there, even if it is against initial popular opinion, to chart a new course. I am not a cautious guy. I have never been. I do not know the political consequences; I will give these kids, the school children of Boston, the best fight I can give them."[43]

"Any mayor who can bring some order to the schools and establish some standards is a candidate for canonization," DiCara commented. "The danger is great—off the charts. It's a crapshoot, and the city's future is on the line. If I were sitting there, I would take the risk."[44]

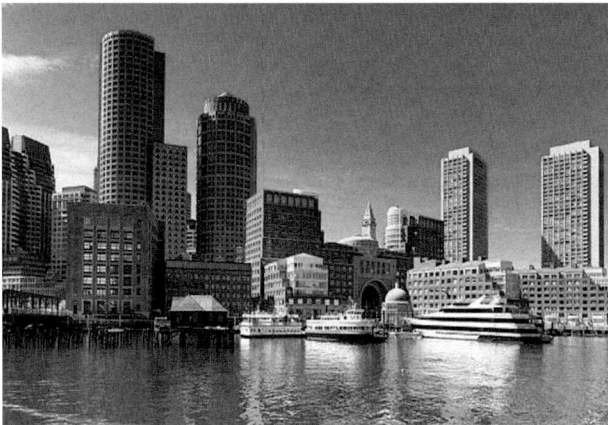

Urban renewal in the 1950s, 1960s, and mid-1970s bulldozed the multiethnic New York Streets and West End areas, making way for luxury housing and high-rise office development. In contrast, the city's public housing and neighborhoods faced disinvestment and abandonment.

"The Soiling of Old Glory" is a Pulitzer Prize–winning photograph by Stanley Forman taken April 5, 1976, the year of the United States Bicentennial. The photo depicts Joseph Rakes assaulting a Black man, lawyer, and civil rights activist, Ted Landsmark, with a flagpole bearing the American flag adjacent to City Hall plaza during the Boston busing crisis. Landsmark would later join the Flynn Administration as Director of the Safe Neighborhoods Campaign.

The proposed highway projects and urban renewal in Boston sparked tenant activism from the 1960s to the present, a testament to the power of grassroots movements. This activism led to the implementation of rent control in the 1970s, but Mayor Kevin White later dismantled the program. Mayor Ray Flynn's attempt to reinstate strong rent control in 1984 was met with opposition from the growth coalition–controlled city council, further highlighting the influence of local politics on urban development.

Boston's 1983 election night was pivotal in the city's history. With a record-breaking 70 percent of the electorate turning out, the highest since 1949, this critical election marked a significant shift in Boston's politics. Ray Flynn's resounding victory with 65 percent of the vote heralded a new era of progressive transformation in the city.

Mel and Joyce King celebrate preliminary election night in 1983 with their Rainbow Coalition, marking a virtual tie in the preliminary election with Ray Flynn. For the first time in Boston's history, an African American was in the final runoff for mayor. King would continue to work on issues important to the community, including the creation of the South End Technology Center at Tent City to assist communities of color in the development of sustainable technology, art, design, and media.

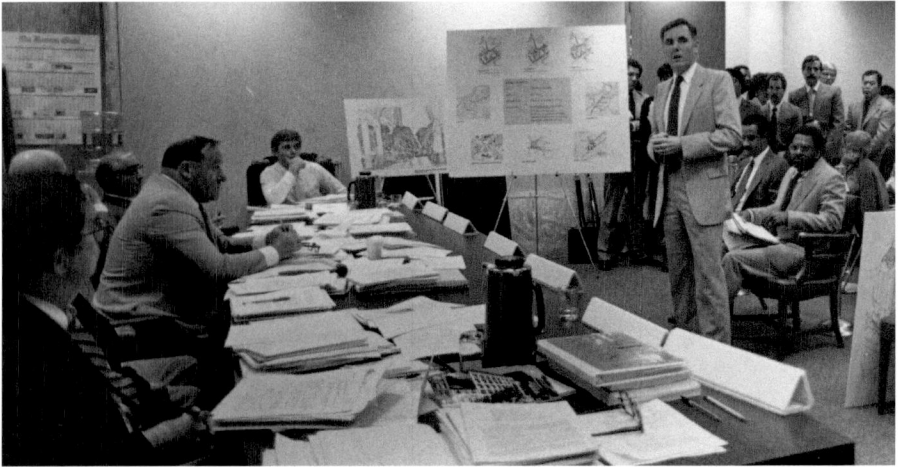

On September 25, 1986, Mayor Flynn introduced the groundbreaking Parcel 18 proposal to the BRA Board and its director, Stephen Coyle. This proposal, which linked a prime downtown parcel to one in the city's Roxbury neighborhood and mandated 30 percent minority equity participation, was a first in the city's history. The policy's pioneering nature continues to shape the city's development landscape.

Boston Mayor Ray Flynn and Police Commissioner Francis "Mickey" Roache meet with youth at the Boys and Girls Club of Boston. Commissioner Roache was a national leader in fighting racial violence, having created the first-in-the-nation Police Community Disorders Unit to identify and prosecute hate crimes, since replicated across the country.

Bill Clinton and Mayor Ray Flynn join supporters at the Erie Pub in Dorchester during the 1992 presidential campaign. Flynn campaigned for Clinton in twenty-two states and was later appointed ambassador to the Holy See (Vatican) in 1993. President Clinton said, "Mayor Flynn's administration made Boston better, fairer, and stronger."

Mayor Ray Flynn, Governor Michael Dukakis, school committee chair Paul Parks, and head of the Greater Boston Chamber of Commerce Fletcher "Flash" Wiley share a laugh at the city-owned Parkman House. When Flynn took office, the posh Beacon Hill building became a site for neighborhood leaders and residents to meet and discuss city policies, ending his predecessors' practice of exclusive private use.

Three mayors—Ray Flynn, Tom Menino, and Kevin White—meet at the city's famous political institution, Doyle's Cafe in Jamaica Plain. Doyle's closed in 2019 after 137 years in the gentrifying neighborhood of Jamaica Plain. (Photo courtesy of Tom O'Malley)

Michael Harrington, the visionary founder of Democratic Socialists of America (DSA) and the celebrated author of *The Other America*, was honored by Mayor Flynn, who declared October 28, 1988, as Michael Harrington Day in Boston—with DSA and Flynn administration members Tom Gallagher (left) and Peter Dreier (right) and the author (center).

Following his release from prison after 27 years on February 11, 1990, Nelson Mandela visited Boston on June 23, 1990, and spoke to over 250,000 people on the Esplanade. He visited Boston to acknowledge the early role the city and the state played in fighting apartheid. Flynn signed legislation in July 1984 divesting the city funds from banks doing business with South Africa. (Photo courtesy of Don West)

City councilor Rosemarie Sansone—who led Women for Flynn and, later, the city Office of Business and Cultural Affairs—greeted Philippines president Corazon Aquino along with Rev. Charles Stith, pastor of the Union United Methodist Church, and Ray Flynn during her visit to Boston in September 1986, where she had lived in exile before Ferdinand Marcos's dictatorship was toppled.

Chicago mayor Harold Washington and Flynn, two political powerhouses, worked hand in hand on progressive urban issues, including organizing mayors for a "fair federal budget." Their collaboration underscores the profound impact of collaboration in shaping urban policies.

Ray Flynn and his grandson Braeden, Mel King, his wife, Joyce, and Mayor Marty Walsh attended Mel's eighty-ninth birthday party on October 20, 2017. Braeden was born with a rare neurological disorder, and Flynn has been searching for a cure as part of his lifelong crusade for special needs children, first with state Chapter 766 and since through sports. Flynn built the city's first playground designed for children with disabilities at Columbus Park and then five similar playgrounds. (Photo courtesy of Bill Brett)

Homeless advocates Mitch Snyder, actor Martin Sheen, and US Conference of Mayors chair Ray Flynn joined forces to press the Reagan administration to fund programs to end homelessness. They successfully lobbied for the enactment of the Stewart B. McKinney Homeless Assistance Act (P. L. 100-77) of 1987, the first major federal legislation to address the welfare of America's homeless population and remains to this day the only such effort.

Billy Crystal and Robin Williams (with Whoopi Goldberg [not shown]) launched *Comic Relief* in 1986 and raised millions of dollars to fund homeless programs in Boston and nationwide. They were frequent visitors to the city's Long Island Shelter.

The unhoused tent encampment at Mass and Cass (Avenues) became a symbol of the failed national policies to address persistent homelessness and poverty.

The Dudley Street neighborhood faced disinvestment and neglect for years, with more than sixty acres used for illegal dumping. The neighborhood organized and took control of their land. Showing respect and confidence in the people in the community to solve problems, Flynn approved eminent domain power for the community land trust, which transformed vacant lots and abandoned buildings into affordable housing, community gardens, and green spaces. Dudley Street Neighborhood Initiative has become a national model for community empowerment and sustainable change.

Boston Celtics players Robert Parish and Larry Bird dropped in on Ray Flynn, a Providence College Academic All-American, following the Celtics' 1984 World Championship victory.

Ray Flynn, eighty-five, an all-star college basketball player and NCAA All-Time Honors Award winner, provides pointers to young people. Flynn believed that "sports is the answer" to addressing neighborhood conflict. He organized numerous sports competitions with professional athletes and neighborhood youth in local parks.

Flynn marched with Benjamin Briscoe, Lord Mayor of Dublin, in the 1993 St. Patrick's Day Parade, the last he would participate in as mayor. Boston and Ireland developed close economic and cultural connections under Flynn. Boston has the tenth-largest Irish population in the United States. In 1989 Flynn issued an executive order requiring Boston companies doing business with the city to adhere to the MacBride Principles, prohibiting discrimination in their Northern Ireland operations against workers because of their religious or political beliefs.

City councilor Ed Flynn, Lieutenant Governor Kim Driscoll, Governor Maura Healey, and Ray and Cathy Flynn at the 2024 St. Patrick's Day Parade, which drew attendees from around the world, including Ireland. They were among the estimated one-million-plus people at the parade in Southie. Healey, Driscoll, and Flynn were also known for their basketball prowess as college stars.

Pope John Paul II, with Ambassador Ray Flynn and President Bill Clinton, at the Vatican, where Flynn served as Ambassador from 1993 until 1997. Ambassador Flynn represented the President in heading up earthquake relief efforts in India and reviewing and reporting on humanitarian aid efforts in Uganda, Kenya, Sudan, Somalia, Haiti, and Bosnia. Ambassador Flynn was involved in peace efforts in Northern Ireland and was instrumental in securing an agreement to begin the formal process of establishing full diplomatic relations between Israel and the Vatican.

Mayor Ray Flynn and Mother Teresa in Boston in June 1988. She was canonized by Pope Francis, St. Teresa of Calcutta, on September 4, 2016. Flynn first met Mother Teresa while a graduate student at the Harvard Graduate School of Education in 1981. A photo of Mother Teresa adorned his city council office.

Ray Flynn was a marathoner, having completed the Boston Marathon, the world's oldest annual marathon, first run on April 19, 1897. The mayor is shown here with State Senator Joe Timilty and Boston Police Patrolmen's Association president Don Murray. Flynn rescued the Boston Marathon, working with corporate executives to increase the prize money for the marathon to attract world-class runners to compete in the race.

On August 11, 2016, Governor Charlie Baker signed the law renaming Boston's Black Falcon Terminal the Flynn Cruiseport Boston while his wife, Cathy, sons Ray and Eddie, and many of his seventeen grandchildren looked on. The city also renamed the adjacent industrial waterfront park Raymond Flynn Marine Park in 2016 to recognize his contributions to the maritime economy.

Boston's fifty-second mayor Ray Flynn with Michelle Wu, Boston's fifty-fifth. Flynn and Wu pursued similar progressive policies nearly forty years apart. They would reject the growth machine coalition and the racial politics of the past. Their social and economic justice agendas engaged community organizers, neighborhood leaders, and residents. (Photo courtesy of Bill Brett)

"A Black guy from the South End and a White guy from South Boston, Flynn and King bonded over basketball. They maintained a lifelong friendship despite being political rivals in one of the city's most storied elections in 1983," wrote Kevin Cullen of the Boston Globe. Flynn and King served in the state legislature together and continued to work as partners on education issues in the city for decades.

Boston's mayoral race in 2013, the first open race in twenty years after Mayor Tom Menino chose not to run for reelection, featured a field of fifteen candidates, eight of whom were people of color. The finalists were two White Irish Catholics, and labor leader Marty Walsh topped the field.

In the mayoral election of 2021, after Mayor Marty Walsh accepted President Joe Biden's appointment as US labor secretary, all five candidates were people of color. Michelle Wu was elected the first woman and person of color in the city's two-hundred-year history. Forty-six White men had led Boston since it was incorporated in 1822.

Flynn subsequently appointed a thirteen-member Special Commission on Public Education to evaluate the public schools' governance structure. He selected Professor James Jennings, dean of the UMass School of Community and Public Service and head of the Black Political Task Force. Jennings had credibility in the city and the Black community. As David Knowles, president of the Federation of Black Directors, said, "Any conclusion James Jennings comes to, I would trust personally."[45] The Special Commission heard testimony from more than 120 people who "were virtually unanimous in the dissatisfaction with the status quo and its call for change in the school committee structure."[46] The special commission recommended two options: the hybrid model with some members appointed and others elected, or the appointment of all members by the mayor. The mayor presented the options to the Boston City Council, which after much debate and rankling agreed to pursue the fully appointed option.

Flynn proposed a nonbinding referendum in the fall of 1990 to eliminate the elected school committee in favor of one appointed by the mayor from recommendations of a nominating panel. The effort was risky since a poll taken earlier that year by the Vault, Boston's growth machine, showed that 61 percent of the electorate disapproved of increased mayoral control of the schools. That led Flynn to create a political action committee, the Better Education Committee, and put his political field organization in motion. It was an uphill battle, with leaders in the minority community actively opposing his efforts. "The Black voting population in Boston is being asked to vote away their vote," Boston NAACP head Jack E. Robinson said about the referendum. "With Blacks and minorities fighting and dying all over the world for this precious right, Boston's Blacks are being sold a bill of goods. No one denies that Boston public schools and public education need drastic reforms. Still, however urgent the need, the quest, and possession of freedom to vote transcends all options of expediency."[47]

The *Boston Globe* initially editorialized against the appointed school committee, opining, "A century ago, when the Irish began to exert political power in Boston, the politically dominant Yankees, in alliance with business interests, tried to break that progress by transferring governmental power from City Hall to the State House. It is troubling that as the Black community edges toward political power, the now-dominant Irish, in alliance with business interests, would try to break that progress by withdrawing the right to vote for School Committee members. In rebuttal, Mayor Flynn and his supporters argue that the appointing power can be used to better represent the city's racial and ethnic cross-section on the committee. That argument would be more impressive if White males, mostly Irish, did not so dominate Flynn's inner circle. The mayor deserves the community's thanks for making the city's schools a central issue in this year's election. His proposal, however, is undemocratic and badly flawed. The Globe urges a 'no' vote on this referendum."[48]

With polling going into the vote showing the measure losing 70 percent to 30 percent, the intensive organizing strategy led by Harry Grill and Flynn's campaign organization managed to have the referendum prevail by a slight margin, 50.8 percent to 49.2 percent, a mere 636 votes. While it gave Flynn and his administration some pause, he went on to say, "The majority of people in Boston rejected the status quo and voted for fundamental change, for a concrete proposal." Asked whether he is claiming a mandate, Flynn said, "Majority vote, I never said a mandate." The referendum's tight margin showed apparent schisms in the city. It lost in the Black and White working-class neighborhoods while winning in the more middle-class White areas of the city. Of the 78,283 voters, 37 percent supported the mayoral-appointed committee, 36 percent were opposed, and 26 percent did not vote. It is not a mandate but a win. Flynn said the following day, "A win is a win, and we will take it any way we can. The people across this city can no longer support a school system that fails their children, and I think yesterday's vote proves that feeling."[49]

"It was the first thing that united Roxbury and South Boston in a long time; they both voted against it," DiCara noted. Following the referendum, Flynn considered abandoning the pursuit of reform, thinking, "People are not for this."[50] The next stop was the Boston City Council and the home rule petition, which Flynn promised to file within a month of the referendum, where passage was not assured.

Although Flynn temporarily abandoned his goal of pursuing changes to the school governance structure to win some reform victory in the face of widespread political opposition, Neil Sullivan proposed to Flynn a modified deal, with four members appointed by the mayor and three elected by reducing the nine districts to three. Sullivan described trying to close the deal with the opposition. "I was promoting a hybrid board proposal that the mayor would appoint four, and three would be elected. I got [school committee president] O'Bryant to agree to do it and Flynn to agree," he recalled. "I arranged a Sunday morning brunch at Doyle's. O'Bryant had suggested meeting there. He walked in with [school committee member] John Grady. Flynn just got up and said, 'It is off. I will make a deal with the Black patronage machine, but I will not make a deal with the White patronage one,' and then he walked out, telling O'Bryant that this was not the arranged meeting."[51]

School committee president O'Bryant was clear about his objections to a school committee appointed by the mayor, as he told city councilor Rosaria Salerno. Salerno, a supporter of the school governance change, recalled their conversation on the issue. "Mel King called me a traitor," she remembered. "I was taken to the cleaners by the communities of color. They discussed disenfranchisement but did not discuss whether this decision would make a better school department for our kids. They never brought up education quality. They spoke about disenfranchisement, but that was not honest. They were talking about the fact that they had four Black elected officials, and if we had an appointed school committee, we would not have four elected Black officials. John O'Bryant called me a racist because I was ready to support the appointed school committee. I explained to O'Bryant that they only had four out of thirteen now. Suppose you have four out of seven, a much better ratio. You are going to be much better off. He said, 'Yes, but they won't be all Black. We will have to have Hispanics and Asians as well. So, the Blacks will lose.' I thought, 'Now, isn't that interesting? I am the racist?'"[52]

Finally, Flynn's increasing frustration led him to file the home rule petition based upon the recommendations of the 1989 Jones and Jennings report, which was widely opposed by the Black elected leadership, the Boston Teachers Union, and many community activists. To the surprise of many, the city council supported Flynn's proposal following what Sullivan called the high school meltdown. "The school committee kept messing up in public," Sullivan said. "We had agreed to set up a commission to decide which high schools would be closed because there were four thousand vacant seats. The school committee voted that the commission would be allowed to choose. Then, on the eve of the commission report, which recommended the closing of Hyde Park High School [school committee members] Peggy Davis-Mullen leaked it to the *Herald* and blew it up. This blow-up reheated the school governance issue and moved the city council forward with a home rule petition to abolish the elected committee and replace it with one appointed by the mayor."[53]

Flynn had forged a coalition with the business community and the media (the *Boston Globe* endorsed the takeover in January 1991 after first opposing it during the 1989 referendum) to get the legislation passed by the city council. Not all members of his administration agreed to move forward with the takeover. Senior policy staff advising him on the issue were divided—one for totally elected, another for a hybrid model (elected and appointed), and yet another senior adviser wanted to maintain the elected body. Consalvo made clear his position on the appointed committee. "If he were not serious about it, he would not have proposed the appointed committee, which I thought was a mistake because then he would own the schools and could never fix them," he said. "It was like this giant battleship just set on automatic pilot, and you could not get into the inner sanctums of the education system of the school department to force any changes. Black leaders, and this is not negative, had control of the school system at the time; it was their system. They wanted it to be their system, and it was their system. They ran it. Any White person had very little say in what went on. You could not break into that at all. It is understandable because the White Irish had it for years, and you could not break into it. School committee member John O'Bryant said to the mayor, 'It is our turn now.' Flynn asked, 'Why can't we do better? Why are you doing this?' He said, 'It is our turn now, our turn to run the system.'"[54]

There was strong support for the mayoral takeover by the business community in Boston, which saw the dysfunction in the school department as an obstacle to students successfully entering the economy. Their role, along with higher education, led to the Boston Compact developed in 1981 by the Boston Private Industry Council, where businesses and universities pledged summer and full-time jobs upon graduation if the schools raised attendance and test scores and lowered dropout rates. Several hundred companies signed the compact. Twenty-five colleges and universities offered to increase the number of Boston public school graduates enrolling in postsecondary education by 25 percent over five years in exchange for more vigorous academic preparation by the schools. In the early 1980s, Boston's climate of business support for education moved from good to excellent.[55] While Flynn's relationship with the business community was often strained, he aggressively worked with companies to provide summer jobs to Boston youth. It was one of his principal requests of the business community and has remained so for subsequent mayors.

Sam Tyler, president of the Boston Municipal Research Bureau, quarterbacked the business community support for the appointed committee. "They had been trying between 1978 and 1991 to define the role of the school committee and the superintendent so that the school committee was just a policy body and not involved with operations," he said. "The result is that the superintendent in Boston is probably the most powerful in the country, statutorily. Still, in 1978, the head of the custodians, the director of the school facilities, and the business manager all reported directly to the school committee. The superintendent was the chief academic officer, not the chief executive officer. We continued our efforts to strengthen the role of the superintendent as the chief executive officer and further define and limit the school committee's role. Finally, we supported the bill that authorized the appointment of school committee members, passed in 1991, and took effect in January 1992. Why did we get involved? It was just part of the culture of the business community in Boston to be engaged in support of public education."[56]

The home rule petition to replace the elected school committee with a seven-member board appointed by the mayor was approved by the city council, 10-3. Then all hell broke loose. The city council approved the plan, and Mel King criticized the council for supporting the appointed board, slamming city councilors for "knuckling under." He saved his harshest criticism for council members David Scondras and Rosaria Salerno, two of the progressive members of the body, saying, "If they roll over on this basis, we don't need them."[57]

Flynn's next challenge was getting the legislature to pass and Republican governor William Weld to sign the home rule measure. The legislature only sometimes supported one of its former colleagues, Ray Flynn. The Black Legislative Caucus was set on killing the home rule petition. "I had a district; it was two-thirds African American and Latino. All these folks were part of my team, totally opposed to an appointed school committee," said one progressive White legislator, John McDonough. "I could not defend the elected school committee. It was a thoroughly politicized body focused on its electoral self-protection and jobs. So I sided with Flynn. One night while at home, I heard some noise outside on my street in Jamaica Plain, and there was a caravan of cars; they were beeping horns and turning their lights on and off directly in front of my house. Part of the school committee member Gerald Anderson's political organization was picketing my house. So, little progress was possible when they were in the way. Many said, 'You are disempowering the community; you are disempowering the one place where folks of color owned power.' I said, 'Yeah, but to me, it is not about them but the kids.'"[58]

In addition to the support of the Republican business community leaders, an essential part of the coalition was the support of the *Bay State Banner*, Boston's newspaper of the Black community, and the Interfaith Ministerial Alliance, which represented twenty churches with over twenty thousand members. Nation of Islam leader Minister Don Muhammad led a State House press conference by the Black ministers in support of the legislation, and the following day, the Senate approved the measure. "The Republican switch was due to a weekly newspaper serving minority neighborhoods and an organization of minority religious leaders that called for the abolition of the elected school board just hours before the senate convened," said Senate president Tom Birmingham, the bill's sponsor. "There had been a suggestion that the Black community was monolithically opposed to the petition. The intervention of leaders, the *Bay State Banner*, and the ministers belied that."[59] The appointed school committee home rule measure was adopted by the legislature in the Senate by a 22-13 vote and by 96-52 in the House, with a provision that there would be a requirement for a binding referendum as to whether to return to an elected school committee five years after the implementation of the appointed board. The next challenge was to get the approval of Republican governor Bill Weld. "It was one thing getting it through the city council," Sam Tyler remembered. "Still, when it got to the State House, Governor Weld thought it might be a problem, particularly in the African American community, to take away the right to vote, which was what this was doing. He thought that it might be a good political move to oppose this bill and gain favor with parts of the Boston population. So it was some business leaders, particularly those who were very active in the Republican Party, that sat down with the governor and made it clear that this was too important to the city, telling him this was not an issue that he should be playing politics with, and in the end, he supported it."[60]

Senator Bill Owens, a vocal opponent of the bill, countered, "The significant factor was that the Vault got into it and had various campaign contributors contact senators. I do not think the ministers had any influence. They saw a win coming and rode the wave of a win."[61] Sullivan recalled getting Governor Weld to agree to sign the legislation over the opposition of the Black elected officials: "Governor Weld said, 'Okay, I will sign it.' We were entitled to consideration by the new governor because of our opposition to John Silber, the Democratic candidate for governor. The famous Flynn-Weld beer lift at J. J. Foley's appeared on the front page of the *Herald* and stuck as an implicit endorsement. Mayor Flynn did not like John Silber, the Democratic candidate for governor. Flynn got the appointed school committee thanks to that beer."[62]

On July 5, 1991, Governor William F. Weld signed the legislation, after much anguish, for fear of alienating the Black community. "The Boston school system desperately needs fundamental change," he insisted. "Educators, parents, and students have well-documented the case for a systematic system overhaul. Simply put, students in the Boston public school system are losing their opportunity for education and any hope for a meaningful and prosperous future. The current situation is unacceptable."[63]

Tyler applauded the governor's action, saying at the time that the change was in the best interests of Boston's students. "This will provide a school board that will serve as a more cohesive, accountable policy body that will more decisively act on the education issues facing the city," he said.[64]

Implementing the governance change would test Flynn and those he appointed to the seven-member committee. In 1992, Flynn made the appointments, and Boston entered another turbulent period in the history of the city's school system. Given the nature of opposing arguments, Flynn was acutely aware of the racially charged nature of those first appointments. He appointed two Blacks, two Hispanics, one Asian, and two Whites, thereby quelling some dissent from Black elected officials. The school committee elected an African American as the chair; this was the first time in history that an Asian had been a school committee member.

As the new members began their first term, they inherited the school superintendent, Lois Harrison Jones, an African American woman hired by the outgoing elected body in May 1991. Flynn and his education adviser Consalvo, who became executive secretary to the new school committee, regularly clashed with Superintendent Jones. "I sat down with Reverend Ray Hammond from the Ten Point Coalition because they wanted to discuss our relationship with Superintendent Lois Harrison Jones," Consalvo said. "I told them, 'These are your kids, and nothing is happening.' You know what they said—I am not kidding—'She is one of us.' I could understand that. 'She is our only hope,' they said."[65]

The issue of race continued to polarize school politics and limit the reforms that the mayor and new school committee sought to adopt. Virtually all those interviewed had strong feelings about the governance change, which generally broke down along racial lines. The elected school committee was referred to as "a joke," "hard to take seriously," "a circus," and "dysfunctional," and those for and against the abolition of the elected committee acknowledged that election to the committee had played a role "as a political stepping-stone" and a platform that gave people of color power. "Structurally, the school department was the sore thumb stuck in the city where they needed to do their job, and everybody who was more thoughtful and had the money was sending their kids to parochial or private school or moving to the suburbs," Vin McCarthy, prominent Boston lawyer, said about the impact of the school committee dysfunction.[66]

Those who opposed the measure in many cases saw the move by Flynn and the business community to "take away the vote" and make the mayor a "czar" as disempowering people of color in the city. Many pointed to the history of the school's segregation and desegregation efforts that had left a significant distrust between the communities of color and the city government.

## Performance and Persistence

In seeking to provide a snapshot of Flynn's key activities regarding the Boston Public Schools and the impacts they may have had, one has first to understand that the schools, the families, and many other variables are directly correlated to their success. These include child poverty, housing insecurity, financial resources, leadership stability, diverse and quality teaching staff, and the engagement of the broader community, including civic and business leaders and the city's other institutions. Student outcomes should not be the only measure of progress, but they help understand what is happening in the classrooms.

Students' performance on several metrics was mixed with successes and failures during the Flynn and Menino tenures. Highlights follow as a few examples:

- Dropout rates decreased significantly, and college-bound rates have improved since 1983. The projected dropout rate for Boston students over the four years of high school declined steadily, from a high of 46 percent in the 1990 class to a projected rate of 36 percent in the 1993 class.[67]
- Moderate gains were achieved in 1987 in median Metropolitan Achievement test scores, and overall performance between 1988 and 1993 remained the same. Various indicators showed slight improvement, whether in 1973 or 1983.
- In 1992, BPS students in eighth grade scored 12 percent above the statewide median in math and 13 percent in science; those in twelfth grade scored 18 percent above the median in math and 14 percent in science.
- Since 2003, Boston has had the most significant gains in fourth- and eighth-grade math scores among eleven cities participating in the National Assessment of Educational Progress.[68]
- At the same time, Boston spent the third highest amount per pupil in Massachusetts after Cambridge and Wellesley. Money has always seemed to be a problem, but Boston has succeeded since 1984 in maintaining and increasing the resource base of public schools.[69]

Near the end of his tenure as mayor, Flynn remained frustrated by school performance. In a possible parting shot, he fired off a letter to the school committee and the superintendent demanding immediate change, not asking for it, which some at the time characterized as harsh. "Change and reform in the Boston Public Schools are going nowhere," he wrote. "I made it clear in my State of the City address this past January that I was unhappy with the slow pace of reform. Now, here it is March, and I am still not happy, and neither are many other people."

He asked for the following:

- An immediate evaluation of the performance of Superintendent Lois Harrison Jones.
- A new school choice plan that allowed children to attend the school of their choice regardless of race.
- Removal of principals unable to improve weak schools.
- Creation of a sports corporation along with the city's professional and collegiate teams.
- Moving early childhood programs into community agencies.

"This is very specific in what he wants to be done; he is putting his credibility on the line," Menino said in reaction to Flynn's directive. Northeastern University president Jack Curry added, "I am very pleased to see him throw down the gauntlet and say to us, 'Help me.' I am pleased he has had the courage to speak out strongly."[70]

In what many saw as the final salvo, Flynn wrote a letter to the candidates hoping to replace him. "Despite the accomplishments of the appointed board, I feel compelled to acknowledge that the loss of the vote for School Committee members has remained a bone in the throat of many Bostonians," he wrote. "The appointed board has done what it had to do. It has accomplished a clean break with the past."[71] Flynn could only reap very few rewards from the appointed board in terms of dramatic school success. His frustration showed; as some suspect, he might have been preserving his future options, knowing full well that, eventually, the tide would turn in favor of an elected body.

The appointed school committee helped to bring governance stability to the system—student performance throughout the system still needed to be more balanced. Public school enrollment went from approximately 97,000 students before busing (1970) to 54,000 when Flynn assumed office (1984) to 60,172 when he was no longer mayor (1994). Enrollment continued to fluctuate, with many new immigrants entering the school system throughout the 1980s and 1990s. The student body continued to change. The *Boston Globe* reported that the number of Black students enrolled in BPS has declined by one-half, losing over 16,000 children between 1994 and 2022, with many families opting for charter or private schools and Metropolitan Council for Educational Opportunity (METCO), a voluntary suburban integration program At the same time, the number of English-language learners was reported to be more than 11,000, with a dramatic increase in

Hispanic students, representing over 40 percent of the school population. BPS enrollment in 2023 was under 48,268 students, with an ever-changing mix of students with new needs more diverse than decades before.

One and one-half years into the new school committee's term, Flynn left for the Vatican. Harrison Jones was still superintendent, and Menino became responsible for moving the schools forward. He was being pressured in 1995 to keep Harrison Jones as school superintendent but was determined to take the Boston Public Schools in a new direction. He faced intense lobbying from Black elected officials and met with a Mel King–led delegation. "The Black community and elected officials have supported her from the very beginning, and we will continue to struggle around this issue until it is resolved," State Representative Gloria Fox said at the meeting with the mayor. "We stand on the side of what is right."[72] Menino made no commitments. A month later, Harrison Jones and the school committee agreed to part ways, saving Menino from taking on the issue directly. By August of that year, Menino and Boston had their newest school superintendent, Thomas Payzant, who would stay at the job for over a decade.

In 1996, as the original 1991 law required, a referendum was held to determine whether to return to an elected school committee. For some in the minority community, sentiments were still raw from Flynn's 1991 campaign to have the mayor appoint the school board. "In campaigning for an appointed body in 1991, Mayor Raymond Flynn successfully co-opted much of the Black clergy, opening deep wounds between them and elected officials, " Joyce Ferriabough, a prominent media and political strategist, observed. "The issue remains [and] so tender are feelings that a meeting of Black activists and elected officials is planned to discuss amicable ways to disagree on the referendum issue."[73]

The referendum to continue the appointed school board was actively supported by Menino and leaders of community, religious, and business organizations. In November 1995, a full year before the referendum was scheduled, a poll showed voters favored returning to the elected board 64 percent to 29 percent. Menino, going into reelection himself in 1997, became concerned about the poll numbers and instructed his political operation, headed by Robert "Skinner" Donahue, to go into full campaign mode. When the polls closed in 1996, the referendum saw the appointed board with 70 percent of the vote and the elected board with 30 percent of the total, a complete turnaround from a year earlier. In the two Black wards, 43 percent of those who voted on the referendum supported maintaining the appointed committee, which was only 5 percent higher than in 1989. In the thirteen overwhelmingly White wards, 72 percent of those voting on the referendum supported maintaining the appointed committee, up from 51 percent in 1989.[74]

Menino shared his thoughts about the value of the appointed school committee, a proposal he supported as a city councilor and actively campaigned to continue as mayor in the 1996 referendum.

Oh, that was a savior. The old-school committee was a swap shop. The custodians' union ran it. The teachers' union ran it. All the unions ran the school committee because the guys running for the school committee had to get campaign funds. Where did they get them? The unions. So they were not dealing with issues that affect the kids. They were dealing with issues that affected the unions, and that was the wrong thing to do. The appointed school board members can never be elected; they want to serve and have done a decent job. There are some issues also, but they have done an excellent job. They devoted a lot of time to it and were a savior to our city. We could move the city schools forward, and people have confidence. Returning to '83 and '84, the people needed more confidence in the schools; classrooms were empty, and we could not hire teachers. When I first became mayor, I had to go to a job fair in Florida to recruit teachers. They did not want to come to Boston. We had to go to Panama to get math teachers. When the job fair opened the following year, we had three thousand applicants. Things have turned around.[75]

Menino dismissed the opponents when asked why he believed that some Black leaders continue to oppose the appointed school committee. "A simple thing is the right to vote," he said. "However, is the right to vote more important than a person's education and the kids' future? I doubt that. Kids' future is more important. They want to have an elected school board because they maintain control of the patronage. That is wrong! I do not care where you come from or who you are. That is wrong! It is the education of children, what goes on in that classroom, what goes on at School Street [school department headquarters], what goes on all over the city. That is what it is all about. If you have a school system that works, your city works, and you know we reduced the dropout rate from 19 percent to 6 percent now. That is a considerable drop."[76]

## Leadership: Instability and Accountability

Menino was successful in recruiting a school superintendent with staying power. Tom Payzant was the Boston school superintendent from 1995 to 2006—eleven years, longer than any modern-day superintendent. Despite some Black community members' objections, Payzant was appointed when Menino declined to reappoint Lois Harrison Jones.

"The appointed committee structure worked well during Menino's first two terms because Menino and Superintendent Tom Payzant were in total sync," Sullivan observed. "Boston was rewarded with a string of national foundation grants—Annenberg, Carnegie, Gates—and then we won the Broad Prize for Urban Education as the nation's best urban school district in 2006 after finishing as a finalist the four previous years."[77]

The Broad Prize is a big deal, awarded to public school systems that have demonstrated the most outstanding overall performance and improved student achievement while narrowing achievement gaps among low-income students and students of color. Menino admitted that he could have done more on public education. "When I left office, there were things that people said I did not do," he acknowledged. "Could I have done better with schools? I could have done much better with schools—no question about that. Schools have come a long way, but they are still not perfect. Schools are still an issue for us."[78]

Many members of the fast-growing Latino community, representing 33 percent of the students in 2006 and 43 percent in 2022, would agree with Menino's assessment. Pablo Calderon, King supporter and Flynn staff member, challenged Menino:

> Well, the number-one issue is the poor work around education. The poor job that the schools are doing, they are still doing the same thing today. In the seventies, we had a 12 percent high school dropout rate yearly in the Latino community. Last year, the numbers came out: 51 percent of Latino students are dropping out of our high schools. I mailed it to Mayor Menino and said to the mayor, first of all, what do you think would happen today if I sent this to Brookline and said to the head of Brookline, 51 percent of your population is dropping out? Would there be a total uproar? What hurts me is that I read this, and there was no uproar by you. Menino sent me one of these apologetic letters saying you know I am trying my best, and blah, blah, blah.[79]

There is much unfinished business in the Boston Public Schools. White let the courts take over the schools. Flynn expended enormous political capital and took control of the schools out of receivership and away from the school committee. Menino continued that practice, at one point early in his tenure—at his 1996 State of the City address, boldly proclaiming, "I want to be judged as your mayor by what happens now in the Boston Public Schools. If I fail to bring about these specific reforms by 2001, then judge me harshly."[80]

King's assessment of the quality of schooling in Boston, an issue he spent his entire career fighting to address, directly criticized the city.

"We do not have in the city a citizenry that says all the children are our children," he said. "One thing that has yet to happen is that we have not become a city where we want all the children to succeed and will challenge the mayor and others to make it happen. It should not be just the parents of the children. This is something that has yet to come together in the city. We have Menino who said to give me control of the schools and, in twenty years, has yet to do it."[81]

Boston has had a revolving door in terms of school superintendents. Thomas Payzant, who served during the Menino administration, was the longest-serving superintendent during this period. The high turnover caused much of the governance instability that has occurred. Boston has moved in less than ten years from a five-member at-large, elected board, to a thirteen-member at-large and district-elected board, to a seven-member board appointed by the mayor. Superintendents hired by one school committee board under one mayor often found themselves at odds with the next set of leaders. This was particularly acute when Lois Harrison Jones was hired by the soon-to-be-outgoing thirteen-member committee just before the mayor appointed the new seven-member board. Flynn tried to get the school committee to hold off selecting a new superintendent or limiting her term, but the school committee refused. Of course, Harrison Jones was never Flynn's superintendent, and despite best efforts, conflict ensued shortly after that, and the school department suffered.

During the period under study, as the summary here demonstrates, governance of the BPS was constantly in flux until Payzant but continued following his departure. Menino's successor, Mayor Marty Walsh, was an ardent supporter of the appointed school committee and appointed most members. "I support the appointed committee—it has taken politics out of education," he said. "You have independent, thoughtful people with expertise." He added, "The schools are a lot of work, and there are many issues; you have twenty-two different school starting times; transportation costs are out of control; and you have a system with fifty-seven thousand kids and ninety thousand seats. You need to have a long game working from prekindergarten to twelfth grade to ensure a kid's career success."[82]

Walsh invested historic funding levels in the school system during his mayoralty, according to his policy chief, Joyce Linehan.[83] When the school committee hired Tommy Chang as superintendent, Walsh noted that three of his appointees to the committee opposed his recommendation, remarking that it showed the committee's independence. Not too far into Chang's tenure, Walsh became frustrated with his missteps and the department's performance. The mayor expressed frustration that student performance has not improved quickly enough.[84] Walsh was blunt.

"They're not performing anywhere near where they need to be," the mayor said of the district's open-enrollment high schools. After a tumultuous three years, confidence had eroded, and the mayor and the superintendent reached what they say is a mutual decision for Chang to step down, two years before his contract expired. [85] Walsh and the school committee hired Brenda Cassellius in 2019 as superintendent. Facing COVID-19-related school closures, remote learning, and a revolt by several principals and headmasters, her tenure was short-lived.[86] In February 2022, she resigned after only three years as superintendent. Hired by Walsh, Wu denied forcing her out, but she was facing a new mayor after Walsh resigned in 2021 and Wu took over the mayor's office.

The department faced many problems that nearly led to a state takeover, which was averted under the Chang and Cassellius superintendencies. When Michelle Wu became mayor, the school committee appointed Mary Skipper as superintendent. Wu and Skipper intervened with the governor and the Department of Education, developing a plan to avoid a state takeover of BPS. Other challenges they faced included implementing a new admissions process for the three exam schools. Cassellius implemented a temporary change; later, a similar plan was made permanent to diversify the student demographics, particularly of Boston Latin School. The policy was challenged, and the US Court of Appeals for the First Circuit in December 2023 upheld a lower court decision in favor of the school department.[87] Wu and Skipper also faced intense criticism from parents and the Boston City Council for their proposal to relocate another of the exam schools, the John D. O'Bryant, to West Roxbury.[88] A particularly incensed O'Bryant mom strode up to Wu and confronted her. "Why West Roxbury?" the parent recalls saying. "Historically, West Roxbury hates Black and Brown people. We can't get there. They don't want us there."[89] This may yet be another example of how race and equity have become issues for city leadership.

"The proposed O'Bryant school move, a steady stream of protests and objections from elected officials, community members, and O'Bryant students, teachers, and parents appeared to wear down the Wu administration's resolve. Last week, Wu announced that the city was withdrawing its plan to move the school. 'It seems like the mayor isn't really thinking through all of the consequences of her decisions,' said Roxbury resident Rodney Singleton. Singleton, who graduated from Boston Technical High School before it was renamed the John D. O'Bryant School of Mathematics and Science, said Wu's proposal was disrespectful. 'She backed down, but the fact that she floated it was a slap in the face,' he said. 'This mayor uses buzz terms like equity, resilience, and affordability. What could be more damaging to long-term equity than taking a school like that from the Black community?"[90]

In a February 27, 2024, letter, Wu outlined her decision to pull the plug on the West Roxbury site for the O'Bryant: "With a lack of consensus around moving the O'Bryant School to the West Roxbury Educational Complex, we are halting those plans indefinitely."[91] She was trying to balance moving quickly with "having the community really feel that these are their decisions and not just something that is sort of dictated or laid out."[92]

Leadership uncertainty continued with the rapid turnover of superintendents: six in ten years from 2013 to 2023.[93] Student performance continued to be uneven, and the challenges facing the BPS today are new and many. The voters' demands to return to an elected school committee can be interpreted as another reaction to Boston children's lack of progress—unlikely to solve the problems that result from poverty amid plenty. As Paul Reville, former state secretary of education, said, "Returning to an elected school committee represents people trying to assign a simple solution to a complex problem. People feel out of control and want to go back to another system; they were no more in control then. Mayoral control gives some coherency to the system."[94]

## Does Mayoral Takeover Work to Improve Public Education?

Is the mayoral takeover of public school governance an effective reform strategy? Boston in 1991 was the first major urban school system to undertake a mayoral takeover. Since that time, a host of other cities have joined suit: Chicago (1995); Cleveland and Baltimore (1998); Detroit (1999); Oakland, Washington, DC, and Harrisburg (2000); and New York (2002)—each has moved to a mayoral-appointed school governance structure, often bitterly contested by the teachers' unions.[95] Analysis and debate on the success and improvement of urban school districts with mayors in charge still need to be more conclusive.

Several leading educational researchers place little or no value on school governance. "Forms of mayoral or other control; state and federal rules and regulations; and policies funded or unfunded do not make a district," Jean Anyon, prominent educational and social policy professor at the City University of New York, suggests. "Describing how these work does not yield an adequate understanding of the possible problems, issues, or solutions."[96] Anyon suggests a critical theoretical approach that looks at the underlying causes of structural inequality. Diane Ravitch, a historian of education and educational policy at New York University and formerly a US Assistant Secretary of Education, does not believe that "elected school boards are obstacles to reform" or in the power of school governance to improve schools. She states, "Mayoral control is not a guaranteed path to school improvement," citing the 2007 National Assessment of Educational Progress tests showing that the cities with the highest scores had elected boards and two of the lowest had mayoral control for over a decade.[97]

Others, such as Brown University political scientist Kenneth Wong, see mayoral takeover as one strategy in the face of significant structural issues, including poverty and race, that have correlated with student achievement. While he presents the overall evidence as inconclusive, Wong develops an empirical analysis suggesting that mayoral takeover districts exhibit higher-quality student performance in the lower grades, and at the lowest-performing schools, increased accountability; reduced conflict, including racial strife; greater civic engagement; and more effective fiscal management.[98]

What factors should we examine when we look at the success or failure of mayoral takeovers, a simple analysis of the test scores, and improvement in closing the achievement gap? Should the research include the level of civic engagement, political and public support for education, the skills and longevity of leadership, or winning the Broad Prize in Urban Education for the most improved urban public school system as Boston did in 2006 and New York in 2008?[99]

## Did the School Governance Structure Change from Elected to Appointed Improve Public Education in Boston?

Only a few people interviewed suggested that governance change has yet to impact education quality and accountability. Education adviser and, for a brief period, secretary to the mayoral-appointed school committee in 1992, Bob Consalvo reflected on whether the governance change has improved the schools. "No, I do not believe it did," he said. "I opposed the governance change but had to keep my mouth shut. The curve will drop steeply if you track the education stories before and after the governance change. There would always be educational stories since the school committee was so crazy. Now, you cannot find stories about education. The *Globe* once wrote a story about no stories on education anymore." Did he believe the appointed board made a difference? "No," he said. "I think MCAS [Massachusetts Comprehensive Assessment System] standardized tests made a difference; I do not think the appointed board made a difference. There was less fighting and less nonsense, but the schools were the same. The test scores were always at the bottom, even then. They are better, and they are better now because the MCAS forced them to be better. There is no other reason; there is no other reason why they are better. It is not [school superintendent] Payzant, this person, or the person before. Once the MCAS came in, people could not hide anymore, which is why they are better. They still need to improve, but they are better because of that."[100]

Long-serving city councilor Charles Yancey, who served from 1984 to 2015 and was an opponent of the appointed board, makes clear his thoughts on the mayoral-appointed school board. "I was very concerned that the appointed school committee would remove from the voters the ability to determine our educational leaders and concentrate the powers within the mayor's office," he said. "It does not remove politics; it just changes politics, and the mayor will have a nominal number of powers regarding the school committee. In terms of what the city and the voters of Boston gave up and what they got in return, the voters lost out."[101]

Ted Landsmark summarized the current state of education in Boston. "Regarding the basic demographics of Boston, 85 to 90 percent of people who live in Boston today did not live here during busing," he said. "Most people who live in the city today have no direct recollection of busing. So the interesting thing is that vestiges drive the conversation about busing; it is primarily a historical artifact. It is not that most of us who live here today are still angry and bitter about what happened; it is a few of us who were here then. So, to a large extent, when people look at schools today and what they see as deficiencies in the education system, a handful of people want to blame busing. Still, the weaknesses exist because we perpetuate particular distinctions within our public schools. One can argue that, in many respects, the same racial and class isolation that existed in Boston in 1976, when I was attacked, continues to exist today."[102]

Margaret Blood, who was an aide to Representative Kevin Fitzgerald and had worked in Mission Hill with a racially diverse group of public school students and families, shared her thoughts on the governance change. "As a Boston homeowner voter, I feel that it has made a difference in that the mayor has made education a priority, and I am not sure that the mayor would have gone out on a limb to do that if he did not have control of the school committee," Blood said. "I have looked at much of the research around the appointed versus elected school committees and governance structures for local early education, and it looked like the jury was out. There was no conclusive evidence about one being better than the other. The failings of public education are not about local control but insufficient and unequal resources for facilities and instruction."[103]

The lingering racial conflict following school busing provided a challenging environment for significant education reform in Boston. Race has been the third rail of Boston politics and was center stage in the school governance debate. The history of school desegregation provided the background and the primary obstacle Flynn encountered when he took on the reform of the school committee. From the perspective of regime theory, was the mayor a central actor in the outcome, or was it the set of relationships he helped coalesce around the goal of reforming educational governance in the city? As Clarence Stone has suggested, did Flynn have "power over," defined as social control, or "power to," defined as social production, to reform the school system?[104]

Did Flynn exercise power over those who opposed the elected school committee? In this instance, he did not have power over the central actors in the debate. The mayor assembled a coalition of influential actors, which might be termed power to achieve the desired result of replacing the elected school committee with an appointed one. He brought together the business community through the Boston Municipal Research Bureau, which also brought on board the Vault. Many saw the business community's motivation as self-serving, ensuring a pipeline of competent business employees. However, their role helped frame the issue as economic rather than racial. Flynn also enlisted support from the media coalition, including the *Boston Globe*, which initially opposed the referendum, writing, "His [Flynn's] proposal is undemocratic and badly flawed. The *Globe* urges a 'no' vote on this referendum."[105] Later, however, the *Globe* reversed course and endorsed the plan, writing, "The Boston public schools have everything to gain by creating an appointed board. Boston's children will be the losers if the current structure remains."[106]

The issue is complex and varies from city to city. Mayoral takeover on behalf of whom? The teachers? Students? Business leaders and the growth machine (who want public schools to run like private companies)? Charter school lobbyists? If the mayor is progressive and wants to build a coalition to support the schools, that is different from a conservative mayor who, with business support, wants to strengthen private charter schools. Mayoral takeover is not a solution. It is a strategy on behalf of a coalition, which varies significantly from city to city and from time to time. The key players in the Boston contest were Hubie Jones, Professor James Jennings, the Black ministers of the Interfaith Ministerial Alliance, and the *Bay State Banner*.

In the 1985 epilogue for his 1967 best-selling book, *Death at an Early Age*, Jonathan Kozol summarized the outcomes of busing and education reform in Boston: "I have often been obliged to ask myself whether the publication of this book did very much to lessen the injustices it describes. *Death at an Early Age* appears to have had some effect in heightening the pressure that would lead in time to the court-ordered integration of the Boston schools; even this may prove at last to be a pyrrhic victory. Today, we see an integrated underclass in Boston in the process of gestation. Poor whites, poor blacks, and poor Hispanics now become illiterate together."[107]

Much needs to be done to break the cycles of poverty and the growth of income inequality in Boston if, as statistics show, those who remain poor and out of the economic mainstream are predominantly people of color in Boston's still-segregated neighborhoods.

# 11 / Rebuilding the City: Urban Finances and Infrastructure

*When Flynn came to office, he inherited a massive annual structural budget deficit of over $40 million. The city was virtually bankrupt and could have been deemed insolvent under certain circumstances. The city's bond rating was suspended in 1981 and was junk.* (Mary Nee, director of capital planning, interview)

## Near Financial Ruin to Balancing the Books

Progressive officials and activists rarely focus on city finances and infrastructure as core issues, but they are critically important. They have difficulty persuading voters to support social justice reforms if the fundamental "civic housekeeping"—potholes, traffic, public safety, financial accountability—is not handled well. They focus more on development policy, community participation, and governance—electing progressives to the mayor or city council offices, and redistributive policies like linkage and affordable housing. Finances and infrastructure are the bedrock of good urban governance. The average family in a neighborhood is concerned about things like functioning police and fire stations. Their kids attend the schools and use parks and playgrounds in their neighborhood. While not often flashy, Mayor Flynn always felt that these quality-of-life issues were the "bread and butter" of running the city. He had to solve the financial problem to do what he wanted for the city and the neighborhoods.

Residents', businesses', investors', and public officials' confidence in the city's financial future is often overlooked. Business leaders were initially wary of Flynn, given his political focus and the staff he surrounded himself with, particularly the left-wing activists. "The critics and skeptics were convinced that this collection of longshoremen and leftists would bankrupt the city," said Neil Sullivan.[1] He needed to provide a break from the past cycle of White's budget deficits and the ongoing fiscal crisis in

Boston, which led to a deterioration of services and the closing of public safety facilities, among other things.

In 1981, the Boston Municipal Research Bureau warned the mayor and the business community about the impending fiscal crisis. "The uncertainty of Boston's financial position has practically closed the market for city bonds. It appears the city will have to seek special financial assistance legislation from the state to avoid either insolvency or critical services and staff reductions—including a total shutdown of the schools." The crisis escalated that year with the layoff of more than 1,400 city workers, 500 from the police and fire department, and the shuttering of seven police stations and nineteen firehouses. These drastic measures led to widespread protests, with residents occupying the police and fire stations and demanding their reopening. The situation was further exacerbated when a later Municipal Research Bureau report revealed that almost 125 of the mayor's ward and precinct workers had managed to survive the cuts and remain on the city payroll, sparking public outrage.[2]

When Flynn became mayor, he inherited a bankrupt city with a massive budget deficit of over $40 million. This was one of the issues the growth machine was concerned about when Flynn was elected—whether he could manage the city's finances to limit their investment risks. Several factors led to the crisis he inherited. First was the impact of Proposition 2½, the tax-limiting measure that lessened tax revenue. The city stood to absorb a cut of $175 million in property tax revenues over the next three fiscal years. Second, it lost a significant tax case, *Tregor v. City of Boston*,[3] which found that the city's assessing practices had disproportionally taxed businesses. That drove further revenue reductions, which required the city to give tax rebates to previously overassessed property owners, estimated to be more than $100 million. There was another pending tax assessment case with utility companies and, finally, the chronic overspending by the school department, over which the mayor had little or no control.[4]

Flynn named a sixty-member financial transition team that produced a seven-hundred-page analysis of the city's fiscal conditions and strategies to solve his inherited crisis. At the release of the report, "Boston in Transition: A Financial Analysis," Flynn said, "Let's open up the entire financial situation, no hidden accounts, no hidden agendas, no mysteries."[5] He began by putting a talented team in place.

Stuart Vidockler, Flynn's first budget director, came to city hall from the Houghton Mifflin publishing company with degrees from MIT and Harvard Business School. He recalls that when he spoke to Flynn about the position, he asked the mayor, "What is your budgeting philosophy?"

Flynn responded, "When you have two quarters and a beer is fifty cents, you put them together and buy the beer. I don't believe in spending what we don't have."[6] Flynn was famous for not having a checking account or credit card. His wife, Cathy, would cash his weekly paycheck at the credit union and pay their bills with money orders.

Vidockler would need to untangle the financial morass left by the White administration, explaining that White's budget operation was a "collection of unusual cultures coming out of a uniquely fragmented style of organization. . . . Some people might call it fiefdoms."[7] He told me, "There were lawyers on every payroll, there were cars that no one knew who they belonged to being paid for, and it took us some time to sort it all out."

He was also responsible for putting together the city's first budget and later bond offering. He said of the process, "It was like Star Wars, a real trial by fire." The city had been out of the bond market for years due to its credit rating and junk bond status. He prepared a "legitimate and credible budget package that presented a 'full view' of proposed expenditures and for the first time disclosed detailed revenues."[8]

Vidockler balanced the budget each year he was director, eliminating chronic deficits. Sam Tyler, executive director of the Municipal Research Bureau, said of Vidockler, "Stuart has done the best job of any budget director since the 1970s. Political budget directors brought the city a decade of deficit spending, which Vidockler has ended."[9] Vidockler added, "It took a while, but we controlled spending. That was the first step to righting the ship so that Flynn could accomplish what he was elected to do."[10]

Flynn's approach to restoring the city's fiscal health was multifaceted. First, he recognized the need for additional revenue to offset the lost tax income. He spearheaded a statewide organizing campaign, rallying other municipalities, the business community, and the media. This collective effort resulted in legislative relief, granting local option taxing authority for jet fuel and a room occupancy excise tax. Additionally, Flynn worked closely with the legislature to amend the local aid distribution formula, which had been unfavorable to Boston.

In other efforts, the city negotiated with the utility companies and reached a compromise resolution on assessments that improved its ability to manage municipal employees' retirement costs. The city also began tracking program performance and spending.

Next, Flynn would focus on gaining the ability to borrow funds to implement a capital plan for the city. There had not been a comprehensive capital plan since the early 1960s, some twenty-three years, and even then it was focused on urban renewal projects rather than the city's neighborhood infrastructure and facilities. "I went to Wall Street with two Black guys, two Jewish guys, a woman, and I was the Irish mayor from South Boston," Flynn said. "They looked at us and wondered, 'Who was this crew?'"[11] Flynn had brought in a team of experienced financial managers. He brought on board as city treasurer George Russell, who came from the State Street Bank with degrees from Clark University and an MBA from New York University, and Leon Stamps as the city auditor, who came from Xerox with degrees from Boston College and a master's degree from Northeastern University. "The first Blacks in the city's history to hold the two key financial jobs," Russell said, commenting on the significance of his appointment regarding racial diversity. "We have a new mayor who has committed to a diverse administration, and my appointment is a statement of that."[12]

They and Vidockler went to Wall Street, as did capital plan director Mary Nee, and the city received several bond upgrades. By 1988, the bond rating was A (bond ratings range from the highest, AAA, to D, which are junk bonds). Flynn's goal was to improve the fiscal climate and the city's bond rating to borrow and spend on significant capital projects. Russell would later reflect on his proudest achievement, improving the bond rating from a noninvestment grade to an A rating. He would still need to close the budget gap and raise additional revenue, which he did by securing local option taxing authority, as mentioned earlier. Flynn ordered every department to identify internal and external capital needs.

Flynn created the Office of Capital Planning in 1984 and hired Mary Nee as director. Nee served as senior budget and policy analyst for the Massachusetts Senate's Ways and Means Committee. Like with his budget office, Flynn consolidated decision-making for all city capital projects under Nee. From a budgeting and capital planning perspective, while there was internal jostling, decision-making was coordinated, and there were clear lines of authority that did not exist previously.

After White closed police and fire stations, parks and playgrounds deteriorated, and upgrades to them were abandoned. The county jails, courthouses, and public schools were in receivership and under federal or state orders to remedy the facilities' conditions. Flynn initiated a significant capital budget campaign to reverse the closings and provide regular and predictable annual investment through the five-year capital plan.

According to Mary Nee, the city's first director of capital planning, the $1.03 billion in investments ($2.758 billion in 2023 dollars) would support 750 projects spanning municipal buildings and equipment, parks, roadways, and bridges citywide. Nee documented the city's most significant investments in its first capital plan in decades.[13]

The 1974 federal school desegregation order mandated that the city develop a unified facility plan for the Boston Public Schools. The court had rejected previous plans, and in 1985 approved a plan to invest $69.7 million for critical repairs in thirty-nine schools and complete the modernization of another thirty schools. Investment in public schools exceeded $165 million. The capital plan targeted $91 million for parks, including five playgrounds for children with special needs, and $5 million for cemeteries and fieldhouses. A master plan was developed to restore the Frederick Law Olmsted Emerald Necklace, a series of parks and open spaces from the Boston Common to Franklin Park in Dorchester.

Public safety was paramount to the mayor from personnel and facilities perspectives. The capital plan funded the construction of four new neighborhood police stations and the renovation of three others, with the Brighton facility housing the city's first sexual assault unit. In 1991, planning was initiated for the replacement of a dilapidated police headquarters in the Back Bay with a new state-of-the-art facility along the Southwest Corridor in Roxbury, which was completed in 1996. Alongside the upgrades of police facilities, the fire department's facilities and equipment needed to be updated. Over thirty-eight firehouses and support facilities were renovated, and all the firefighting trucks were replaced during the plan. Both investments were critical for public safety and the protection of Boston residents.

Other facilities critical for Bostonians were incorporated into the first five-year plan. The Boston Public Library, the first public library in the nation, operated a central library and twenty-six neighborhood branch libraries. Each neighborhood branch and the main library were renovated through a $34 million investment. Two of the nation's oldest and historically significant buildings, Faneuil Hall and the Old State House, dating back to 1761 and 1712, were also addressed.[14] Significant investments were made in economic development, housing,[15] and the often-unnoticed but vital bridges, streets, and light infrastructure.[16]

Allan Stern, who led the city's Management Information Systems Department, reported that its IT infrastructure was nonexistent in 1983. "We opened up the doors to the outside world. We went on to bring the city into the twentieth century, and before long, employees had PCs at their desks and even email!"[17]

One area of importance to Flynn from his experience as a kid growing up in South Boston was the city's gyms, pools, and recreation facilities, which were in similar disrepair and neglect. Twenty-four million dollars was invested in these facility upgrades to provide thousands of neighborhood residents with opportunities for play and community connections.

When Flynn was a kid, he and his friends would go to the beach during the summer only to find signs that said, "No Swimming—Polluted." His family was poor and, unlike middle-class families, could not afford to go to Cape Cod or New Hampshire. Flynn spoke of his commitment to restoring the harbor, economy, and beaches. "I grew up and depended upon this harbor for my livelihood," he said. "As a youngster, I used the beaches. My father was a longshoreman, and I unloaded ships, too. I wanted to see a renaissance in the harbor so that Boston would again be known worldwide as a prosperous port. I've been diving into polluted water since I was four years old. My kids are doing it now."[18]

In October 2019, on the thirty-fifth anniversary of the Harborwalk, Boston Harbor Now recognized Flynn's "1984 vision and all that has been achieved on the Boston waterfront." The Boston Harborwalk now encompasses forty-three of the forty-seven miles of Boston's shoreline along eight neighborhoods: East Boston, Charlestown, North End, Wharf District, Seaport District, Fort Point Channel, South Boston, and Dorchester, with nine public beaches.[19]

Stephen Coyle, the BRA director who led much of the harbor planning, along with Lorraine Downey, head of the Environment Department, required developers of waterfront property, against their wishes, to build and extend Harborwalk. He believed that the design of Harborwalk would bring Blacks and Whites together in the city. Coyle invoked Olmsted, responsible for the Emerald Necklace, and his philosophy of "communitiveness."

> "It was the notion that, instead of coming in the front door with reform and saying, 'you must do this, you should do that,' coming in the back door," Coyle added. "Plan and design the city so that people will come together. It is not the reformer's job to say, 'Your day must include two hours of talking to your neighbors.' It is to say, 'There will be a great esplanade by the river. It will be beautiful, and you will enjoy it. Whether you are a Catholic, a Protestant, a Jew, [B]lack, a [B]rown or a [W]hite, a landlord or a tenant, a manufacturer, or a laborer, you will take your family out here on a Sunday afternoon, and you will behave in a way that doesn't encourage confrontation or conflict.'"[20]

Flynn led the cleanup of the Boston Harbor and the beaches, for which the state agencies responsible were placed into receivership by State Superior Court Judge Paul Garrity. During his first week in office, he received a letter from the Environmental Protection Agency regarding the polluted harbor. Flynn and Governor Michael Dukakis advocated for creating the

Massachusetts Water Resources Authority (MWRA), with a mandate to take over responsibility for Boston's water and sewer responsibilities and the surrounding communities. The effort was costly and controversial, and the mayor secured three seats on the MWRA board so that Boston's interests would be represented.[21] Downey, who was appointed along with Rick Innes and Bob Ciolek, stopped the flow of sludge from the Deer Island treatment plant into Boston Harbor in December 1991, calling it "a Christmas present to Boston Harbor" after working for decades to stop the pollution of the harbor.[22] Downey recalled Garrity calling Flynn "a visionary" for cleaning up the polluted harbor.[23]

Probably Flynn's highest priority was the replacement of the aging Boston City Hospital (BCH), built in 1864, the first municipal hospital in the United States, to treat Boston's poor. When he took office, a sprawling campus of seriously deteriorated buildings was on the verge of losing accreditation. Flynn was advised that it should be closed. He was born there, and his parents died there. There was no way he was closing the hospital for people with low incomes. Instead, he wanted it to be the best health service in Boston. With the leadership of Senator Ted Kennedy, Flynn accessed a federal financing tool to fund the redevelopment of the $170 million 356-bed BCH inpatient facility so that it could continue to provide health care to Boston's poor and needy residents. After Flynn left office, in 1996 BCH merged with Boston University Medical Center Hospital to form the Boston Medical Center. Some, including Flynn, still question the wisdom of transferring the public hospital to Boston University. A doctor at the new Boston Medical Center told me he thought the poor were losing out by merging the hospital of the poor with the university hospital for the well-to-do.

During Flynn's administration, Nee and her team addressed the enormous backlog of deferred capital needs in every neighborhood and function of city government. Their success was due mainly to the mayor's support, community residents, and small businesses that had a seat at the table in planning the neighborhood development and infrastructure improvements. Without the stability of city finances during this period, due to the financial team's leadership and the state legislature's support, much of this story would not have been possible. This comprehensive approach and improved maintenance moved the city from crisis and court orders to a revitalization felt in every corner of the city.[24] He later created a budget program evaluation department to track performance in each agency. He appointed Bob Ciolek, who had joined the administration from Cleveland working for Mayor George Voinovich, to lead the effort.[25]

According to Rosemarie Sansone, who oversaw the Office of Business and Cultural Development, while the business community was initially wary of Flynn, they later thought, "Flynn was not bad for business; they were impressed with the team of people he assembled around him who they thought were quite competent."[26]

This approach continued under the Menino administration with regular comprehensive capital investment plans. His last plan in 2013, as he prepared to leave city hall, was investing $1.8 billion to fund 341 projects.[27] When he left office, the city's bond rating had risen to AA under his financial stewardship.

Walsh's $3 billion capital plan had a lasting impact on everything from affordable housing to climate resiliency. It included the first firehouse in thirty years, new schools, and renovated libraries.[28] As Joyce Linehan, Walsh's policy chief, said, "Walsh was proudest of the work they did to renovate the Central Library's McKim Building, a National Historic Landmark in Copley Square, and every branch library in the city, remembering what libraries meant to us as kids."[29] They succeeded with the capital plan, and the city's first perfect AAA bond rating based upon solid fiscal management unlocked unprecedented investments in parks, libraries, and public safety. The city had received the AAA rating for eight years since 2014, leaving the city finances in good shape for Wu.

Wu initiated her Boston Capital plan in fiscal year 2023 to make $3.6 billion in critical investments in the city's infrastructure—including roads, bridges, bike lanes, and libraries—and new infrastructure funds supporting affordable housing, revitalized parks, multimodal transportation improvements, and school improvements.[30] As of 2023, there was an understanding of the critical importance of investing in the city's infrastructure. In 1984, after twenty-three years without a capital plan, Flynn set the course for sound fiscal investments by his successors.

# 12 / Confronting Poverty and Homelessness

> *Poverty and homelessness were related. The state of homelessness was poverty in its most visible, savage, and lethal form.* (Tracy Kidder, *Rough Sleepers*, 2023)

> *I considered Ray Flynn an emotional leader. He understood the issue; he felt it.* (Dr. Jim O'Connell, Boston Health Care for the Homeless, interview)

## Poverty in Boston

Poverty and its root causes have been a central consideration in how the city invests, from early childhood education to jobs and housing programs. The period in the 1980s, with even a tiny decrease in poverty, demonstrates that improvements can be achieved with leadership, redistribution strategies, and adequate and effective deployment of resources.

Boston's official poverty rate—using the federal definition based on income and family size—has remained relatively stable for the past fifty years, between 18 and 20 percent of the population. Demographic and income data mapped by the Boston Foundation's Persistent Poverty Project over the past several decades reveal that the same neighborhoods have faced poverty and inequality throughout this period. Boston has struggled to address the root causes: the interrelated lack of jobs and skill levels, generational poverty and unemployment, quality of education and attainment, access to affordable housing, and ladders of opportunity out of poverty. City governments by themselves lack the resources to address these root causes, and the federal and state governments do not provide nearly the resources necessary to help with address poverty's persistence.

Boston's poverty reduction efforts during the late 1980s led to significant reductions and a period of remarkable progress, with family poverty, which stood at 18 percent in 1980, dropping to 11.5 percent in 1988. This decline was primarily attributed to increased employment and active government programs to reduce poverty across all racial and ethnic subgroups. This achievement should be celebrated as a testament to the effectiveness of targeted interventions.

MIT professor Paul Osterman's study for the Boston Foundation revealed a significant reduction in poverty among Boston families from 1980 to 1989. Overall poverty fell to 19 percent from 23.5 percent, with single parents experiencing a decrease from 60.5 percent to 40.5 percent and single individuals from 22.5 percent to 5.9 percent. However, a closer look at the data by race reveals a stark reality. Among White single parents, the poverty rate declined to 25.7 percent from 56 percent over that period. For Black single parents, there was a decline to 35.2 percent from 59.9 percent. This breakdown underscores the disparities that persisted even as the economy improved, highlighting the need for continued efforts to address these inequalities.[1]

Poverty in Boston increased from 16 percent in 1970 to 20 percent in 1980. As Charles Kenney wrote as part of a special report, "Poverty amidst Affluence," for the *Boston Globe* in 1985, "For many of Boston's residents, the city's booming economy and population revival point to excellent prospects for growth as a place to work and a place to live. However, the transformation has been largely downtown-oriented, and fewer benefits have yet flowed into the poorer neighborhoods where most of the city's population lives. While Boston achieved new growth records in employment and development investment, poverty spread in the city's neighborhoods. Boston is a city of 'poverty amidst affluence,'" according to a Boston Redevelopment Authority report.[2]

TABLE 3. Boston Poverty Rates, 1980 and 1989

| | % Total | % White | % Black | % Hispanic |
|---|---|---|---|---|
| **1980 Boston Poverty Rates** | | | | |
| Singles | 23 | 19 | 32 | 38 |
| Single Parents | 61 | 56 | 60 | 74 |
| Families | 24 | 15 | 37 | 53 |
| **1989 Boston Poverty Rates** | | | | |
| Singles | 6 | 3 | 9 | 23 |
| Single Parents | 41 | 26 | 35 | 79 |
| Families | 19 | 8 | 22 | 45 |
| All Residents | 17 | 8 | 23 | 46 |

Source: The Boston Foundation, 1989

"A person seeing Quincy Market at five p.m. on a Friday would say, 'Wow, what a thriving, bustling city we live in,' but you have to get on the Red Line and see those people getting off at Fields Corner and going into the bank and cashing their checks," Mayor Flynn observed. "What is the take-home pay? It is not enough. They bring that envelope home and must pay rent, food, heat, and kids' education."[3]

As a result of the high housing costs, poverty in Boston was on the rise during the White years; in 1975, the number of families in poverty was 12 percent, gradually reaching 21 percent in 1985.[4] Factors contributing to the escalating poverty included rapidly rising housing prices and the immigration of low-income new immigrant families. The 1985 BRA Household Survey found significant differences in income by race and ethnicity. "Households headed by a [W]hite householder had a higher mean household income in 1984 than households headed by [B]lack or other minority householders," the authors reported. "The average household income of [W]hite householders was $25,750. Households headed by [B]lack householders had an average household income of $18,150, significantly lower than [W]hite households. White households' mean income increased by 3.5 percent between 1979 and 1984. At the same time, [B]lack households did not change significantly, falling from the 1979 mean of $18,400 in 1984 constant dollars to $18,150 in 1984."[5]

The BRA survey reported,

The distribution of household income by race and ethnicity highlights the disparity among the incomes of these different groups. While 28 percent of all Boston households earned less than $10,000 in 1984, only 22 percent of [W]hite households fell into this category, significantly lower than non-[W]hite households, with 35 percent of [B]lack households and 43 percent of other minority households reporting incomes below $10,000. Twenty-two percent of all households earned over $35,000, with 27 percent of [W]hite households earning this much, but only 14 percent of [B]lack households at or above this level. Although there was no significant difference by race in the proportion of households reporting their largest source of income as wages and salaries, a more significant proportion of [W]hite households reported Social Security benefits, veterans' benefits, pensions, or annuities as their largest source, 20 percent higher than any other race. A higher proportion of Black and other minority households reported unemployment compensation, SSI, AFDC, or welfare payments as their largest income source.[6]

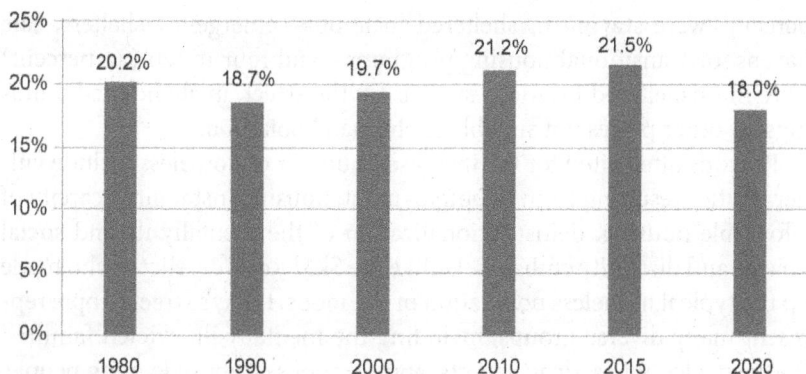

**CHART 13. Boston Poverty Rates, 1980–2020**
Source: Boston Planning and Development Agency

A combination of market forces, local and national public policies, social forces, and demographic change in the city fueled poverty and the housing crisis. How the city invests—from early childhood education to jobs, schools, and housing programs—is a response to these factors.

## Homelessness

Flynn saw the connections between homelessness and poverty, between affordable housing and jobs, and in those connections the need for a broad progressive agenda for Boston. Homelessness and poverty were emblematic of a more extensive set of problems he sought to address. The preceding chapters detail these interrelated housing, discrimination, and education issues. Flynn tells several stories of his interactions with people experiencing homelessness and the "rough sleepers" whom Dr. Jim O'Connell, who worked with homeless people on the streets and in the shelters, eloquently describes in Tracy Kidder's book *Rough Sleepers*.[7]

Gauging the number of homeless people in the United States is an inexact science, with some estimating that one-fifth of 1 percent of the US population experience homelessness on a given night in the country, which translates to about 568,000 people. Other estimates place the number well over a million people, with roughly 5 percent experiencing homelessness in their lifetime. This should be put into the context of over 34 million Americans living below the federal poverty line in 2019.[8] A 2022 HUD report stated, "On a single night in 2022, roughly 582,500 people were experiencing homelessness in the United States. Six in ten (60 percent) were staying in sheltered locations—emergency shelters, safe havens, or transitional housing programs—and four in ten (40 percent) were in unsheltered locations such as on the street, in abandoned buildings, or other places not suitable for human habitation."[9]

Reasons often cited for the increased number of homeless include vulnerabilities resulting from unemployment, housing instability, scarcity of affordable housing, deinstitutionalization of the mentally ill, and social service and disability cutbacks. Unlike the Skid Row "derelicts" who made up the typical homeless population of the 1960s, today's street people represent many diverse groups, including the mentally ill, evicted families, the aged, alcoholics, drug addicts, abused spouses, abused young people, and cast-off children.[10] These are sometimes called the *individual* factors, often seen as personal pathology.

Others see that *structural* factors, such as market conditions, housing costs, racism, discrimination, and inequality, causally explain the prevalence of homelessness. Under the structural explanation, homelessness is a consequence of broader and more profound societal factors driving people at the margins of society out of their housing. Finally, individual and structural factors both lead to the problem of homelessness, where the bottom line is housing.[11]

## Crisis of the Unhoused

As a city councilor and mayor, Flynn took the lead in addressing the homelessness crisis. In 1982, while on the city council, he sponsored legislation to create an emergency shelter commission to respond to the growing homelessness problem in Boston. White vetoed Flynn's proposal, and the council later approved the creation of the Emergency Shelter Commission and opened the vacant and unused Long Island Hospital to house people without housing, initially with 100 shelter beds. In 1982, the city administration estimated the city had more than 2,400 homeless people, but only 643 shelter beds were available combined at the Salvation Army, Rosie's Place, and the Pine Street Inn. The number of unhoused would increase annually, and under White, the city would play catch-up to provide shelter beds to house most of Boston's homeless.[12]

One of Flynn's first acts as mayor was to issue an executive order in January 1984, doubling the capacity of the city's shelter at Long Island and committing more than $1 million to help the homeless. The following month, he proposed a women's shelter and responded to the rapidly increasing homeless population, including allowing a ten-day tent city encampment of more than 200 homeless people on Boston Common in

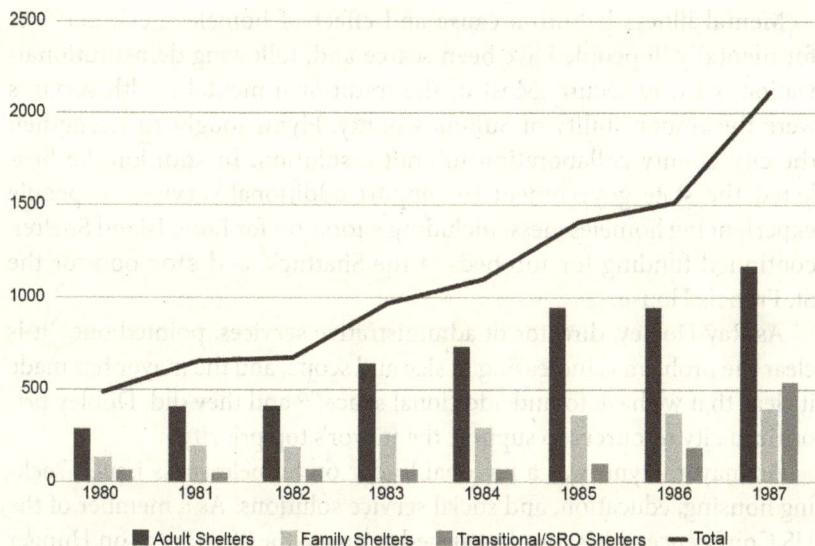

CHART 14. Shelter Beds in Boston, 1980–1987
Source: "Making Room: Comprehensive Policy for the Homeless," City of Boston, 1986

June of that year. Flynn said, "No society can call itself civilized when its people must sleep in alleys, parks, and bus stations. The real solution is not more shelters, but more decent affordable housing."[13] Emergency Shelter Commission executive director Joseph Vallely suggested, "There is no indication that the numbers of homeless are leveling off. More family shelters are needed. Given the demand, you could fill them up yesterday."[14]

In the first two years of Flynn's administration, the city spent approximately $6 million, leveraging an additional $13.6 million in state, federal, foundation, and private funds for homeless services and shelters. During this period, the number of shelter beds in Boston increased from 972 to 1512—a 56 percent increase. These include adult shelters, family shelters, and transitional housing for women and children.[15] As Chart 14 shows, the dramatic increase in shelter capacity occurred beginning in 1984 and was projected to continue into 1987 and beyond to respond to the growing need. As discussed in Chapter 5, housing production and regulation were seen as the most effective strategies to reduce homelessness. Katherine Mainzer, executive director of the Massachusetts Coalition for the Homeless, said, "The key is to develop more housing. The mayor has been very articulate on it. We can't lose sight of the action and agenda that are needed."[16]

Mental illness is both a cause and effect of homelessness. Services for mentally ill people have been scarce and, following deinstitutionalization, hard to secure. Most of the traditional mental health services were the responsibility of Suffolk County. Flynn sought to strengthen the city-county collaboration to craft a solution. In addition, he brokered the state government to support additional services to people experiencing homelessness, including $400,000 for Long Island Shelter, continued funding for 100 beds at the Shattuck, and $100,000 for the St. Francis House.[17]

As Ray Dooley, director of administrative services, pointed out, "It is clear the problem is increasing in size and scope, and the mayor has made it clear that we have to find additional space,"[18] and they did. Dooley prioritized city resources to support the mayor's top priority.

As mayor, Flynn was a national leader on homelessness issues, seeking housing, education, and social service solutions. As a member of the US Conference of Mayors, he pushed to create the Task Force on Hunger and Homelessness, which he chaired. To respond to the growing national homelessness crisis each year, the committee issued a report between Thanksgiving and Christmas based upon a survey of cities to encourage Congress and President Ronald Reagan to act. He would hold press conferences nationwide to fight for the issue to receive attention. During the 1988 presidential primary, Flynn invited candidates to visit Boston homeless shelters and make homelessness an issue in the campaign. Candidates Paul Simon, Al Gore, and Jesse Jackson took him up on the offer and toured several Boston homeless facilities.[19] In 2023, the committee continued this work under the leadership of Los Angeles mayor Karen Bass.

Flynn met with Governor Charlie Baker at the Parkman House when he was secretary of health and human services in 1992. Flynn told him how he rescued a homeless man in a blizzard and took him to Boston City Hospital. Governor Baker often reminded the mayor about "Jimmy the Broom," the homeless man the mayor had rescued. Dr. Jim O'Connell reminded the author that a facility on Long Island bears the given name of Jimmy the Broom: Woods Mullen.

"Flynn opened Long Island Shelter—he got it up and running to meet the winter shelter needs," recalled Susan Tracy, whom Flynn first appointed to head the Boston Emergency Shelter Commission. "Long Island, before it was closed in 2014 because of an unsafe bridge, played a pivotal role in serving the homeless and providing addiction and mental health services." Tracy, who created and led, along with Allan Stern, the city's Management Information Services director, the first empirical annual census of people without housing in the nation, knew that accurately and scientifically quantifying the homeless population was critical for securing funding and developing a strategy to respond. Past census attempts have varied widely on the number of homeless individuals, and Flynn wanted a methodology that would give the city credence. The census consisted of sending volunteers, led by the mayor—generally on a frosty night in January—to try and locate those homeless sleeping on the streets and those housed in shelters. The census process went on to become a national model. "Regardless of the number, however, one person homeless in a city like Boston and a nation like America is one person too many, Flynn added."[20]

Flynn and key administration staff, including Howard Leibowitz and Peter Dreier, convened all the city's homeless providers to develop a coordinated response to the growing problem. Flynn led the US Conference of Mayors and lobbied the White House and Congress to create a national response to increasing homelessness. At the urging of Leibowitz—who had a deep set of relationships with members of Congress—and with Flynn's connections with mayors across the country, Congress passed the McKinney-Vento Homeless Assistance Act of 1987.[21] The act provides federal funds for homeless shelter programs and support services. It was the first significant legislation to respond to homelessness, signed into law by Reagan, and has been reauthorized since.

In 1987, the widening crisis of homeless children and families led Flynn to compete aggressively for federal funding to respond. Boston was awarded $367,000 in the first year of the new act, primarily due to the mayor's leadership (personally lobbying members of Congress) and the city's response to the growing crisis already underway. As chair of the US Conference of Mayors Task Force on Hunger and Homelessness, Flynn pushed a resolution calling on the nation's lawmakers to increase spending for programs to feed the hungry and shelter people without housing. "It is an implicit bill of indictment of the failure of our national leaders to develop an effective urban policy to wipe out the disgrace of homelessness in this country," he said. He joined Philadelphia's mayor, Wilson Goode, and Chicago's mayor, Harold Washington, to call for housing and community development funds to ease the crisis.[22]

The Boston Healthcare for the Homeless Program (BHCHP) was founded in 1984, shortly after Flynn was elected mayor. "When I think back to the beginning of BHCHP, to that winter of 1984, I recall then-mayor Raymond Flynn convening a broad coalition of shelter and social service agencies, city and state representatives, hospital and health care leaders, and a feisty group of homeless persons and advocates," said Jim O'Connell. O'Connell learned early that the advocates were serious when Kip Tiernan, the women's shelter Rosie's Place founder, grabbed his tie during an interview. "Charity is scraps from the table, social justice is a seat at the table, and remember, we want a *seat*," Tiernan told him.[23] They would go on to develop a plan to create a charter for this new program—with a mandate to end the existing fragmented state of medicine for this marginalized population by providing continuity of high-quality health care from street and shelter to hospital to respite care to home. Dr. Joseph Cohen, chair of the BHCHP governing board and chief of medicine at the Lemuel Shattuck Hospital, was critical in pursuing grants from the Robert Wood Johnson Foundation and the Pew Charitable Trust, mobilizing state support to open the Shattuck for people experiencing homelessness. The proposal created three medical teams at various sites in Boston: BCH, Mass General Hospital, the Shattuck, Long Island Shelter, the Pine Street Inn, St. Francis House, and several small family shelters.

In December 1984, the city received a four-year, $1.4 million grant to integrate people experiencing homelessness into the city's medical system. "The warm message of support from the conference of mayors and the Johnson and Pew foundations contrasts with the chilling message America's cities have received from Washington," Flynn said at the announcement of the grant award. "In Boston, we have seen a troubling increase in low-income families seeking emergency shelter. In Washington, we are witnessing a shocking decrease in the funds to provide emergency shelter and health care for the homeless."[24]

The terms of the agreement by the funders required that a medical doctor lead the team of nurses, social workers, and other key staff. Flynn could not find a doctor to do so. Friends at Mass General Hospital, medical partners in the creation of the BHCHP along with the BCH and Shattuck Hospital, approached Massachusetts General Hospital's Dr. Tom Durant and Dr. John Potts, who both nominated someone to take on the role for a year—a newly minted doctor, James O'Connell. O'Connell said he felt he had been "conscripted" but could think of no way to refuse. On July 1, 1985, O'Connell began his mission, first caring for individuals experiencing homelessness in clinics located at the Pine Street Inn, Long Island Shelter, Boston City Hospital (now Boston Medical Center), and Massachusetts General Hospital and on the city's streets. O'Connell has led BHCHP since 1985 and continues as the country's leading homeless healthcare provider.[25]

"Ray Flynn was everywhere, met the van, gave us any support we needed from the police, fire and EMS, and BCH, and he was magic with the homeless," O'Connell said, reflecting on that experience. "*I considered Flynn an emotional leader. He understood the issue; he felt it.*"[26]

Flynn guaranteed a shelter bed for anyone who needed and wanted one but clearly understood more had to be done. The focus on afford-able housing was a priority, and the development of supportive housing facilities began under Flynn and continues to this day. Kidder would re-count when O'Connell tried to draw a picture of what had gone wrong in Boston and pointed to the massive development in the former New York Streets area. "Look at these new buildings all along here," O'Connell said. "There has to be at least four thousand new units there right next to the Pine Street Inn. But not a single one for homeless people."[27] He was refer-ring to the Ink Block, a luxury condominium redevelopment of parcels in the New York Streets area bulldozed in 1958, also the former home to the *Boston Herald*, built under the Menino administration.

The magnitude of homelessness can be elusive. On the one hand, the city homeless census would count between fifteen hundred and two thousand homeless during that snapshot on a winter's night. The BH-CHP serves ten thousand unduplicated homeless patients annually in its various programs. According to official estimates, between 2012 and 2017, homelessness had risen by nearly one-third, and the number of homeless families had doubled.

Comic Relief, the organization that featured Robin Williams, Whoopi Goldberg, and Billy Crystal, is a nonprofit that uses comedy fundrais-ing performances to aid America's homeless. It would frequently come to Boston to raise funds for the BHCHP and visit with people experiencing homelessness at the Long Island Shelter. "Williams came down to the Long Island Shelter, a hospital that I had just built, a shelter for homeless people in Boston, getting them off the freezing streets, and he was phenomenal," Flynn recounted after Williams's death. "He was extraordinary, entertain-ing all the homeless and staff."[28] Ann Maguire, who headed the Emergency Shelter Commission in 1987, talked about Flynn and the homeless. "It was his issue. It mattered to him, so you could go out there and get things ac-complished. When she told Flynn she needed twenty-five emergency shel-ter beds, he told her to do it. When she returned and had been told they couldn't do it, he said, 'Who told you that?'; lo and behold, we got the beds." She remembers walking with the mayor to St. Francis House. Once inside, he was at home with the residents; "he had a gentleness that made him care about the people and the issues the way he did."[29]

Flynn recalls bringing homeless people to sleep on the couch in his home's parlor on chilly winter nights and in the mayor's office. "I was walking by this homeless person on the street and thought I must do more to build housing in Boston," he said. "I can give him a buck, take him to Dunkin' Donuts, and buy him a roll and a coffee. He cannot wait for me to build more housing because he has no money. You can do something immediately, even though it's a short-term answer. It begins with heart; you don't return to city hall, walk up to the fifth floor, and say, 'I want a new project.' It's all about doing something now. That is what you have to do here."[30]

Massachusetts Housing and Shelter Alliance president and executive director Joe Finn wrote about Ray Flynn in 2018, "As Mayor of Boston, Ray Flynn was one of the first mayors nationwide to highlight the serious issue of homelessness. His approach to homelessness was rational and pragmatic, and he highlighted the unique convergence of social and economic conditions that created the reality of people living on our streets. He advocated for the investment of federal resources to respond to homelessness. He believed in the 'common good,' and his hope became Boston's legacy as Boston continued to address the issue of homelessness and recognized that the problem was not intractable but solvable."[31]

Did Boston's strategies for dealing with homelessness work? The city has not succeeded as long as one person or family is homeless, Flynn asserted. But the city's "emotional homeless leader" set a high bar for policy and personal interventions to make a difference. Mayors Menino, Walsh, and Wu have continued the city's commitment to people experiencing homelessness. During Walsh's tenure, the facilities at the city's Long Island Shelter campus were closed because of an unsafe bridge to the island, which was torn down. Walsh and Wu have allocated the necessary capital funding and worked hard to overcome challenges from neighboring Quincy to build a new bridge and renovate the Recovery Campus for homeless, mental health, and substance abuse services. Fortunately, the efforts initiated by Flynn and the work of the city's Emergency Shelter and Public Health Commissions have continued to this day, as has O'Connell at the Boston Health Care for the Homeless Program. One needs to have observed Mass and Cass, the former site of the city's largest and longest-running homeless encampment, to know the challenge is Sisyphean.[32]

# 13 / The 2013 and 2021 Mayoral Elections: New Directions for Boston

*We will expand the opportunity to reach every person in every corner of our city. We cannot tolerate a city divided by privilege and poverty. We will bring up neighborhoods that haven't seen prosperity in a long time.* (Marty Walsh, inaugural address and interview).

*Boston had the most significant income inequality of any American city in 2014. Five percent of households earned $266,224; the bottom 20 percent earned $14,942.*[1]

## Thomas Michael Menino

After Flynn formally resigned as mayor on July 12, 1993, a special election was called for the fall of that year. The city council petitioned the state legislature, which approved a change in the election cycle so that instead of filling out the remaining two and one-half years of Flynn's term, the next mayor would be elected to a full four-year term.

As city council president, Tom Menino became acting mayor and a candidate to succeed Flynn. Joining him in the preliminary election would be city councilors Bruce Bolling and Rosaria Salerno, Suffolk County Sheriff Robert Rufo, State Representative Jim Brett, police commissioner Mickey Roache, and Christopher Lydon. Councilor John Nucci decided not to run, as he said later about Menino's advantage, "Being acting mayor during the mayoral campaign is like being able to start the Marathon in Kenmore Square. It brings a huge advantage."[2] Menino and Brett would face off in the final election, with Menino prevailing 64 percent to Brett's 36 percent.

Menino ran unopposed for reelection as mayor in 1997, unheard of in Boston politics since 1834, and won decisively in each general election after that, beating Peggy Davis Mullen in 2001 by 76 percent to 24 percent, Maura Hennigan in 2005 by 68 percent to 32 percent, and, in his final election, defeated Michael Flaherty in 2009 by 57 percent to 42 percent.[3]

On October 30, 2014, Boston's longest-serving mayor, Tom Menino, died after a courageous battle with cancer. The seventy-one-year-old mayor served the people of Boston admirably for over thirty years, first as a city councilor elected in 1983 representing Hyde Park and Roslindale, and then five terms as mayor—twenty years, five months, and twenty-five days. I had the pleasure of interviewing Menino for this book. His contributions to Boston, its public schools and neighborhoods—which barely resemble the areas of distress and decay from decades earlier—were significant. However, his leadership during the tragic Marathon bombing on April 15, 2013, truly showcased his resilience and dedication to the city, forming a part of his lasting legacy.

His administration is referenced throughout the book concerning major themes that are explored—race relations, housing, development, and public school governance, among others.

On March 28, 2013, Menino made a historic announcement at Faneuil Hall, declaring that he would not seek an unprecedented sixth term. Solemnly stated, this decision surprised many and marked a turning point in Boston politics. At least one city councilor had already announced a challenge before Menino's statement, and soon a flurry of candidates would enter the race, eager for a chance at the first open seat for mayor in twenty years.

Just a few days before his announcement, Menino delivered a speech to the Boston Municipal Research Bureau that some saw as reflecting his legacy. "'Boston has a record of success when it comes to connecting residents with the necessary technology,' he said, 'and the city's housing market grew faster than it has in the last five decades,' two of which he was in charge of, by adding 20,000 housing units between 2000 and 2010. He proudly proclaimed, 'Our test scores are up. Our graduation rates are the highest they have ever been. Our students are outperforming their peers in other big cities. Our schools are better than ever but aren't as good as they will be.' Menino told the crowd that there are more jobs than ever in Boston, along with a growing rate of development and 'more young workers per capita than in any other city.'" These achievements, among many others, were a testament to Menino's dedication and vision for Boston.[4]

## The 2013 Mayoral Contest—Succeeding Tom Menino

Tom Menino claimed to be staying out of the race to succeed him. "I have no plans to pick the person to fill this seat," he said. "I just ask that you choose someone who loves this city as much as I do."[5] However, he reportedly told his political organization who they could work for in the preliminary election. City councilor John Connolly was not one of them, having earned Menino's scorn by announcing a challenge to Menino in February 2013 before he called it quits. Menino first blessed his Hyde Park neighbors, Suffolk County district attorney Dan Conley and city councilor Rob Consalvo. He also approved of his housing director, Charlotte Golar Richie, who was African American. Several were not on the list of acceptable candidates for his political organization's support. In addition to Connolly were city councilors Felix Arroyo and Charles Yancey, Cape Verdean community activist John Barros, and Codman Square Health Center director Bill Walczak.

After thirty years with two White mayors (Irishman Ray Flynn and Italian Tom Menino), the majority-minority city seemed poised to elect a person of color in 2013. Boston is one of two cities among the twenty-five largest that had never elected a mayor of color as of 2021.[6] Menino talked about this, apparently signaling support for Golar Richie, while several of his political operatives were assisting her campaign.[7] "She is a person of color [and] a woman," he said during the campaign. "The first woman elected mayor of the city of Boston. That would be national news." He later walked that back and insisted it was not an endorsement.[8]

The media, especially the *Boston Globe*, wrote about the issue. Kevin Peterson, director of the New Democracy Coalition, tried and failed to orchestrate Arroyo, Barros, and Yancey to clear the field for Golar Richie. The other candidates of color would not hear of it and were offended by the effort. Peterson circulated a letter seeking "consensus on who the consensus candidate from the Black community is." Latino mayoral candidate Felix Arroyo said in response to the effort to preselect an acceptable candidate of color, "We have a process for that. It's election day."[9]

During the primary election cycle, an editorial in the *Boston Globe* by Andy Sum and I stated that the top priority for the next mayor must be confronting the growing income inequality and reducing poverty, especially among the city's thirty-six thousand poor kids. "While we have seen impressive results in some neighborhoods being rebuilt and many positive changes in Boston over the past 20 years, including the enriching ethnic, racial, and economic diversity of the growing city, some neighborhoods are teetering on the brink from foreclosures, crime, and a lack of investment," the editorial said. "The next mayor must work with our poorer communities to identify how to collectively increase the social and economic capital of the city's families and raise our neighbors out of poverty."[10]

## Race and Class as Factors in the Mayor's Race

The mayoral candidates discussed the issues of race and class at many of the dozens of forums on the campaign trail. When asked about race relations during Boston's 2013 mayoral election, Michael Curry, president of the Boston chapter of the NAACP, said, "It is the elephant in the room none of us want to talk about." James Jennings, a specialist in race and politics at Tufts University, referring to the discussion of racism in Boston, added, "They uttered a word that has not been part of the public discourse around the social, economic, and demographic challenges facing the city of Boston."[11]

Unlike the 1983 election, during which the candidates discussed race issues—still raw from the racial conflicts surrounding the 1974 desegregation of the schools—most did not want to label the city as racist. Fast-forward thirty years, and half the candidates in the 2013 preliminary election were people of color. As the campaigns progressed, and each candidate's organization sought to capture every vote, the issue of race and identity politics continued to overshadow the election. The minority candidates had trouble raising campaign funds, and pundits consistently raised the specter of a White man becoming mayor of the majority-minority city. As the *Boston Globe* reported, "A united block of African Americans, Hispanics, and Asians is not a given. Research on how Black mayors get elected indicates that a coalition of Blacks and liberal Whites is more likely to succeed. The basis of political math means White voters will decide whether Boston elects a mayor of color."[12]

In a poll in late August 2013, nearly 60 percent of decided voters planned to support a candidate of their race, compared to 31 percent who said they did not, pointing to the ongoing issue of identity politics in Boston.[13] That contrasted with the 1983 election, when the two finalists disagreed with characterizing that race as coming down to identity politics. "In 1983, so-called 'identity politics' based on race didn't happen because Mel and I were talking about, and had a record on, the issues most people cared about: affordable housing, condo conversion, and using linkage to spread the wealth of the downtown to the neighborhoods," Flynn said. "It will not necessarily happen in 2013, either. It will depend on the two candidates who choose to get behind the issues people most care about, many of which are still the same."[14]

"Boston is a very different city now," King said about the 2013 mayor's race. He had been propelled into the 1983 final primarily by overwhelming majorities in communities of color. "I am always tickled," he added, "when I hear the assumption that people of color can only get votes from minority communities. No one talks about that for the White candidates. No one is asking if there are too many of them. No matter who it is, White, Black, Hispanic, or anything else, they must secure the backing of a good chunk of the minority community."[15]

Like Flynn, King also believed that how the candidates address the issues important to people is more important than the composition of the field. "The community is demanding affordable housing, access to high-quality schools, and an end to the 'lock-'em-up' prison culture," he said. "Interestingly, most candidates waited until Menino revealed he would not seek reelection to announce they would run. If folks had that burning desire to change things, why wouldn't they try to change them while he was in office? If you were going to do it, do it."[16]

Marty Walsh and John Connolly were the top two vote-getters in the 2013 nonpartisan election. Of the 113,000 voters who went to the polls (in the 1983 preliminary mayoral election, 169,309 voted), Walsh captured 20,284 votes or 18.5 percent of the total. Connolly received 19,425, 17.2 percent of the total. Third in the preliminary election was African American Charlotte Golar Richie, with 15,546 votes or 14 percent. The next three finishers were Suffolk County district attorney Dan Conley, who received 12,775 votes (11 percent), and two of the candidates of color, Felix Arroyo, with 9,895 votes (9 percent), and John Barros, with 9,146 votes (8 percent). The six White candidates received 58 percent of the votes, and the six candidates of color garnered 35 percent. Although Boston was a majority-minority city, the votes were not there for the candidates of color. Part of the reason may have been that people of color constituted less than half of registered voters, closer to 38 percent. With a total turnout of 31 percent, there was no opportunity for a candidate of color to emerge as a frontrunner with the highest-voting wards of West Roxbury and Dorchester, home bases to Connolly and Walsh, respectively, turning out the most voters.[17]

On November 5, 2013, the final mayoral election would pit two White Irish candidates against one another: Walsh, state representative and head of the Greater Boston Building Trades, and Connolly, a member of the Boston City Council whose family has a long political history in Massachusetts. Immediately following the preliminary election, both men aggressively courted the endorsements of Golar Richie, Barros, and Arroyo. Connolly and Walsh had garnered few votes in communities of color in the preliminary election. As a Connolly top campaign operative said, it made a difference for the Irish labor candidate once Walsh secured the endorsements of the three leading candidates of color, Golar Richie, Barros, and Arroyo. "He [Walsh] reeled off nine endorsements of people of color, which is what the race became about. It catalyzed everything." As Walsh's adviser said, "These endorsements validated Marty in a way that we could not have done otherwise. Most of these people had an intimate knowledge of both candidates, and everyone chose Marty, which speaks to his character. That was one of the biggest differences in the campaign. They trusted him."[18]

The *Boston Globe* suggested in a post-election analysis that people of color were the key to Walsh's victory:

> He won neighborhood after neighborhood in communities of color, precincts that neither he nor Connolly did especially well in during the preliminary election. That was the home base for the three candidates of color who earned the most votes during the preliminary. Charlotte Golar Richie, John F. Barros, and Felix G. Arroyo became Walsh allies during the final election, endorsements that appeared to translate into votes at the polls Tuesday. Walsh won in many places where Golar Richie, Barros, and Arroyo had their best showing in the preliminary. They captured the most votes in September in nine of Boston's 22 wards. Walsh topped Connolly in seven of those nine wards Tuesday. Voters weighed their options differently because Walsh had the backing of Golar Richie, Barros, Arroyo, and most of the state's elected officials of color. Voters may have disregarded their concerns about Walsh or believed in his cause even more because Walsh had the stamp of approval from trusted sources.[19]

Beyond race, class issues resonated in the election. Walsh labor supporters began to characterize Connolly as a "son of privilege," seeking to draw distinctions between the Irish pols. As Joan Vennochi of the *Boston Globe* wrote, "Some Walsh backers are trying to reduce that broad concern to something personal. Fliers that describe John Connolly as a 'son of privilege' who 'doesn't understand working-class people' are part of an effort to frame this race as 'Mahty' Walsh, son of Irish immigrants, versus John R. Connolly, offspring of a well-connected political family. The emphasis on whose roots are more humble also turns the bigger concern, the growing gap between rich and poor, into petty caricature."[20]

As a top official in the Connolly campaign conceded, "He was brilliant—playing the underdog, playing the class divide. At the very same time, he's pulling every power lever there is, moving the race. I do not know what we could have done differently."[21]

The results were clear. Class and race mattered in the 2013 mayoral election. Walsh won in precincts with a lower per capita income ($25,000 compared with $42,000 for Connolly). Connolly won precincts with a higher percentage of children enrolled in private schools (30 percent Connolly to 13 percent Walsh). Walsh toped Connolly in precincts where residents have lived there for more than a year, whereas newcomers went more heavily for Connolly. Walsh overwhelmingly won the blue-collar votes and those of people working in service occupations, while Connolly won the support of white-collar workers and those in management positions.[22]

Menino publicly stated right before the election that he was not backing any candidate: "I don't care who wins."[23] Reports surfaced about a feud between his son-in-law and Walsh, both residents of the Savin Hill area of Dorchester.[24] Reportedly, Menino's chief of staff sent a strong message to "Team Menino" about where the mayor stood on the election. On Election Day, Menino was riding around his neighborhood of Hyde Park and driving by his polling place. According to two independent sources, he gave a thumbs-down to Representative Angelo Scaccia, a longtime friend and ally, when he spotted him holding a Walsh campaign sign.

In the final election, 142,007 voters went to the polls, representing 38 percent of those registered (compared to 201,118 in 1983 when Flynn beat King and 70 percent of registered voters went to the polls). Walsh received 72,583 votes, 4,889 more than Connolly's 67,694 votes, taking eleven of the city's twenty-two wards and propelling him into the mayor's office.[25]

## The Legacy of Race in Boston

After the progress on race relations made under the administrations of Flynn and Menino, why was a candidate of color not in the final election in 2013? Why, nearly forty years after court-ordered school desegregation and the violent reaction to busing, are leading political figures still calling Boston a racist city? "There is racism in all of Boston, systemic, institutional, and structural," Connolly said about Boston during the campaign. Walsh also weighed in. "We have racism in the City of Boston that we have to deal with," he said. "We talk about one Boston, but we do not see one Boston in the City of Boston right now."[26]

Leaders have discussed class and race issues in Boston for some time, but income inequality and racial disparities continue to grow. When Menino was asked about his most significant achievement as mayor, he cited helping change Boston's reputation as a bitterly racist city to one that prizes its diversity. "I think I brought people together more than before," he said. "Boston was a real racist city at one point. You don't read about that anymore. We provided an opportunity to many people in our city who did not have one."[27]

He was right that you don't read about it anymore, but that does not mean that racism and inequality do not exist in the city. A report in the *Boston Business Journal* (*BBJ*) in December 2012 claimed, "Boston ranked second among all U.S. cities in the number of hate crimes reported in 2011. Approximately half of Boston's reported hate crimes were race-related, a fact that pokes holes in the idea the city has come a long way since the chaos following mandated school busing in the 1970s." The *BBJ* even went as far as to say, "One could even say Boston is the hate crime capital of the country, at least on a per capita basis."[28]

Walsh spoke about the "elephant in the room" on the campaign trail and vowed to address it. "We will expand opportunity so it reaches every person in every corner of our city," he said in his inaugural speech on January 6, 2014. "We cannot tolerate a city divided by privilege and poverty." But Boston was just that. When Walsh took office in 2014, Boston had the most significant income inequality of any American city. Five percent of households earned $266,224; the bottom 20 percent earned $14,942—5.6 percent of the top earners.[29]

As the founding vice chair of the US Conference of Mayors Cities of Opportunity Task Force dealing with income inequality, Walsh took many innovative steps in that direction. He focused on the net worth disparities in Boston and the country, knowing that the year he took office, 2014, the median net worth of a White family in Boston was $247,500, while the median net worth of a Black family was $8.[30] "The most important thing that was said at the table or was not said at the table was that this isn't a Democrat thing, this isn't a Republican thing, this is the right thing to do, and this is a bipartisan effort that we need to continue to move forward and close that gap," he said at the inaugural meeting of the Task Force in August 2014 alongside the chair, New York mayor Bill de Blasio.[31] Walsh told me he believed that mayors could do things to address income inequality, jobs, and opportunity but probably would not see the results in one's term in office.[32]

## Walsh Responds to Racial Challenges

Mayor Walsh responded to President Obama's call to address disparities for boys and young men of color by appointing a task force in Boston for the president's My Brother's Keeper initiative and following the release of a report by the Boston Public Schools that pointed out the significant educational disparities between boys who were Black and Latino and those who were White and Asian. "We know that nearly two-thirds of the young men in the city of Boston are Black or Latino," Walsh said. "We know that 78 percent of the males of our student population in Boston high schools are Black or Latino, so the success of our school system is riding on how we support them; it's time to stop talking and start taking action. This conversation needs to happen. This conversation is long overdue. These changes we are talking about will happen in our system. I didn't run for mayor for the status quo; I ran for mayor to make a difference in these young kids' lives, to create a truly level playing field and truly a just society."[33]

"One of those conversations that some of us choke on a little bit is we don't know if we have racism in Boston," said Walsh, Boston's fifty-fourth mayor, during a discussion following the screening of the film Selma. "There is a need for a conversation, not just a conversation but with action following it. There is a need to have conversations about race in Boston and beyond. We have to go beyond racial lines. The conversation on inequity and inequality in this country has to be discussed; we are having that conversation in Boston."[34] He admitted initially having shied away from the conversation but that he got a lot more comfortable discussing the issue of racism. It is not only racial violence but, as Mel King said, also that Boston must confront the politics of "class cleansing"[35] to make the city more just and equitable for all residents.

When George Floyd was murdered in Minnesota by a White police officer, Derek Chauvin, on May 25, 2020, more than two thousand cities and towns in all fifty states saw some form of demonstration in the weeks after Floyd's death, as did major cities around the globe.[36] According to Joyce Linehan, "Young Black members of our administration were walking around in a daze. . . . They were hurting big time. Mayor Walsh saw people's pain and could take one-on-one help he was used to giving out and make it universal."[37]

Walsh's legacy on race relations wasn't without its challenges. Controversy erupted over a proposed "slave memorial" at Faneuil Hall initially conceived by local African American artist Steve Locke. Walsh endorsed the Auction Block Memorial at Faneuil Hall. The city was to provide funding until it received vague opposition from the Boston branch of the NAACP. The project was abandoned.[38] After hours of hearings by the Boston Arts Commission on the proposed removal of a statue of President Lincoln and a formerly enslaved person, Archer Alexander, titled Emancipation Group, Walsh removed the statue from its Park Plaza location in December 2020 to be dealt with later.

Capping his racial healing efforts before resigning to become US secretary of labor, Walsh issued an executive order on June 12, 2020, declaring racism to be a public health crisis in Boston.[39] After a series of town hall meetings on race, he said, "We are not going to let this moment or this movement pass us by," pledging to reallocate 20 percent of the police overtime budget, about $12 million, to community public health and other initiatives to fight racism. Walsh had agreed to reallocate some funding from the city's $414 million police budget, arguing that arbitrary cuts don't fix big problems. "I mean cutting the budget, just cutting the budget, doesn't solve anything; cutting the budget doesn't deal with racism. Cutting the budget doesn't deal with systemic issues. That doesn't resolve anything."[40]

## New Housing, Development, COVID, the Arts, and Early Education Strategies

On January 14, 2019, Boston mayor Marty Walsh took to the historic Boston Symphony Hall stage to give his fifth State of the City address since his election in November 2013 and first since his reelection in 2017. Walsh boasted of the city's low unemployment rate, the construction of thousands of new housing units—many of which are affordable to low- and moderate-income families—and the city's attack on the persistent racism that plagued Boston and other American cities.

"Today, more people are working than at any time in our city's history," Walsh noted. "Unemployment is 2.4 percent, the lowest ever recorded; we are ranked number two in the nation for moving people up and into the middle class. And we've been named the best city in the world to find a job."

The previous week, he and his administration proposed altering the long-standing linkage formula that required developers to dedicate money and space in the projects to low- and moderate-income housing. The mayor and Boston City Council members also proposed imposing a luxury tax on real estate sales of property worth $2 million or more. These proposals would have raised millions of dollars in additional funds to construct affordable housing.

The proposals immediately received criticism from the *Boston Globe* editorial pages and growth machine interests, as they did when they were first introduced in the mid-1980s. Linkage in Boston is a settled policy. Still, the ability of any administration to maximize the resources available in robust economic times to share the benefits of growth was challenged by the growth machine and its political supporters. The formula remained relatively the same since the Flynn administration expanded the linkage policy to add job training in the 1980s. Menino only had the opportunity for an increase in linkage every three years based on the consumer price index. As a result, during Menino's twenty-year tenure, the funding level remained unchanged and stagnant. Finally, near the end of his term, Walsh significantly increased linkage, increasing fees on large new commercial buildings by 42 percent, from $10.81 per square foot to $15.39. That compares with the 8 percent hike Walsh signed off on in 2018. He persuaded the legislature to allow the city more flexibility in setting the fee structure, which hampered both him and Menino.[41] Walsh changed the inclusionary housing formula to double the contributions for affordable housing, the first change in nine years.[42]

During his tenure, Walsh made significant investments in housing with an ambitious plan, setting records for new affordable and middle-class homes. As he said in an interview during his second year in office, he was "holding off changing the linkage and inclusionary housing policies until he understood how they would affect the business climate. He also claimed that the city developed the largest number of low-income housing units in Boston in just one year and that he was well on his way to meeting his 2030 housing goal of thirty thousand housing starts."[43]

Walsh was cautious when he first took office, saying he didn't want to take actions that would slow growth. The opposite occurred. The *Boston Globe* reported, "Boston's total assessed value grew to $190.7 billion last year, a $14.5 billion increase over the previous year, thanks to new construction and building renovations—mostly in residential properties. Since January 2014, 86 million square feet of development worth more than $43 billion has been approved in Boston; this led to 80,972 construction jobs and 69,613 long-term jobs, part of the claim of having helped create 120,000 jobs since 2014. Lew Finfer suggested Walsh will leave a legacy of "his empathy for hard-working people."[44]

When Walsh met in his office with the leaders of Boston's CDCs to discuss the transit-oriented development planning effort on Dorchester Avenue, one CDC leader asked, "Do we need to do six stories?" The mayor retorted, "Can we do twelve to fifteen?" The density issue in Dorchester and Jamaica Plain had its detractors. Lori Hurlebaus, whose neighborhood in Dorchester was undergoing dense development, said, "Neighborhood by neighborhood, we see these developments prioritizing luxury housing. It is not housing that's being developed to meet the needs of working people."[45]

In an interview, Marie Turley, a Jamaica Plain neighborhood activist and senior official in the previous three city administrations, worried that "the density is hurting the abutting residential neighborhood. Prices are increasing, and there is no plan for neighborhood stabilization."[46] The neighborhood underwent a lengthy—and, some might argue, contentious—planning process, which led to significant changes on Washington

Street in Jamaica Plain. The mayor saw the plan as a strategy to address income inequality in the city. "We are very quickly, as all the stats show, becoming a city of those who have it and those who do not," he said.[47] The goal was to drive down housing prices through density, inclusionary zoning, and reduction of parking spaces. Jamaica Plain, South Boston, and Dorchester each faced significant challenges in maintaining a robust supply of affordable housing. As of 2024, whether the strategy delivered as intended remained unanswered.

Walsh fought aggressively to fulfill his 2013 campaign pledge to implement early childhood education by adding hundreds of high-quality pre-kindergarten seats, championing extended learning time and advanced curriculum at more schools, and securing tuition-free community college for Boston Public Schools graduates. As he prepared to leave office, he proposed $15 million in the fiscal year 2020 city budget to complete the rollout of pre-K for all four-year-olds in the city, estimated to reach four thousand kids by 2025.

Long a champion for immigrant rights, Walsh created the Greater Boston Immigrant Defense Fund, partly in response to President Trump's crackdown on immigrants. Walsh had long pledged that Boston would offer safe harbor for undocumented immigrants and, in 2017, famously offered city hall as a shelter of last resort for immigrants in need, saying, "They can use my office. They can use any office in city hall."[48] Walsh added in response to Trump, "We will not be intimidated by a threat to federal funding. We will not retreat one inch. To anyone who feels threatened or vulnerable, you are safe in Boston."[49]

He led the city's effective response to the COVID pandemic, which saw the schools and city hall close for long periods. Other milestones include the nation's first municipal Office of Recovery Services to prevent and treat substance abuse, and the first equity and inclusion cabinet was appointed in 2013. Walsh could take credit for improving the city's quality of life, with crime down 30 percent during his time in office and arrests down 33 percent after his police department took five thousand guns off the streets.[50]

An area of city life that often received low priority was the arts. Walsh created the first cabinet-level Office of Arts and Culture and led the city's first cultural plan in a generation, Boston Creates, to restore Boston's identity as an arts leader. According to Joyce Linehan, Walsh's chief of policy who led the planning initiative, the city's efforts to save the Huntington Theatre, built in 1925 as America's first nonprofit playhouse, were significant.[51] "The Walsh administration has done a sensational job as a steward of keeping these legacy theaters in place, particularly the Huntington and the Colonial," theater critic Ed Seigel wrote. "The consensus of these various entities now is that the mayor's office had the backs of the arts organizations."[52] Linehan added, "We saved the Huntington Theatre in perpetuity."[53]

## The 2021 Mayoral Contest: Progressivism Reemerges in Boston

Walsh's departure from city hall to the White House in 2021 marked a historic moment for Boston. It led to the elevation of Councilor Kim Janey, the city council president, as acting mayor. Janey's ascent was a personal achievement and a significant milestone for the city. She became the first African American and first woman to hold the mayor's office. While race played a significant role during the 2013 mayoral election, in 2021, most believed it was not as prominent an issue. Segun Idowu, executive director of the Black Economic Council of Massachusetts, said, "The fact that there are so many candidates of color is one measure of that. The conversation has shifted from 'We'll never have a person of color as mayor' to 'Which one will we have?'"[54]

Although Janey ran for the permanent job in the city's 2021 preliminary election, she was edged out by city councilor Annissa Essaibi George of Dorchester and city councilor Michelle Wu of Roslindale. Wu became the first woman and person of color elected to the post, a testament to the city's growing diversity and inclusivity, and showed the city's changing political landscape. She arrived in the mayor's office and built upon the mayors who preceded her, paving the way for a more inclusive Boston. Her win by a wide margin marked a clear shift toward a profounder progressivism in the city.

Wu was born in Chicago, the daughter of Taiwanese immigrants. She assumed significant responsibilities for her family, caring for her ailing mother and raising her sisters. As she has said in the context of her life and as a political leader, she often felt "alone, invisible, and powerless."[55] As a young small businesswoman, she started a tea café in Chicago. She later attended Harvard University, graduating in 2007, and went on to Harvard Law School, receiving her law degree in 2012. While at Harvard, she met Professor Elizabeth Warren and became her political and constituency group organizer in Warren's US Senate campaign. She also worked as the state coordinator for Asian and Pacific Islander American Vote (APIA Vote), the largest nonpartisan political nonprofit focusing on Asian–Pacific American civic engagement and political mobilization in Massachusetts.[56] Wu's first city government experience was working for Mayor Menino as an "urban mechanic" on the mayor's civic research and design team.[57]

In 2013, Wu made her first bid for public office at age twenty-eight, running for an at-large seat on the Boston City Council. She was successful and reelected in 2015, 2017, and 2019. She was in her fourth term when she announced her candidacy for mayor of Boston in September 2020. Wu was the first Asian American woman to serve on the council. In January 2016, she was unanimously elected president of the city council by her colleagues, becoming the first woman of color to serve as council president. She had frequently criticized Walsh in the media. After criticizing a city coronavirus fund, Walsh said, "It would be better if the city councilor just took time out of her schedule to call me and maybe talk to us about her concerns."[58] She had been positioning for a run for mayor, having told one Boston civic leader that was her plan from the beginning.

Wu announced a run for mayor before Walsh was appointed US Department of Labor secretary. Like the mayoral election in 2013, when Connolly announced his candidacy for mayor before Menino decided not to run, her announcement was preempted by Walsh, who announced that she was challenging him for his job. He was criticized for stealing her thunder and stepping on her announcement.[59]

The 2021 mayor's race saw six candidates vie for the office: Wu; city councilor Andrea Campbell from Mattapan (who also announced before Walsh announced he was resigning); acting mayor Kim Janey from Roxbury; councilor Annissa Essaibi George from Dorchester; John Barros, city economic development chief under Walsh, from Dorchester; and Representative Jon Santiago, a South End physician who dropped out of the race in July 2021. The election would be the first time in the city's history that a White man would not be mayor.

The preliminary election held on September 14, 2021, would see as the finalists Wu with 36,060 votes (33.4 percent) and George with 24,268 votes (22.5 percent), edging out Campbell by less than 3,000 votes to secure the second spot for the final election ballot. Janey trailed 250 votes behind Campbell. Advocates in the Black community had hoped that with several Black candidates in the race, one would make the final. If Janey or Campbell were in the race alone, some argued one of them would have been a strong contender in the final, given their combined 42,346 votes representing 29.2% of the total vote.[60]

Wu ran on a progressive platform, including making the MBTA fare-free for Boston residents, reforming the police department, enacting rent control, confronting the climate crisis, and, among other issues, eliminating the Boston Planning and Development Agency. Renamed by Walsh, it still was the Boston Redevelopment Authority and the Economic

Development and Industrial Corporation, the two major city development agencies, by another name.

Essaibi George was also the daughter of immigrants. Her father was from Tunisia, and her mother was Polish (she identified as a person of color). She was considered a moderate traditional political leader hailing from more conservative Dorchester. She taught at East Boston High School for many years and ran a small business in Dorchester. Her platform included dealing with the homeless crisis at Mass and Cass, rejecting calls for reallocation of police funding, and supporting adding mental health staff to help the police. She supported the expansion of the city housing stock targeted at middle-income homeowners and larger units, opposed rent control, and supported a more significant role for the city in public housing. She proposed responding to the climate crisis by making school buildings green and expanding open space. And she proposed prioritizing tackling the opioid crisis.

Wu and Essaibi George raised considerable campaign funds, with Essaibi George slightly outpacing Wu by about $335,000 (Wu raised $2.653 million and Essaibi George $2.688 million). Outside groups continued the financing of mayoral contenders that began in the 2013 election. They gave more to Essaibi George at $1.209 million than Wu's $879,000, while Wu had outside groups opposing her with $343,000 in campaign funds. Both were less than the 2013 election, where Walsh and Connolly raised $9.4 million in addition to $3.8 million in outside funds.[61]

Wu outpaced Essaibi George in the endorsement battle, although each received several union endorsements. Wu received more endorsements from elected officials, including acting mayor Kim Janey, Congresswoman Ayanna Pressley, and Senator Elizabeth Warren. The *Boston Herald* endorsed Essaibi George. After supporting Andrea Campbell in the preliminary election, the *Boston Globe* endorsed Wu in the final. "The Globe endorses at-large City Councilor Michelle Wu of Roslindale, the first-place finisher in the preliminary election with an expansive vision for the city's following chapters and a proven record of ethical leadership," the *Globe* wrote. "In this election, she has sketched an agenda for a greener, more equitable city. She's committed to tackling one of Boston's stubborn, entrenched problems—a police department lacking too many residents' trust. She's a persistent advocate for mass transit and rightly sees it as a way to both clean up the environment and ease the crippling traffic congestion that has been an unfortunate byproduct of the city's growth. She envisions setting up a system to help families navigate the bewildering complexity of the Boston Public Schools."[62]

Walsh's role in the 2021 election was unclear. He said then that he had no plans "to put my thumb on the scale." Reports referred to him as an "ally" of Essaibi George. The Local 223 Laborers' Union, Walsh's union headed by his cousin, endorsed Essaibi George, as did several of his labor allies. The *Globe* reported that Essaibi George escorted Walsh's mother to the polls. Ironically, Wu won the home precinct where Walsh and Essaibi George grew up.[63]

When the votes were counted in the final election for mayor on November 2, 2021, Wu received 91,974 votes, representing 64.0 percent of voters, and Essaibi George received 51,125 votes, representing 35.6 percent. Overall, the voter turnout was 33 percent of registered voters, down from the 38 percent who voted in the 2013 election when Walsh was elected. Compared to the 1983 election between King and Flynn, voter turnout in 2013 and 2021 was significantly down from the historic 70 percent turnout when Flynn received 128,575 votes (65 percent), and King received 69,015 votes (35 percent).

Wu won nineteen of the city's twenty-two wards with a diverse mix of voters from Roxbury's Black community to the more liberal wards of Jamaica Plain, the South End, Back Bay, Allston Brighton, and Roslindale. Essaibi George gathered support from South Boston, parts of West Roxbury, and Dorchester. Wu had received the endorsement of many progressive organizations, including one hundred Latino leaders in Boston. Her coalition earned significant votes that had gone to Janey and Campbell in the preliminary election. Her deep voter support, evidenced by being the top city council vote-getter twice in her three terms, served her well. Wu had no large natural political base like many of the other candidates. So how did she win? State Representative Aaron Michlewitz, chair of the powerful Ways and Means Committee and a friend of Wu's, offered, "The old-school way of winning in Boston was always, 'I come from this neighborhood, and I'm going to pick up that neighborhood, and then that neighborhood.' I can't even tell you where her base is from a neighborhood standpoint. That changes the entire campaign dynamic to something many people aren't used to."[64] Still, her vote and neighborhood totals mirrored Menino's 1993 election bid. Wu essentially won based on policy and ideology, moving beyond the ethnicity, race, and geography of past mayoral elections.

Because Walsh resigned before the election, Wu was sworn in earlier than would have happened in a normal election cycle and assumed office on November 16, 2021.

The *Washington Post* weighed in on the Wu election:

> The wonky, very progressive Michelle Wu won the mayoral election in Boston on Tuesday, illustrating that left-wing ideas can appeal to a broad swath of Democratic voters and a major test of whether

these ideas can work in practice. The resurgent progressive movement hasn't won a lot of executive roles across the country, so it's usually in the position of just talking about its big ideas. Now, Wu must run a city of nearly 693,000. And while Boston hasn't had the recent crime surge that other big cities have, it has other problems of urban America, such as a lack of affordable housing and a huge racial wealth gap. Boston is an ideal place to advance a progressive agenda.[65]

It has been tried before; Bostonians will find out if it can be done again.

## Wu's First Term in Office: Successes, Challenges, and Political Battles

On January 25, 2023, Mayor Michelle Wu delivered her first State of the City address, the first time it was given since 2020 because of the pandemic. She highlighted the progress of her first year in office and the challenges ahead. She outlined many bold plans, as during her campaign, to change the way the city does business: for example, to address the affordable housing crisis—including her proposals for rent stabilization and using the city-owned property for housing, infrastructure improvements and climate resilience, and abolishing the Boston Planning and Development Agency:

> As we look to the year ahead, our administration is focused on building a green and growing city for everyone. When the "Boston Redevelopment Authority" was created nearly 70 years ago, its purpose was singular: to clear the way for new development, even if that meant displacing tens of thousands of working-class, immigrant, and Black and brown residents. Since 2016, it's been called the Boston Planning and Development Agency, or "BPDA." Still, the focus on building buildings rather than community has held back the talent of its staff and deepened disparities in our city. Over the last decade, Boston saw the most prominent building boom in generations: cranes in the sky and jobs on the ground. But that growth wasn't harnessed for the benefit of all our communities.[66]

There were no significant incidents of racial conflict in Wu's first three years in office, although some community leaders saw race emerge in several policy proposals. Wu defeated two African American women and one African American man for the mayor's office, and she would go on to tout the diversity she has brought to city hall in her 2023 State of the City address. "That team is here tonight. Our Cabinet is two-thirds people of color! We are BPS parents and graduates. We speak Spanish and Arabic, Vietnamese, Haitian Creole, and more. We speak honestly about Boston's past, present, and future because we have lived the challenges and shared the dreams of the families we now get to serve."[67]

African American community members were still smarting from not electing a Black mayor. After the preliminary election, which sent Wu and Essaibi George to the final, members of the Black community reacted, "My community is in grief." State Representative Russell Holmes said the results were tougher to take than in 2013, the last open mayoral election that produced a diverse set of candidates. This time around, he noted, "The city had a Black acting mayor and could not hold on to her."[68] Wu acknowledged then, "We have a lot of work to do in Boston. We are at a moment when no Black finalist is in the election. However, this is still a moment for the Black community."[69]

The Black community has gone on to organize to change that for the future, analyzing the results of the mayor's race and found that "roughly 30 percent of White Boston voters cast ballots in Boston's 2021 mayoral preliminary, but only 25 percent of Black voters and 14 percent of Latino voters participated." But the big question raised by the mayoral election never went away: "What would it take to boost Black turnout, to give Dorchester, Roxbury, and Mattapan greater sway in a city that has given them short shrift for too long?"[70]

During Black History Month in 2023, Wu highlighted Black leaders, acknowledging the work the city must do to reverse policies that have harmed Black residents. "I have the chance to be surrounded by Black excellence, Black joy, Black brilliance, Black persistence, every single day here working for the city of Boston," she said.[71] Not long after that, she announced the formation of a Reparations Task Force at the African Meeting House. "For four hundred years, the brutal practice of enslavement and recent policies like redlining, the busing crisis, and exclusion from city contracting have denied Black Americans pathways to build generational wealth, secure stable housing, and live freely," she said. "Our administration remains committed to tackling long-standing racial inequities, and this task force is the next step in our commitment as a city to advance racial justice and build a Boston for everyone."[72]

Wu knew she needed to respond to the concerns of Blacks and other people of color—indeed, all residents of Boston's neighborhoods—and she began to do that immediately after taking office, not without criticism. The rising violence and increased shootings in early 2023 had some community religious leaders criticizing the mayor. "This is a disgrace, and she's ducking and dodging the issue," Rev. Eugene Rivers said about Wu. "This indifference would not happen under [Mayors] Walsh, Menino, Flynn."[73] At a Violence Reduction Task Force meeting at the Charles Street AME Church in Roxbury, Rev. Gregory Groover asked leaders of all faiths to unite. "We can turn this around. We did it before, and by God's help, we can do it again," Rivers said, adding, "We're asking Mayor Wu; you have to be leadership for all of the city. You cannot ignore the Black community." Wu's office said, "There is no greater priority for our city than ensuring people feel safe and welcome in their communities."[74] In an interview, Wu was prideful of the city's efforts in response to crime, touting "our remarkable numbers on safety, the huge declines we have been seeing in crime statistics. We have undertaken new approaches for how to bring the community into safety."[75]

Jimmy Hills, a Dorchester talk show host of *Java with Jimmy*, says, "Black Bostonians would give Wu a C-plus to a B-minus so far waiting for economic development, housing, and equitable education policies to come a little quicker."[76]

David Hopkins, associate professor of political science at Boston College, said, "The outstanding question now is whether Wu can create a legacy that leaves lasting impacts on the day-to-day lives of people in Boston. It's tough to do. You're always up against many powerful people who are invested in the status quo . . . . and voters who sometimes can favor change in the abstract but not so much when it gets to be about a specific change. She's made her mark symbolically, but does that translate into tangible differences in the policy of the city government and differences in the way that city government related to the state government and other relationships in the political system? That really is not yet clear that she'll be able to do that. . . . I think, after two years or three years or four years, maybe it'll be a better place to answer it."[77] "There are bound to be moments when some of her big ideas collide with the messy reality of how things get done and the pace at which change happens, if at all. I think activists are at some point going to be disappointed," said Gintautas Dumcius, editor of the *Dorchester Reporter*, calling that "part and parcel of what happens when a candidate shifts from campaigning to governing."[78]

## Early Results and Political Controversies

Her bold, progressive agenda framed Wu's first three years in office. While there were difficulties and predictable opposition from the growth machine coalition and others that placed their economic self-interest above all else, she has successfully increased linkage and inclusionary development by raising the percentage of affordable units required in housing developments. She had fended off the charge of killing the goose that laid the golden egg, the common refrain from the growth machine.

She talked about her strategy, "We are finding ways. . . . For example, as part of our antidisplacement strategy, part of our zoning reform is to ensure that we are bringing equitable growth across the city and more affordability for our residents. We are building new affordable homeownership units. We are investing in the Boston Public Schools. All of these are efforts to close gaps and invest in equality."[79]

The city council adopted her home rule petitions for rent control, a high-end real estate excise tax, expanding liquor licenses in underserved neighborhoods, restructuring the city's development agencies, and—importantly—tax reclassification. However, four of the five home rule petitions, each of which she supported with testimony in the State House, have languished. Only the expansion of liquor licenses was enacted. Lacking seemingly was a well-understood or articulated political strategy to see the petitions achieve their purpose. There appeared to be an absence of organizing efforts with those who got Wu elected to push Beacon Hill legislators to implement her and their agenda.

Wu has predictably faced some controversy following her honeymoon period in the mayor's office, from bike lanes to parks, outdoor dining, and zoning. There is discontent with Wu among some groups that supported her during her campaign. The Alliance of Downtown Civic Organizations, which advocates for nine of the most prominent resident associations in downtown Boston, had supported Wu for mayor, but now "association members' sentiments toward Wu skew negative."[80] "The problem with their process is they come into the community with a plan and say they want to hear from you, but they've already made up their minds," said city councilor Tania Fernandes Anderson, whose district includes Franklin Park and the O'Bryant School.[81]

The leadership in the North End Chamber of Commerce and twenty-one restaurants filed suit against the city regarding outdoor dining restrictions imposed only on the North End neighborhood. Many residents supported the outdoor dining ban, and according to the mayor, the North End has several serious, unique challenges with density and parking. Former city councilor and Italian American historian Larry DiCara said, "The North End is being treated differently than everyone else. If I were mayor, I'd figure out a way to make it work. It's not a good use of the legal system."[82] DiCara's quote in the *Globe* earned him the ire of Mayor Wu, who called him the same day the story appeared to share her displeasure.[83]

THE 2013 AND 2021 MAYORAL ELECTIONS / 265

As Wu's administration proceeded with an aggressive and focused agenda, many longtime activists have perceived that the city does not support meaningful engagement regarding zoning and development. "The tides have turned a little bit away from Wu because she's not living up to the expectations created in her campaign," said Alison Frazee, executive director of the Boston Preservation Alliance, who supported Wu in her first election but said she wouldn't vote for the mayor again if the election were held today. "We give our feedback, and it's completely ignored." "We want the city to make decisions with us, not for us," added Connie Forbes, chair of the Roxbury Neighborhood Council.[84]

Wu has a clear perspective on the current zoning and development process. "There's near universal agreement that the status quo is broken," Wu said, adding that she "knew headed into this role that taking action can come at a political cost." But this is about "bringing more people into setting the new foundation," she said. Former city councilor Matt O'Malley, a strong Wu supporter and appointee of Governor Healey to the BPDA board, views the conflict differently: "You sometimes have a small group of people who are self-appointed guardians for a neighborhood, who dictate what can and cannot be built. And that's inherently unfair and stymies a lot of good development. A fairer, streamlined, more understandable process benefits everyone. Will there be some political fallout? Of course, but it's a risk well worth taking."[85]

Wu announced in an emotional flourish at her 2024 State of the City address the establishment of a pilot program twice monthly for Boston Public School families to provide free access to the city's major cultural institutions—an exciting and long-overdue initiative to connect Boston students to these tax-exempt institutions that, in most cases, they cannot afford, with admission for a family of four costing over one hundred dollars. The administration demurred when several city leaders and parents advocated expanding the program to the other primarily low-income Boston families attending the charter or METCO schools. "While the program was welcome news for the 46,000 students in the Boston Public Schools, the roughly 13,000 Boston students who attend public charter schools are out of luck, as they aren't included. Neither are the 2,800 Boston students who attend suburban school districts through the METCO program," wrote Michael Jonas in the *Commonwealth Beacon*.[86] After significant pressure, Wu agreed to expand the BPS Sundays program to all Boston school-age children and their families in 2025.[87]

In an interview, Wu said, "We have seen progress when it comes to stabilizing and building out a vision for the Boston Public Schools, which have had a lot of instability over the last several years." She also described expanding upon Walsh's efforts to increase the number of pre-K seats in the Boston Public Schools and address the lack of child care available or affordable to many families. "Child care has huge gaps in different parts of the city. We have over the last several years increased the number of pre-K seats dramatically, opened up new classrooms for early education, and created a one-stop shop where families can finally see in one place all of the options available to them. I know that child care was important to Mayor Flynn as well. My kids went through the City Hall child care program that he started when he was mayor. He really was forward-thinking about how working families need support to balance everything."[88]

Another major issue that emerged early in the mayor's tenure was to press ahead, absent a broad community consensus, to bring in a private group to run a women's soccer franchise at the city's White Stadium in Franklin Park. The Boston Public Schools manage White Stadium, which is in serious disrepair. The city had allocated $50 million for renovations contingent on $30 million in funds from Boston Unity Soccer Partners (later raised to $50 million), who would bring the women's soccer franchise to Boston. Some find this to be an exciting and ambitious proposal. There has been a mixed reaction from others in the community, and when I discussed this with Mayor Wu, she seemed to acknowledge mistakes.

The Franklin Park Coalition, a fifty-year-old community-based park advocacy organization that serves as a voice for the park and the diverse communities of park users, surveyed about the city's proposed White Stadium renovation project. "More than 700 park users from the neighborhoods surrounding Franklin Park responded with fifty-six percent 'all for it' or 'cautiously support,' and forty-five percent were having 'some concerns' or are 'against it.'" The coalition has endorsed the project, says Rickie Thompson, the coalition board president and lifelong park user. "Renovation of White Stadium is long overdue."[89]

The Emerald Necklace Conservancy, a nonprofit group that raises funds to maintain, restore, and protect the parks, challenged the mayor's proposal in Superior Court along with more than 20 residents seeking a preliminary injunction to halt the project until the case's merits could be adjudicated. More than 140 community leaders and six organizations signed a Statement of Principles supporting the Conservancy position. "The plan as it was developed and announced did not include significant consultation with community groups immediately adjacent to the stadium," said Ted Landsmark, who serves on the board of the Boston Planning and Development Agency as well as on the board of directors of the Emerald Necklace Conservancy. Landsmark said there is still a way "for the parties to come together."[90] The Parks Department and Boston School Committee went on to approve the project in September 2024.[91]

On March 22, 2024, the judge denied the request for a preliminary injunction. Mayor Wu praised the judge's ruling in a statement: "I'm thrilled to see the court's clear ruling that this frivolous lawsuit from the Emerald Necklace Conservancy must not block our ongoing community engagement to deliver a generational investment in White Stadium and Franklin Park."[92] Renee Stacy Welch, a plaintiff and community leader from Jamaica Plain, responded to the mayor's statement: "Black and Brown residents are not being heard, and our voices and concerns are being dismissed as frivolous," she said. "This decision bulldozes my community's rights to public land."[93] Lisa Fliegel, a trauma specialist who works in Dorchester, questioned what she sees as a team of affluent, primarily White outsiders placing their vision at a site that has historically served Boston's communities of color. "This is a group of White women who are investing in what they think is this cool feminist project, and of all the places in the world to do it, they're doing it in Franklin Park," she said.[94]

Several days later, the city convened a meeting led by city councilor Tania Fernandes at the Trotter School, attended by many community residents opposed to the project filling the school auditorium. Attendees brought up issues of transportation, environmental justice, and privatization. Nefertiti Lawrence of Roxbury stood up at the microphone to express what may be the central issue: "An awesome area with a beer garden? It's not for folks like us. Many people won't feel welcome," she said.[95]

Plaintiff Jean McGuire of Roxbury, the first African American woman elected to the Boston School Committee (in 1981), executive director of METCO, and a community activist who lives four blocks from Franklin Park, said, "Franklin Park, as Fredrick Law Olmsted originally designed it over a century ago, is for the people who live here. It's not for any private group to profit from; it's for the public's free use." And finally, plaintiff Rodney Singleton, a Roxbury resident, said the group is fed up with the disregard by city officials in response to concerns raised about the planned renovation of the stadium. "Would the city give Boston Common or the Public Garden to private hands? No," he said.[96] The plaintiffs, calling themselves the Franklin Park Defenders, announced on April 23, 2024, their intention to proceed with the lawsuit despite the court's denial of their preliminary injunction request. The lawsuit, absent an agreement between the mayor and the plaintiffs, is scheduled for trial in 2025 after the stadium is slated to be demolished.

Wu responded in an interview about the White Stadium proposal opposition, saying, "I think there has been some misunderstanding of what we are trying to do, some misrepresentation of the facts. Many groups have been engaged in this process. The Franklin Park Coalition and many neighborhood associations have used and are in the park daily. Some people involved in the opposition don't spend time in Franklin Park; I don't know if they have ever been to White Stadium." In response to criticism that BPS students would not have sufficient access to the facility, Wu said, "I can guarantee that this would open up the stadium for far, far more public uses than currently happens right now," saying the renovation plan would "at least triple" the hours Boston Public Schools can use the stadium, which has fallen into disrepair and currently sits "locked up" most of the time. Meanwhile, the women's soccer team's thirteen to fifteen home games a year "would end up taking less than 10% of the available hours."[97]

Wu evoked Frederick Law Olmsted's concept of communitiveness, as referenced earlier by Steve Coyle discussing the Boston Harbor Walk, saying the park is a place for both active and contemplative use, calling it "the DNA of what Franklin Park is, and we are trying to restore the full usage of it."[98] Olmsted viewed parks as restorative places that could help individuals be more inclined to "serve others and to be served by others"—what he called "communitiveness." "He believed that healthy civil societies bring people together. In good times and times of crisis, parks and open spaces give people from all walks of life a place to connect. They offer a setting for diverse individuals and groups to find common ground, whether playing host to family celebrations, local festivals, political rallies or other activities," according to the Olmsted Network.[99]

Joan Vennochi summarized in the *Boston Globe* the concerns of many: "Wu's failure to build a loud and public network of support for the White Stadium plan—before she announced it—took the gloss of what could otherwise be seen as bold and creative leadership. The same thing happened with her proposal—later withdrawn—to move the John D. O'Bryant School of Mathematics and Science from Roxbury to West Roxbury without first getting the O'Bryant community on board. You could blame those challenges to Wu's vision on the forces of 'no,' which are undoubtedly strong in Boston. But it also shows an inability or unwillingness to build trust by listening and responding to concerns before unveiling her grand vision."[100] Wu characterized the "community process playing out how it was intended" in each of these controversies.[101] The *Boston Globe* endorsed Wu's plan in 2023, when first announced, and again in 2024 with the headline, "Despite Shaky Rollout, Wu's White Stadium Plan Is Good for Student-Athletes."[102]

Wu shared her thoughts on her approach to change, expressing her sense of urgency to get things done:

> It's always complicated to introduce change even when it is much-needed change, like issues that everyone agrees we need action on. We are learning and growing every day in how we build that muscle across the communities to do more than one thing at one time. I came in at a time when there is a lot we have to catch up on. Not only that, new things, but there many things that need to happen all at the same time because we have run out of time for fixing them. So, it's a combination of multiple areas where it can feel overwhelming."[103]

Many people in Boston cheered for Michelle Wu's success in creating a new progressive urban agenda. The city had a unique opportunity to build the progressive and inclusive city many in Boston struggled to achieve for nearly three decades, if not longer. What a number of the issues raised earlier indicate—including the reorganization of the development agencies and the ill-fated proposal to move the O'Bryant to West Roxbury—is that if the neighborhoods and important constituent groups are not engaged in a meaningful way in the process of change, many of the bold and brilliant ideas will remain just that: ideas.

## How Did Flynn, Menino, Walsh, and Wu Differ, and How Were They the Same?

Each mayor provided a foundation for Boston's economic and social success. As described in the previous chapters, Flynn was hyperkinetic about what he wanted to accomplish for working people in Boston. His policies were geared toward the poor and needy residents, whether in public housing or a homeless shelter. His focus was the same—sharing the benefits of the city with its neighborhoods and engaging city residents as active partners through neighborhood councils and other participatory mechanisms. His efforts at race relations were unmatched by any mayor—probably before and since his departure in 1993.

Menino continued some of Flynn's key redistributive policies but never supported rent or condo controls and was not aggressive in realizing affordable housing benefits from the massive luxury housing developments that shot up across the city or pursuing affordable housing resources from the Community Preservation Act or the expansion of linkage. He was captured more by the growth machine than were his predecessor and successors. Menino focused on essential city services as the "urban mechanic" and supported the growing influx of immigrants to the city.

As discussed earlier, he prioritized the schools, and the fact that the city had a ten-year superintendent in Tom Payzant was undoubtedly a plus. Flynn would acknowledge that he and Menino had "different philosophies."[104]

Like Flynn, Walsh leaned more on the side of working people, and his history with the building trades helped direct his efforts to increase construction activity in the city. He sought significant benefits from development from linkage and affordable housing set-asides. However, he received some criticism for overdevelopment with more lax development density policies. In his nearly seven years in office (2014–2021), he could not significantly affect the performance of the public schools. He led in other areas, as mentioned, including recovery services, the arts, and early childhood.

Completing her first term as mayor in 2025, Wu had focused significant attention on climate change policies for city and private buildings and energy consumption, telling me, "We now live in a moment where weather events are more and more intense. We recently avoided a hurricane directly hitting the city, but it's only a matter of time."[105]

She expanded on Walsh's redistributive housing and development policies and was not a friend of the growth machine. Some suggested that could be a weakness. The growth machine interests resurrected the old mantra of her killing the goose that laid the golden egg. She had a bold, and in some ways risky, agenda with the public schools, and time would tell how successful she would be. Wu's and Flynn's policy approaches were the most similar. However, at different social and economic times, they both pressed for progressive housing, development, and racial and economic equality policies that the growth machine opposes. She came to office with many forward-thinking ideas in her first term; however, in several parts of her agenda, she found it challenging to build a broad public consensus with many of the longtime neighborhood activists. It's unclear if this is a conscious strategy, a lack of understanding, the inexperience of her or her staff, or a misstep. She had remained incredibly popular with the public. In a poll in 2024, "Fifty-seven percent of registered voters believe she is doing a good job, while 35 percent rate her negatively."[106] While Wu would likely be reelected in 2025, no incumbent mayor has lost reelection since 1949; the confidence of the city's engaged citizenry in its progressive mayor is critical to its successful future. Pierre Clavel articulates how practical progressive politics operates, gaining people's motivation and commitment to "increase public participation so that it rested more on mass base and less on organized interest groups."[107] Wu would be well served to heed the calls of neighborhood leaders for more significant consultative planning and power sharing and increase the involvement of her progressive base that put her in office in that complex process.

Boston changed dramatically between the election of Flynn in 1983 and Wu in 2021. The population grew younger, wealthier, and, in some instances, more racially and culturally diverse while economically unequal; some neighborhoods continued to be segregated by race and class. There is much to be learned from understanding the approach of each Boston mayor, where they succeeded, and where they fell short. The city is counting on it.

# 14 / How Does Urban Progressivism Succeed?

*The legacy of Ray Flynn, a transformative figure in his time, is yet to be fully recognized and documented. His impact on racial harmony, economic development, and wealth distribution in Boston is often overlooked. Flynn's efforts played a pivotal role in the city's transformation.* (Fletcher "Flash" Wiley, Boston business leader, interview)

## Creating a Progressive City

What are the ingredients of progressive cities that challenge and defeat (or at least weaken) the corporate-centered growth machine, transform city governments, and respond to racial divisions and discrimination? This book tries to answer that overarching research question. It highlights several cities with periods of progressivism, with Boston as the detailed case study.

Seventy-plus personal interviews, archival research, and study of the "civic diaries" of the time have uncovered a sociologically relevant story about progressive city policies. The Boston story also illustrates how the use of politics and power is a critical component of what makes cities progressive.

This book delves into the concept of a progressive city, which can be elusive. It ultimately boils down to three fundamental questions: Who organizes? Who gets their voices heard? Who benefits? This complexity is what makes the study of urban progressivism so intriguing.

The concept of a progressive city is multifaceted. It's not a simple matter of being progressive on all fronts. Urban governments can champion specific issues, such as the environment, workers' rights, or race relations, while lagging on others, like housing policy, transportation, or LGBTQ equality.

This book's definition of a progressive city encompasses the social, political, and economic challenges that Ray Flynn was determined to address. While he succeeded in some areas, his efforts were only partially successful in others, and he fell short of his aspirations for Boston in particular issues. Flynn's work was a constant effort to redefine the relationship between city hall and its constituents.

According to Pierre Clavel, Flynn "found ways to recast planning as a link between a vital grassroots citizen movement and the desire of progressive political leaders to formulate redistributive policies."[1] Cities, on their own, can't solve big problems without the support of state and federal governments. However, within the limits of what cities *can* do, the critical question is how well Boston achieved Flynn's goal of redistributing wealth and income from private sector growth and how well the city addressed the vexing issues of urban poverty and racial inequality.

Throughout the city's history, were the Brahmin elites, and later the so-called growth machine, in total control of Boston's economy and politics? Did it change, and if so, how, when, and by whom?

Some argue that the mayoralty of James Michael Curley was a type of ethnic progressivism. He championed the clash between its immigrant majority—"the people"—and a wealthy Brahmin elite—"the interests."[2] His political history was long and complex. Elected as mayor, governor and, a member of Congress, and serving a stint in jail, some saw his ethnic machine politics and him personally as corrupt, and his opponents consistently attacked him as such. One of his defenders, Helen McDonough, his longtime housekeeper at his Jamaicaway home, responded to a Brahmin member of the good government National Civic Association, Mrs. Ames, who said to her, "We all know he is a crook." McDonough replied, "He's no crook, Mrs. Ames; I don't like what you are saying about the Governor. I wouldn't work for you if I never worked again," in response to a job offer. Mrs. Ames then called her so impressed with Helen's loyalty to Curley that she wanted to give her the job. She refused, saying, "Tell her to stick it."[3] In Curley's biography, *The Rascal King*, Jack Beatty wrote, "For many Bostonians, his good works would ever stay their dudgeon at his bad deeds."[4]

The city took a new turn after the city's business elites orchestrated Curley's defeat for mayor in 1949. It ushered in a period when city leaders pursued the growth machine strategy over a more progressive one. Following Curley's last term, under a succession of mayors from 1950 to 1983—Hynes, Collins, and White—the city focused on "revitalizing" its downtown. Urban renewal, redlining, disinvestment, and then the first phases of gentrification took their toll, displacing tens of thousands of working-class low-income families of all races, but particularly egregiously in predominantly Black and Brown neighborhoods.

Many had hoped that Kevin White, elected in 1967, would change the tide and challenge the corporate-dominated growth machine. In contrast to his opponent, the virulent racist school committeewoman Louise Day Hicks, White looked like a liberal. As Ira Jackson, White's chief of staff, said about White in 2017, "A young progressive took on a traditional pol, and the city held its breath as the final count came in. City government became a magnet for talent and an incubator for innovations, like Little City Halls, Summerthing, and community schools."[5] But by the end of his first term, White decided to join forces with the corporate and real estate growth machine. His 1971 reelection campaign was a hint of things to come, but after he came close to losing his 1975 reelection bid, he turned his back on tenants, the poor, working families, and blue-collar neighborhoods. In 1977, he proposed a charter change that would provide, among other things, for partisan elections, consolidate his power, and give him, as the *Boston Globe* called it, "political immortality."[6] He even once described his plan as a "democratic dictatorship" that would make the mayor of Boston "the single-most powerful municipal office-holder in America."[7] Add the taint of corruption that engulfed White's city hall, and the one-time liberal reformer had become a business-oriented politician.

White reversed his previous support of rent control, adopted the "machine politics" model of cities like Chicago under Richard J. Daley, and helped lead the growth machine to transform Boston's downtown at the expense of the city's neighborhoods. The moniker of progressivism no longer fit, if it ever did. As George Higgins, author of *Style versus Substance: Boston, Kevin White and the Politics of Illusion*, recalled, White went to the neighborhoods to "strike a posture as something of a populist," knowing he had the support of the "growth machine" businesspeople downtown.[8]

The political balance between business and neighborhood interests began to change in 1981. That's when progressives in Boston pushed the city to adopt a new charter allowing district representation in the city council and school committee. City councilors Rosemarie Sansone and Ray Flynn led the Committee for Change, while State Representative Mel King and his top political adviser, Pat Walker, helmed the Campaign for District Representation. These campaigns were not coordinated, and some questioned whether the progressives could cooperate. "They are now completely independent; there is, in fact, some hard feeling. Many in Sansone's group feel that King is putting too much emphasis on race. Many in King's group feel that they gathered most of the necessary signatures and that Sansone wants to take over; separate organizations might run a successful campaign, but not hostile ones," *Boston Globe* columnist

Robert Turner wrote.[9] Here, Boston's progressives were playing out the transformative versus redistributive populist dichotomy and that problem of progressives each doing it their way.

Despite opposition from all the incumbent city councilors, except Flynn, the electorate overwhelmingly approved the district representative charter change proposal. James Kelly, leader of the anti-busing South Boston Information Center, opposed the proposal. Kelly was elected to the city council in 1983 because of district representation.

As detailed in chapter 3, the two progressive candidates, Flynn and King, defeated the more establishment candidates in the primary and advanced to the general election in November 1983. At that point, their campaigns went in different but still overlapping directions. Many of Flynn's supporters joined his new administration. Some King supporters went to work for Flynn, and despite overtures to King himself and others, many became the "movement in opposition." Throughout the early years of Flynn's tenure, there were conversations about the two progressive coalitions—King's Rainbow Coalition and the Flynn administration's progressive community organizers—joining forces, but it did not materialize. King's campaign manager, Pat Walker, thought the reason was that Ray Dooley, Flynn's campaign manager and top political strategist, "wanted to minimize his exposure on the left. He was more concerned with the right side, the more Irish traditional working-class base."[10]

"Some of my progressive friends who worked on Mel's campaign were angry at those of us progressives who sided with Ray," Peter Dreier said. "Some of that anger spilled over after the election when some of us went to work for Ray in city hall, and others continued to support him from the outside as activists."[11]

Pat Walker reflected on Mel King's role in bringing progressives together after his passing in 2023. "I think perhaps the most important goal for Mel was to overcome the division in Boston by building a coalition of all colors dedicated to building community and institutional power, guided by the values of love and compassion," Walker said. "Those were important times for all of us, and we all owe Mel our gratitude for inspiring and leading us. We had an amazing and challenging opportunity back in 1983—and I do believe we, the progressives, on both sides, helped to dramatically redirect the future of Boston, which was then carried on by Rosaria, Tom, and many others—that was the meaning of chain of change [the title of King's book] as I understood it."[12]

These informal progressive coalitions had played alongside one another in the 1981 district representation campaign and competed in the mayor's race. When Flynn won the mayoral election, some of King's supporters remained in opposition, trying to hold the mayor's feet to the fire during Flynn's nine-and-a-half-year tenure. As this book describes, Flynn and King had different approaches but a widely shared agenda around the poor, fairness, and justice. While Flynn succeeded in many of his progressive policies, he lacked the support of a largely conservative city council and many of King's most loyal followers, particularly the more ideological leftists. On the other hand, in his two reelection campaigns, Flynn won a significant majority of votes in the predominantly Black and Latino parts of the city.

Flynn's administration directly and consistently challenged the downtown power brokers, including the developers, landlords, bankers, and leaders of the high-tech and healthcare sectors. With the support of community organizers and activists, Flynn's administration waged powerful grassroots campaigns against the growth machine. They were not successful at every turn. However, every policy battle enlisted neighborhood, labor, tenant, and small business groups—the people—and knew how to target the growth machine—the interests—to achieve progressive goals. As Joan Vennochi wrote in the Boston Globe on Flynn advising Wu, "Take it from Ray Flynn—the last Boston mayor to terrify the downtown real estate and development community with a populist agenda that critics said would kill the city's economy. When elected in 1983, many in that crowd considered his commitment to wealth redistribution—what he calls 'values'—a major threat to their ability to profit from the city's emerging skyline. Yet, at a time when Boston was much less prosperous than it is today, and 'woke' meant not asleep, Flynn was able to achieve significant success in the areas of rent control and linkage, which requires commercial developers to set aside money for affordable housing and job training."[13]

In other cities that developed progressive coalitions that led to the election of progressive mayors and city council members, success was based on identifying allies, enemies, and opportunities. Having good policy ideas isn't enough. Political skills and savvy are necessary to navigate the political waters. In nearly all cities, like Boston, longevity and perseverance were the winning ingredients. Political leaders come and go, and as we saw in Boston and other cities, without a sustainable coalition, victory will come and go because, as sure as hell, the growth coalition will do anything in its power to control the decision-making process.

In San Francisco, winning the mayoral and city supervisors' contests bore fruit early, but as the progressive leaders changed, so did the politics. When Mayor George Moscone and Supervisor Harvey Milk were assassinated in 1978, the promising progressive political leadership ended, with pro-growth board of supervisors member Diane Feinstein replacing

Moscone as mayor. The enactment of the referendum process sustained San Francisco's progressive coalition for longer than most cities—placing various progressive propositions before the voters. This allowed progressives to implement change outside the traditional mayor-council process and build winning coalitions.

When Mayor Harold Washington died in 1987 after only five years in office in Chicago, his followers were widely dispersed politically. The coalition that elected him and governed ceased to exist. Chicago's longest-serving mayor, Richard M. Daley, son of the infamous Chicago ward boss Richard J. Daley and the most powerful mayor in the country at the time, became an ally of the city's growth coalition, which favored the development of the downtown loop at the expense of the neighborhoods. (See Appendix 1: Cities Defined as Progressive.)

Each city pursued progressive city governance policies in the 1970s, 1980s, and beyond, and many attempted to sustain those efforts over time. Boston's political leaders differed from those in other progressive cities, if only because Flynn had been in office for nearly ten years. "When Flynn left office in 1993 to become ambassador to the Vatican, there was a weakened progressive base and no logical progressive to succeed him. His successor, Tom Menino, was a classic centrist downtown Democrat," Bob Kuttner wrote in *American Prospect*.[14]

Subsequent mayors in Boston did not share all of Flynn's progressive agenda or hire community organizers in key positions. Still, many of his progressive policies—linkage, affordable housing, community participation, racial inclusion, immigrant and human rights—largely survived. His successor, Tom Menino, pursued the growth machine model to a greater or lesser extent, often at the expense of neighborhoods and poor and working-class families. Menino was socially progressive, and although he retained a small number of Flynn's progressive staff, as the book outlines, he allowed the growth machine to dominate development in the city. The next mayor, Walsh, was also socially progressive and, as a union leader, paid particular attention to the working men and women of the city.

Walsh can be credited for building thousands of housing units during his tenure, having permitted thirty-six thousand after coming into office, setting records for new affordable and middle-class homes. His relationship with the growth coalition was nuanced, as he supported growth and was a proponent of equity and fairness. Joyce Linehan called him a "good solid liberal; an Elizabeth Warren democratic capitalist that puts guard rails on capitalism so working people get a fair shake."[15] Walsh took on the progressive issues Flynn identified in the twentieth century and developed twenty-first-century solutions. He addressed issues related to race, affordable housing, increasing linkage, and identifying new revenue through the Community Preservation Act. He also managed growth in an attempt to benefit Bostonians.

Moreover, in the context of those progressives who were not in Flynn's administration, there were issue alliances. While significant, they did not sustain a robust enough coalition to build upon Flynn's social and economic policies when he left office. Wu has the opportunity, as Vennochi suggests, to build upon her impressive voter approval and continue to organize grassroots activists while building alliances in the legislature and business community.

As Pierre Clavel makes the point in his book *Activists in City Hall,*

> What role then did Flynn and Washington play relative to Menino and Daley? Certainly, the former was more uncomfortable for the middle class. But their single-minded focus on redistributive policies made it easier for their successors. More abstractly, they pushed the fundamental structures of economic bias and political power a bit more toward equality in a decade when the nation was moving toward an insupportable inequality. Their programs tended to persist over time—most remained in place under subsequent mayors, whether or not progressive policies continue to have the same salience in the general local consciousness and the face of a general drift away from redistributive or participatory approaches at the national level.[16]

Where is Boston today? In 2021, Councilor Wu was elected mayor and was called the most progressive Boston mayor yet. Wu's platform, among other things, seeks to complete the unfinished business initiated nearly forty years ago by the progressive populist mayor, Flynn. Flynn had pledged to share Boston's promise with those left behind. While his economic justice program was primarily implemented since leaving office in 1993, Menino did not pursue an aggressive progressive agenda. Flynn faced an initial defeat of his proposal for full rent control due to a conservative majority on the city council, including the future mayor, Menino, and strong opposition from the growth machine led by the real estate industry. A largely progressive city council enacted Wu's rent control proposal, many of whom were pushing her to do more. The real estate community led the growth machine to oppose vigorously infringement on their industry. They sought the unfettered ability to maximize profits, even if it meant displacing families in Boston's neighborhoods. The change in the leanings of the city council to a more progressive majority will make a significant difference. Wu's rent control proposal faced uncertainty from the state legislature, and it is unclear if the Wu team that got her elected was organized effectively enough to enact the bill.

During her first term, Wu sought to emulate some of Flynn's policy ideas for the twenty-first century by building upon her impressive voter approval. But Boston was a much different city by then. In some ways, the progressive forces—particularly labor and community organizing groups —were more aligned and politically engaged. But by the time she was elected, many of the city's working-class areas—including South Boston, the South End, Charlestown, the North End, Jamaica Plain, and parts of Roxbury, Mattapan, and Dorchester—had been significantly gentrified. These changes were reflected in Wu's inability to get many of the Boston delegation members in the state legislature to back her campaign to win home rule powers so that Boston could adopt rent control, transfer fees, and property tax changes. The real estate lobby had restored its influence after Flynn left office, and the base of low-income and working-class renters had diminished in size and organization.

The progressive coalitions in the city went through a significant transition period between the 1970s and today. Several groups ceased to exist, including the Massachusetts Tenant Organization, organized by Peter Dreier, Lew Finfer, and John McDonough in the 1980s, and Massachusetts Fair Share, another major player that went out of business in the mid-1980s. In its heyday, Fair Share had more than one hundred thousand members, dozens of chapters, and community organizers statewide. Many of the leaders of both organizations helped Flynn get elected in 1983. Still, other organizations like the Massachusetts Communities Action Network, a coalition of faith-based groups, and the Boston Tenants Coalition would emerge to battle for rent control and tenant protections against displacement. The Mass Alliance of HUD Tenants would win victories for tenants in subsidized housing. City Life, founded in the Jamaica Plain neighborhood, expanded to be more regionally based and celebrated its fiftieth anniversary in 2023. Groups that led the Community Preservation Act campaign—like the Massachusetts Association of Community Development Corporations, Greater Boston Interfaith Organization, Mass Affordable Housing Alliance, and others—achieved specific victories. Statewide, a coalition of labor representing service workers, teachers, and others joined with community, tenant, and faith-based groups to form Raise Up Massachusetts in 2013. They have successfully won ballot campaigns to raise the minimum wage; get paid medical, family, and sick time leave; and levy a so-called millionaires tax to fund education and transportation projects. The millionaires tax has far outpaced early projections to provide several billion dollars for these projects. These largely issue-specific groups or coalitions have emerged following what some argue was a period of dormancy in Boston during the twenty-year mayoralty of Tom Menino, whom they claim was not particularly supportive. Longtime neighborhood associations and neighborhood councils initiated by Flynn have received a warmer reception over the past decade.

One historic failing of Boston's progressives was that there had been no concerted effort to gain control of the city council during Flynn's tenure, absent successful efforts by several progressive candidates—including David Scondras, Brian McLaughlin, Charles Yancey, and Bruce Bolling, and later by Rosaria Salerno—and failed attempts by Michael Kane and Frank Costello. Progressives Felix Arroyo Sr. and Sam Yoon arrived on the council during Menino's years as mayor. "In 1985, many political analysts said Flynn's decision to stay out of the council race cost him an opportunity to change the makeup of the council, which routinely defeated his key legislation by a 7-to-6 vote. Many of the city's progressive leaders have predicted this strategy could come back to haunt him again."[17]

Nearly forty years later, the city council, like much of Boston, has become more progressive socially and politically. In 2009, Ayanna Pressley was elected to the city council, becoming the first Black woman in the body's hundred-year history and who would be the top vote-getter in 2011. Pressley later upset the establishment by challenging Democratic congressman Michael Capuano in 2018 and handily defeating him to secure Boston's seventh Congressional seat.

In 2007, the Boston City Council had three people of color and eleven White members. Fast-forward to 2019: seven seats were people of color, and six were White members. The council has continued to change to represent Boston. Wu, elected to the city council in 2013, was the first Asian American woman to serve on the council. She was elected president in 2016, the top vote-getter in the 2017 council election, and would become mayor in 2021. Andrea Campbell, elected in 2015, was elected as council president in 2018, the first African American woman to hold that spot. She would run for mayor in 2021 and, after placing third, become Massachusetts attorney general in 2023. Lydia Edwards was elected to the city council in 2017 and became a state senator in 2022. Kim Janey was elected in 2017, and as council president in 2020 who would become acting mayor in 2021 was the first African American and woman to serve in that role; Ricardo Arroyo and Julia Mejia were both elected in 2019; and Kendra Lara, Tania Anderson, and Ruthzee Loujienne elected in 2021 would join the council's then-progressive majority.[18] In 2023, the council went through some readjustment, with two of the progressive candidates in office, Arroyo and Lara, surprisingly unable to make it past the September preliminary election;

some argued, in part, their losses resulted from ethical issues, but outside conservative PACs' money was also a factor in opposing them. Four new self-proclaimed progressives were elected in 2023 with Wu's active support.

"It is like the old days," Flynn said of Ayanna Pressley's election to Congress. "The Irish came into political power. And then the Italians. Now, you are seeing the immigrant population and the people of color, and they are starting to gain real political strength in Boston. That is a good thing. That means that they feel empowered. They feel like they are part of Boston."[19]

Flynn was talking about "government communalism," the way Dan Monti does, to build a community that is more inclusive of those historically left out of the mainstream of a city's civic and political culture. Those elected to the Boston City Council and mayor's office over the past decade have taken a decidedly progressive turn. When you dig deeper, some of the progressive candidates call upon neighborhood or ethnic constituencies, but in considerable measure, with a population that has grown by more than one hundred thousand between 1980 and 2020 from the influx of new immigrants and higher-income working professionals—the progressive candidate benefits from a generally more progressive electorate, borne out in the past decade. The city can build upon these successes and end progressive "parallel play," the city will be better off, and a true progressive agenda that Ray Flynn and Mel King introduced to Boston in 1983 could become a reality for Michelle Wu and future city leaders.

## Outside Money in Boston Politics

As *Globe* reporter Larry Harmon recalled, "In 1983, money did not talk. Mayoral Candidates Ray Flynn and Mel King could barely rub two nickels together."[20] Things have changed since, mainly due to the *Citizens United* decision by the US Supreme Court in 2010, which ruled that money is speech and that limiting "independent political spending" violates First Amendment rights to free speech.[21]

All political campaigns require resources to pursue one's agenda, reach voters, hire staff, and advertise. In Boston, campaign fundraising has always attracted the growth coalition, as in 1983, when candidates Finnegan, Kearney, and DiCara received most of the contributions from real estate interests. Ultimately, it was not determinative that King and Flynn received most of their funds from small donations.

Some candidates for local or state office, or even Congress, can be outspent by their opponents and still win, but in the post–*Citizens United* era, that's become more complex. Outside political action committees' (PACs) funding of local elections is changing. In the 2013 mayoral race, outside groups representing business, labor, and environmental causes spent an estimated $3.8 million. Walsh outspent Connolly, receiving a significant portion of his funds from national labor organizations; Working America, the political arm of the AFL-CIO and American Working Families, spent more than $1 million, and One Boston PAC spent $480,000 on a television advertising buy on behalf of Walsh. Connolly received funds from Democrats for Education Reform, a national education reform group led by corporate donors who favor charter schools, which spent an estimated $1 million.[22]

The 2021 mayoral race saw early political action committee expenditures. Acting mayor Kim Janey received support from the Unite Here PAC, which hoped to raise $500,000, and the Better Boston PAC, which raised $776,000 in donations and supported councilor Andrea Campbell.[23] The two eventual finalists, Annissa Essaibi George, received approximately $1.209 million from the Real Progress Boston PAC, and Michelle Wu was funded by the Boston Turnout Project PAC and the Environmental Action League of Massachusetts Action Fund, providing an estimated $1 million in their efforts to bolster her candidacy.

Following the 2013 and 2021 mayoral elections, which set a new record for outside political action committee spending, some of the same interest groups financed candidates in the 2023 city council election, an unprecedented development. A conservative business group led by New Balance chairman Jim Davis and other Trump fundraisers in the Forward Boston PAC spent $320,000. At the same time, the Bold Boston PAC, a coalition of labor unions, backed four progressive-leaning candidates with $100,000.[24]

Does the outside spending help? Vanessa Snow, an activist with the Right to the City Vote coalition, said, "The conservative's relatively poor showing demonstrates the limitations of outside funding. Money could not deliver the boots on the ground that the labor unions and city workers produced."[25]

As Harvey Molotch, author of "The City as Growth Machine" and analyst of urban politics, writes, "Those who stress the relative autonomy of elected officials pay very little attention to how politicians get nominated, elected, appointed, or promoted in the electoral, government agency, and business systems. Campaign contributions remain the mother's milk of U.S. politics, and these funds, especially at the local level, come overwhelmingly from growth machine sectors. Whether liberal or conservative on other issues, candidates tend to depend on growth coalition support. Sometimes all major candidates in local elections receive their largest contributors from property entrepreneurs, and such interests certainly tend to dominate the winning side."[26]

Progressives must keep a close watch on the unfettered influence of outside funds. Several mayoral and city council candidates refused the PAC funds. Still, the fact that they are "independent" means the organizations make their determinations with or without the candidate's support—to meet their ideological and political objectives. In Boston, since the 2013 mayoral election, the conservative "old guard" and the progressive "new" leadership have jostled to win elections, and each "side" has drawn upon outside funding from unions, and environmental, education, and business groups. History shows that money makes a difference, but only voters can elect city leadership.

## Economic, Governance, and Cultural Challenges Addressed

The central question in this book has been whether and how cities can adopt progressive policies that redistribute wealth, income, and power. I answer this question by examining three overarching sets of issues that Boston faced during this period: *economic challenges,* including affordable housing, income inequality, and access to jobs; *governance challenges,* which focus on mayoral leadership in public education, fiscal management, and urban infrastructure; and *cultural issues* from immigration and the assimilation of newcomers to racial discrimination, animosity, and conflict.

In exploring these questions, how did each governing regime respond to and shape race and ethnic relations, inequality, economic development policy, and public education governance? Were the policies of each administration progressive?

The book reviews evidence that the municipal government *could* promote greater social tolerance *and* economic equality at the same time. The Flynn administration, in particular, worked to reduce poverty, improve education, lessen racial conflict, and increase economic opportunity for city residents. Flynn sought to democratize decision-making in municipal affairs. However, the impact of these efforts on the period under study was affected by the fact that during Flynn's period as mayor, his administration was sandwiched between the White and Menino regimes, both of which pursued a growth machine path that led to more significant, even unprecedented, concentrations of wealth among the city's residents.

The Menino philosophy of "build it and [the builders] will create jobs" did not work for the majority of Boston residents, who did not benefit from undirected (or unfettered) growth in either the construction of new office buildings or permanent well-paying jobs inside those buildings.[27] When it came to housing, the results were even worse. "Since 2000, more than 50 sizable developments featuring multimillion-dollar condos—new construction and renovations—have opened in Boston," according to the *Boston Globe*. "In a flurry of activity in the seven years from 2015 to 2021 alone, that included more than 1,000 new condos now worth $2 million and up. Who can afford such pricey real estate? Less than 2 percent of the Boston population."[28]

Chuck Collins from the Institute for Policy Studies calls this type of housing "swanktuaries," symbols of "grotesque wealth inequality. These are not homes but 'safety-deposit boxes in the sky.'"[29] Most of this luxury housing was built or permitted during the Menino and later Walsh administrations.

Walsh and later Wu proposed a 2 percent transfer tax on these developments, which would have produced almost $384 million for affordable housing from 2019 to 2022. The growth machine, represented by business and real estate interests, opposed this legislation, claiming that transfer taxes would increase the cost of housing and dissuade new investment. While Governor Maura Healy supports local options like the transfer tax she included in her $4 billion housing bond bill. The bill passed, but the transfer tax provision was deleted after strong lobbying from the growth machine.

Wu didn't buy into the "build it and [the builders] will create jobs" argument. In 2003, she said, "We are in a very dire moment. We need to create more housing. And we need more affordability. And we need more housing that is appropriate for families," not believing that "no matter what you create, even if you only create luxury housing, it will somehow trickle down and have a positive impact."[30]

Flynn initially increased linkage, and Walsh and Wu have significantly changed linkage requirements. Since 1986, linkage has generated "more than $227 million in housing funds—$36.8 million in 2022 alone and $55 million in job training money."[31] These are essential steps to respond to the housing crisis, which in 2023 included more than thirty-seven thousand families on the public housing waiting list.[32]

"People need to start looking at the bigger picture here, which is what our city becomes when so many people can't afford to live here," said Adam Guren, an associate professor of economics at Boston University. "It's a city without diversity and essential workers—a city for the wealthy."[33]

The climate of open racial hostility in the city fluctuated during the period under study. Hate crimes decreased under Flynn but later escalated under Menino. As Sullivan described, Flynn's approach was "to bring the noise, to bring the attention, to bring the focus"[34] on racial violence.

According to Jim Jordan, "Flynn took the power of the mayor's office and focused on civil rights,"[35] significantly impacting the city's mood and manner of conducting its racial affairs. Menino took a different approach, consciously refusing to speak about racial conflict, fearing it would divide the city. Menino defended this approach by saying, "I always try to be moderate and be as honest as possible to the public and not call it racial; it was racial, but I would not do it. I would not divide the city."[36] While racial incidents increased during Menino's administration, particularly with integrating public housing in South Boston and across the city, race was no longer a significant part of the public discourse.

The racial struggles of Codman Square and other neighborhoods in the 1970s and '80s, and later success in creating more peaceful neighborhoods, made for an ideal site to help Catholics and Protestants of Northern Ireland learn how to work together. As Bill Walczak describes, "Following the Good Friday Peace Accord, Codman Square Health Center was chosen as a site to teach Catholic and Protestant community leaders how to work together. Small integrated groups would work on public health projects together in a neighborhood that wasn't their neighborhood but seemed familiar."[37] An unprecedented period of civic peace came over the city under study.[38]

The 2013 and 2021 campaigns for mayor of Boston saw race emerge less as an election issue. In 2013, the two White Irish finalists acknowledged the prevalence of persistent institutional racism in the city, and in the 2021 election, all the candidates were persons of color.

The lack of much "noise" about race during the campaigns was a tribute to all the hard work done in the past to produce a calmer and more even-tempered way of discussing racial differences. Walsh chose his path to confront this issue. The verdict on Wu and race relations isn't yet in place.

## Social Science and Urban Politics

Sociologists, political scientists, geographers, urban planners, and economists look at the same realities of urban life from slightly different perspectives, all helpful in understanding how cities work (or don't work). This book draws on all those disciplines to examine the limits and possibilities for cities to adopt progressive policies. Paul Peterson's view that cities were severely constrained in adopting such policies—which, he claimed, would push business, jobs, and middle-class residents out of cities—dominated the social science literature about cities for many years. At the same time, Mollenkopf, Molotch, Stone, Dreier, Swanstrom, and other scholars looked at cities from a different angle—challenging Peterson's view of limits, which was based on accepting the business perspective about what cities could or couldn't do. Instead, they explored how different forces could forge electoral and governing coalitions of different governing regimes to set agendas, including a progressive one. The "limits" perspective reflected how local growth machines (or growth coalitions) viewed cities. It was a kind of economic determinism based on the corporate worldview. But could another kind of coalition rooted in working-class interests govern cities differently? To put this question in a broader context, can a vocal class-based progressive approach to confronting racism and racial conflict be effective in addressing inter-racial tension as well as economic inequality?

Dan Monti does not think so, at least not in a significant or transformational way.[39] He believes that the more friendly turn in Boston's civic culture took place *despite* the continuation of marked economic inequality and that this improvement had to happen before the issue of economic inequality could be addressed more forthrightly. This book presents evidence that Peterson's and Monti's views do not fully capture the realities of urban politics and the abilities of politically savvy progressive coalitions and elected officials to significantly address issues like income inequality, poverty, and racial peace. In fact, by prioritizing these issues, Flynn's administration showed substantial gains in each arena.

We use three theoretical concepts to explore these questions: mayoral leadership and community power; inequality, economic development, and redistribution; and race relations, racial conflict, and public-school governance. We draw on a rich case history and use a historical-sociological lens. Through this lens, we show how Flynn's administration was able to adopt progressive policies that made a significant difference in the lives of most Boston residents, especially those with few economic resources.

## Theme One: Mayoral Leadership and Community Power

Clarence Stone categorizes four ideal types of urban regimes: *maintenance* or *caretaker regimes*, which support the status quo and focus on the delivery of essential services; *development regimes*, which pursue policies identified with growth machine coalition theory; *middle-class progressive regimes*, which seek to negotiate community benefits as part of the development process; and *lower-class opportunity regimes*, which pursue a redistributive agenda to alter the actions of the private sector without stifling investment. The redistributive agenda has been the central strategy of progressive regimes.[40]

Urban regime theory suggests that coalitions must be built between governmental and nongovernmental actors to manage a complex urban city successfully. The data point to Flynn's having created governing capacity through the effective political management of the pockets of coalitions that led to his election in 1983.

The 1983 mayoral contest, highlighted in chapter 3, came down to a match between Mel King and Ray Flynn, the two candidates of the nine who ran as self-described populists. Both Flynn and King were, in fact, different kinds of urban populists. Todd Swanstrom, writing about Mayor Dennis Kucinich of Cleveland, defines urban populism by what it tries to accomplish and how: "Urban populism tries, at first, to displace the divisive social issues that arose in the 1960s around race, religion, lifestyle, and sex, with fundamental economic issues. The claim is that busing and abortion divide natural political allies; urban populism attempts to displace the growth issue with the distributive issue."[41]

The contest broke along racial lines, however, with the King campaign characterizing its candidate as a "transformative populist" who emphasized and celebrated diversity and "explicitly introduces derived ideology in the process of mutual education of coalition members, and targets as its central goal the transformation of consciousness through empowerment."[42] In essence, transformative populism's central focus is to fight racial oppression and promote self-determination. King's campaign strategists characterized Flynn as a "redistributive populist," by which they implied that he sought to "build unity by emphasizing what people have in common and downplaying or even overlooking differences such as race; such populists value community organization as a means to the end of redistribution of resources and economic justice."[43] I suspect that Flynn would agree with that charge.

Flynn campaign worker and later housing aide Jerry Rubin ruminated on the failure to broaden the alliance with the King campaign: "I do not believe in revolutionary politics as an organizing strategy," he said. "Now, could you have an alliance between race-based politics and populism, progressive populism? Yes. In some ways, we did. The Ray Flynn campaign had deep roots in the African American community, in some ways deeper than Mel King's campaign. So, I think you can bridge White economic populism with the perspective of race, which has its own set of dynamics, even independent of class. Can you bridge progressive populism and revolutionary theory? I still believe in class-based populist organizing; that is my perspective, and I think it can cut across race lines."[44] While there were efforts at alliances with King's followers after the 1983 election, the transformative populists saw themselves as a "movement in opposition," which would play itself out on numerous fronts during Flynn's mayoralty.

Flynn expanded his political reach through policies that unified a racially fractured city with a diverse community of political and business leaders. Unlike Stone's insistence that the business elites are necessary to the governing coalition, Flynn broadened his administration's reach into neighborhoods and constituencies that had not supported him in the 1983 election. His aggressive push early on in his administration for rent control and linkage created strong opposition from the business elites in Boston.

Rent control was opposed not only by the representatives of the Greater Boston Real Estate Board, but by the majority of the Boston City Council and some conservative members within the Flynn administration. Linkage was a different matter altogether. Broad political consensus, excepting the real estate industry, had emerged in reaction to the development policies of Flynn's predecessor, White. Following the period under White, during which the mayor had sought to centralize power and control on both the development front and the delivery of city services for political purposes, the city was ready for a new type of leadership.

Urban regime theorists would characterize the Flynn administration as a lower-class opportunity regime, which "pursues a redistributive agenda to alter the actions of the private sector without stifling investment," leaning into a middle-class progressive regime because of the "focus on such measures as environmental protection, historic preservation, affordable housing, and the quality of design, affirmative action, and linkage funds for various social purposes."[45] Flynn had the active political support of the electorate to implement his redistributive policies, which gave him the power to go well beyond redistribution symbolically and in his actions. Early and throughout his administration, Flynn supported progressive causes such as a human rights ordinance to protect gays and lesbians. He aggressively pursued the removal of city funds from banks doing business with South Africa; he fought for the expansion of home mortgages to the low-income neighborhoods of Boston, particularly the communities of color that had been denied access to capital; Flynn expanded services to people experiencing homelessness and for people with AIDS, including receiving approval from the city council for the nation's first clean needle exchange program, over significant political opposition, including the governor and cardinal; and he instituted jobs and training policies that favored Boston residents, people of color, and women. In one of his proudest moments he, working with Holocaust survivor and friend from his days as a youth worker, Stephan Ross, helped to build the New England Holocaust Memorial in downtown Boston.[46] "Ray became the mayor of the Black people, the gay people, and the wealthy people had to put up with him," Vin McCarthy said.[47]

Symbolizing Stone's "alternative social production mode of power," Flynn had "power to" rather than "power over" the city.[48] He derived that power from tapping into his pockets of coalitions, which encompassed housing organizations, pro-life groups, labor, Irish leaders, local boards of trade, community groups, and neighborhood activists. Effectively managing these coalitions helped him implement policies that transformed participatory democracy and enabled some redistribution of the economic benefits of growth over his decade-long tenure. As described in chapter 4, he followed a community organizing model in creating his administration and enacting key policy objectives.

## Theme Two: Inequality, Economic Development, and Redistribution

In analyzing the Boston city government's response to poverty, income inequality, housing affordability, economic development, and redistribution policies in chapters 5, 6, and 7, I drew upon growth machine and progressive city theories.

Growth machine theory posits that the growth imperative results from elites' control of the political process to enhance land values and corporate profits. The goal is to maximize exchange values at the expense of use values. The growth imperative was evident during the period of urban renewal in Boston when neighborhoods were decimated in favor of higher and more expensive land uses benefiting wealthier Bostonians.

The role of the mayor is one of broker of who gets what, who gets rich, and who derives maximum benefit from the city development policy. A focus on growth politics can help discern in which periods between 1980 and 2000 changes in this distribution of benefits and social and economic reform occurred in Boston. As Harvey Molotch observes in "The City as Growth Machine," "First, 'symbolic' politics comprise the 'big issues' of public morality and the symbolic reforms featured in the headlines and editorials of the daily press. The other politics is the process through which goods and services come to be distributed in society. Largely unseen and relegated to negotiations within committees (when it occurs within a formal government body), this politics determines who, in material terms, gets what, where, and how."[49]

As demonstrated, the mayoralties of White, Flynn, and Menino each pursued different strategies in building the physical side of Boston. The growth machine coalition strategy was in full swing at the end of White's final term as he sought to place his imprimatur on Boston's skyline to build a "world-class city." He was the sole decision-maker regarding "who got what, where and how." This was symbolized best by his having the Boston Redevelopment Authority model room moved to the city-owned Parkman House and summoning developers of major projects there before they received city approval. Flynn's counter to White's use of the Parkman House—which Flynn claimed he had never visited before winning the 1983 election when White invited him and his wife, Cathy, for lunch—was to use the Parkman House to host community events and hear directly from community leaders on a wide range of issues, including development policy.

Mayoral leadership priorities were transformed during the Flynn era to respond to the electorate's growing dissatisfaction at the close of the White period. Progressive city government, also taking hold in other cities across the United States, meant, as Flynn put it in his first inaugural speech:

> The tall and beautiful buildings which grace our city's skyline are monuments to a broad vision which every great city must possess. But these towers of granite and glass must not come at the expense of displacement or neighborhood neglect. We are committed to continuing the progress of downtown revitalization. But we are equally committed to ensuring that no neighborhood in Boston is left behind. We see growth as progress; that progress must be our servant, not our master. The true test of our greatness will be the protection we afford the weak, the needy, the poor, not at some future date, but now.[50]

Flynn's progressive city would manage growth for the benefit of the residents of Boston over the special interests that had for too long been the only voice at city hall. The redistributive populism that Flynn employed resulted in the establishment of policies that remain firmly entrenched in Boston. His BRA director, Stephen Coyle, characterized Flynn's transition in his approach to economic development and theory of change as "social contract theory." Linkage, inclusionary zoning, the parcel-to-parcel linkage program, and the authorization of eminent domain power to the Dudley Street Neighborhood Initiative section of Roxbury were all part of Flynn's social contract with the neighborhoods—reflecting a strategy aimed at sharing power and the benefits of growth. This new social contract also guided Flynn's housing and economic development team and led to the development and institutionalization of related policies that held up his commitment to the contract.

As discussed in chapter 5, housing affordability was a crucial issue in Boston during the decades under study. White initially supported rent control but later succumbed to pressure from the growth machine and implemented vacancy decontrol, which eliminated protections against significant rent increases for most of Boston's tenants. In the election to succeed White, King and Flynn, the two mayoral finalists, supported the reenactment of strong comprehensive rent control and regulations limiting condominium conversions, rapidly leading to gentrification and displacement. While I suggest that the issue of gentrification is a result of policies of the growth machine, other scholars view gentrification as a process whereby cultural actors have noneconomic motivations, notably social preservation.[51]

When Flynn won, he immediately planned to return to full rent control, including protections for tenants from condominium conversion. As Flynn's progressive housing adviser Dreier said, "The real estate interests had captured control of the city council, and Flynn could not get strong tenant protections passed by that body."[52] One of the opponents of rent control at the time was Menino. He would go on to become mayor when Flynn resigned, continue to support the growth machine, and oppose strong protections for tenants.

Linkage was the most significant redistributive policy implemented in the face of opposition by the growth machine coalition. The linkage policy, initially proposed by Bruce Bolling in early 1983, was established later that year but only reached its full realization when Flynn expanded it in 1985. Challenged by the developer of the urban renewal project in the West End, Jerome Rappaport, Flynn and his BRA director Stephen Coyle aggressively fought back against the growth machine coalition, which sought to overturn the law. Coyle used the development approval powers of the BRA to thwart the challenge and enlist members of the growth coalition, if not as allies, at least as not-vocal opponents. The final resolution of the linkage challenge and the law's expansion to raise additional revenue would lead to thousands of affordable housing units in Boston's neighborhoods. Other housing initiatives, notably the use of all publicly owned land for affordable housing, were a significant change from the previous policy of selling it to the highest bidder, and the redevelopment of thousands of units of public housing during the 1980s would help reduce the city's stubborn poverty rate. Between 1980 and 1989, poverty in Boston declined from 23 percent for singles to 6 percent and from 25 percent for families to 19 percent, as shown in Table 3.[53]

Neighborhood leaders felt empowered to have a seat at the table in economic development and the revitalization of their parks, business districts, and housing stock, as well as a role in improving essential service delivery. Under Flynn, Boston's neighborhoods changed dramatically regarding their physical character and demographic composition. The coalition of left-leaning progressives, more traditional unions, and conservative leaders worked together to bring a new governing style to Boston. Progressive cities theories, developed by Pierre Clavel, helped frame Flynn's democratization of the historically closed development approval process by opening the decision-making process to neighborhood groups and organizations. Several examples include the creation of neighborhood councils, planning and zoning advisory committees, and project-specific review panels, such as the Prudential Project Advisory Committee (PRUPAC). In addition, to share the benefits of downtown development with Boston's poor and working-class neighborhoods and people of color, Flynn expanded linkage, affordable housing production, and, through the parcel-to-parcel linkage program, required minority developer equity participation in this first-of-its-kind development process.

Regime and growth machine theories help to understand the challenge of governance during the Flynn era, which replaced a strict growth machine regime with a progressive cities' regime.[54] A managed growth approach replaced the growth machine over the previous three decades with a goal of shared prosperity. This progressive city agenda led to substantive changes in the urbanization of heretofore forgotten neighborhoods through the first comprehensive capital plan in the city's history, including the building of thousands of units of affordable housing; the reopening, rehabilitation, and construction of new parks, police stations, and fire stations; and other long-stalled capital projects. "The city had not had a capital plan in twenty-three years," Mary Nee, director of capital planning for the city, said. "It had not been in the bond market after Proposition 2½; it lost its rating and had been out of the bond markets for three, maybe pushing four years. Its ratings were junk, and Ray Flynn inherited a $40 million deficit. The city was virtually bankrupt at the end of the White administration, and it was hemorrhaging. To do what Ray Flynn wanted for the city and the neighborhoods, he had to solve that financial problem."[55] And he did.

Flynn led affirmative action in the parcel-to-parcel linkage program in Roxbury. This program linked the last unsold city-owned downtown garage site with a vacant parcel in Roxbury and required minority participation in the development. He held steadfast in negotiations with banks following the race-based mortgage lending scandal, first uncovered by the Federal Reserve Bank of Boston, to secure below-market loans for low-income families. He turned city land over to community groups and CDCs, and, in the case of Roxbury, bucked his own BRA board and granted eminent domain power, previously used to displace residents through urban renewal, to the neighborhood organization Dudley Street Neighborhood Initiative (DSNI)—the first such example of ceding eminent domain power to a community organization in the nation's history. The BRA board was poised to deny approval of eminent domain power to DSNI because its chair, Robert Farrell, questioned the legality until Flynn intervened. He called the board into his office and read the riot act to the board, which reversed its opposition. The board also questioned a study Coyle and Dreier were pushing on discrimination in mortgage lending. Again, Flynn needed to intervene, and the study was approved and completed, showing the same discriminatory practices as the Boston Fed study had uncovered. Farrell subsequently resigned after nearly twenty years on the board.

There are many examples in which Flynn not only used the power of his office to implement redistributive development policies but was also conscious of the symbolic value of his actions. His team worked tirelessly to build the South End neighborhood development known as Tent City, which had been the symbol of failed urban renewal policy when Mel King and South End leaders took over the site on April 28, 1968, to protest urban renewal.[56] As King said on March 7, 1986, eighteen years later, during the groundbreaking for the $28 million, 270-unit, mixed-income residential complex, "The people have outlasted their opposition. I have always believed that we would be able to get that together. It was the only just thing to happen on that land."[57] Flynn received credit for completing the project and said at the groundbreaking, "Tent City is a significant victory for the people. This is a symbol of what we want to see happen in Boston—a symbol of building bridges between government and neighborhood and between neighborhood and neighborhood."[58]

Another symbolic victory for Flynn and the city was the redevelopment of the last vacant parcel in the West End, designated initially for Jerome Rappaport, the controversial developer whose plan led to the urban renewal clearance of the West End in the 1950s and 1960s. The BRA de-designated Rappaport, who fought the issue in court. While the suit was pending, BRA director Coyle had a sign erected on the vacant lot reading, "Coming Soon! Affordable Housing. A public/private partnership," thereby irking Rappaport, who, Coyle believes, had it removed several times. After a five-year legal battle, the BRA won the suit and designated the Archdiocese of Boston to build 270 cooperative housing units, including a museum about the West End. For Coyle, the fight over the West End parcel was personal. He said, "Winning gives us a chance to fulfill a commitment to the people whose neighborhood was destroyed." Flynn added, "I am pleased that the city has prevailed in each challenge [by Rappaport on linkage and condo conversion] and that we will soon add Lowell Square to the long list of vacant land sites transformed into affordable housing opportunities."[59]

When Flynn left office in 1993 to become ambassador to the Vatican, Menino inherited precedents established by Flynn in terms of linkage, affordable housing policy, capital planning, and democratic participation. During Menino's tenure, after the slow-growth period of the early 1990s, the building of Boston accelerated and moved forward unabated, primarily driven by the expansion of nonprofit institutions (universities, hospitals, and other nontaxable organizations). This led straight to a return to the growth machine model of the White administration. The democratization process continued in form only, as Fenway community activist Helen Cox described trying to get Menino to engage residents of the Fenway in the development process: "Menino may have started in the right place when he first came in, but the BRA and the mayor were the same," she said. "The community felt helpless in dealing with the BRA. It was a constant battle with the administration. Getting community residents on the project advisory committees [PACs] takes much work. The administration was not into that. They had a lot of pro-development people, real estate people, and representatives of developers on PACs. We once submitted twenty to thirty names, and only one was selected. The Flynn administration was more responsive to the neighborhoods than the Menino administration. While that may seem to contradict the sentiments about Menino, who is considered a neighborhood mayor, the reality is that the things that mattered to our neighborhood—that were under the control of the BRA, thus his control—were not pro-neighborhood, but pro-development. That is not to diminish other things he may have done. We had big battles with the Menino administration."[60]

"The community process now is not like the Kevin White era, but it is much less involved than the Ray Flynn era," Coyle suggested. "I do not know if that is good."[61] Michael Reiskind, a Jamaica Plain activist and member of the neighborhood council created by the Flynn administration, shared his views on whether Menino supported the neighborhood council and neighborhood participation in decision-making. "Grudgingly," he said. "I do not think he likes it. I think he sees it more as a way to get information to his administration on the issues so he could decide on them before the neighborhood might."[62] Sandee Story, *Jamaica Plain Gazette* editor, echoed Reiskind, telling me, "Menino didn't like the neighborhood councils. He thought they were 'extraneous.'"[63]

Chuck Turner, community activist and Boston city councilor, described Menino's approach to neighborhood empowerment this way: "What began to happen is that Menino was willing to invest in communities of color and establish ties to particular business and organizational leaders," he said. "However, because of his ego, he demanded fierce loyalty, where people would be 'punished' if they challenged how he was doing things. Moreover, while he was somewhat progressive regarding sharing resources, he was an old-style pol in his heavy-handed, controlling style of politics. The result was a shallow level of activism in the community because people wanted to avoid irritating Menino for fear of losing funds."[64]

Reiskind praised Menino for his work with neighborhood businesses, saying, "Menino put money in the business districts and main streets, saying the business district is the heart of the community. Pumping money and organization into the neighborhood business district has turned those around."[65]

Menino governed in a "caretaker regime" model early in his twenty-year tenure, becoming dubbed the "urban mechanic." As Clarence Stone characterizes, a "regime devoted to a caretaker style of governance has a much less demanding task than a regime devoted to an activist style of governance."[66] This approach created little affordable housing through linkage or inclusionary housing in Boston's neighborhoods, which, as shown earlier, was one of Flynn's highest and most successful priorities.

The city's linkage program, which assesses fees for commercial and retail developers to finance affordable housing, produced an average of a third fewer such units every year under Menino than under Flynn. During Menino's first six-and-one-half years in office, 1,080 affordable units were built with linkage funds, while 3,096 were constructed between 1986 and mid-1993 under Flynn.[67]

As a result of the settling, by and large, of the most egregious racial and cultural conflicts during the Flynn period, Menino was later poised to take advantage of development opportunities, particularly in the education and medical sectors because they were countercyclical to commercial development, which had slowed in the early 1990s. The nonprofit institutional industry was allowed to grow almost unregulated during Menino's tenure. Little in the way of redistributive benefits accrued to Boston residents in terms of jobs. The residents' job policy enforcement could not have been more lax. As the *Boston Globe* reported in 2009,

> The proportion of Boston residents, people of color, and women working on city construction projects has dropped sharply since Mayor Thomas M. Menino took office, even as a boom in real estate development brought tens of thousands of construction jobs to the city. City officials are reluctant to impose legal sanctions because they fear the law might not survive a court challenge. Workers' advocates say the mayor wields considerable influence over developers, who must get City Hall approval for their building projects and should use that power to get more work for residents, people of color, and women. "The law is supposed to create an uplifting opportunity for working residents," said Kerrick Johnson, director of the Roxbury Builders Guild. "But the working population is losing its toe hold. They are getting driven out."[68]

Mel King observed, "I stood up with the Workers Alliance and challenged the police station going up in Roxbury and what they had to do to get jobs. We were not getting the jobs."[69]

Menino, like White, began a process where he selected developers for significant projects, picking the winners in a style eerily reminiscent of the White administration. One prominent example is that during the approval of a project in the Back Bay, Menino was said to have drawn the rooftop design on a napkin, which was later incorporated into the approved project beginning of the period of Menino's "rooftop" designs. As a 2009 story in the *Boston Globe* put it, "Never before in Boston, and perhaps nowhere else in the nation, has a mayor obsessed so mightily, and wielded power so exhaustively, over the look, feel and shape of the built city. Routine construction projects on remote streets need City Hall approval; prominent towers that climb the downtown skyline carry his mark; independent city boards bow to his will."[70]

Menino was proud of his iron fist on the development process and the city, saying in his 2014 book, *Mayor for a New America,* "The only check on Boston's emperor/mayor was the emperor/mayor."[71]

Following Flynn's exit, Boston's population grew, fueled by the construction of luxury housing in downtown and through new immigrants, mainly from Asia and South America. With population growth and housing attracting a "new class" to Boston, the city's income inequality grew to the highest point in its history.[72] As BRA director under Menino, Tom O'Brien described it, "One of Mayor Menino's significant contributions is the development of downtown residential buildings. At the restaurants there, on Thursday and Friday nights, there is a Mercedes parked out front, there are BMWs parked out front, there are very expensive cars, and there are a lot of empty nesters."[73]

Menino belatedly issued an executive order early in 2000 for inclusionary zoning, the setting-aside of units in luxury housing developments for low- to moderate-income families after he had promoted significant luxury housing development downtown, including the long-vacant Filene's building, which with lucrative city tax breaks was developed into 350 units of luxury condos with not a single affordable unit. *Boston Globe* reporter Stephen Kurkjian wrote that in late 1999, Menino approved 830 units of high-priced luxury housing without a single contribution for affordable housing:

> The new buildings will house more than 830 high-priced condominiums along Boston's skyline. Still, none will contain, or finance, a single unit of moderate-income housing, even though such concessions were commonplace during the previous administration of Raymond Flynn. Mayor Thomas M. Menino has frequently cited affordable housing as one of his main priorities, acknowledged in an interview last week that his administration has been slow to force such trade-offs. "It's something we should have been doing before now," Menino said. "As we moved forward, there should have been a percentage of the luxury units set aside for affordable housing." While receiving favorable treatment from City Hall, some luxury housing developers gave generous contributions to Menino's campaign committee. Menino denied that the developers were receiving better treatment from the city. The new condo buildings could have yielded more than 100 affordable units under the rules used by the Flynn administration.[74]

"Tom Menino unleashed market-rate luxury development, which drove up rents in surrounding neighborhoods," Michael Kane, director of Mass Alliance of HUD Tenants, said. "When you look at the Seaport development, it was a crime; it could have been a historic treasure for Boston. He gave away the store to a handful of wealthy investors."[75] BRA director Steve Coyle explained, "When you permit almost unrestrained commercial development, there is a major consequence in land values that prices out affordable housing. It is tough for working families to live in the city anymore. We built thousands of low, moderate, and upper-income units, one-third, one-third, one-third, that working families could move into. Under Menino, the balance shifted toward capital from community."[76]

The *New York Times* reported on Menino's tenure as mayor: "There were challenges that Mr. Menino could not overcome. Housing was another problem area. The city created millions of dollars of high-priced housing, leaving longtime residents priced out of their newly gentrified neighborhoods."[77]

As Logan and Molotch suggest, the growth machine "must influence government decisions to maximize returns from their holdings, and they must also make campaign contributions (or bribes) to public officials."[78] The *Boston Globe* reported in 2009 that Menino personally selected nearly every developer for every project from a select few: Menino would argue, as he did in the *Boston Globe* report cited above, "What you're talking about is my integrity, and there is no price on that, absolutely none." One developer's employees donated $3,000 to the mayor's campaign just one day before submitting plans to the BRA for approval, though Menino himself claimed, "Donations did not determine my decisions. They were one among many factors. Suppose you had to choose between a proposal from a friend and one from a stranger. Other things being equal, you'd do what I did. You'd favor the friend."[79] While there may be no direct link, the growth machine developers certainly knew how to be successful.

Did Menino's return to the growth machine coalition model and abandonment of aggressive redistributive policies facilitate the growth of income inequality? A study prepared by the Brookings Institute in late 1999 showed that "Boston is one of four U.S. cities in which the income of the richest households is at least fifteen times the earnings of the poorest 20 percent." At the same time, the incomes of the upper 5 percent continued to increase, and those in the bottom 20 percent remained unchanged.

Menino did recognize the issue of income inequality. "We have inequalities, a big issue today, more than ever before," he said. "There's a big division between the rich and the poor in our country, city, and world. The middle class is being squeezed out. That's one of the things I see as an issue today."[80] The data bear him out when, at the end of his tenure as mayor, "Boston has the least equitable income distribution in the country, among cities of population over 500,000."[81] Ed Glaeser at Harvard University thinks, "It is important not to view the coexistence of wealth and poverty as something damning about Boston. The city should take pride in having a thriving financial sector, a thriving tech sector, and well-paid doctors."[82] And it should take pride in responding to the challenges of poverty, "the defining issue of our time." As Walsh said in his first inaugural address, "We cannot tolerate a city divided by privilege and poverty."[83]

Menino did not believe the city could do much to "reverse the greatest threat to social hope in America, economic inequality. Against inequality, cities do what *can* be done by passing living wage ordinances, for example, not all that *needs* to be done. Legislation to address inequality must come from Washington."[84] Boston's business elites and growth machine would agree with Menino's approach to development: "Build it, and they will work. Buildings create jobs," not confronting who will do what work and the quality of the jobs created.[85]

The growth coalition opposed the policies Flynn pursued, which prolonged their frosty relationship with him and his administration. Their relationship with the city became warmer when Menino took office, as one prominent business leader, former US Attorney Wayne Budd, said: "I think for the last many years they've felt they were on the outside looking in, that their presence was not viewed as particularly important. I think the mayor [Menino] is determined to do all he can to assure that companies know they are welcome here."[86] As the *Boston Globe* wrote following Menino's election as mayor, "The Ray Flynn era of social justice for the have-nots appears to be giving way to a new era, where the haves and have-nots share equal claim to City Hall."[87] Whether there was indeed equal access for both groups is a point of significant contention.

## Theme Three: Race Relations, Racial Conflict, and Public School Governance

An analysis of Boston's governance and social and cultural structures—particularly racial politics, as discussed in chapters 8 and 9—demonstrates that the urbanism of Boston, the culture, and the way of life were transformed, and political conflict in the city shifted from ethnicity to race and later to class in the period under study. I sought to answer whether the Flynn governing regime could make progress on race relations and reduce racial conflict. The discussion of public school governance in chapter 10 sought to answer whether the new school governance structure successfully achieved the results the reformers envisioned.

The theoretical frameworks used in these chapters were those of government communalism and urban regime theory. Government communalism theory analyzes how the government can help build a community and be more inclusive of individuals left out of the mainstream civic culture. Race became a more central issue in Boston following the 1974 court order requiring the busing of school children; the handling of school desegregation's legacy of racial conflict by White, Flynn, and Menino is a focus of this book. Each political leader would confront racial conflict during their terms in office. However, how leaders use the government to make rules that favor the rights of individuals not otherwise protected from harm is an essential quality of mayoral leadership.[88]

Later in his term, White was seen as aloof from the Black community's concerns, as Hubie Jones recounted. When asked why he did not hire more people of color in significant positions in his administration, White said, "Well, I have an answer for you. Vote for someone else."[89] As Flash Wiley said, Flynn changed that equation: "Flynn brought more Blacks to his administration." Ken Wade added, "The Flynn administration worked very hard to change the perception of the city to do more to get more people of color involved in significant roles within the administration, and that had not happened under Kevin White."[90] Mel King commented, "Flynn took some of the people on my campaign and put them on his staff. The significance was his [Flynn's] recognition that these people could make a difference in the city."[91] King also said that he "declined an offer by Flynn to be a paid administration advisor, adding that he often gave Flynn advice 'and they do not need to pay me to do that.'"[92]

Flynn was widely credited with bringing more people of color into city government. "The percentage of people of color in the municipal work-force climbed from 24.2 percent in 1983, the year before Flynn took office, to 30 percent last year," the *Boston Globe* reported in 1990. "City officials say people of color have also benefited from a 1988 executive order directing the administration and all city departments to award 15 percent of outside contracts to minority-owned firms. 'Something has to be said for a program with 16 percent of city contracts going to minority firms,' said Rev. Joseph Washington, Flynn's equal rights adviser."[93] Fearing a legal challenge, Menino would eliminate the minority and women-owned business program in favor of a resident-focused effort, which failed to deliver results for people of color, according to observers.

The remnants of the 1974 court-ordered school desegregation and busing under White and the ensuing racial and cultural conflict were transformed through an aggressive police response and civic engagement during Flynn's tenure. As shown in chapter 9, top city priorities were responding to racial violence and working toward the peaceful integration of the city's public housing in the majority-White neighborhoods of Charlestown and South Boston, as well as enforcement of civil rights violations and hate crimes by the Community Disorders Unit (CDU) of the Boston Police Department. As illustrated in Chart 12 in chapter 9, the period of the late 1970s to the early 1990s was punctuated by many hate crimes. In 1984, when Flynn took direct aim at the issue, the number of incidents began to decline. The data show that incidents continued to decline in 1991, with a 20 percent reduction from 1990.

The CDU was fully supported by the Flynn administration and proved effective in contributing to the decline in hate crimes in the city. It was not without its detractors, however, particularly in South Boston. A frequent critic of the CDU was city councilor James Kelly. "When the victim is a minority, they come down like the Gestapo, but when the victim is White, you never hear from them again," he said. "There is a great distrust of the CDU out there."[94] As described in chapter 9, some South Boston leaders continued to resist vigorous enforcement of civil rights violations. There were periodic increases in hate crimes during public housing integration. Later, when Menino took control of the mayor's office, the city's support for the CDU was reduced.

The *Boston Globe*, which closely tracked the city's release of hate crime statistics, wrote that there was a 20 percent drop in rights violations in 1992.[95] Several years later, in 1994, under Flynn's successor Menino, the *Globe* reported that racially motivated incidents were rising in the city. As the 1992 report stated, "Between 1978—when the Boston police became the first department in the nation to track racially motivated crime—and 1988, reports of bias crimes dropped from 607 to 152 annually, according to department figures obtained by the *Globe*. Then, Mayor Raymond L. Flynn would hold press conferences, heralding the annual reports of the CDU. It was used as a model for civil rights training by the FBI, and within the Police Department, the unit was considered a launching pad for star detectives."[96]

Later, as described in chapter 9, the *Boston Globe* reported in 2000 that things had changed dramatically under Menino. "Twenty years after Massachusetts became one of the first states in the country to enact a hate

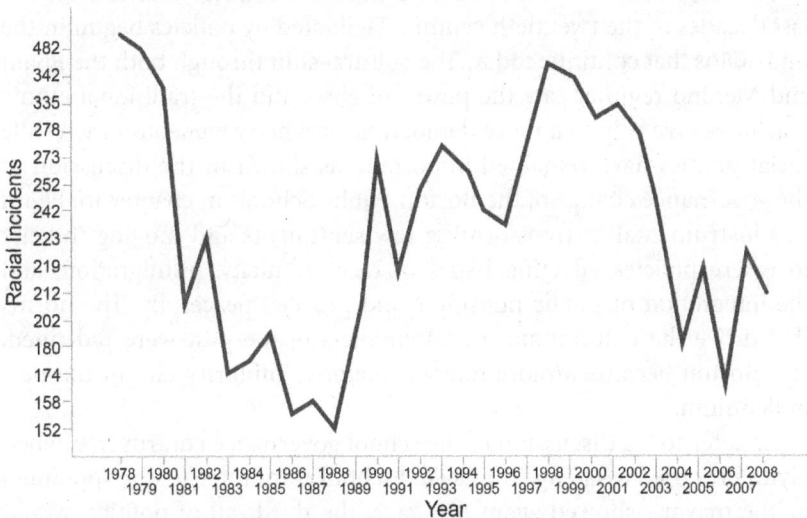

CHART 15. Racial Incidents in Boston by Year
Source: City of Boston Police Department

crimes bill, the squad is a shell of what it used to be, undercut by political pressure from heavily voting South Boston," the author wrote. "The decline of the CDU is a case study in both the exercise of raw Southie muscle and the erosion of a bulwark against racism that was widely seen as a significant contributor to the cleansing of Boston's image in the traumatic aftermath of busing in the 1970s."[97]

Menino said during an interview that he resisted calling racial incidents hate crimes because he felt this would divide the city. He didn't often discuss race issues, as Sandee Story, *Jamaica Plain Gazette* editor, told me in an interview. "Menino called me at 8 a.m. one morning, the first time he ever called me directly, asking me about a letter to the editor we had published in the *Hyde Park Gazette* about racism. He said, 'What were you thinking?'" Story went on to say, "Tom Menino had a real sensitivity to racism and prejudice of any kind, and while it bothered him, he didn't want it talked about."[98] The question remains: Was the Menino strategy for dealing with hate crimes one that swept the issue under the rug and pretended that it did not exist? Or was it simply that his administration was preoccupied with other crime issues?

Flynn would have to confront other racially polarizing events in Boston during his tenure. These included the Mandela campaign effort by some in Boston's Black community to secede from the city and the aftermath of the Stuart incident described in chapter 9. These issues kept the matter of race squarely in the city's consciousness.

The city's culture has undergone a dramatic transformation since the last decades of the twentieth century, facilitated by policies begun in the mid-1980s that continue today. The cultural shift through both the Flynn and Menino regimes saw the power of elites and the traditional ethnic machines give way to a more democratic and heterogeneous city. While racial politics have remained important, as shown in the discussion of the governance change of the Boston Public Schools in chapter 10, Flynn was instrumental in transforming raw sentiments and moving the city to where policies affecting issues of race, ethnicity, immigration, and the integration of public housing could proceed peacefully. The norms that drove the cultural and racial conflicts of the past were redefined, and Boston became a more tolerant majority-minority city in the new millennium.

Chapter 10—a discussion of the school governance controversy, when Flynn proposed to change the elected school committee to one appointed by the mayor—showed again that race, the third rail of politics, would be a significant issue in the debate. Notwithstanding having the support of the business community and many civic leaders, including the Black ministers, can it be claimed that Flynn exercised power over those who opposed the elected school committee? I suggest that he did not, in this instance, have power over the central actors in the debate. The mayor assembled a coalition of influential actors, which Clarence Stone termed "power to" achieve the desired result: replacing the elected school committee with an appointed one.[99] Flynn brought together the business community through the Boston Municipal Research Bureau, which also brought onboard the Vault. The role of the business leaders helped frame the issue as economic rather than racial. Flynn also enlisted media support in the coalition of the *Boston Globe*, which initially opposed the referendum, writing, "Flynn's proposal is undemocratic and badly flawed. The *Globe* urges a 'no' vote on this referendum."[100] The paper later reversed course and endorsed the plan. Still, the key players in this contest appear to have been both the highly visible and trusted Hubie Jones and Professor James Jennings, the Black ministers of the Interfaith Ministerial Alliance, and the *Bay State Banner*, the newspaper of Boston's Black community, which also editorialized in favor of the change. With their support, Flynn undermined the opposition efforts by many Black elected leaders, portraying them as protecting the status quo at a time when, following the turbulent 1970s, it was clear the city's educational system needed dramatic improvement.

Menino continued the reforms with his own appointed school committee and superintendents. Ken Tangvik, Jamaica Plain activist and Mel King campaign organizer, shared his thoughts on the schools and the appointed school committee. "You know, it is funny because we blamed the schools being a mess on the White Louise Day Hicks types, and now clearly, the schools' leadership is Black and brown, and it is slowly getting better," he said. "If you have kids in the schools, and you don't get your kid into an exam school, you're fucked, your kid's fucked. The appointed school committee has stabilized the schools as much as we notice how bad they are still. Looking back, I see that the appointed school committee was positive; it had to happen. The school committee was a training ground for city council candidates. The committee now is a group of exceedingly committed, well-minded people who are trying to do the right thing, but what you are asking them to do is an overwhelming task: deal with the whole equity issue."[101]

Chuck Collins, the parent of Boston Public School students, author, activist on economic inequality, made the point equally clear: "I do think that the multigenerational inequalities are the big issue, you know, race and class, poverty, disparities, how that plays out in education," he said. "It is one place where you can make a difference."[102]

304 / HOW DOES URBAN PROGRESSIVISM SUCCEED?

Menino had promised in 1996 to transform the student assignment
process. After a lengthy planning effort led by Dr. Theodore Landsmark,
Menino abandoned implementing changes in student assignments.
Hubie Jones explained why Menino balked at taking on school assignments then. "Menino wakes up, realizing political power is coming into
the Black community," he said. "He gets the message when Andrea Cabral beats Stephen Murphy for the sheriff's job. She took half of Roslindale and Hyde Park against an Irish Catholic sitting city councilor. Two
weeks before, they talked about a new assignment plan they would ram
through, even though they were getting negative feedback from Black
leadership and neighborhood folks. They were going to ram it. Cabral
won, and two days later, they abandoned the assignment plan. So, he
says whoa. This is a different deal, you know. Okay. This political voting
power is in the Black community, and I better take heed. You can see a
complete change of behavior in the future and being respectful of what
the Black leadership says about all kinds of issues. Menino's paying attention and respectfully dealing with it. He goes on to talk all about it: this
is a majority-minority city."[103]

Released from the fear of a backlash as he prepared to leave office,
Menino embraced a change in the school assignment plan in the final
months of his mayoralty. Neil Sullivan said, summarizing the transition
from White to Flynn and Menino, "Though we focused on the economic
issues that crossed racial lines, race continued to be a driving issue—
from the Mandela secession movement to public housing integration
to gang violence, the Stuart murder, and the school committee debate.
It is also important to point out that Boston went through a significant
economic recession at the turn of the decade in 1990, leading to layoffs
and service cutbacks. Most of these issues had been resolved, one way
or the other, by the time Menino took office. The city was becoming
more diverse, and the economy was improving. Many of the policies
we implemented during the Flynn era came to fruition during Mayor
Menino's tenure."[104]

While Flynn made progress in reducing racial violence and hostility
in the city, the problem did not disappear. As demonstrated in chapter 8,
Menino took a different approach, refusing to discuss the issue publicly.
The record shows an increase in hate crimes during his tenure. Is the les-
son for future city leaders that to address the problems of racial conflict
and racism, you need to confront them publicly? When I spoke to Marty
Walsh about this strategy, he told me his thoughts on issues of race: "You
have to talk about it. You can't get to the point of comfort if you aren't
talking about it; you can't get people to realize there is an issue here if

you don't talk about it; you can ignore it and hope it goes away, hope the tensions go away; as a person, I couldn't do that."[105] Both Flynn and Walsh disagree with Menino on this point.

Dan Monti captured the cultural transformation that was occurring in Boston when, in 2013, he wrote in *Engaging Strangers,*

> Bostonians have come to practice and embrace a kind of *public civility* in their dealings with each other that makes the city different from the way it used to be. Life in Boston has settled down even as people unfamiliar with the locals have continued to move in. The city is much less rambunctious and mean-spirited today, and its people are not nearly as prickly or openly intolerant. Crime, the great bellwether for how poorly big-city people treat each other, has been dropping consistently for at least two decades. Something big and important has changed in Boston, nothing to do with how people make a living, how much richer or poorer they are, where they or their parents came from, what religion they practice, and how odd they look and sound. What has changed are the customary ways the different groups living in Boston talk about each other in public and act in each other's presence.[106]

Following Monti's public civility frame, Menino symbolically responded to Boston's communities of color. Every year during his mayoralty, he would tour the troubled Bowdoin-Geneva neighborhood on Christmas Eve, bringing toys, a practice his family continued after his death. He was widely praised by many in minority neighborhoods. "He does not make much fanfare about the work being done," Landsmark said, "but there is no African American community in Boston that one can drive through today without seeing dramatic, positive physical changes."[107]

Not all agreed with Landsmark's assessment. "I think people have been complacent because things have been a lot worse," Lisa Martin of Dorchester said. "From where I sit, things have not changed. When I walk through here, I still see boarded-up housing. Crime in the area is increasing, even when crime overall is down."[108] Kevin Peterson of the New Democracy coalition added, "Boston's black community supports the mayor but feels let down. Menino's administration has promised to improve the quality of life in urban areas that have fallen short of community expectations. If you ask the average black person in the city, they would say they have not been overwhelmingly positively impacted during his tenure."[109]

While Menino received widespread praise in some quarters of the community, the growth of race-based income inequality is an issue that has not been addressed.

## Conclusions

Boston is a different city than it was in 1970. Each of Boston's recent mayors made their mark during their tenure. The city's culture has changed, and it is better for it. It is more open, less insular, and more tolerant. There is less racial segregation within and between neighborhoods, although more income segregation is based on class. There were significant transformative moments in Boston during the period under study. However, policies instituted to make Boston more equal in the 1980s ceded to policies that favor the haves over the have-nots.

Implementing redistributive policies, primarily created by Flynn's progressive middle-class and working-class regime, has continued. Still, they have not been adjusted to keep pace with the city's growing poverty and inequality. Linkage, the foundation of Boston's shared prosperity, has not effectively addressed the current affordable housing needs of Boston's low- to moderate-income families. Efforts pushed by Flynn to expand protections for Boston's renters, particularly low-income and elderly tenants, were thwarted first by the growth machine–controlled Boston City Council and later by the successful statewide effort in 1994 to repeal the rent control enabling law ballot initiative led by the real estate industry. Inclusionary zoning policies, formally enacted during the Menino administration and expanded during the Walsh and Wu tenures, have similarly provided minimal relief from escalating housing costs. Still, they were driven mainly by the rapid development of luxury housing downtown, now expanding to other parts of the city.

Finally, the racially discriminatory banking and lending policies that were uncovered first by community activists and later confirmed by the Federal Reserve Bank of Boston seem to have reemerged as a result of a lack of vigilance by city hall. As Jim Campen commented on a 2001 Massachusetts Community and Banking Council report he authored, "Race continues to be an issue. It is a bigger issue now than in 1990 with African Americans being denied loans three times more often than whites."[110]

The book has revealed how the redistributive policies of the 1980s, coupled with the city's "managed growth" of the economy, led, in part, to a reduction in poverty. When attention to this strategy waned in the 1990s, poverty significantly increased in Boston, especially among children and families. Between 1989 and 2011, poverty increased by 4.4 percent for children under eighteen and 3 percent for families.[111] At the same time, in the Boston area, "Net worth (or wealth), the sum of total assets minus the value of debts, shows racial differences. While White households have a median wealth of $247,500, Dominicans and U.S. Blacks have a median wealth of $8."[112]

The transition from the school controversies lingering from the busing crisis to a more focused set of governance policies for the Boston Public Schools contributed to continued racial divisions; even today, the majority of Black residents in the city prefer an elected school committee. However, the city reached the historic milestone of becoming a majority-minority city in 2000. This reflected the city's diversity; electing a mayor of color was only achieved in 2021 with the rise of Michelle Wu.

Each area under study constituted sociologically significant, transformative shifts. Boston's new and future administrations should understand these lessons—hopefully, by embracing strategies to respond to racial conflict, equal access, income inequality, and protecting the most vulnerable citizens.

The book has also focused on race relations, economic development, and inequality. An aggressive redistributive strategy to reduce poverty is needed in Boston and across America to respond to the growing income inequality and attendant racial inequality. The city should also focus on expanding linkage, rent stabilization, the transfer tax on high-end real estate transactions, and the inclusion of more affordable housing in development projects. In addition, Boston's corporate and large nonprofit institutions should be required to guarantee employment for city residents. The current Boston Residents' Jobs Program policies must first be enforced beyond construction employment to provide permanent jobs from growth. Menino was correct in saying that development in Boston creates jobs. Still, more people in the city need to realize the benefits from growth, other than the growth machine interests that reap plenty of benefit from maintaining control of the city's economy.

Boston is home to forty-seven private institutions from the educational, medical, and cultural sectors identified as owning tax-exempt property, each valued more than the $15 million threshold established in the Payment in Lieu of Tax agreements (PILOT) guidelines to encourage contributions from nonprofit institutions toward city services.[113] There are hundreds more nonprofits in Boston as well. Some make small PILOT payments; others do not. These nonprofit institutions contribute to the richness of the city culture and employment base. Still, as Flynn suggested, one of his regrets was that he did not work with the colleges and universities to do more. "We could have got a lot more out of them," he said in an interview. "How was it that, with Boston being the higher education center of the world, we have one of the worst public school systems in the country? How does that happen? Why do the kids living in the shadows of Harvard and MIT, BU and Boston College, these colleges that their mothers work at, like in the cafeteria washing dishes, and these kids cannot get an education?"[114]

As the *Boston Globe* editorialized on January 6, 1993, "Universities and hospitals have thrived and expanded in Boston's worst economic times. Some have been magnanimous in their voluntary payment in lieu of taxes. Others have been disdainful. Flynn's pointed message should at least stimulate institutions of higher learning to direct more of their educational know-how into local schools."[115]

Flynn's approach to lessening racial conflict and hate crimes was to use power over the police and courts to quell the racial conflict and the power to bring people together to initiate collective action. Leaders must address race and racial conflict issues publicly, not refuse to talk about them for fear of causing divisions. As Mel King explained, the solutions to the historical problems of race and inequality, first and foremost, require action by the community. "Race is an issue for many folks in this country and this city. It is imperative that if things are going to change in the city for everybody, then a significant push from the community can make this place work in ways that it can. Until that gets mobilized and people say they are deserving, I see no change. Unfortunately, what will happen is, as the Metropolitan Planning Council survey says, that 30 percent of folks of color will be out of the city, and if we are going to sit by and allow class cleansing, that is on us. Frankly, it is in our hands."[116]

Joyce Ferriabough, a prominent leader in the Black community and media and political strategist, offered her thoughts on Flynn's legacy on race relations:

> Flynn faced some strong racially tinged headwinds during his term. Besides the Stuart debacle, the Mandela initiative was where Black areas of Boston threatened to secede from the city. I don't think we give Flynn enough credit for what he did around racial inequities. He signed Bruce Bolling's linkage legislation into law, a promise he and his mayoral opponent Mel King made. Linkage gave Flynn BRA chief Steve Coyle the tools to develop parcel-to-parcel linkage that finally gave minority developers a shot at major development opportunities in the city for the first time. Ministers like Don Muhammad, Bruce Wall, and Eugene Rivers worked with police commissioner Mickey Roache to craft a community policing initiative hailed as a model for the nation. Public housing was desegregated without the kind of animus previously brought about by busing. No doubt he moved the city forward in that regard.[117]

Rev. Eugene Rivers, a Black minister who has long been on the front lines of matters involving race in Boston and isn't known for his conciliatory ways, said, "Ray Flynn is a complicated story in a complicated city. On balance, he is a decent man, coming up in a tough town. He was objectively trying to heal the city. There's no question."[118]

Walsh made strides in this area by talking about racism and the issue of race and convening several citywide conversations with community, business, faith-based, and political leaders. In June 2020, he issued an Executive Order declaring racism a public health emergency and redirected 20 percent of the police overtime budget to address the issue. Now, Boston's newest mayor, Michelle Wu, has had the unique opportunity during her first three years in office to balance the needs of all Bostonians and make Boston a place where all its citizens can realize their potential and share in the prosperity of America's "city upon a hill."

## Final Thoughts

Ray Flynn is a progressive—a term he has never used to describe himself—having steered Boston's economy toward greater fairness and opportunity for poor and working-class residents while embracing the city's racial, ethnic, and cultural diversity. Born sixty-five years after James Michael Curley, his progressivism took on many characteristics that depicted the city's public life during Curley's time as a clash between its immigrant majority—the people—and a wealthy Brahmin elite—the interests.[119] Perhaps a symbolic event in 1993 was the night when, along with the mayor of Galway, Ireland, Flynn was asked to leave the Ritz-Carlton Hotel because he was not wearing a coat and tie. The mayor, myself, and an entourage from Ireland decamped to J. J. Foley's, an Irish working-class bar in the South End, which the owner Jerry Foley described as "the place where the common people gather."[120] There Ray Flynn was comfortable and always centered his public life working to advance the interests of Boston's poor and working families—the people.

Steve Coyle spoke about his time leading the BRA for Flynn: "It was a tremendous opportunity, for all of us, to put into motion what we believed in. We all enjoyed it, even though the hours were long and the stress was significant. For the communities, development was different than having it jammed down their throats. There was a different mood about development, and we engaged everybody we could about building Boston."[121] During these years, the progressive regime effectively managed the growth machine.

Neil Sullivan affirms the experience of many who had the unique opportunity to govern a city at a turning point in its history. "We accomplished so much together, yet, all the while, we did not see ourselves as anything other than a loose coalition, held together by our respect for

Ray Flynn as a person and leader. Some within our administration called themselves 'Real Americans.' Some of us were called 'Sandinistas,' and we never really objected to the label. We were young and saw ourselves as revolutionaries of one sort or another. From 1983 through 1993, the Flynn era was perhaps the most exciting and progressive ten years in this or any city's history. In a mere ten years, we reoriented city government and ensured that every mayor that followed would strive to be the next mayor of the neighborhoods. Plus, no group of people ever had more fun winning a campaign or governing a city."[122]

# Acknowledgments

First, I would like to thank those who took the time to share their stories with me: the mayors of Boston—Raymond L. Flynn, Thomas M. Menino, Martin J. Walsh, and Michelle Wu—and the many activists, organizers, officials, community and business leaders I interviewed, and people who believe in Boston's capacity to be a great, inclusive, and equitable city. I greatly respect the many people who have engaged inside or outside the Boston city government to help make the city a better place for thousands who live and work in Boston. I want to acknowledge with sorrow that too many of those I interviewed, or who have been so active in civic life in our city, are no longer with us. I want to thank them and their families for their contributions to our city and for letting their memories tell their story.

As I reference in the book, this research emerged from work I undertook while a PhD student in sociology at Boston University. I am grateful for the support I received from the BU Department of Sociology members of my dissertation committee: Nazli Kibria was supportive throughout my later-in-life university journey; the late professor John Stone's advice and guidance on race relations were instrumental; Professor Japonica Brown-Saracino helped me frame issues in urban sociology; and Professor Bruce Fraser was an invaluable teacher and mentor in qualitative research methods. A warm thank-you goes to Professor Dan Monti, an urban scholar who advised and mentored me at BU before he moved to Saint Louis University. He continued to provide guidance, support, and inspiration as chair of the Polis: Fordham University Series in Urban Studies Advisory Board. I wouldn't

312 / ACKNOWLEDGMENTS

have completed this book without him. I also thank Professor Peter Dreier, Occidental College, for his guidance and suggestions for better organizing and communicating the voluminous material. Peter was a fellow activist during our years at Boston City Hall, trying to build a "progressive city." We made some progress in Boston, which I try to capture in this book. They and others have reviewed parts of the manuscript and helped me tell the story of the community organizers and leaders who changed Boston. The manuscript's peer reviewers provided insightful comments and a productive critique. My thanks to Fordham University Press for making this book possible, its director Fredric Nachbaur and his capable team, copy editor Bob Land, and for the assistance I received from LSU professor Bob Mann. Several people reviewed and commented on chapters along the way. I want to thank Sunny Schwartz, Neil Sullivan, Susan Tracy, John Riordan, Mary Nee, Joyce Ferriabough, and Lew Finfer for their invaluable advice. I want to thank Pierre Clavel, Professor Emeritus at Cornell University, for sharing the interviews he conducted for his book *Activists in City Hall*. I quoted from several of his interviews, and his book helped frame Boston's story as a progressive city. I want to thank my sister, Jane Gillis, and brother, Robert Gillis, for their assistance with the images and graphics. The book was made immeasurably better through the contributions of so many people. I couldn't have done it without them, and they bear no responsibility for the errors or omissions of the author.

Undoubtedly, those who stand by us during the arduous nights of writing and editing are often our closest ones. I want to express my deepest appreciation to my family, Megan and Sally Gillis, and Sunny and Ilana Schwartz, for their unwavering support throughout this journey. Their understanding, patience, and encouragement have sustained me while writing this book, making it a true family endeavor.

And finally, much of the book is about one person, Ray Flynn. While I got to know Ray while working in South Boston, in his 1983 campaign, and during his tenure as mayor, I learned and gained a deeper understanding of him, and his values of family, community, and sacrifice, through our many hours spent together in his living room and at the family kitchen table. Along with his wife, Cathy, their six children, and seventeen grandchildren, they were inviting, open, and wonderful to be around. I learned what many of us often took for granted in his administration: the tremendous personal sacrifices he and his family would undergo during his tenure in public life. As the book recounts, many did not always support his difficult decisions to move the city forward. At times, he and his family paid the price. As his son city councilor Ed Flynn said at the fortieth anniversary celebration of his father's mayoral election attended by hundreds of former members of the administration and city leaders, "It was difficult as a child living in the city when my father was mayor, knowing that the integration of public housing had a tremendous impact not only on the city and the residents and families but also on our family. My father never took the easy way out." Undeterred, Boston is better in so many ways, and I want to thank the entire Flynn family for their friendship and kindness throughout the years; they have enriched the narrative of this book and the City of Boston.

October 2024

# Appendix 1: Cities Defined as Progressive

## San Francisco, California

San Francisco followed a similar model to Boston's in enacting progressive housing and economic development policies. Both cities are roughly the same regarding geography and population; they have grappled with and developed an antifreeway coalition to oppose highway construction through neighborhoods and massive downtown development at the expense of the city's neighborhoods. San Francisco's process to bring about progressive change was centered on the ability to put important questions before the voters in binding referenda. The coalition of neighborhood activists and progressive board of supervisors (city council) members was responsible for several significant referenda and policy changes.

Most notable was San Francisco's linkage program, the first in the nation. Approved by the mayor and Board of Supervisors in 1981, a one-time development fee of $5 per square foot on commercial development was used to pay for public transit. Later, the slow growth coalition could not get their San Francisco Plan growth control proposal to severely limit commercial development approved, losing by less than 1 percent. The Downtown Plan supported by the growth machine was adopted in 1985 over the objections of the slow growth coalition, so they pursued yet another ballot measure—Proposition M, a ballot initiative that would place tight controls on growth in both downtown and the neighborhoods. Winning that historic battle in 1986 led some to believe that Proposition M did not represent merely a change *in* the system but a change *of* the system (DeLeon 1992). The city had been steadily expanding linkage during this period, including housing. It strengthened the relationship with local community development corporations to take the lead in building more affordable housing. The new focus on the neighborhoods and slowing growth led to Proposition M, including growth caps on office space, linkage fees for affordable housing, provisions for neighborhood protection, historic preservation, abatement of traffic, protection of small businesses serving neighborhoods, along with a powerful weapon for communities called "discretionary review," which allowed those near a project to call for a special review, making it possible to cause deal-killing delays or exact concessions (Beitel 2004).

During all the battles of this period, San Francisco saw dramatic changes in the city's political leadership. When George Moscone was elected mayor in 1975, he was considered the "people's mayor." He went on to open up city hall with diverse appointments for people of color and the gay community and expanded citizen participation at all levels of city government. The loose progressive coalitions saw Moscone as an ally and were devastated when he was assassinated along with Supervisor Harvey Milk on November 27, 1978, just two years into his term. Milk was the first openly gay member of the board of supervisors. The gunman, former supervisor Dan White, killed Moscone over a disagreement over reappointing him to the board of supervisors and Milk because he was gay. The board of supervisors had just passed an antidiscrimination ordinance with Moscone's signature over White's lone vote against it.

As president of the Board of Supervisors, Dianne Feinstein would become mayor. She was very popular, reelected twice, and later became a US senator from California. She was considered a moderate and was in the corner of the growth machine during her tenure. After she was term-limited, the longshot California state assemblyman Art Agnos ran for mayor. Although he jumped into the race as the underdog, he ended up with 70 percent of the final vote. He would go on to lead a progressive administration that focused on the major urban issues of the time: public housing, increasing affordable housing production from 342 units when he took office to 2,240 units; the AIDS epidemic; homelessness; hiring minorities and members of the LGBTQ community for city positions; and putting the city on a solid financial footing so that he could invest in neighborhood infrastructure. Agnos received support from the progressive and neighborhood leaders for his reelection bid in 1992; however, they were not enough to save him from losing by a mere few thousand votes.

Activism was strengthened in San Francisco due to the prevalence of ballot initiatives, which chalked up both wins and losses. Battles came and went between the growth machine and their political supporters, whether in the mayor's office or on the board of supervisors, and activists fought for tenants' rights, against unfettered development, and for stronger environmental regulations and historic preservation. Activists won a ballot initiative to have the supervisors elected by districts, giving some impetus to those seeking seats on this body. Housing was another of the victories in San Francisco. With a tight rental market, a 1998 ballot initiative supported by tenant activists, labor, and the board of supervisors to control rents and evictions was enacted and widely praised. San Francisco had some of the most far-reaching publicly enacted legal regulations over the private housing market of any major US city. Success came once the movement emphasized ballot initiatives that required grassroots mobilization (Domhoff 2011; Beitel 2004; Shaw 1998).

## Chicago, Illinois

Chicago was the poster child for the machine-style form of government in the mid twentieth century. The twenty-one-year tenure of the late Mayor Richard J. Daley (1955–1976) was notable not only for its longevity but also Daley's ability to deliver on ethnic progressivism as defined by author James Connolly and have a tight grip on the ward politics like his earlier Boston counterpart James Michael Curley. As the head of the city and local Democratic machine, he controlled the patronage jobs and all major development decisions. The growth machine supported the early phases of development in the downtown area alongside a dramatic loss of manufacturing and deterioration of the city's neighborhoods.

Following Mayor Daley's death on December 20, 1976, two interim mayors served until the election of Jane Byrne in April 1979. She was the first woman to be elected mayor of a major city in the United States. Mayor Byrne had a mixed review of her tenure. She ran on a platform of taking on and dismantling Daley's political machine and the grip of the so-called Vrdolyak 29, moniker for the all-white Chicago City Council's majority bloc. She once called Vrdolyak and his allies a "cabal of evil men." Her election appealed to the antimachine forces, White lakefront liberals, and a cross-section of ethnics and, surprisingly, members of the African–American community who had been poorly treated by the Daley machine (Ferman 1996). Byrne is often remembered for her decision to move into the crime-ridden Cabrini–Green Homes housing project on the north side of Chicago after thirty-seven shootings resulting in eleven murders in three months. She stayed in the project for three weeks, in an effort to bring attention to the crime and lack of maintenance in the development. She was criticized for appearing to use the project as a publicity stunt. She ran for reelection in 1983 against Mayor Richard J. Daley's son, Richard M., and Harold Washington. Washington would win the Democratic primary by less than 3 percent over Daley and Byrne with the largest turnout in twenty-five years. Washington prevailed in the general election against Republican Bernard Epton by only 3 percent, unheard of in the Democratic-dominated city with over 82 percent turnout.

Washington had run for mayor in 1977 to fill the remaining term of Daley but lost badly. At one time, he was a machine precinct worker under Daley who later became a congressman from the South Side (Clavel 2010). In 1983, he was recruited to run for mayor again. He would mount a formidable campaign with solid support from Chicago's growing African American population, liberal Jews, progressive leaders and organizations, and those disgruntled with the growth machine's singular focus on downtown while ignoring the city's manufacturing base, which provided many thousands of working-class jobs.

Chicago underwent a significant transformation in its politics with the election of Harold Washington in 1983 as mayor. Washington was the fifty-first mayor of Chicago and, like Kurt Schmoke of Baltimore, was the first African American to be elected to the mayor's office. Chicago politics had been dominated by the political machine of Mayor Richard J. Daley for decades. Washington built a progressive coalition during his brief time in the mayor's office (he died on November 25, 1987, early in his second term). He drew upon much of the community organizing and social activism emerging in Chicago then, a legacy of the civil rights movement and the New Left. The work of renowned community organizer Saul Alinsky and the history of the settlement house movement would help shape the progressive coalition's support of Washington.

Within hours after Washington had concluded his swearing-in speech in April 1983, one of the most dramatic moments in the city's history segued from thunderous applause and triumphant music at Navy Pier to the bitter realities of city hall: "council wars." The control exercised by the city council wreaked havoc throughout most of the first term of Chicago's first African American mayor, pitting Mayor Washington against the Vrdolyak 29, led by Alderman Edward "Fast Eddie" Vrdolyak of the Tenth Ward and Edward Burke of the Fourteenth. Despite its reputation as a "boss-dominated" city, Chicago's governing structure was "strong council, weak mayor." The Vrdolyak 29 blocked the mayor's replacements of council committee chairs and appointments to the patronage-heavy Park District, Chicago Transit Authority, Board of Education, city colleges, and other vital agencies (The Encyclopedia of Chicago 2004).

Washington struck back by using the mayoral power of executive order to cut the city's payroll from an estimated forty thousand down to
less than thirty thousand, erase the city's deficit, balance the budget, and
broaden freedom of information "as public policy." As a result, Chicago's
bond rating dramatically improved, enabling the mayor to push through
a $100 million bond issue and deploy Federal Community Development
Block Grant funds to resurface and repair miles of city streets in each
of the fifty wards. He also moved to improve housing for people experiencing poverty, afterschool and food pantry programs for the homeless,
police-community relations, equity in Tax Increment Financing (TIF),
and city economic planning.

The council wars ended in May 1986, when federal court–ordered
special elections were completed in seven wards, remapped to reflect
Chicago's Black and Hispanic population growth. Washington supporters on the city council increased from twenty-one to twenty-five—a tie
with the twenty-five in power from the Vrdolyak 29. With the mayor's
tie-breaking vote activated, the council, on May 9, 1986, approved twenty-
five mayoral appointments to fourteen boards and departments.

In his short tenure, Washington ushered in several progressive policy
changes. His administration notably focused on preserving and retaining
the city's manufacturing base. The policy favored jobs over real estate and
promoted the balance between the Loop (downtown) and the neighborhoods in development investments. The Chicago Works Together plan,
built upon the mayoral campaign, involved hundreds of people who
sought to "counter and challenge the hegemonic position of the business
community and its machine allies. He invested heavily in the manufacturing strategy, including, between 1984 and 1987, $1.2 million in business
incubators, resource recycling, microenterprise, capital pools, sectoral research, and worker buyout opportunities, and did joint projects focused
on building early warning plant closing networks, industrial displacement
organizing, and city purchasing from youth enterprises" (Clavel 2010)

Although Washington ran on a platform of expanding neighborhood
participation in city development and service delivery, he balked when
it came time to implement the reforms necessary to achieve the policy
objective. Washington was unwilling to create structural power in the
neighborhoods for fear the council would coopt them. This was despite
neighborhood support for the idea of neighborhood planning councils
that he promoted during the 1983 campaign.

Washington sought to create alternative mechanisms for neighborhood
empowerment that had been central to his campaign for mayor. There
were advisory committees for industrial retention; the city identified

other groups as "delegate agencies" to redirect resources to the neighborhoods. He allocated $7 million to support 124 new delegate agencies. Most
notable were the creation of the Local Economic and Employment Development Council and Planned Manufacturing Districts. The goal was to
engage community leaders and businesses, primarily manufacturers, in
devising a plan to "protect factories and jobs against the influx of wealthy
residents and upscale office and commercial development" (Clavel 2010).

After Washington's short tenure, Richard M. Daley—son of the former mayor—won election and was the city's longest-serving mayor at
twenty-two years, one more than his father. Daley returned to the growth
machine model, focusing more on the downtown Loop than Chicago's
neighborhoods. He had to adopt many of the changes put in place by
Washington, so he was not the autocratic boss like his father and adopted
some liberal/progressive measures. He accomplished this balancing act
because the growth machine was not as unified and robust as it had been
during his father's mayoralty.

## Baltimore, Maryland

In Baltimore, the election of Kurt Schmoke in 1987, the city's first
Black mayor, was the result of a progressive coalition led by Baltimor-
eans United in Leadership Development (BUILD), which targeted affordable housing production as the critical driver. In partnership with James
Rouse, a thriving shopping mall developer responsible for revitalizing
Quincy Market in Boston, in Baltimore, many of his urban redevelopment initiatives led to the unintended consequence of deterioration in
the downtown urban commercial core (Gillette 2022, 17).

Baltimore was transformed under Mayor Schmoke during his three
terms in office. The city had been a leader in the national effort to tear
down dilapidated, crime-plagued high-rise public housing developments and replace them with lower-density, low-rise communities that
better support the healthy development of families. He demolished
the Lexington Terrace high-rise housing project, Pleasant View Gardens, and the former Murphy Homes high-rise public housing project
to make way for new middle-income neighborhoods. Schmoke's other
housing initiatives include establishing the Baltimore Community
Development Financing Corporation, which pools private and public
resources to renovate abandoned city dwellings, and developing the
Settlement Expense Loan Program, which gives homebuyers up to five
thousand dollars to meet settlement costs. Mayor Schmoke has made
Baltimore a national model for neighborhood revitalization. At the

same time, during his tenure, he led the early stages of the renewal of the Inner Harbor on Baltimore's waterfront.

Schmoke led efforts to establish needle exchange programs to combat the spread of AIDS, initiating in Baltimore what was the nation's most extensive local government-sponsored needle exchange program. He sought to have drug abuse declared a "public health problem" instead of a crime directed at the estimated sixty thousand drug addicts; he sought to promote the "medicalization" of drug use over significant opposition (Schmoke 1995). In his first inaugural address, Schmoke announced his intention to make Baltimore "The City That Reads," where in a city of over 720,100, it was estimated that 200,000 adults were considered functionally illiterate. Schmoke, in partnership with Baltimore's public and private sectors, established a cabinet-level city agency and a private foundation to fund, coordinate, and expand adult literacy programs throughout the city (Valentine 1990).

As mayor, Schmoke was known for his progressive and effective policies. However, he also struggled to address some of Baltimore's more enduring social problems, notably the city's crime and murder rate, which was directly a result of the drug plague. The city is depicted in the award-winning HBO series *The Wire*, in which Schmoke made a cameo appearance.

Schmoke's predecessor, William Donald Schaefer, mayor for four terms who went on to become governor, had strong support from the city's growth machine. With the decline of the city's manufacturing base, he promoted downtown development. Schmoke helped shift the city's focus from the Inner Harbor to the neighborhoods.

## Cleveland, Ohio

Cleveland elected Dennis Kucinich mayor in 1977 and had one of the most controversial mayors in the city's history. Kucinich governed for his short two-year term as an urban populist. Urban populism can best be understood as Saul Alinsky–style community organizing carried into the electoral arena, promoting policies that favored serving inner-city residents over corporate interests. On the agenda of local politics, urban populism attempts to displace the growth issue with the distributive issue (Swanstrom 1985).

As the youngest mayor of any major US city, the city's growth machine challenged him early and often. The primary issue he confronted while in office was the public ownership of utilities in Cleveland, specifically the beleaguered city-owned electric utility firm Municipal Electric Light or Muny Light (later renamed Cleveland Public Power). Kucinich was cast as valorous David against the rapacious Goliath (Perloff 2017). Despite pressure from the growth machine, he was adamant that the city would not sell Muny Light. The other issue Kucinich derided was the city's policy to provide tax abatements to downtown businesses, a stand that undoubtedly helped propel him into the mayor's office.

Cleveland, like other Midwest cities, underwent a population and economic transformation. "Cleveland's population peaked at 914,808 in 1950 and had declined to 750,903 by 1970. The city lost nearly 100,000 jobs during the same period, and its population changed character: Nonwhites numbered 149,544 in 1950 and had increased to 282,819 in 1970. Along with this demographic change, the city became poor compared to the rest of the Cleveland metropolitan area and the nation" (Clavel 1986).

Kucinich had grown up poor, and as a politician, he learned to tap into the deep class resentment growing in Cleveland, a city caught between deindustrialization and the expanding downtown service sector. The scourge of urban renewal sweeping the country did not leave Cleveland unscathed. While not as robust as other major American cities, the growth machine nevertheless led efforts to replace "slums" with moderate- to upper-income housing. He came to power appealing to the voters based on grievances, perceived or actual. His most significant confrontation was with the growth machine, which wanted the mayor to privatize the public utility, something he steadfastly refused to do. The city's fiscal interests, most notably the banks, put tremendous pressure on Kucinich to sell the municipal electric system and forced the city to default on its debt when he refused. The default significantly affected Kucinich's ability to deliver on his promises made during the election.

Kucinich was fortunate that he was able to draw upon the planning expertise of Norman Krumholtz, first hired by Carl Stokes, the nation's first Black mayor of a major city. Krumholtz would go on to harness the neighborhood movement in Cleveland, which emerged in the 1970s focused on empowerment. Organizing occurred around plant closing and downtown tax abatements. Kucinich could ride the anti–tax abatement tide and maintain the municipal electric system into the mayor's office. From these efforts, "Kucinich deduced that the proper direction for city policy was a shift in the agenda away from divisive race and social issues to deal directly with economic questions: most important, the redistribution of wealth from corporate concentrations to popular constituencies (Clavel 1986). Based on his approach since he was elected, Kucinich was subject to constant attacks from the media, the city council, and business and commercial interests. He faced a recall in 1978 and later a default on city loans from the Cleveland banks.

The history of the progressive or urban populist mayor of Cleveland can be instructive. He challenged the growth machine and placed himself and the city in political and economic jeopardy. He was a one-term mayor for only two years and had to confront a recall election halfway through his term. Although he survived the recall, he was politically damaged goods. He became a flash-in-the-pan progressive mayor serving as a poster child of how not to govern. Could he have done things differently and survived? The die was cast partly owing to his personality and the alignment of the growth machine forces squarely against him. The neighborhood movement did continue in Cleveland but failed to unite a political alliance of Blacks and neighborhood organizations. So the Cleveland experiment cannot be seen as sustainable. Following his departure as mayor, the growth machine was back in complete control with the election of his successor, George Voinovich. Kucinich went on to run unsuccessfully for several positions, including his former office, and he did win several terms in Congress in 1996, where he served until 2013. Kucinich was an unsuccessful candidate for president in 2004 and again in 2008.

Several smaller cities also underwent a progressive transformation during the same period. Cities like Santa Cruz, Santa Monica, and Berkeley, California; Burlington, Vermont; Cambridge, Massachusetts; and Madison, Wisconsin—all midsize cities dominated by universities—elected progressive regimes and began moving away from growth machine politics toward more inclusive citizen participation in development decisions and becoming more responsive to community housing and service needs.

## Santa Cruz, California

Santa Cruz, with a population of approximately fifty-eight thousand people, is located on the US West Coast about one hundred miles south of San Francisco. Known for its beautiful beaches and tourist attractions, Santa Cruz became the beachhead in the small town's progressive government.

For example, the city elected a progressive majority on the board of supervisors (city council) and the board of county commissioners (many cities in America are part of the dual governing system of county government). With a city manager form of government, the power rested with the board of supervisors. Over ten years, between 1984 and 1994, the progressives gained total control of the seven supervisor seats. Three issues were at the top of the agenda: increasing social services, rent control, and development policies and management. While there was agreement on the first, social services, the progressives were divided regarding rent control and development. Some factions struggled with the no-growth versus managed-growth approaches, with many following the framework—that growth could be about jobs, not profit. The issue of rent control was hotly contested by the real estate community and small landlords, and three attempts to enact rent controls and regulations lost at the ballot box (Gendron and Domhoff 2009).

On October 17, 1989, the city and its politics were shaken up. A 6.9-magnitude earthquake struck Santa Cruz, and along with the death and destruction came an altering political environment. As one would expect, there was a significant push to rebuild the city, and the growth machine was in the driver's seat here, upsetting the progressive balance of power.

## Burlington, Vermont

Burlington took a somewhat different path. A city of 37,712, Vermont's largest city had seen an influx of young people and progressives in the 1970s. In 1981, Burlington made it into the progressive camp with the election of Bernie Sanders as mayor (1981–1989). Sanders was constrained not only by his socialist politics but also by the fact that the board of aldermen (now the city council) was unfavorable to his proposals. When he was elected, he had two supporters out of thirteen aldermen. The numbers increased, and after his major reelection victory in 1983, by 1984, he had support from six of the thirteen.

For a small city, Burlington had a highly active core of neighborhood organizations focused on utility rates, affordable housing, and opposition to highway construction. Sanders has sought to increase the engagement of neighborhood organizations and city workers in government decision-making. He created Neighborhood Planning Assemblies, which would handle short- and long-term planning and development issues in each city ward. The committees serve as organized, democratic forums where neighbors can learn about public issues that affect them and advise the city of their concerns and needs. They remain active to the present day.

The city planning commission supported two significant issues: the Southern Connector—a four-lane roadway through the city—and the Lake Champlain waterfront area development with hundreds of luxury condominiums. Sanders opposed both issues. Neither issue went anywhere quickly, as Sanders and the neighborhood leaders organized against the growth machine spearheading the projects. The roadway was primarily stopped, and the waterfront development became more balanced due to Sanders and neighborhood cohesion. Burlington remains a city with a sizeable progressive majority, and due to their efforts, Sanders and his allies helped to create the city's most extensive housing development, now resident-owned; its largest supermarket is a consumer-owned cooperative, one of its largest private employers is worker-owned; and most of its people-oriented waterfront is publicly owned. Its publicly owned utility, the Burlington Electric Department, recently announced that Burlington is the first American city of any decent size to run entirely on renewable electricity (Dreier and Clavel 2015).

Some would argue that many other cities are or were progressive. That is undoubtedly true, and those stories should be told. The economic lessons from those cities that have implemented progressive policies must also be shared.

# Appendix 2: Urban Theories Used in Boston Analysis

## Urban Regime Theory

Urban regime theory—the view that city governance is the result of a coalition between public and private actors—became prominent following Clarence Stone's study of Atlanta and has guided significant research in other urban areas (Burns 2003; Domhoff 2006; Ferman 1996; Gendron 2006; Stone 1989). Most urban sociological and political theorists would agree that there are limits to localism and to the ability of an urban regime to single-handedly increase economic opportunity, reduce poverty, solve racial conflict, and fix the social problems that face urban America (Dreier, Mollenkopf, and Swanstrom 2014; Peterson 1981). Paul Peterson argues, "The rivalry among groups, the patterns of coalition formation, the presence or absence of competitive political parties, the power of local elites, or the vagaries of political campaigns influence policy outcomes. Moreover, parties, groups, the news media, bureaucracies, and other political institutions function similarly in local and national contexts" (1981, 3). Peterson argues that even the most progressive elected officials in cities have difficulty adopting redistributive policies because they will lead private businesses and affluent residents to leave, thus undermining the local tax base and reducing the revenues available to redistribute. Peterson's view—which justifies conservative approaches to governance—argues that cities have a Catch-22 that they cannot escape. He identifies some of the areas of inquiry and the key institutions, issues, and actors that are the focus of this study of Boston. In another approach to urban regime theory, in *Place Matters*,

Dreier, Mollenkopf, and Swanstrom (2014) distinguish the characteristics of progressive, liberal, and conservative regimes to show variations in urban regimes and their attention to issues of equity and justice.

Scholars disagree about the precise nature and structure of growth politics. Stone (1989) theorizes that urban regimes govern through collaboration by institutional leaders (government, business, labor, religious, and nonprofit institutions). He characterizes the governing model as "the social production model" (8). While most agree that the primary goal of the urban regime or growth machine is to promote economic development (Peterson 1981), scholars such as Logan and Molotch, along with Richard Gendron and G. William Domhoff, view the process and purpose of the coalition as exploiting land use to maximize the private profit that accrues to the dominant coalition partners in the urban regime. How this process led to the urban renewal plans executed between 1950 and 1970 in Boston is explored.

## Growth Machine Theory

Growth machine theory emerged from the Chicago School of urban sociology and the social science field of community power studies. The main power studies frames were the power elite—the capitalist class in total control of the economy and decision-making—and the pluralist model, where power is dispersed among competing governmental, business, and civic groups. Growth machine theory, primarily formulated by Harvey Molotch, comprises the local power structure, led by real estate interests, or "place entrepreneurs," which joined with other corporate interests (banks, landlords, developers), government, and to a lesser extent organized labor (mainly in the construction unions) to promote the fundamental transformation of the city (Gendron and Domhoff 2009). In Boston, as in other places, it could be argued that the dominant actors are the banks, the real estate developers, and the property owners or landlords. John Mollenkopf (1983) suggests that the rise of the growth machine was the Democratic Party's response to urban industrial transformation during and following World War II. The "political entrepreneurs" developed "a kind of banker government" to support redevelopment and transformation of the urban core into a hub of postindustrial administrative and service centers (1983, 139).

Growth machines formed in cities across the United States following World War II, and in Boston, they resulted in the elections of Mayors John Hynes (1950), John Collins (1960), and Kevin White (1968). This trend is juxtaposed with the election to the office of mayor of the populist candidate Ray Flynn (1984) and his successor Thomas Menino (1993), who was in office until 2014, Marty Walsh (2014), and Michelle Wu (2021) (Kimelberg 2011; Mollenkopf 1983; Molotch 1976).

The literature on growth machines focuses on their primary goal of growing the economy. The coalition of real estate, business, construction unions, and newspapers want more jobs, people, wealth, and profits. The coalition is less interested in the distribution of economic prosperity, the quality and wages of jobs, the development of housing affordability, the success of public schools, and the environment's health. Only when these latter issues pose problems for business success do key elements of the growth machine seek to join forces to address them. Examples include the sporadic efforts to support public education and housing while not being willing to sacrifice profits and achieve affordable housing options for their employees. This book has examined how regime and growth machine theories align with the experiences of critical actors in Boston.

The growth machines in many cities underwent a fundamental change—even lost some of their power and influence—with the consolidation of large corporations and the migration of many corporate headquarters away from big cities. Increasingly, nonprofit hospitals and universities and the outgrowth of research centers, "eds and meds," have become key players in employment, development, and expansion. This was often true during recessionary periods. While the nonprofits paid little or no property taxes (some voluntary limited payment instead of tax agreements) to the municipality, they acted like the for-profit corporations that had driven the growth machine.

One window into the theoretical questions of growth machine theory is whether governing regimes can implement redistributive policies and how they do so. I examined here how regime and growth machine theories align with the experiences of political actors in Boston. Exploring political, community, and governmental actions and decisions during the study period will help better understand why Boston is where it was by the end of 2023.

Growth machine theory and practice were challenged in many cities across the country by activists seeking a more balanced distribution of economic rewards from the growth of urban areas. Of note was the reaction to the urban renewal policies of federal and local governments of the 1950s and 1960s, which sought to facilitate a postwar economic revival of the postindustrial city. While the growth machines were successful in the initial phases of the physical transformation of urban areas, the political, neighborhood, and cultural revolt soon formed the basis of a new set of politics and policies.

## Progressive City Theory

Progressive city theory, developed by Pierre Clavel in the 1970s and 1980s, is an outgrowth of the civil rights and antiwar movements in the prior decades. Urban political and community leaders were fostering the creation of a new type of social organization in many cities centered on redistributive and participatory reforms. Clavel's research on several cities revealed that "many of the programs had a populist tone reminiscent of the great democratizing of the period around the turn of the century" (Clavel 1986, 1; 2011).

The first wave of "progressive city" victories and accomplishments occurred in the 1970s, catching the imagination of activists and showing the potential for winning office. Activists who identified as progressives captured city council seats, city council majorities, and mayoralties in dozens of places (Clavel 2013).

## Government Communalism Theory

"Government communalism" is a phrase coined by Daniel Monti (1999), who uses it to distinguish one of the main ways in which Americans "do community." Monti argues that government communalism principles are exclusivity, accountability, and tolerance. Only some persons are deemed worthy enough to be welcomed as citizens (exclusivity). Those allowed in are expected to treat others in public in a way that respects other citizens' needs (accountability). People who make it as citizens are treated more leniently than those who do not (tolerance). The Flynn administration was pivotal because it worked with an organized Black community seeking to gain political legitimacy and rights that came with citizenship through Mel King's mayoral campaign. Flynn had to deal with that in the electoral arena and gain legitimacy as Boston's mayor. In other words, Blacks were already citizens but had to fight to claim and win the rights that came with citizenship. The city government could work in a way that enabled Black Bostonians and the growing immigrant populations to be considered and treated like every other group or class that had been granted citizenship and political power. The government could help build community by being more inclusive of those left out of the mainstream of the civic culture (Monti 1999).

# Interviews by Author

| | |
|---|---|
| Muhammad Ali-Salaam | October 3, 2012 |
| Margaret Blood | June 13, 2012 |
| Ed Burke | June 11, 2012 |
| Pablo Calderon | June 25, 2012 |
| Chuck Collins | December 5, 2012 |
| John Connolly | February 11, 2013 |
| Bob Consalvo | November 12, 2009 |
| Frank Costello | June 15, 2010 |
| Helen Cox | May 22, 2014 |
| Steve Coyle | April 1, 2014 |
| Larry DiCara | September 12, 2012 |
| Bernie Doherty | May 3, 2023 |
| Conny Doty | March 10, 2023 |
| Lorraine Downey | June 3, 2024 |
| Frank Doyle | February 6, 2023 |
| Peter Dreier | April 23, 2013 |
| Larry Dwyer | October 7, 2024 |
| Joyce Ferriabough | November 17, 2023 |
| Lew Finfer | June 1, 2012 |
| Ray Flynn | May 12, 2010 |
| Jovita Fontanez | May 5, 2023 |
| Clara Garcia | February 21, 2013 |
| Harry Grill | July 24, 2013 |
| Mossik Hacobian | April 26, 2013 |
| Hubie Jones | May 24, 2012 |
| Jim Jordan | January 24, 2014 |
| Michael Kane | March 11, 2023 |

| | |
|---|---|
| Dennis Kearney | October 2, 2012 |
| Mel King | November 13, 2014 |
| Judith Kurland | June 22, 2012 |
| Ted Landsmark | October 15, 2009 |
| Joyce Linehan | December 8, 2023 |
| May Louie | June 14, 2012 |
| Michael Patrick MacDonald | October 7, 2010 |
| Ann Maguire | September 3, 2013 |
| Jose Masso | May 15, 2012 |
| Vin McCarthy | October 11, 2012 |
| Kristin McCormack | February 21, 2013 |
| John McDonough | February 11, 2013 |
| Pat McGuigan | December 28, 2023 |
| Tom Menino | June 25, 2014 |
| Bart Mitchell | April 16, 2013 |
| Mary Nee | August 8, 2013 |
| Tom O'Brien | March 8, 2013 |
| Jim O'Connell | April 12, 2023 |
| Tom O'Malley | May 10, 2023 |
| Michael Reiskind | June 21, 2012 |
| John Riordan | January 17, 2018 |
| Mickey Roache | October 30, 2009 |
| Jerry Rubin | September 18, 2013 |
| Rosaria Salerno | February 13, 2023 |
| Rosemarie Sansone | January 21, 2010 |
| Nancy Snyder | January 13, 2010 |
| Allan Stern | April 12, 2023 |
| Sandee Story | February 10, 2023 |
| Neil Sullivan | August 25, 2009 |
| Ken Tangvik | June 6, 2012 |
| Michael Taylor | February 22, 2013 |
| Susan Tracy | January 9, 2024 |
| Marie Turley | May 10, 2023 |
| Sam Tyler | February 21, 2013 |
| Stuart Vidockler | January 2, 2024 |
| Ken Wade | March 11, 2013 |
| Bill Walczak | February 12, 2013 |
| Pat Walker | June 14, 2012 |
| Marty Walsh | March 25, 2016 |
| Joseph Washington | March 22, 2010 |
| Flash Wiley | October 19, 2010 |
| David Williams | February 15, 2013 |
| Michelle Wu | August 14, 2024 |
| Charles Yancey | August 26, 2013 |

# Notes

## Preface: A City in the Twenty-First Century

1. Child 2021.
2. Don Gillis and Peter Dreier, "Mayor Wu's Rent Control Proposal Is Pro-business," *Boston Globe*, February 27, 2023.
3. Adam Reilly, "The Good, the Bad, and the Ugly of Mayor Wu's First Year," *Talking Politics*, WGBH, November 18, 2022.
4. Marty Walsh interview; Michelle Wu interview.
5. Gillis and Dreier, "Mayor Wu's Rent Control Proposal."
6. Rebecca Ostriker, "Reckoning with Boston's Towers of Wealth," *Boston Globe*, November 1, 2023
7. Simon Rios, "WBUR Poll: Rent Control Supported by Most Boston Voters," WBUR, April 14, 2021.
8. Emma Platoff, "New Statewide Poll Shows Strong Support for Rent Control," *Boston Globe*, March 9, 2023.
9. Wu interview.
10. Joan Vennochi, "Ray Flynn Knows What Mayor Wu Is Going Through. He Has Some Advice," *Boston Globe*, June 5, 2023.

## Introduction: Can Cities Be Economically and Socially Progressive?

1. Maria Karagianis, "The Ambitions of Raymond Leo Flynn," *Boston Globe*, April 11, 1982.
2. Logan and Molotch 1987, ix.
3. Key 1955.
4. Kerry Picket, "Trump Pushes Law-and-Order Policy in First D.C. Speech since Leaving White House," *Washington Times*, July 26, 2022.
5. Trump tweet, December 26, 2019.
6. Trump tweet, July 27, 2019.
7. Eric Brander, Kristin Holmes, and Alicia Wallace, "Trump Proposes Building 10 'Freedom Cities' and Flying Cars," CNN, March 3, 2023.

8. Trump tweet, August 22, 2020.

9. Remarks by President Biden at the National League of Cities Congressional City Conference, March 14, 2022.

10. Paul Waldman, "Trump and Vance Are Deploying a Particularly Nasty Anti-urban Strategy," MSNBC, October 20, 2024.

11. Joan Vennochi, "For Flynn, a Hectic, Fulfilling First Day," *Boston Globe,* January 3, 1984.

12. Vennochi, "For Flynn."

13. *Down the Project* 1982.

14. Jim Gomez, "Gillis, of Neighborhood Services, Works as an Advocate from Within," *Boston Globe,* July 28, 1987.

15. Peterson 1981.

16. Suffolk University 2013.

17. Benjamin Kail, "Boston Election 2021: Voters Overwhelmingly Vote Yes on Question 3 to Bring Back Elected School Committee System," Masslive.com, November 3, 2021.

18. David Abel, "Homeless at Record Levels, Survey Finds," *Boston Globe,* December 14, 2002.

19. Strauss and Corbin 1990.

## 1 / City Limits and Opportunities

1. Connolly 1998.

2. William Schneider, "The Suburban Century Begins," *The Atlantic,* July 1992.

3. Glyn and Drenkard 2013.

4. Molotch 1976.

5. Dreier, Mollenkopf, and Swanstrom 2014.

6. Stone 1989.

7. Molotch 1976.

8. Clavel 1986.

9. Monti 1999.

10. Wirth 1938.

11. Borer 2006.

12. Du Bois 1899; Gans 1962; Gottdiener 1994; Liebow 1967; Monti 1985; 1994; Park 1915; Park, Burgess, and McKenzie 1967 [1925]; Small 2004; Stack 1979; Suttles 1968; Whyte 1993 [1943].

13. Boyer 1992; Lees 1985.

14. Patton 2002.

15. Clavel 1986; 2010; Hackworth 2007.

16. Peterson 1981, 4.

17. Domhoff 2006; Mills 1956.

18. Dahl 1961; Levine 1974.

19. Peterson 1981.

20. Stone 1989; Dreier 2014.

21. Peterson 1981, 7.

22. Tyack 1974.

23. Stone 1993, 2.

24. Clavel 1986; Dreier et al. 2000; Stone 1989; 1993.

25. Swanstrom 1985.

26. Gendron and Domhoff 2009, 206.

27. DeLeon 1992, 159.

28. DeLeon 1992, 198n19.

29. Peterson 1981, 148.

30. Monti 1999, 271.

31. Dreier et al. 2000.

32. Logan and Molotch 1987, 157.

33. Kennedy 1992; Logan and Molotch 1987; Molotch 1976.

34. Logan and Molotch 1987, 13.

35. Peterson 1981; Stone 1989; Clavel 1986; 2010; Logan and Molotch 1987; Gendron and Domhoff 1985; Dreier 2000.

36. Clavel 1986; 2010; Dreier et al. 2000; 2004.

37. Boston Redevelopment Authority 2003.

38. Clavel 2010; Dreier et al. 2000; 2004, 206; Swanstrom 1985.

39. Kennedy 1992, 2.

40. Monti 1999.

41. Monti 2013.

42. Lofland 1998, 4.

43. Levine 2005, 179–80.

44. Levine and Harmon 1992.

45. Masur 2008.

46. Beitel 2004; Domhoff 2011; Shaw 1998; Gillette 2022; Valentine 1990; Perloff 2017; Dreier 2004; Clavel 2010w.

47. Lofland and Lofland 1995.

48. Friedman 1990, 61.

49. Patton 2002; Holt 2003; Duncan 2004.

50. Friedman 1990, 64; Patton 2002.

51. Friedman 1990, 62.

52. Friedman 1990, 60–66.

53. Thernstrom 1973, 3.

54. Mahoney and Dietrich 2003, 6.

55. Thernstrom 1973, 3.

56. Kimelberg 2011, 77.

## 2 / Political, Social, and Economic History of Boston

1. Kennedy 1992, 2.

2. Tebbetts 2004.

3. Kearns-Goodwin 1982, 107.

4. Tebbetts 2004.

5. Holli 1999.

6. Connolly 1998.

7. Connolly 1998.

8. O'Connor 2001.

9. Horan 1990, 496.

10. Horan 1990; Mollenkopf 1983.

11. *Mission Hill and the Miracle of Boston* 1978.

12. Mollenkopf 1983, 159.

13. *Mission Hill and the Miracle of Boston* 1978.

14. Bulger 2009, 72.

15. Kennedy 1992; King 1981; Gans 1962.

16. Boston Redevelopment Authority, 1964.

17. Gans 1962.

18. Gans 1962; King 1981.

19. O'Connor 1993.

20. Powers 1967.

21. Mollenkopf 1983, 184.

22. Cited in Leon Neyfakh, "How Boston City Hall Was Born: Fifty Years after a Groundbreaking Competition, Two Architects Look Back at the Project That Polarized the City—And Gave It a New Lease on Life," *Boston Globe*, February 12, 2012.

23. Bluestone and Stevenson 2000, 13.

24. Bluestone and Stevenson 2000.

25. Medoff and Sklar 1994; Wilson 1978; 1996.

26. Matthew L. Wald, "Mayor Assesses Boston: Progress, and Problems," *New York Times,* January 11, 1987.

27. Boston Redevelopment Authority 2008; 2011.

28. Handlin 1969, 52.

29. Medoff and Sklar 1994, 23.

30. Brown-Saracino 2010.

31. The Boston Foundation 2011.

## 3 / The New Boston and the 1983 Race for Mayor

1. Mollenkopf 1983; King 1981; Kennedy 1992; Small 2004.

2. Weinberg 1981.

3. Sam Tyler interview.

4. DiCara 2013, 124.

5. Crockett 2018.

6. Vrabel 2014.

7. *Morgan v. Hennigan.* 379 F. Supp. 410.1974, p. 410.

8. Key 1955.

9. King 1981.

10. Mollenkopf 1983 210.

11. Green 1986, 115.

12. Larry DiCara interview.

13. Menino with Beatty 2014.

14. "The Future of Kevin White," *Boston Globe* editorial, July 14, 1982.

15. Stone 1989, 164.

16. "Dan Shaughnessy, "For More Than a Half-Century, the Boston Neighborhood Basketball League Has Brought Peace to and Love for the City," *Boston Globe*, July 9, 2024.

17. "The Secret Search for Racial Peace," *Boston Globe,* May 25, 1975.

18. Allen 2005.

19. Ray Flynn interview.

20. Wallace 2022.

21. Bud Collins, "Flynn Turns on TV Blackouts," *Boston Globe*, April 15, 1972.

22. Flynn interview.

23. Mary Nee interview.

24. Charles Kenney, "Raymond Flynn Announces Candidacy for Boston Mayor," *Boston Globe,* April 27, 1983.

25. Flynn interview.

26. Neil Sullivan interview.

27. Maria Karagianis, "The Ambitions of Raymond Leo Flynn," *Boston Globe,* April 11, 1982.

28. Mary Baker interview with Pierre Clavel, April 25, 1992.

29. Nancy Snyder interview.

30. Rosemarie Sansone interview.

31. Sansone interview.

32. Marie Turley interview.

33. Kristin McCormack interview.

34. Karagianis, "The Ambitions of Raymond Leo Flynn."

35. Peter Canellos, "Aides Guard Flynn Legacy in Tight Times," *Boston Globe,* December 21, 1992.

36. Vrabel 2014, 209.

37. Harry Grill interview.

38. Karagianis, "The Ambitions of Raymond Leo Flynn."

39. Clavel 2010, 209n58.

40. Flynn interview.

41. Robert Turner, "Mel King's Endorsement Setbacks," *Boston Globe,* July 12, 1983.

42. *Radical America* 1983–1984, 3.

43. Rosaria Salerno interview.

44. Lew Finfer interview.

45. Kevin Cullen, "The Long, Sweet Friendship of Mel King and Ray Flynn," *Boston Globe,* March 30, 2023.

46. King 1981.

47. David Hugh Smith, "Mel King Has Spent a Lifetime as an Advocate for Boston Families," *Christian Science Monitor,* September 24, 2015.

48. King 1981, 28.

49. Annual Report of the Election Department for the Period July 1, 1983, to June 30, 1984, City of Boston [Document 10-1984].

50. Jose Masso interview.

51. Mossik Hacobian interview.

52. Louie interview.

53. Wiley interview.

54. *Radical America* 1983–1984, 3.

55. Walker interview.

56. Horan 1990.

57. DiCara 2013, 181.

58. Vin McCarthy interview.

59. *Radical America* 1983–1984, 3.

60. Louie interview.

61. Charles Kenney, "Poll: How Boston Voters Rate Issues and Their City," *Boston Globe,* August 9, 1983.

62. Allan Stern interview.

63. Kenney 1983.

64. Menino with Beatty 2014, 35.

65. Larry DiCara interview.

66. Dennis Kearney interview.

67. Walter Robinson and Charles Kenney, "The 9 Running for Mayor Keep the Debate Easygoing," *Boston Globe*, September 15, 1983.

68. Robinson and Kenney, "The 9 Running for Mayor."

69. Ed Quill, "Flynn Rebuts 3 of 5 Finnegan Charges," *Boston Globe*, October 8, 1983.

70. Joan Vennochi and Charles Kenney, "It's Coming to a Boil; Finnegan, Flynn Clash," *Boston Globe*, October 7, 1983.

71. Vennochi and Kenney, "It's Coming to a Boil."

72. Vennochi and Kenney, "It's Coming to a Boil."

73. Wallace 2022.

74. Vennochi and Kenney, "It's Coming to a Boil."

75. Joan Vennochi, "Four Mayoral Candidates Call Boston a Racist City," *Boston Globe*, August 15, 1983.

76. Kennedy, Tilly, and Gaston 1990.

77. DiCara interview.

78. Fogelberg 1996; Vrabel 2014.

79. Annual Report of the Boston Election Department, 1984.

80. Bruce A. Mohl and Desiree French, "The Day After, Business Appears Conciliatory," *Boston Globe*, October 13, 1983.

81. Adam Reilly, "Racial Healing: Former Mayoral Opponents Ray Flynn and Mel King Discuss How Far Their City's Come, and How Far It Hasn't, since 1983," *Boston Phoenix*, November 10, 2008.

82. Reilly, "Racial Healing."

83. Mel King interview.

84. Peter Dreier interview.

85. Wiley interview.

86. McCarthy interview.

87. Flynn interview.

88. DiCara interview.

89. Michael Rezendes, "Mayor's Reputation as Racial Healer Gets Some Tarnish," *Boston Globe*, September 10, 1991.

90. Ken Wade interview.

91. David Nyhan, "Populism Was the Big Winner in This Election," *Boston Globe*, October 13, 1983.

92. David Nyhan, "A Step Forward for Boston," *Boston Globe*, November 17, 1983.

93. Walter Robinson, "Survey Shows Flynn Leading the Race; Globe Poll Also Finds King's Popularity Up," *Boston Globe*, October 31, 1983.

94. Robert A. Jordan, "Flynn Wins in a Big Way, 66%-34%; Win for City, Too—King," *Boston Globe*, November 16, 1983.

## 4 / Community Organizing as Political Governance

1. Jerry Rubin interview.

2. Ray Flynn interview.

3. Flash Wiley interview.

4. Ken Wade interview.

5. Wade interview.

6. Wade interview.

7. Pat Walker interview.

8. Pablo Calderon interview.

9. John Connolly interview.

10. Peter Dreier interview.

11. Neil Sullivan interview.

12. Jim Jordan interview.

13. Ray Flynn interview.

14. Flynn interview.

15. Raymond L. Flynn, inaugural address, January 2, 1984.

16. Peter Carlson, "Although As Crooked As They Come, This Boston Politician Was Beloved," *HistoryNet*, August 29, 2023.

17. Flynn interview.

18. Flynn inaugural address.

19. Ed Quill, "Mission Hill Neighborhood Session Opens Flynn Town Meetings Tonight," *Boston Globe*, January 31, 1984.

20. Diego Ribadeneira, "Designing Its Own Zoning Plan, Community Wields a New Control," *Boston Globe*, November 18, 1988.

21. Bernie Doherty interview.

22. Muhammad Ali-Salaam interview.

23. Steve Coyle interview.

24. Coyle interview.

25. Ali-Salaam interview.

26. Ted Landsmark interview.

27. Don Aucoin, "Mayor of Neighborhoods Faces Dismay in the Street," *Boston Globe*, September 9, 1991.

28. John Riordan interview.

29. Aucoin, "Mayor of Neighborhoods Faces Dismay."

30. Riordan interview.

31. Joan Vennochi, "Ray Flynn Knows What Mayor Wu Is Going Through. He Has Some Advice," *Boston Globe*, June 5, 2023.

32. Riordan interview.

33. Ann Maguire interview.

34. "Mayor Appoints Cape Verdean Liaison," *Boston Greater News*, March 17, 1989.

35. Jacqueline Kerstner, "Refugees Face Obstacles, Defy Stereotypes," *Allston Brighton Journal*, December 28, 1988.

36. Shelley Murphy, "City Sandwiches 'Sausage Wars' Vendors," *Boston Herald*, September 8, 1998.

37. Andrew Blake, "Flynn to Create Resource Office for Immigrants." *Boston Globe*, August 25, 1987.

## 5 / Confronting the Housing Crisis and Landlords

1. Allan R. Gold, "Racial Pattern Is Found in Boston Mortgages," *New York Times*, September 1, 1989.

2. Michael Kane interview.

3. Janet Riddell, "A Carnival Flavor about Tent City," *Boston Globe*, April 29, 1968.

4. Janet Riddell, "Hub's Rising Rents Hit Poor Hardest," *Boston Globe*, March 11, 1969.

5. Muzzio and Bailey 1986; Bluestone and Huff 2000.

6. Peter Dreier interview.

7. Report to the Mayor on the Linkage between Downtown Development and Neighborhood Housing, Boston Mayor's Advisory Group on Linkage, 1983, https://archive.org/details/reporttomayoronlo0bost.

8. Michael Taylor interview.

9. David Williams interview.

10. M. E. Malone, "Flynn Forgoes Housing Goals, Shortfall Is Feared in Sluggish Market," *Boston Globe,* February 8, 1988.

11. City of Boston 1986, "Making Room: Comprehensive Policy for the Homeless."

12. Tom O'Malley interview.

13. Sarah Snyder, "South End Residents, Activists Hit Plan to House Homeless Women," *Boston Globe,* August 26, 1986.

14. Katherine Yung, "Only Money Is Standing in the Way of Chinatown Affordable Housing Units," *Boston Globe,* August 22, 1992.

15. Ted Chandler, "Steve Coyle Left a Legacy of Building Nearly 100,000 Homes," National Housing Conference newsletter, January 7, 2024.

16. Steve Coyle interview.

17. Ray Flynn, personal communication with author on receipt of an award from the West End Museum, March 31, 2014.

18. Pat McGuigan interview.

19. McGuigan interview.

20. Janet Riddell, "Rent Control! The Cry Grows Louder in Boston Area," *Boston Globe,* June 1, 1969.

21. Vrabel 2014, 138.

22. Ed Burke interview.

23. David Rogers, "Rent Tampering Innocent Pleas," *Boston Globe,* July 19, 1979.

24. David Rogers, "White Backs Rent Control," *Boston Globe,* July 19, 1979.

25. Joan Vennochi, "DiCara: A Sense of Destiny to His Quest," *Boston Globe,* September 28, 1983.

26. DiCara 2013; Vennochi, "DiCara."

27. Joan Vennochi, "Flynn Housing Plan Goes to City Council; Rent Control Stressed," *Boston Globe,* June 27, 1984.

28. Vennochi, "Flynn Housing Plan Goes to City Council."

29. Dreier interview.

30. Joan Vennochi, "Tenants' Group Charges Real Estate Interests Spent at Least $182,000 to Defeat Rent Control," *Boston Globe,* October 17, 1984.

31. Logan and Molotch 1987, 157.

32. Joan Vennochi, "Flynn to Push for Amendments to Council Rent Control Measure," *Boston Globe.* October 10, 1984.

33. Joan Vennochi, "Flynn's Rent Package Rejected; Council Adopts Kelly Substitute," *Boston Globe,* October 4, 1984.

34. Lew Finfer interview.

35. John McDonough interview.

36. Dreier interview.

37. "Boston Measure Limits Rent Rises and Condominium Conversions," *New York Times,* October 24, 1984.

38. "A Defeat for Boston," *Boston Globe* editorial, October 5, 1984.

39. Vennochi, "Flynn's Rent Package Rejected."

40. Ed Quill, "Council OK's a Permit Rule on Some Condo Conversions," *Boston Globe,* December 19, 1985.

41. John H. Kennedy, "SJC Kills HUB Condo Rule," *Boston Globe*, July 10, 1986.

42. M. E. Malone, "HUB Condo Conversion Rate Climbed in 1987," *Boston Globe*, April 5, 1998.

43. Peggy Hernandez and Steven Marantz, "Council Approves Flynn Condo Bill," *Boston Globe*, June 30, 1988.

44. Susan Diesenhouse, "New Ordinance Would Stem Condominium Tide in Boston," *New York Times*, August 7, 1988.

45. John Riordan interview

46. Connie Doty interview.

47. Daniel Golden and David Mehegan, "Changing the Heart of the City," *Boston Globe*, September 18, 1983.

48. Ed Quill, "Tenants' Group Says Kelly Given $5000 in Landlords Contributions," *Boston Globe*, September 28, 1984.

49. Vennochi, "Flynn's Rent Package Rejected. 1984."

50. "A Defeat for Boston."

51. Finfer interview.

52. Joan Vennochi, "An Electoral Feast for Third-Termer Menino," *Boston Globe*, November 8, 2001.

53. Renee Loth, "A Bright Spot for Massachusetts," *Boston Globe*, November 14, 2016.

54. Loth, "A Bright Spot for Massachusetts."

## 6 / Redlining, Blockbusting, and Fighting Bank Discrimination

1. Bob Consalvo interview.

2. Ron Rosenbaum, "Surviving in Codman Square; Not Long Ago, Some People Thought This Diverse Dorchester Neighborhood Was Doomed, with Crime on the Rise, Burned-Out Buildings, Stores Closing," *Boston Globe*, February 8, 1991.

3. Pietila 2010, 61.

4. Michael Reiskind interview.

5. Daniel Golden and David Mehegan, "Changing the Heart of the City," *Boston Globe*, September 18, 1983.

6. Bradbury, Case, and Dunham 1989.

7. Lew Finfer, "The 'Good Intentions' Program That Devastated Boston's Neighborhoods," *Boston Globe*, January 18, 2019.

8. "Statement of Demands" n.d.

9. Levine and Harmon 1992, 171.

10. Lew Finfer interview.

11. Levine and Harmon 1992, 272.

12. Levine and Harmon 1992.

13. Peter Canellos, "A Lingering Urban Folly: Impact of the '60s Redlining and Blockbusting Still Felt in Mattapan," *Boston Globe*, December 11, 1988.

14. White 1978.

15. Bill Walczak interview.

16. Lukas 1985.

17. Bill Walczak interview.

18. Kristin McCormack interview.

19. Canellos, "A Lingering Urban Folly."

20. Rosenbaum, "Surviving in Codman Square."

21. Levine and Harmon 1992, 270.

22. Lukas 1985.

23. Canellos, "A Lingering Urban Folly."

24. Muhammad Ali-Salaam interview.

25. Ken Hartnett, "Arson Case Laurels Earned by Bellotti as White Lost Out," *Boston Globe*, October 29, 1977.

26. Michael Kenney, "The Key: Scarred Symphony Road," *Boston Globe*, October 18, 1977.

27. Medoff and Sklar 1994.

28. Raymond L. Flynn, "From City Hall to Neighborhoods, It's War on Arson," *Boston Globe*, February 7, 1984; "Arson and Reality," *Boston Globe* editorial, March 15, 1986.

29. Brady 1983.

30. Campen 1992, 39.

31. Steve Marantz, "Inequities Are Cited in Hub Mortgages: Preliminary Fed Finding Is 'Racial Bias,'" *Boston Globe*, January 11, 1989.

32. Peter Dreier interview.

33. Steven Marantz and Teresa Hanifin, "Report of Lending Bias Draws Mix of Reactions," *Boston Globe*, January 12, 1989.

34. Dreier interview.

35. Lew Finfer interview.

36. Finfer interview.

37. Steve Marantz, "Two Lending Advocacy Groups Split: Emphasis on Bank Mortgage Credit for Boston Minorities Is at Issue," *Boston Globe*, July 8, 1989.

38. Dreier interview.

39. Ken Wade interview.

40. Teresa M. Hanifin, "Roxbury Group Vows to Sue on Loan Bias," *Boston Globe*, August 11, 1989.

41. Steve Marantz, "Group to Seek $2.1B in Loans to Community," *Boston Globe*, August 24, 1989.

42. Richard Saltus and Steve Marantz, "Flynn to Order Linked Deposits," *Boston Globe*, September 10, 1989.

43. Bradbury, Case, and Dunham 1989.

44. Steve Marantz, "Study Finds Racial Pattern in Lending: Inequities Cited for City's Blacks," *Boston Globe*, September 1, 1989.

45. Dreier interview.

46. Bart Mitchell interview.

47. Steve Marantz, "Flynn to Lobby Bankers on Mortgage Program," *Boston Globe*, November 14, 1989.

48. Steve Marantz, "Boston Banks, City Officials Divided over Remedy for Lending Disparity," *Boston Globe*, December 24, 1989.

49. Finn 1989; Steve Marantz, "Disparity Found in Mortgage Loans: Boston Study Shows Minority Areas' Needs Unmet," *Boston Globe*, December 20, 1989.

50. Steve Marantz, "Hub Bankers Postpone Unveiling of $1 Billion Reinvestment Plan," *Boston Globe*, December 21, 1989.

51. Marantz, "Boston Banks, City Officials Divided."

52. Steve Marantz, "$400M Investment Plan for Hub Minority Areas: Low- to Moderate-Income Homebuyers Targeted," *Boston Globe*, 1990.

53. Adrian Walker, "Hub Banks Rate Higher at Serving Minorities," *Boston Globe*, September 30, 1993.

54. Steve Marantz, "Bankers Report on Status of $1b Loan Plan," *Boston Globe,* July 1, 1990.

55. Finfer interview.

56. Edward Mason, "Mortgage Denials Rise for Boston Blacks," *Boston Business Journal,* December 30, 2002; "New Report Documents Persistence of Racial and Ethnic Disparities in Mortgage Lending in Boston," *University Reporter* [University of Massachusetts–Boston] 7, no. 6 (February 2003): 124.

57. Marantz, "Boston Banks, City Officials Divided."

58. US Census Bureau, Decennial Censuses, BPDA Research Division. Does not include Hispanic Black residents. *Redlining in Boston: Black People, Place and Policy,* BPDA Research Division, February 2023.

## 7 / Challenging the Growth Machine: A New "Social Contract"

1. Clavel 1986; 2010; King 1981.

2. Daniel Golden and David Mehegan, "Changing the Heart of the City," *Boston Globe,* September 18, 1983.

3. Golden and Mehegan, "Changing the Heart of the City."

4. Boston Mayor's Advisory Group on Linkage, 1983, report to the mayor on the linkage between downtown development and neighborhood housing, https://archive.org/details/reporttomayoronloobost.

5. Jennings and King 1986, 61.

6. Clavel 1986; Clavel 2010, 209n58.

7. Charles Kenney, "2 Referendum Questions Will Be on Tuesday Ballot," *Boston Globe,* November 12, 1983.

8. Gerald O'Neill and Dick Lehr, "McCormack Amassed Millions as White Left Office," *Boston Globe,* January 29, 1989.

9. Boston Mayor's Advisory Group on Linkage, 1983.

10. Joan Vennochi, "White Backs Linkage Plan for Housing," *Boston Globe,* October 15, 1983.

11. Charles Kenney, "A Poll of How Boston Voters Rate Issues and Their City," *Boston Globe,* August 9, 1983.

12. Charles Kenney, "Finnegan Takes Stand on Housing-Fund Issue," *Boston Globe,* August 18, 1983; Ed Quill, "Finnegan Denies Switch on Linkage," *Boston Globe,* August 13, 1983.

13. Vennochi, "White Backs Linkage Plan."

14. John Kennedy, "SJC Kills Boston Condo Rule: Flynn Calls Decision Temporary Setback," *Boston Globe,* July 10, 1986.

15. Kennedy, "SJC Kills Boston Condo Rule."

16. John Powers, "Boston Developers Lawsuit Challenges Linkage Requirement," *Boston Globe,* June 20, 1985.

17. Steve Coyle interview.

18. Michael Frisby, "Jobs Policy to Go Private," *Boston Globe,* July 10, 1985.

19. Coyle interview.

20. Frisby, "Jobs Policy to Go Private."

21. John Powers, "Boston's Plan: Build with Caution; Flynn Asks 'Economic Justice' for Residents, as Guidelines Are Proposed for Developers," *Boston Globe,* July 22, 1985.

22. John Kennedy, "SJC Reverses Ruling against Linkage Law," *Boston Globe,* August 22, 1986.

23. Muzzio and Bailey 1986.

24. Michael Frisby, "Development Plans Come with a Link," *Boston Globe*, March 29, 1986.

25. Coyle interview; Boston Redevelopment Authority 1986.

26. Boston Redevelopment Authority 1986.

27. Michael Frisby, "Flynn Due to Back Minority Linkage Plan," *Boston Globe*, September 25, 1986.

28. John Powers, "A Linkage Proposal with Downtown Lure," *Boston Globe*, March 30, 1986.

29. John Chesto, "City Puts Property Owners on Notice: Diversity Matters," *Boston Globe*, August 13, 2020.

30. Powers, "A Linkage Proposal with Downtown Lure."

31. City of Boston Archives 1984a.

32. "Downtown Plans." *Boston Globe* editorial, November 3, 1984.

33. Peggy Hernandez, "For Builders, Linkage Now Part of the Landscape," *Boston Globe*, December 5, 1989.

34. Tom O'Brien interview.

35. Marie Kennedy interview with Pierre Clavel.

36. Neil Sullivan interview.

37. Boston Redevelopment Authority 2003.

38. Neighborhood Housing Trust Report, nht_report_2017_170102.pdf (boston.gov).

39. Neighborhood Housing Trust Report.

40. Charles Radin, "Nonprofit Groups Lead Housing Drive," *Boston Globe*, August 16, 1987.

41. Christopher S. Pineo, "After 25 Years, Dudley St. Initiative Still Going Strong," *Bay State Banner* (MA), April 23, 2009.

42. Kennedy 1992; Medoff and Sklar 1994; "Roxbury Group to Get Eminent Domain Right," *Boston Globe* editorial, November 11, 1988.

43. David J. Barron and Gerald E. Frug, "Make Eminent Domain Fair for All," *Boston Globe*, August 12, 2005.

44. Medoff and Sklar 1994.

45. Medoff and Sklar 1994.

46. Kirk Scharfenberg, "Resident Jobs Plan Passes a Milestone," *Boston Globe*, July 21, 1985.

47. Scharfenberg, "Resident Jobs Plan."

48. Scharfenberg, "Resident Jobs Plan"; Frisby, "Jobs Policy to Go Private."

49. Michael Rezendes, "Fewer Building Jobs Stay in City," *Boston Globe*, May 3, 1990.

50. Matt Rocheleau, "Hiring Goals Not Met in City," *Boston Globe*, May 18, 2015.

51. Ed Quill, "Mel King Criticizes Flynn on Handling of Rent Control Plan," *Boston Globe*, October 10, 1984.

52. Sarah Schweitzer and Alice Gomstyn, "Construction Hiring Goals Unmet," *Boston Globe*, August 16, 2002.

53. Mel King interview.

54. Laura Crimaldi, "Honoring a Pioneer," *Boston Globe*, April 8, 2015.

55. Rocheleau, "Hiring Goals Not Met in City."

56. Rocheleau, "Hiring Goals Not Met in City."

57. "Mayor Walsh Files Boston Residents Jobs Policy Update," City of Boston, November 28, 2016, https://www.boston.gov/news/mayor-walsh-files-boston-residents-jobs-policy-update.

58. Paul Singer, "Boston's Diversity Hiring Mandate for Construction Projects Is All Bark, No Bite," WGBH, October 13, 2020.

59. Chris Burrell, "City Commission Issues Its First Fines under Boston Residents Jobs Policy," WGBH, February 1, 2023.

60. Peter J. Howe, "Boston Agency Eyes Six Industries for Growth in Jobs," *Boston Globe*, February 3, 1991.

61. Peter Canellos, "Flynn Cites Michigan Ruling, Urges Bid to Keep Digital," *Boston Globe*, February 12, 1993.

62. Andrew Ryan, "A Brand New Boston, Even Whiter Than the Old," *Boston Globe*, December 11, 2017.

63. Ryan, "A Brand New Boston."

64. Shirley Leung, "The Seaport Has Become Boston's Innovation District. Somewhere Former Mayor Tom Menino Is Saying, 'I Told You So,'" *Boston Globe*, January 30, 2021; Don Gillis, "Boston's Seaport District: A Gleaming Disappointment," *Boston Globe*, February 6, 2021.

65. Dumcius Gintautas, "Mayoral Candidates Sound Off on Seaport as 'Playground for the Rich,' Future of Work," *Dorchester Reporter*, July 16, 2021; Bruce Mohl, "Most Mayoral Candidates Pan the Seaport," *Commonwealth Magazine*, July 15, 2021.

66. Ryan, "A Brand New Boston."

67. Coyle interview.

68. Catherine Carlock, "As Market Hits Pause, Wu Pushed on Reforms," *Boston Globe*, May 21, 2023.

69. Catherine Carlock, "Board Pushes Back on Wu's Plan to Remake BPDA," *Boston Globe*, February 18, 2023.

70. Joan Vennochi, "Wu Is Short on Details about Planning Equity," *Boston Globe*, February 23, 2023.

71. Greg Ryan, "Boston City Council Votes to Replace BPDA in Combative Vote," *Boston Business Journal*, March 28, 2024.

72. "Mayor Wu Marks Creation of New City Planning Department with Signing Ceremony," Mayor's Office, April 2, 2024.

73. "A City United? Letter to the Mayor," *Boston Guardian*, January 5, 2024.

74. Michelle Wu interview.

## 8 / Boston's Racial Politics: Ending Racial Violence

1. Lukas 1985, 61.

2. Lukas 1985, 60.

3. O'Donnell 1983.

4. "Honoring a Moral Obligation," *Boston Globe* editorial, March 16, 1984.

5. Michael Rezendes, "Race Issues Once Again Stir Tension in Boston," *Boston Globe*, March 4, 1990.

6. Ted Landsmark interview.

7. Dennis Kearney interview.

8. Akilah Johnson, "Boston. Racism. Image. Reality," *Boston Globe*, December 10, 2017.

9. Johnson, "Boston."

10. Rosemarie Sansone interview.

11. Bill Walczak interview.

12. Bob Consalvo interview.

13. Jon Keller, "Ground Rules for the City's Racial Healing," *Boston Globe,* August 26, 1995.

14. "Where Is Mayor White?" *Boston Globe* editorial, October 8, 1980.

15. Tager 2001; Lukas 1985.

16. Hubie Jones interview.

17. Chapter 636, Racial Imbalance Law of 1965, https://repository.library .northeastern.edu/downloads/neu:rx914f96w?datastream_id=content.

18. Tager 2001, 184–85.

19. Levine 269; Harmon 1992.

20. Weinberg 1981, 92.

21. Text of Mayor Kevin White's Inaugural Address, *Boston Globe,* January 8, 1980.

22. "Mayor White: Sounds of Silence," *Boston Globe,* September 3, 1980.

23. "Where Is Mayor White?"

24. Jennings and King 1986, 62.

25. Jones interview.

26. *The Busing Battleground: The Decades Long Road to School Desegregation* 2023.

27. Al Larkin, "The 1970s Served Up Turmoil; Second in a Three-Part Series Examining the Four Terms of Boston Mayor Kevin H. White," *Boston Globe,* July 25, 1983.

28. Joan Vennochi, "Mayor Hailed for Hub Spirit, but the Verdict Is Still Out," *Boston Globe,* November 6, 1984.

29. Ray Flynn interview.

30. Charles Kenney, "The Popular Populist Is Put to the Test," *Boston Globe,* May 5, 1985.

31. Nancy Snyder interview.

32. Kenney, "The Popular Populist."

33. Kenney, "The Popular Populist."

34. Vennochi, "Mayor Hailed for Hub Spirit."

35. Bill Walczak interview.

36. Vin McCarthy interview.

37. Michael Frisby, "Flynn Seeks Advice on Next Police Head," *Boston Globe,* June 20, 1984.

38. Mickey Roache interview.

39. Neil Sullivan interview.

40. Ed Quill, "Roache to Be Sworn In Today as Permanent Commissioner," *Boston Globe,* March 13, 1985.

41. Steven Marantz, "Lots of Praise from Community on Appointment," *Boston Globe,* February 1, 1985.

42. Gregory Witcher, "Activists See Progress in Boston Police-Minority Relations," *Boston Globe,* April 10, 1986.

43. David Nyhan, "Flynn Setting an Example in Racial Harmony," *Boston Globe,* January 5, 1987.

44. Fox Butterfield, "Boston Ignores a Trend in Re-electing a Mayor," *New York Times,* November 11, 1991.

45. Katherine Seelye, "Ailing Mayor of Boston Says He's Still Up to the Job," *New York Times,* December 16, 2012.

46. Peter Canellos, "Melee a Test of Mayoral Approach. In Past, Menino, Brett Worked behind Scenes," *Boston Globe,* October 21, 1993.

47. Canellos, "Melee a Test of Mayoral Approach."

48. Brian Mooney, "Mayor Lauded on City's Race Issues," *Boston Globe*, October 16, 2005.

49. Tom Menino interview.

50. Adrian Walker, "Menino Calls Race Relations the Overriding Issue for City," *Boston Globe*, September 19, 1994.

51. Walker, "Menino Calls Race Relations the Overriding Issue."

52. Menino interview.

53. Patricia Nealon and Kate Zernike, "W. Roxbury Fire Raises the Specter of Bigotry: Arson Investigated at Home Being Bought by Blacks," *Boston Globe*, September 23, 1996.

54. Brian MacQuarrie, "West Roxbury Residents Gather to Condemn Racism," *Boston Globe*, September 27, 1996.

55. Menino interview.

56. Walker, "Menino Calls Race Relations the Overriding Issue."

57. Walker, "Menino Calls Race Relations the Overriding Issue."

58. Maureen Goggin, "Excerpts from Reports on Police Raid," *Boston Globe*, May 12, 1994.

59. Brian McGrory and Toni Locy, "Minister Dies after Botched Drug Raid: Suffered Heart Attack in Apartment," *Boston Globe*, March 26, 1994.

60. Menino interview.

61. Judy Rakowsky, "US Asked to Probe Hub Police Case," *Boston Globe*, September 27, 1996.

62. Brian McGrory, "One Disgrace after Another," *Boston Globe*, January 12, 1999.

63. McGrory, "One Disgrace after Another."

64. Lehr 2009.

65. Francine Latour, "Rivers Calls for Probe of Police Racism," *Boston Globe*, May 28, 1999.

66. Daniel Vasquez and Tatsha Robertson, "Police Said to Tolerate Racism; Noose Incident Latest in Pattern, Sources Say," *Boston Globe*, April 28, 1999.

67. "Prosecution Gap," *Boston Globe* editorial, June 13, 2000.

68. M. E. Malone, "Minority Firms to Get 15% of City Contracts," *Boston Globe*, December 18, 1987.

69. Donavan Slack, "Minorities, Women, Lose Business Edge," *Boston Globe*, February 10, 2003.

70. Corey Dade, "City Won't Restore Minority Program," *Boston Globe*, February 20, 2003.

71. "Backpedaling in Boston," *Boston Globe* editorial, February 12, 2003.

72. Adrian Walker, "Memo Assails Menino on Black Issues," *Boston Globe*, July 25, 1995.

73. Menino with Beatty 2014, 59.

74. Jackson and Winship 2006, 14.

75. *Hurley v. Irish-American Gay, Lesbian, and Bisexual Group of Boston, Inc.*, 515 U.S. 557 (1995).

76. Ann Maguire interview.

77. Kearney interview.

78. Neil Sullivan interview.

## 9 / Civil Rights and Wrongs: The Search for Racial Justice

1. Boston Police Department, "2008 Crime Summary Report," Office Research and Development, Office of Police Commissioner.

2. Michael Rezendes, "Boston Had 20% Drop in Rights Violations," *Boston Globe*, May 13, 1992.

3. *US Department of Justice: Jane Doe No. 1, et al., Plaintiffs, v. The City of Boston and the Boston Housing Authority*, Defendants, Agreement and Order, 1999.

4. Judy Rakowsky, "As Reported Hate Crimes in Boston Surge, Prosecutions Drop," *Boston Globe*, June 12, 2000.

5. The Boston Police Department reports listed 342 hate crimes in 1999, not the 433 number reported by the *Boston Globe*. Hate crime incidents against African Americans that year had increased by over 30 percent from both 1993 and 1998.

6. Rakowsky, "As Reported Hate Crimes in Boston Surge."

7. Rakowsky, "As Reported Hate Crimes in Boston Surge."

8. Diego Ribadeneira, "In Divided Era, A Decade of Healing: Police Racial Unit Marks 10 Years of Protecting Rights," *Boston Globe*, April 7, 1988.

9. Rakowsky, "As Reported Hate Crimes in Boston Surge."

10. Rakowsky, "As Reported Hate Crimes in Boston Surge."

11. Steve Marantz, "Walking Boston's Racial Hate Beat, Where No Crime Is Minor," *Boston Globe*, September 1, 1990.

12. Jack Thomas, "Was Globe Story on Boston Hate Crimes Unfair?," *Boston Globe*, September 11, 2000.

13. Thomas, "Was Globe Story on Boston Hate Crimes Unfair?"

14. Rakowsky, "As Reported Hate Crimes in Boston Surge."

15. Jim Jordan interview.

16. Judy Rakowsky, "Handling of Hate Crimes Is Debated," *Boston Globe*, June 13, 2000.

17. Marantz, "Walking Boston's Racial Hate Beat."

18. Dick Lehr, "Doubt Cast over Tiffany Moore Verdict," *Boston Globe*, May 14, 2014.

19. Neil Sullivan interview.

20. Michael Rezendes, "Mayor's Reputation as Racial Healer Gets Some Tarnish," *Boston Globe*, September 10, 1991.

21. Hubie Jones interview.

22. *Murder in Boston: Roots, Rampage & Reckoning* 2023.

23. Ron Bell in *Murder in Boston: Roots, Rampage & Reckoning* 2023.

24. Neil Sullivan in *Murder in Boston: Roots, Rampage & Reckoning* 2023.

25. Brian McGrory in *Murder in Boston: Roots, Rampage & Reckoning* 2023.

26. Howard Bryant in *Murder in Boston: Roots, Rampage & Reckoning* 2023.

27. Sullivan interview.

28. Mickey Roache interview.

29. Roache interview.

30. Elizabeth Koh, "The Five Most Surprising Findings from the Globe's Charles Stuart Investigation," *Boston Globe*, December 18, 2023.

31. Michelle Caruso in *Murder in Boston: Roots, Rampage & Reckoning* 2023.

32. Ray Flynn interview.

33. Frank Doyle interview.

34. Kristin McCormack interview.

35. Jones interview.

36. Ken Wade interview.

37. Michael Rezendes, "Youth Plan Helps Flynn Renew Ties with Blacks," *Boston Globe*, July 8, 1990.

38. Sullivan interview.

39. Michael Rezendes, "Tarnished Healer," *Boston Globe*, May 20, 1990.

40. Roberto Scalese and Hilary Sargent. "The Charles Stuart Murders and the Racist Branding Boston Just Can't Seem to Shake," *Boston Globe*, October 22, 2014.

41. Hubie Jones, personal communication with author, October 9, 2024.

42. Diego Ribadeneira, "A Gentle Side," *Boston Globe*, November 1, 1989.

43. Ribadeneira, "A Gentle Side."

44. Adrian Walker, "Wu's Eloquent Apology Can Be the Start of Healing," *Boston Globe*, December 20, 2023.

45. Adrian Walker, Evan Allen, Elizabeth Koh, and Andrew Ryan, "Nightmare in Mission Hill: The Untold Story of the Charles and Carol Stuart Shooting," *Boston Globe*, December 1, 2023.

46. Jim Jordan interview.

47. Rezendes, "Mayor's Reputation as Racial Healer."

48. Rezendes, "Tarnished Healer."

49. Bob Consalvo interview.

50. Peter Canellos, "Legacy of Racial, Neighborhood Progress," *Boston Globe*, March 18, 1993.

51. Canellos, "Legacy of Racial, Neighborhood Progress."

52. Walker et al., "Nightmare in Mission Hill."

53. Rezendes, "Tarnished Healer."

54. Rezendes, "Tarnished Healer."

55. Stone and Rizova 2014.

56. Charles Kenney, "The Aftershock of a Radical Notion, the Mandela Debate Is Still Very Much Alive—in the Painful Issues It Raised and the Enemies It Created," *Boston Globe*, April 12, 1987.

57. Kenney, "The Aftershock of a Radical Notion."

58. *Bay State Banner*, November 11, 2010.

59. Kenney, "The Aftershock of a Radical Notion."

60. Charles Stith, "Vote No; The Entire City Is Making Progress," *Boston Globe*, November 1, 1986.

61. Kenney, "The Aftershock of a Radical Notion."

62. Kenney, "The Aftershock of a Radical Notion."

63. Jones interview.

64. Kenney, "The Aftershock of a Radical Notion."

65. Allan Stern interview.

66. Robert A. Jordan, "Many Winners in Mandela Vote," *Boston Globe*, November 8, 1986.

67. Matthew L. Wald, "Mayor Assesses Boston: Progress, and Problems," *New York Times*, January 11, 1987.

68. Constance L. Hays, "Boston's Black Areas Mount New Secession Drive," *New York Times*, December 10, 1989.

69. Sullivan interview.

70. Joseph Washington interview.

71. Charles Kenney, "Raymond Flynn Announces Candidacy for Boston Mayor," *Boston Globe*, April 28, 1983.

72. *Perez vs. Boston Housing Authority*, 368 Mass. 333 (masscases.com).

73. Judge Paul Garrity Receivership files, University Archives and Special Collections, Joseph P. Healey Library, University of Massachusetts–Boston.

74. Roache interview.

75. Frank Costello interview

76. Roache interview.

77. Stephanie Chavez, "A Quiet Move to Charlestown Project," *Boston Globe*, April 9, 1984.

78. "Mrs. Bunte Out, She'll Appeal," *Boston Globe*, July 13, 1971.

79. "The Selection of Bunte Is One of Great Boldness," *Boston Globe* editorial, October 20, 1984.

80. M. E. Malone, "Flynn: Projects in S. Boston to Be Integrated," *Boston Globe*, October 29, 1987.

81. Malone, "Flynn."

82. Adrian Walker, "This Hope Is Home-Grown," *Boston Globe*, June 16, 2009.

83. Raymond Flynn, "No Hiding on Flynn's Part," *Boston Globe*, June 20, 2009.

84. Andrew Blake, "South Boston Sends Its Mayor a Message," *Boston Globe*, November 4, 1987.

85. Flynn interview.

86. Roache interview.

87. Steve Marantz, "Walking Boston's Racial Hate Beat, Where No Crime Is Minor," *Boston Globe*, September 1, 1990.

88. Judith Kurland interview.

89. Flynn interview.

90. Michael Frisby, "Housing Stand Holds Some Risks," *Boston Globe*, October 31, 1987.

91. Frisby, "Housing Stand Holds Some Risks."

92. Larry Dwyer interview.

93. Dwyer interview.

94. Malone, "Flynn."

95. Jonathan Kaufman and M. E. Malone, "Suit Charging Discrimination Puts the BHA Back in Court," *Boston Globe*, May 18, 1988.

96. Norman Boucher, "People Live Here, Too," *Boston Globe*, March 12, 1989.

97. Kaufman and Malone, "Suit Charging Discrimination."

98. Joanne Ball, "Integration: A Higher Profile for Law," *Boston Globe*, May 23, 1988.

99. Peggy Hernandez, "Service Illustrates Change in Racial Climate, Leaders Say," *Boston Globe*, May 23, 1988.

100. Sally Jacobs, "Outside the Church, Some Send a Message: We Say No," *Boston Globe*, May 23, 1988.

101. Sean Murphy, "600 Gather in S. Boston to Pray for Racial Harmony," *Boston Globe*, May 23, 1988.

102. Flynn interview.

103. Murphy, "600 Gather."

104. "NAACP and Boston Settle Challenge to Housing Plan," *New York Times*, August 27, 1988.

105. *NAACP v. Boston Housing Authority*, 723F. Supp. 1554, D. Mass. 1989.

106. Adrian Walker, "BRA Chief Quits under Pressure." *Boston Globe,* November 3, 1994.

107. Judith Gaines, "New Team Will Police Developments," *Boston Globe*, September 19, 1994.

108. "Remodeling Job at the BHA," *Boston Globe* editorial, December 19, 1995.

109. Adrian Walker, "A House United: Knitter of Neighborhoods in Public Projects Steps Down," *Boston Globe*, July 8, 2019.

110. Rezendes, "Mayor's Reputation as Racial Healer."

## 10 / "Death at an Early Age": Public Education Debates

1. Anyon 1997; *Equality of Educational Opportunity* 1966; Elizabeth Evitts Dickenson, "Coleman Report Set the Standard for the Study of Public Education," *Johns Hopkins Magazine*, Winter 2016, https://hub.jhu.edu/magazine/2016/winter/coleman -report-public-Education/; Conant 1961; Cronin 1973; 2008; Jencks 1972; Jencks and Phillips 1998; Karabel and Halsey 1977; Kozol 1967; 2005.

2. *Equality of Educational Opportunity.*

3. Kozol 1967; DiMaggio and Mohr 1985.

4. Park, Burgess, and McKenzie 1967 [1925]; Boyer 1992.

5. Gans 1962.

6. Emirbayer 1992; Labaree 1988.

7. Cronin 1973.

8. Portz, Stein, and Jones 1999; Reville 2007.

9. *Plessy v. Ferguson*, 163 U.S. 537 (1896).

10. *Brown v. Board of Education of Topeka*, 347 U.S. 483 (1954); National Archives, "Brown v. Board of Education," https://www.archives.gov/milestone-documents/brown -v-board-of-education.

11. *Brown v. Board of Education of Topeka*, 349 U.S. 294 (1955).

12. *Swann v. Charlotte-Mecklenburg Bd. of Educ.*, 402 U.S. 1 (1971).

13. Gillis 2015.

14. US Commission on Civil Rights, "Twenty Years after Brown: Equality of Educational Opportunity—A Report of the U.S. Commission on Civil Rights, March 1975," https://eric.ed.gov/?id=ED102285.

15. Formisano 2004, 34.

16. Formisano 2004; Masur 2008.

17. Kozol 1967.

18. "Anti-Bias March on City Hall," *Boston Globe,* June 12, 1963.

19. Seymour R. Linscott, "8260 Stay Out—But All Calm," *Boston Globe,* June 19, 1983.

20. Cronin 2008.

21. *Morgan v. Hennigan,* 379 F. Supp. 410 (D. Mass. 1974); Formisano 1991; 2004; Masur 2008; Cronin 2008 (italics added).

22. *Morgan v. Hennigan*, 1974, 410 (italics added).

23. Michael Patrick MacDonald interview.

24. PBS 2023.

25. Levine 2005, 179–80.

26. Ray Flynn interview.

27. PBS 2023.

28. Tom Menino interview.

29. Dennis Kearney interview.

30. Larry DiCara interview.

31. MacDonald interview.

32. May Louie interview.

33. Clara Garcia interview.

34. Al Larkin, "The 1970s Served Up Turmoil; Second in a Three-Part Series Examining the Four Terms of Boston Mayor Kevin H. White," *Boston Globe*, July 25, 1983.

35. Flynn interview.

36. Menino with Beatty 2014.

37. Aja Antoine, "Black History Month Profile: Ruth Batson," Boston.gov, May 19, 2017, https://www.boston.gov/news/black-history-month-profile-ruth-batson.

38. "Flynn Speech to Education Panel a Signal," *Boston Globe* editorial, February 28, 1984.

39. Nancy Snyder interview.

40. Bob Consalvo interview.

41. Snyder interview.

42. Hubie Jones interview.

43. Peter Howe, "Flynn: This School Plan Is Doomed," *Boston Globe*, October 1, 1989.

44. DiCara interview.

45. Patricia Wen, "Flynn Names Panel to Study School Board," *Boston Globe*, May 3, 1989.

46. Diego Ribadeneira, "Overhaul School Board, Study Says," *Boston Globe*, July 21, 1989.

47. Diane Lewis, "Opponents See Vote Loss with Appointed Board," *Boston Globe*, September 19, 1989.

48. "No on Question Two," *Boston Globe* editorial, November 1, 1989.

49. Peter Howe, "Councilors Leery of School Plan," *Boston Globe*, November 9, 1989.

50. Patricia Wen and Peggy Hernandez, "Flynn Hedges on Panel's Advice for School Board," *Boston Globe*, May 2, 1989.

51. Neil Sullivan interview.

52. Rosaria Salerno interview.

53. Sullivan interview.

54. Consalvo interview.

55. Cronin 1989.

56. Sam Tyler interview.

57. Joe Battenfeld, "Black Leader Criticizes School Referendum, Vote," *Boston Herald*, October 5, 1989.

58. John McDonough interview.

59. Michael Rezendes, "Ministers Want New School Board in Split with Minority Politicians; Church Leaders Back Mayor's Plan," *Boston Globe*, May 28, 1991.

60. Tyler interview.

61. Rezendes, "Ministers Want New School Board."

62. Sullivan interview.

63. Scott Lehigh, "Elected School Panel Is Abolished; Weld Signs Bill; Mayor to Name 7," *Boston Globe*, July 6, 1991.

64. Lehigh, "Elected School Panel Is Abolished."

65. Consalvo interview.

66. Vin McCarthy interview.

67. Don Aucoin, "Dropout Rate: Down but . . . ," *Boston Globe,* January 27, 1992.

68. Jim Stergios, "After Payzant," *Boston Globe,* March 28, 2006.

69. Dentler 1994.

70. Patricia Nealon, "Mayor Sets School Reform Deadline, Seeks Evaluation of Superintendent," *Boston Globe,* March 13, 1993.

71. Adrian Walker, "Flynn in Shift, Backs Elected School Board," *Boston Globe,* July 8, 1993.

72. Adrian Walker, "Black Leaders Rally for Harrison-Jones; Plan Menino Protest," *Boston Globe,* January 13, 1995.

73. Adrian Walker, "The Committee in Question: The Fight to Return an Elected School Board Has Quietly Lost Its Steam to—what!—success," *Boston Globe,* May 5, 1996.

74. Taylor 2001, 12.

75. Menino interview.

76. Menino interview.

77. Sullivan interview.

78. Menino interview.

79. Pablo Calderon interview.

80. Geeta Anand, "Menino Pledges Better Schools, Tells City: 'Judge Me Harshly' If I Fail," *Boston Globe,* January 18, 1996.

81. Mel King interview.

82. Marty Walsh interview.

83. Joyce Linehan interview.

84. Katharine Q. Seelye, "Boston Schools Chief to Depart after a Short, Rocky Tenure," *New York Times,* June 25, 2018.

85. Michael Jonas and Bruce Mohl, "The Codcast: Marty Walsh Talks Taxes, Baker, and More," *Commonwealth Magazine,* June 25, 2018.

86. Malcolm Gay, "Boston Superintendent Facing Revolt among High School Headmasters," *Boston Globe,* July 16, 2020.

87. James Vaznis, "Appeals Court Upholds Legality of Boston's Temporary Exam School Admission Policy," *Boston Globe,* December 20, 2023.

88. Christopher Huffaker, "Opposition Heats Up over Plan to Move the O'Bryant to West Roxbury," *Boston Globe,* July 4, 2023; Deanna Pan and Danny McDonald, "Boston City Council Passes Resolution Opposing Moving O'Bryant School to West Roxbury," *Boston Globe,* December 6, 2023.

89. Catherine Elton, "Inside the Bunker with Michelle Wu," *Boston Magazine,* November 1, 2023.

90. Yawu Miller. "Civic Leaders Say Wu Ignoring Community Input," March 6, 2024.

91. Letter from Mayor and Superintendent to O'Bryant and Madison Park School Communities, February 27, 2024.

92. Ross Cristantiello, "Wu Explains Where She Went Wrong in Failed Plan to Move O'Bryant School," Boston.com, March 4, 2024.

93. Boston Public Schools, Office of the Superintendent, "Past Superintendents," Accessed July 1, 2024, https://www.bostonpublicschools.org/Page/7879

94. Julian E. J. Sorapura, "Elected School Committee Put on Hold," *Boston Globe*, November 29, 2022.

95. Ravitch 2010; Wong 2003.

96. Anyon 2009, 3.

97. Ravitch 2010, 91.

98. Wong and Shen 2002, 21.

99. Portz, Stein, and Jones 1999; Reville 2007.

100. Consalvo interview.

101. Charles Yancey interview.

102. Ted Landsmark interview.

103. Margaret Blood interview.

104. Stone 1989; 1993.

105. "No on Question Two."

106. "A Vote for the Schoolchildren," *Boston Globe* editorial, May 20, 1991.

107. Kozol 1967; 1985, 233.

## 11 / Rebuilding the City: Urban Finances and Infrastructure

1. Neil Sullivan interview.

2. Scott 1984.

3. In *Tregor v. Board of Assessors of City of Boston*, 377 Mass. 602 (1979), the Supreme Judicial Court held that the victim of a disproportionate assessment had the right to have the assessment reduced so that it was "proportional to the assessments of the class of property valued at the lowest percentage of fair cash value."

4. Bob Ciolek, personal memorandum to the Boston City Council Raymond L. Flynn Commission, May 27, 2015.

5. Joan Vennochi, "Hub to Spend Hidden Funds," *Boston Globe*, January 18, 1984.

6. Stuart Vidockler interview.

7. Joan Vennochi, "New Director Races Time to Produce Hub Budget," *Boston Globe*, March 18, 1984.

8. Vennochi, "New Director Races Time."

9. Michael Frisby, "Flynn's Budget Puts 2 Officials in Competition," *Boston Globe*, April 11, 1986.

10. Vidockler interview.

11. Ray Flynn interview.

12. Ed Quill, "Flynn Appoints 4 to Key City Financial Posts," *Boston Globe*, February 4, 1984.

13. Mary Nee interview and personal communication with author, February 12, 2023.

14. With $14.5 million in federal funding, the city addressed the structural and mechanical conditions and handicapped accessibility of Faneuil Hall and the Old State House.

15. More than $76 million in infrastructure investments supported economic development, including affordable housing, neighborhood business districts, the marine industrial park, and economic redevelopment efforts.

16. The capital plan invested $258 million, 30 percent of the entire budget, in eleven hundred miles of streets and sidewalks, fifty thousand streetlights, seven hundred traffic signals (mainly ignored by Boston drivers), and rehabilitation of the city's thirty-four bridges.

17. Allan Stern interview.

18. Charles Radin, "Changing Tides: The Future of Boston Harbor—Commerce, Community and Condos," *Boston Globe,* November 3, 1985.

19. Boston Harbor Now, bostonharbornow.org.

20. Jonathan Kaufman, "Changing Tides: The Future of Boston Harbor—Neighborhoods 'Want It All,'" *Boston Globe,* November 3, 1985.

21. Ciolek, personal communication.

22. Dianne Dumanoski, "Sludge Reaches End of the Line," *Boston Globe,* December 25, 1991.

23. Lorraine Downey interview.

24. Mary Nee interview.

25. Ciolek, personal communication.

26. Rosemarie Sansone interview.

27. Jeremy Fox, "Menino Details Five-Year, $1.8 Billion Capital Plan," *Boston Globe,* May 18, 2013.

28. Milton J. Valencia, "His Legacy Build on Relationships and Action, But To-Do List Remains," *Boston Globe,* March 23, 2021.

29. Joyce Linehan interview.

30. FY23 Capital Plan W&M Overview for April 25, 2022 (boston.gov).

## 12 / Confronting Poverty and Homelessness

1. Sum 2013; Osterman and Jones 1989.

2. Charles Kenney, "The Poor Get Poorer," in *Boston Globe* special report, December 15, 1985.

3. Kenney, "The Poor Get Poorer."

4. City of Boston Archives.

5. O'Brien and Oriola 1985, 3–5.

6. O'Brien and Oriola 1985.

7. Kidder 2023.

8. Colburn and Aldern 2022.

9. HUD 2022.

10. Karen Spar and Monique C. Austin, "The Homeless: Overview of the Problem and the Federal Response," Congressional Research Service, Washington, DC, September 14, 1984.

11. Colburn and Aldern 2022.

12. Ed Quill, "Council OK's Aid to Homeless," *Boston Globe,* December 19, 1982.

13. Andrew Andrews, "100 Camp at Common's Tent City," *Boston Globe,* June 5, 1884.

14. Philip Bennett, "Many Families Find No Room at Homeless Shelters," *Boston Globe,* December 5, 1985.

15. "Making Room: Comprehensive Policy for the Homeless," December 1986, City of Boston.

16. Bonnie V. Winston, "Recent City Census Shows Boston Has 2,863 Homeless Persons," *Boston Globe,* October 12, 1986.

17. Andrew Diablis, "Mass Hiking Aid to Homeless," *Boston Globe,* November 15, 1984.

18. Dick Lehr, "Mentally Ill Homeless to Get Help," *Boston Globe,* December 9, 1985.

19. M. E. Malone, "Flynn, Simon Tour Shelter for Homeless," *Boston Globe,* January 26, 1988.

20. Bonnie V. Winston, "Recent City Census Shows Boston Has 2,863 Homeless Persons," *Boston Globe,* October 12, 1986.

21. Stewart B. McKinney Homeless Assistance Act (P.L. 100-77).

22. Michael Frisby, "Federal Money Needed for Homeless, Says Flynn," *Boston Globe,* June 15, 1986.

23. Kidder 2023.

24. John Ellement, "Two Foundations Give Cities $25m to Provide Health Care to Homeless," *Boston Globe,* December 20, 1984.

25. Kidder 2023.

26. Jim O'Connell interview.

27. Kidder 2023.

28. "Robin Williams Remembered Fondly in Boston," CBS Boston News, August 12, 2014.

29. Ann Maguire interview.

30. Ray Flynn interview.

31. Joe Finn, "Ray Flynn's Dedication to Ending Homelessness," *Massachusetts Housing & Shelter Alliance Newsletter*, January 30, 2018.

32. Mass and Cass is the site in the Roxbury/Newmarket area of the city where an ongoing homeless encampment was established and remained for years. With City Council approval in 2023, Mayor Wu adopted a new ordinance to clear the tent encampment. The unhoused were offered alternative services in shelters, emergency, and transitional housing.

## 13 / The 2013 and 2021 Mayoral Elections: New Directions for Boston

1. Holmes and Berube 2016.

2. Danny McDonald (2021), "Need a Precedent for Mayoral Race? Take a Look at '93," *Boston Globe,* January 19.

3. Boston Election Department 1993, 2001, 2005, 2009.

4. Steve Annear, "After 20 Years, Mayor Menino Is Leaving the Job That He Loves," *Boston Magazine,* March 28, 2013.

5. Andrew Ryan, "Menino, Pick a Tough Call," *Boston Globe,* August 7, 2013.

6. Kenneth Cooper, "A Mayor of Color," *Boston Globe,* August 18, 2013.

7. Jim O'Sullivan, "Political Group Could Break Barrier for Golar Richie," *Boston Globe,* May 17, 2013.

8. Ryan, "Menino."

9. Akilah Johnson, "Minority Leaders Split on Mayoral Race Strategy," *Boston Globe,* September 6, 2013.

10. Don Gillis and Andy Sum, "Poverty Must Be Top Priority for Candidates," *Boston Globe,* August 17, 2013.

11. Akilah Johnson, "Mayoral Hopefuls Confront Racism," *Boston Globe,* November 5, 2013.

12. Cooper, "A Mayor of Color."

13. Simon Waxman, "Can Boston Break Identity Politics?," *Boston Globe,* September 8, 2013.

14. Joan Vennochi, "Mayoral Race—A Battle of Two Bostons," *Boston Globe,* May 26, 2013.

15. Wesley Lowery, "Historic Diversity in Mayor's Race," *Boston Globe*, July 29, 2013.

16. Akilah Johnson, "After Decades of Activism, Mel King Looks Only Ahead," *Boston Globe*, July 8, 2013.

17. Boston Election Department 2013.

18. Jim O'Sullivan and Stephanie Ebbert, "From the Inside: How Walsh Came Out on Top," *Boston Globe*, November 10, 2013.

19. Akilah Johnson, "Minority Voters Were Key in Victory," *Boston Globe*, November 7, 2013.

20. Joan Vennochi, "Class and Boston's New Mayor," *Boston Globe*, October 24, 2013b.

21. O'Sullivan and Ebbert, "From the Inside."

22. Economic Justice Research Hub, "Boston Mayoral Vote 2013 Analysis," 2013, http://www.ejresearch.org/boston-mayor.

23. David Abel, "Menino Weighs Offer from Academic World," *Boston Globe*, October 22, 2013.

24. Richard Weir, "The Feud: Why Mayor Menino Is Giving Marty Walsh the Cold Shoulder," *Boston Herald*, October 28, 2013.

25. Boston Election Department 2013.

26. Akilah Johnson, "Mayoral Hopefuls Confront Racism," *Boston Globe*, November 5, 2013.

27. Abel, "Menino Weighs Offer."

28. Craig Douglas, "Boston Ranks 2nd in U.S. for Hate Crimes; Race a Factor in Half of All Incidents," *Boston Business Journal*, December 14, 2012.

29. Holmes and Berube. 2016.

30. Muñoz et al. 2025.

31. Somers and Webb 2014.

32. Marty Walsh interview.

33. My Brother's Keeper Boston, Boston.gov.

34. Walsh interview.

35. Mel King interview.

36. Audra D. S. Burch, Weiyi Cai, Gabriel Gianordoli, Morrigan McCarthy, and Jugal K. Patel, "How Black Lives Matter Reached Every Corner of America," *New York Times*, June 13, 2020.

37. Joyce Linehan interview.

38. Murray Whyte, "Boston Lost a Powerful, Poetic Work When Artist Pulled His 'Auction Block' Slave Memorial," *Boston Globe*, August 17, 2019.

39. Mayor Martin J. Walsh, "Declaring Racism an Emergency and Public Health Crisis in the City of Boston," Executive Order, June 12, 2020, https://www.boston.gov/sites/default/files/file/2020/06/racism-as-public-health-crisis-ocr.pdf.

40. Danny McDonald and Milton Valencia, "'Cutting the Budget Doesn't Deal with Racism': Mayor Walsh Says Slashing Police Funding Isn't Enough to Bring Change," *Boston Globe*, June 10, 2020.

41. Tim Logan, "Boston to Big Developers: Pay Up," *Boston Globe*, February 9, 2021.

42. Tim Logan, "City Will Raise Its Fees on Builders," *Boston Globe*, December 9, 2015.

43. Walsh interview.

44. Milton Valencia, "Legacy Built on Relationships and Action but To-Do List Remains," *Boston Globe*, March 23, 2021.

45. Tim Logan and Shelby Grebbin, "Growing Pains Coming to JP," *Boston Globe*, February 8, 2017.

46. Marie Turley interview.

47. Walsh interview.

48. Jeremy Fox, "Walsh's Budget Includes $50,000 for Immigrant Legal Defense," *Boston Globe*, April 20, 2019.

49. Megan E. Irons and Cristela Guerra, "Walsh Rails against Trump, Calls Immigration Actions 'Direct Attack,'" *Boston Globe*, January 25, 2017.

50. Valencia, "Legacy Built on Relationships."

51. Linehan interview.

52. Ed Siegel, "The Walsh Administration's Success Story with the Huntington and the Colonial," WBUR, June 13, 2016.

53. Linehan interview.

54. Yawu Miller, "Is Boston Finally Past Tribal Politics?," *Bay State Banner* (MA), April 21, 2021.

55. Wu for Mayor campaign website, 2024, michelleforboston.com.

56. Wu for Mayor campaign website; Ellen Barry, "Boston, Long Led by White Men, Votes in New Guard," *New York Times*, November 6, 2019.

57. City of Boston, "New Urban Mechanics," accessed November 3, 2024, https://www.boston.gov/departments/new-urban-mechanics.

58. Barry, "Boston."

59. Shirley Leung, "In Confirming Michelle's Wu Run for Mayor, Marty Walsh Committed a Political Faux Pas," *Boston Globe*, September 9, 2020.

60. Boston Election Department 2021.

61. Mass Office of Campaign and Political Finance.

62. Editorial Board, "Michelle Wu for Mayor," *Boston Globe*, October 22, 2021.

63. Emma Platoff and Milton J. Valencia, "Michelle Wu Wins Historic Boston Mayor's Race, Marking a New Era for the City. 'We Are Ready to Meet This Moment,' Wu Said during a Celebration," *Boston Globe*, November 3, 2021.

64. Catherine Elton, "Inside the Bunker with Michelle Wu," *Boston Magazine*, November 1, 2023.

65. Perry Bacon Jr., "The Progressive Breakthrough in Boston," *Washington Post*, November 2, 2021.

66. Mayor Michelle Wu, State of the City address, January 25, 2023, https://www.boston.gov/news/mayor-wus-2023-state-city-address.

67. Wu, State of the City address.

68. Meghan Irons and Andrew Ryan, "In the Race for Boston Mayor, Wu and Essaibi George Are Focusing on a Crucial Part of the Electorate: Black Voters," *Boston Globe*, September 27, 2021.

69. Meghan Irons, "Both Finalists Are in Full Courtship of a Crucial Bloc," *Boston Globe*, September 27, 2021.

70. David Scharfenberg, "Black Voter Turnout in Massachusetts Isn't Nearly as High as It Could Be," *Boston Globe*, January 26, 2023.

71. Sonel Cutler, "Boston Must Work to Address Its Role in Disparities, Wu Says," *Boston Globe*, February 3, 2023.

72. "Members of Reparations Task Force Announced," February 7, 2023, Boston.gov.

73. WCVB, "Faith Leaders Critical of Boston Mayor Michelle Wu's Response to Deadly Violence," February 22, 2023.

74. WCVB, "Faith Leaders Critical."

75. Michelle Wu interview.

76. Elton, "Inside the Bunker."

77. Saraya Wintersmith, "One Year in, The Jury Is Still Out on Boston Mayor Wu's Ability to Make Sweeping Changes," WGBH News, August 7, 2023.

78. Michael Jonas, "What Will Boston's New Wuniverse Bring?" *Commonwealth Magazine*, November 8, 2021.

79. Wu interview.

80. Elton, "Inside the Bunker."

81. Yawu Miller, "Civic Leaders Say Wu Ignoring Community Input," *Bay State Banner* (MA), March 6, 2024.

82. Joan Vennochi, "North End Restaurateurs' Dispute with Mayor Wu Is about More Than Outdoor Dining," *Boston Globe*, April 10, 2024.

83. Mass Historical Society, "Italian Influence on Boston's Culture, Economy and Politics," April 10, 2024.

84. Emma Platoff and Catherine Carlock, "Mayor Wu Wants to Overhaul Boston's Rules for What Can Be Built Where. She's Stepping into a Political Minefield," *Boston Globe*, February 20, 2024.

85. Platoff and Carlock, "Mayor Wu Wants to Overhaul."

86. Michael Jonas, "Boston's Free Museum Plan Leaves Out Thousands of Kids," *Commonwealth Beacon*, February 7, 2024.

87. Niki Griswold, "Mayor Michelle Wu Says City Working to Extend Free Sunday Museum Program to All School-Aged Children in 2025," *Boston Globe*, September 10, 2024.

88. Wu interview.

89. "Franklin Park Coalition Survey Neighborhood for Advancing White Stadium Renovation," press release, March 11, 2024.

90. Joan Vennochi, "Mayor Wu Plays Hardball over White Stadium Soccer Deal," *Boston Globe*, March 18, 2024.

91. Mandile Mpofu, "Boston School Committee Approves White Stadium Lease Agreement," *Bay State Banner* (MA), September 18, 2024.

92. Esteban Bustillos, "Judge Denies Request for Injunction against White Stadium Renovation Project," WGBH News, March 22, 2024.

93. Nick Stoico, "Court Ruling Allows White Stadium Renovation Project to Proceed," *Boston Globe*, March 22, 2024.

94. Maliya Ellis and Tiana Woodard, "White Stadium, a 'Treasure That Needs Some Love,' Could Get a $30 Million Renovation under New Proposal," *Boston Globe*, July 12, 2023.

95. Richard Heath, "Mayor Wants Her Stadium; Majority Says 'No Thanks,'" *Boston Bulletin*, April 4, 2024.

96. Adam Swift, "Franklin Park Defenders to Continue Lawsuit against White Stadium Development," *Jamaica Plain Gazette*, April 26, 2024.

97. Rupa Shenoy, "Town Hall with Mayor Michelle Wu," WBUR, March 20, 2024.

98. Shenoy, "Town Hall."

99. Olmsted Network, "Principles, Values and Impact, accessed July 1, 2024, https://olmsted.org/frederick-law-olmsted/legacy/.

100. Joan Vennochi, "Wu's Fumble on White Stadium Renovation," *Boston Globe*, April 24, 2024.

101. Shenoy, "Town Hall."

102. "Despite Shaky Rollout, Wu's White Stadium Plan Is Good for Student-Athletes," *Boston Globe* editorial, May 10, 2024.

103. Wu interview.

104. Danny McDonald, "Need a Precedent for What's Going On in Boston Politics? Look to 1993," *Boston Globe*, January 15, 2021.

105. Wu interview.

106. Gintautas Dumcius, "Wu Gets High Marks from Voters in Think Tank's Survey," *Commonwealth Beacon* (MA), April 7, 2024.

107. Clavel 1986.

## 14 / How Does Urban Progressivism Succeed?

1. Clavel 2010, 64.

2. Connolly 1998.

3. Beatty 1992, 427.

4. Beatty 1992, 489.

5. Ira A. Jackson, "The Great Boston Comeback Story," *Boston Globe*, November 2, 2017.

6. "White Sends Charter Reform to Hill," *Boston Globe*, January 6, 1977.

7. Andrew Ryan, Adrian Walker, and Todd Wallock, "For Blacks in Boston, a Power Outage," *Boston Globe*, December 15, 2017.

8. Higgins 1984, 72; O'Connor 1993.

9. Robert Turner, "City Charter Reform, 1981 Model," *Boston Globe*, August 9, 1981.

10. Pat Walker interview.

11. Peter Dreier interview.

12. Pat Walker, personal communication with author, March 29, 2023.

13. Joan Vennochi, "Ray Flynn Knows What Mayor Wu Is Going Through. He Has Some Advice," *Boston Globe*, June 5, 2023.

14. Robert Kuttner, "Community Organizing and Electoral Politics," *American Prospect*, March 8, 2023.

15. Joyce Linehan interview.

16. Clavel 2010, 198.

17. Michael Frisby and M. E. Malone, "A Landslide for Flynn," *Boston Globe*, September 23, 1987.

18. Ellen Barry, "Boston, Long Led by White Men, Votes in New Guard," *New York Times*, November 6, 2019.

19. Katharine Q. Seelye and Matt Flegenheimer, "Ayanna Pressley's Victory: A Political Earthquake That Reflects a Changed Boston," *New York Times*, September 5, 2018.

20. Lawrence Harmon, "No Clues from 1983 Mayoral Race," *Boston Globe*, May 4, 2013.

21. *Citizens United v. Federal Election Commission*, No. 08-205, 558 U.S. 310 (2010), http://www.supremecourt.gov/qp/08-00205qp.pdf.

22. Wesley Lowery, "Outside Spending Hit $3.8m in City Race," *Boston Globe,* December 18, 2013.

23. Gintautas Dumcius, "Hotel Workers Form Super PAC to Back Janey in Mayor's Race," *Dorchester Reporter* (Boston), June 25, 2021.

24. Gintautas Dumcius, "New Balance Chairman Turns to City Council Races after Spending Big in Mayoral Contest," *Dorchester Reporter* (Boston), September 6, 2023; Yawu Miller, "Progressives Triumph in Council Election, but Activists Wary of Wu's Policy Shifts," *Bay State Banner,* November 15, 2023.

25. Miller, "Progressives Triumph."

26. Molotch 1988.

27. Menino with Beatty 2014, 175.

28. Rebecca Ostriker, "Reckoning with Boston's Towers of Wealth," *Boston Globe,* November 1, 2023.

29. Ostriker, "Reckoning with Boston's Towers of Wealth."

30. Ostriker, "Reckoning with Boston's Towers of Wealth."

31. Catherine Carlock, "BPDA Approves Hike on Housing Fees for Lab and Commercial Buildings," *Boston Globe,* February 18, 2023.

32. Diti Kohli, "'A Nightmare of Epic Proportions': Thousands of Mass. Residents Languish on Subsidized Housing Wait Lists," *Boston Globe,* July 7, 2023.

33. Andrew Brinker, "'A Housing Market for Almost No One': Rising Prices and Interest Rates Have Made Home Buying Feel Impossible," *Boston Globe,* February 25, 2023.

34. Neil Sullivan interview.

35. Jim Jordan interview.

36. Tom Menino interview.

37. Bill Walczak interview.

38. Monti 2013.

39. Monti 2013.

40. Clavel 2010; Stone 1989; 1993.

41. Swanstrom 1985, 122–23.

42. Kennedy, Tilly, and Gaston 1990, 302.

43. Kennedy, Tilly, and Gaston 1990, 306.

44. Jerry Rubin interview.

45. Stone 1989, 19.

46. Raymond Flynn, "Farewell to Steve Ross, Who Gave So Much to So Many," *Boston Herald,* February 27, 2020.

47. Vin McCarthy interview.

48. Stone 1989.

49. Molotch 1976, 313.

50. Raymond L. Flynn, inaugural speech, January 2, 1983.

51. Brown-Saracino 2009, 245.

52. Dreier interview.

53. Osterman 1991.

54. Molotch 1976; Clavel 2010; Stone 1989.

55. Mary Nee interview.

56. King 1981.

57. Joanne Ball, "Tent City: 18-Year Cause Culminates in Triumph," *Boston Globe,* March 7, 1986.

58. Paul Hirshson, "Start of Work at Tent City Is Full of Symbols," *Boston Globe*, March 9, 1986.

59. Michael Rezendes, "Tarnished Healer," *Boston Globe*, May 20, 1990.

60. Helen Cox interview.

61. Steve Coyle interview.

62. Michael Reiskind interview.

63. Sandee Story interview.

64. Chuck Turner interview, with Pierre Clavel.

65. Reiskind interview.

66. Stone 1989, 188.

67. Stephen Kurkjian, "Menino's Missed Chance on Housing Didn't Set Tie-In to New Luxury Units," *Boston Globe*, January 10, 2000.

68. Donavan Slack, "Fewer Residents Get Building Jobs under Menino, Number of Minority, Women Workers Sink," *Boston Globe*, September 10, 2009.

69. Mel King interview.

70. Stephanie Ebbert, Michael Levenson, and Donavan Slack, "A Well-Tuned Political Machine, Powered by Zeal," *Boston Globe*, September 13, 2009.

71. Menino 2014, 211.

72. Benjamin Swasey, "Report Shines New Light on Boston's Inequality," WBUR, February 20, 2014.

73. Tom O'Brien interview.

74. Kurkjian, "Menino's Missed Chance."

75. Michael Kane interview.

76. Steve Coyle interview.

77. Katherine Seelye, "Thomas M. Menino, Mayor Who Led Boston's Renaissance, Is Dead at 71," *New York Times*, October 30, 2014.

78. Logan and Molotch 1987, 157.

79. Menino 2014, 212.

80. Menino interview.

81. Swasey, "Report Shines New Light."

82. David Scharfenberg, "Walsh Targets Inequality, but What Can a Mayor Actually Do?," *Boston Globe*, February 14, 2014

83. "Transcript of Martin Walsh's Inauguration Speech," *Boston Globe*, January 6, 2014; Scharfenberg, 2014.

84. Menino 2014, 209.

85. Menino 2014, 175.

86. Adrian Walker, "Menino Burnishes Links to Business; Development Agencies Get an Overhaul," *Boston Globe*, March 6, 1994.

87. Peter Canellos, "Middle Class Was Central in Election," *Boston Globe*, November 7, 1993.

88. Monti 2013.

89. Al Larkin, "The 1970s Served Up Turmoil; Second in a Three-Part Series Examining the Four Terms of Boston Mayor Kevin H. White," *Boston Globe*, July 25, 1983.

90. Ken Wade interview.

91. King interview.

92. Ed Quill, "Mel King Criticizes Flynn on Handling of Rent Control Plan," *Boston Globe*, October 10, 1984.

93. Rezendes, "Tarnished Healer Mayor Flynn."

94. Michael Rezendes, "Boston Had 20% Drop in Rights Violations," *Boston Globe*, May 13, 1992.

95. Rezendes, "Boston Had 20% Drop."

96. Indira A. R. Lakshmanan, "Hate-Crime Reports Rise in Boston," *Boston Globe*, June 20, 1994.

97. Judy Rakowsky, "As Reported Hate Crimes in Boston Surge, Prosecutions Drop," *Boston Globe*, June 12, 2000.

98. Sandee Story interview.

99. Stone 1989.

100. "No on Question Two," *Boston Globe* editorial, November 1, 1989.

101. Ken Tangvik interview.

102. Chuck Collins interview.

103. Hubie Jones interview.

104. Sullivan interview.

105. Marty Walsh interview.

106. Monti 2013, 5.

107. Ted Landsmark interview.

108. Meghan Irons, "Blacks Appreciate Menino, Yearn for More," *Boston Globe*, March 29, 2013.

109. Irons, "Blacks Appreciate Menino."

110. Edward Mason, "Mortgage Denials Rise for Boston Blacks," *Boston Business Journal*, December 30, 2002; *University Reporter* (University of Massachusetts–Boston), "New Report Documents Persistence of Racial and Ethnic Disparities in Mortgage Lending in Boston," 2003.

111. Sum 2013.

112. Muñoz et al. 2025.

113. City of Boston Assessing Department, September 28, 2022.

114. Ray Flynn interview.

115. "The State of the Mayor," *Boston Globe* editorial, January 6, 1993.

116. King interview.

117. Joyce Ferriabough, interview and personal communication with author, January 4, 2024.

118. Joan Vennochi, "What Is Ray Flynn's Legacy in Light of the Charles Stuart Case?," *Boston Globe*, January 4, 2024.

119. Connolly 1998.

120. Peter Canellos, "No Putting On the Ritz for Dressed-Down Flynn," *Boston Globe*, February 25, 1993.

121. Coyle interview.

122. Sullivan interview.

# BIBLIOGRAPHY

Allen, Henry L. Interview by Rhea Ramjohn. 2005. Boston, MA: *John Joseph Moakley Archive and Institute*, Suffolk University.

Anderson, Elijah. 1990. *Streetwise: Race, Class, and Change in an Urban Community*. Chicago: University of Chicago Press.

Anyon, Jean. 1997. *Ghetto Schooling: A Political Economy of Urban Educational Reform*. New York: Teachers College Press.

———. 2005. *Radical Possibilities*. New York: Routledge.

———. 2009. *Theory and Educational Research: Toward a Critical Social Explanation*. New York: Routledge.

Beatty, Jack. 1992. *The Rascal King: The Life and Times of James Michael Curley, 1874–1958*. New York: Addison-Wesley.

Beitel, K. E. 2004. *Transforming San Francisco: Community, Capital, and the Local State in the Era of Globalization, 1956–2001*. PhD dissertation, University of California–Davis.

Bernard, H. Russell, Peter Killworth, David Kronenfeld, and Lee Sailer. 1984. "The Problem of Informant Accuracy: The Validity of Retrospective Data." *Annual Review of Anthropology* 13: 495–517.

Berrien, Jenny, Omar McRoberts, and Christopher Winship. 2000. "Religion and the Boston Miracle: The Effects of Black Ministry on Youth Violence." In *Who Will Provide? The Changing Role of Religion in American Social Welfare*, ed. Mary Jo Bane, Brent Coffin, and Ronald Thiemann, 266–85. New York: Routledge.

Berrien, Jenny, and Christopher Winship. 1999. "Lessons from Boston's Police Community Collaboration." *Federal Probation* 63, no. 2 (December): 25–32.

Bluestone, Barry. 1972. "Economic Theory and the Fate of the Poor." In *Power and Ideology in Education*, ed. Jerome Karabel and A. H. Halsey, 335–39. New York: Oxford University Press.

Bluestone, Barry, and Mary Huff Stevenson. 2000. *The Boston Renaissance: Race, Space, and Economic Change in an American Metropolis*. New York: Russell Sage Foundation.

Borer, Michael Ian. 2006. "The Location of Culture: The Urban Culturist Perspective." *City and Community* 5, no. 2: 173–97.

———. 2008. *Faithful to Fenway: Believing in Boston, Baseball, and America's Most Beloved Ballpark*. New York: New York University Press.

Bourgois, Philippe. 1996. *In Search of Respect*. New York: Cambridge University Press.

Boyer, Paul. 1992. *Urban Masses and Moral Order in America, 1820–1920*. Cambridge, MA: Harvard University Press.

Bradbury, Katharine L., Karl E. Case, and Constance R. Dunham. 1989. "Geographic Patterns of Mortgage Lending in Boston, 1982–1987." *New England Economic Review* (Federal Reserve Bank of Boston) (September): 3–30.

Brady, James. 1983. "Arson, Urban Economy, and Organized Crime: The Case of Boston." *Social Problems* 31, no. 1 (October): 1–27.

Brown-Saracino, Japonica. 2009. *A Neighborhood That Never Changes*. Chicago: University of Chicago Press.

———, ed. 2010. *The Gentrification Debates*. New York: Routledge.

Bulger, William, M., 2009. *James Michael Curley: A Short Biography with Personal Reminiscences*. Beverly, MA: Commonwealth Editions.

Burawoy, Michael. 1991. *Ethnography Unbound*. Berkeley: University of California Press.

Burns, Peter. 2003. "Regime Theory, State Government, and a Takeover of Urban Education." *Journal of Urban Affairs* 25, no. 3: 285–303.

Campen, James T. 1992. "The Struggle for Community Investment in Boston, 1989– 1991." In *From Redlining to Reinvestment: Community Responses to Urban Disinvestment*, ed. Gregory D. Squires, 38–72. Philadelphia: Temple University Press.

Child, Christopher. 2021. "Mayors of Boston." *New England Historic Genealogical Society*. February 22.

Clavel, Pierre. 1986. *The Progressive City: Planning and Participation, 1969–1984*. New Brunswick, NJ: Rutgers University Press.

———. 2010. *Activists in City Hall: The Progressive Response to the Reagan Era in Boston and Chicago*. Ithaca, NY: Cornell University Press.

Colburn, Greg, and Clayton Page Aldern. 2022. *Homelessness Is a Housing Problem: How Structural Factors Explain U.S. Patterns*. Berkeley: University of California Press.

Cole, Donald B. 1963. *Immigrant City, 1845–1921*. Chapel Hill: University of North Carolina Press.

Conant, James B. 1961. *Slums and Suburbs*. New York: McGraw Hill.

Connolly, James J. 1998. *The Triumph of Ethnic Progressivism: Urban Political Culture in Boston 1900–1925*. Cambridge, MA: Harvard University Press

———. 2003. "Beyond the Machine: Martin Lomasney and Ethnic Politics." In *Faces of Community: Immigrant Massachusetts, 1860–2000*, ed. Reed Ueda and Conrad Wright, 189–218. Boston: Massachusetts Historical Society.

Crockett, Karilyn. 2018. *People before Highways: Boston Activists, Urban Planners, and a New Movement for City Planning.* Boston: University of Massachusetts Press.

Cronin, Joseph, M. 1973. *The Control of Urban Schools: Perspective on the Power of Educational Reformers.* New York: The Free Press.

———. 2008. *Reforming Boston Schools, 1930–2006: Overcoming Corruption and Racial Segregation.* New York: Palgrave Macmillan.

Dahl, Robert. 1961. *Who Governs? Democracy and Power in an American City.* New Haven, CT: Yale University Press.

DeLeon, Richard Edward. 1992. *Left Coast City: Progressive Politics in San Francisco 1975–1991.* Lawrence: University of Kansas Press.

Dentler, Robert A. 1994. "Key Issues Facing the Boston Public Schools." *New England Journal of Public Policy* 10, no. 1: 271–82. Article 14.

DiCara, Lawrence. 2013. *Turmoil and Transition in Boston.* Lanham, MD: Hamilton Books.

DiGaetano, Alan. 1989. "Urban Political Regime Formation: A Study in Contrast." *Journal of Urban Affairs* 11, no. 3: 261–81.

DiGaetano, Alan, and John S. Klemanski. 1999. *Power and City Governance: Comparative Perspectives on Urban Development.* Minneapolis: University of Minnesota Press.

DiMaggio, Paul, and John Mohr. 1985. "Cultural Capital, Educational Attainment, and Marital Selection." *American Journal of Sociology* 90, no. 6: 1231–61.

Domhoff, G. William. 2006. "The Limitations of Regime Theory." *City & Community* 5, no. 1: 47–51.

———. 2011. "Why San Francisco Is (or Used to Be) Different: Progressive Activists and Neighborhoods Had a Big Impact," Who Rules America?, November, http://whorulesamerica.net/local/san_francisco.html.

Dreier, Peter. 1991. "Redlining Cities: How Banks Color Community Development." *Challenge: The Magazine of Economic Affairs* 34, no. 6 (November–December): 15–23.

———. 1993. "Ray Flynn's Legacy: American Cities and the Progressive Agenda." *National Civic Review* 82, no. 4: 380–403.

Dreier, Peter, and Pierre Clave. "What Kind of Mayor Was Bernie Sanders?" *The Nation*, June 2, 2015.

Dreier, Peter, and Bruce Erlich. 1991. "Downtown Development and Urban Reform: The Politics of Boston's Linkage Policy." *Urban Affairs Quarterly* 26, no. 3: 354–375.

Dreier, Peter, and W. Dennis Keating. 1990. "Limits of Localism: Progressive Housing Policies in Boston, 1984–1989." *Urban Affairs Quarterly* 26, no. 2: 191–216.

Dreier, Peter, John H. Mollenkopf, and Todd Swanstrom. 2014. *Place Matters: Metropolitics for the Twenty-First Century.* Third ed. Lawrence: University Press of Kansas.

Du Bois, W. E. B. 1899. *The Philadelphia Negro: A Social Study.* Philadelphia: University of Pennsylvania Press.

Duncan, Margot. 2004. "Autoethnography: Critical Appreciation of an Emerging Art." *International Journal of Qualitative Methods* 3, no. 4: 28–39.

Emirbayer, Mustafa. 1992. "Beyond Structuralism and Voluntarism: The Politics and Discourse of Progressive School Reform, 1890–1930." *Theory and Society* 21, no. 5: 621–64.

Esping-Anderson, Gosta. 2007. "Sociological Explanations of Changing Income Distributions." *American Behavioral Scientist* 50, no. 5: 639–58.

Ferman, Barbara. 1996. *Challenging the Growth Machine.* Lawrence: University Press of Kansas.

Finn, Charles. 1989. "Mortgage Lending in Boston's Neighborhoods, 1981–1987: A Study of Bank Credit and Boston's Housing." Hubert Humphrey Institute of Public Affairs, University of Minnesota.

Fogelberg, Michael. 1996. "Electoral Activism and Progressive Coalition Building in Boston, 1983–1993." Unpublished thesis, Tufts University.

Formisano, Ronald P. 2004. *Boston against Busing: Race, Class, and Ethnicity in the 1960s and 1970s.* Second ed. Chapel Hill: University of North Carolina Press.

Friedman, Norman L. 1990. "Autobiographical Sociology." *The American Sociologist* 21, no. 1: 60–66.

Gans, Herbert, J. 1962. *The Urban Villagers: Group and Class in the Life of Italian-Americans.* New York: The Free Press.

———. 2009. "Some Problems and Futures for Urban Sociology: Toward a Sociology of Settlements." *City and Community* 8, no. 3: 211–19.

Gendron, Richard. 2006. "Forging Collective Capacity for Urban Redevelopment: 'Power To,' 'Power Over,' or Both?" *City & Community* 5, no. 1: 5–22.

Gendron, Richard, and G. William Domhoff. 2009. *The Leftmost City: Power and Progressive Politics in Santa Cruz.* Boulder, CO: Westview Press.

Gillis, Don. 2015. "Busing (School Desegregation)." *The Wiley Blackwell Encyclopedia of Race, Ethnicity, and Nationalism*, ed. A. D. Smith, X. Hou, J. Stone, R. Dennis, and P. Rizova, 1–5. Hoboken, NJ: Wiley and Sons.

Gillette, Howard, Jr. 2022. *The Paradox of Urban Revitalization.* Philadelphia: University of Pennsylvania Press.

Gittell, R., and A. Vidal. 1998. *Community Organizing: Building Social Capital as a Development Strategy.* Thousand Oaks, CA: Sage.

Glazer, Nathan, and Daniel Patrick Moynihan. 1970. *Beyond the Melting Pot: The Negroes, Puerto Ricans, Jews, Italians, and Irish of New York City.* Cambridge, MA: MIT Press.

Glyn, Noah, and Scott Drenkard. 2013. "Prop 13 in California, 35 Years Later." *Tax Foundation.* June 6.

Gonzalez, Juan. 2017. *Reclaiming Gotham: Bill de Blasio and the Movement to End America's Tale of Two Cities.* New York: The New Press.

Goodman, Michael D., and Daniel J. Monti. 1999. "Corporately Sponsored Redevelopment Campaigns and the Social Stability of Urban Neighborhoods: St. Louis Revisited." *Journal of Urban Affairs* 21 (Spring): 101–27.

Gottdiener, Mark. 1994. *The New Urban Sociology.* New York: McGraw Hill.

Green, James. "The Making of Mel King's Rainbow Coalition: Political Changes in Boston 1963–1983," in Jennings and King 1986.

Hackworth, Jason. 2007. *The Neoliberal City: Governance, Ideology, and Development in American Urbanism.* Ithaca, NY: Cornell University Press.

Handlin, Oscar. 1969. *Boston Immigrants: 1790–1880.* Cambridge, MA: Harvard University Press.

Hawley, Amos H. 1971. *Urban Society: An Ecological Approach.* New York: John Wiley and Sons.

Henig, Jeffrey, and Clarence Stone. 2008. "Rethinking School Reform: The Distractions of Dogma and the Potential for a New Politics of Progressive Pragmatism." *American Journal of Education* 114, no. 3: 191–218.

Hess, Frederick M. 2008. "Looking for Leadership: Assessing the Case for Mayoral Control of Urban School Systems." *American Journal of Education.* May.

Higgins, George V. 1984. *Style versus Substance: Boston, Kevin White and the Politics of Illusion.* New York: Macmillan.

Holli, Melvin G. 1999. *The American Mayor: The Best and Worst Big-City Leaders.* University Park: Pennsylvania State University Press.

Holmes, Natalie, and Alan Berube. 2016. "City and Metropolitan Inequality on the Rise, Driven by Declining Incomes." Brookings Institution. January 14.

Holt, Nicholas L. 2003. "Representation, Legitimation, and Autoethnography: An Autoethnographic Writing Story." *International Journal of Qualitative Methods* 2, no. 1: 1–22.

Horan, Cynthia. 1990. "Organizing the 'New Boston': Growth Policy, Governing Coalitions & Tax Reform." *Polity* 22, no. 3: 489–510.

———. 1991. "Beyond Governing Coalitions: Analyzing Urban Regimes in the 1990s." *Journal of Urban Affairs* 13, no. 2: 119–35.

Jackson, Ronda, and Christopher Winship. 2006. "Race Relations in Boston: A Tale of Two Mayors, Raymond L. Flynn and Thomas M. Menino." Hauser Center for Nonprofit Organizations.

Jacobs, Jane. 1993. *The Death and Life of Great American Cities.* New York: Modern Library.

Jencks, Christopher. 1972. *Inequality: A Reassessment of the Effect of Family and Schooling in America.* New York: Basic Books.

Jencks, Christopher, and Meredith Phillips. 1998. *The Black-White Test Score Gap.* Washington, DC: Brookings Institution.

Jennings, James. 2003. *Welfare Reform and the Revitalization of Inner-City Neighborhoods.* East Lansing: Michigan State University Press.

———, ed. 2007. *Race, Neighborhoods, and the Misuse of Social Capital.* New York: Palgrave.

Jennings, James, and Mel King. 1986. *From Access to Power: Black Politics in Boston.* Cambridge, MA: Schenkman Books.

Judd, Dennis R., and Todd Swanstrom. 1994. *City Politics: Private Power and Public Policy.* New York: HarperCollins.

Kearns-Goodwin, Doris. 1987. *The Fitzgeralds and the Kennedys.* New York: Simon & Schuster.

Kennedy, Lawrence W. 1992. *Planning the City upon a Hill: Boston since 1630.* Amherst: University of Massachusetts Press.

Kennedy, Marie, Chris Tilly, and Mauricio Gaston. 1990. "Transformative Populism and the Development of a Community of Color." In *Dilemmas of Activism: Class, Community, and the Politics of Local Mobilization.* ed. Joseph M. Kling and Prudence Sarah Posner, 301–23. Philadelphia: Temple University Press.

Key, V. O., Jr. 1955. "A Theory of Critical Elections." *The Journal of Politics* 17, no. 1: 3–18.

Kidder, Tracy. 2023. *Rough Sleepers.* New York: Random House.

Kimelberg, Shelley McDonough. 2011. "Inside the Growth Machine: Real Estate Professionals on the Perceived Challenges of Urban Development." *City & Community* 10, no. 1: 76–99.

King, Mel. 1981. *Chain of Change: Struggles for Black Community Development.* Boston: South End Press.

Kling, Joseph M., and Prudence Sarah Posner, eds. 1990. *Dilemmas of Activism: Class, Community, and the Politics of Local Mobilization.* Philadelphia: Temple University Press.

Kozol, Jonathan. 1967. *Death at an Early Age: The Destruction of the Hearts and Minds of Negro Children in the Boston Public Schools.* New York: Penguin.

———. 2005. *The Shame of the Nation: The Restoration of Apartheid Schooling in America.* New York: Three Rivers Press.

Labaree, David. 1988. *The Making of an American High School: The Credentials Market and the Central High School of Philadelphia, 1838–1939.* New Haven, CT: Yale University Press.

Lazerson, Marvin. 1971. *The Origins of the Urban School: Public Education in Massachusetts, 1870–1915.* Cambridge, MA: Harvard University Press.

Lees, Andrew. 1985. *Cities Perceived: Urban Society in European and American Thought, 1820–1940.* New York: Columbia University Press.

Lehr, Dick. 2009. *The Fence: A Police Cover-Up along Boston's Racial Divide.* New York: Harper.

Lemann, Nicholas. 1991. *The Promised Land: The Great Black Migration and How It Changed America.* New York: Knopf.

Levine, Bertram J. 2005. *Resolving Racial Conflict: The Community Relations Service and Civil Rights, 1964–1989.* Columbia: University of Missouri Press.

Levine, Charles H. 1974. *Racial Conflict and the American Mayor.* Lexington, MA: Lexington Books.

Levine, Hillel, and Lawrence Harmon. 1992. *The Death of an American Jewish Community: A Tragedy of Good Intentions.* New York: The Free Press.

Liebow, Eliot. 1967. *Tally's Corner: A Study of Negro Streetcorner Men.* New York: Little Brown.

Lofland, John, and Lyn Lofland. 1995. *Analyzing Social Settings: A Guide to Qualitative Observation and Analysis.* Belmont, CA: Wadsworth.

Lofland, Lyn H. 1998. *The Public Realm.* New York: Aldine de Gruyter.

Logan, John R., and Harvey L. Molotch. 1987. *Urban Fortunes: The Political Economy of Place.* Berkeley: University of California Press.

Lukas, J. Anthony. 1985. *Common Ground: A Turbulent Decade in the Lives of Three American Families.* New York: Knopf.

MacDonald, Michael Patrick. 1999. *All Souls: A Family Story from Southie.* Boston: Beacon.

Mahoney, James, and Dietrich Rueschemeyer, eds. 2003. *Comparative Historical Analysis in the Social Sciences.* New York: Cambridge University Press.

Masur, Louis, P. 2008. *The Soiling of Old Glory: The Story of a Photograph That Shocked America.* New York: Bloomsbury.

Medoff, Peter, and Holly Sklar. 1994. *Streets of Hope: The Fall and Rise of an Urban Neighborhood.* Boston: South End Press.

Menino, Thomas M., with Jack Beatty. 2014. *Mayor for a New America.* Boston: Houghton Mifflin Harcourt.

Mills, C. Wright. 1956. *The Power Elite.* New York: Oxford University Press.

Mollenkopf, John H. 1983. *The Contested City.* Princeton, NJ: Princeton University Press.

Molotch, Harvey. 1976. "The City as a Growth Machine: Toward a Political Economy of Place." *American Journal of Sociology* 82, no. 2: 309–32.

———. 1988. "Strategies and Constraints of Growth Elites." In *Business Elites and Urban Development: Case Studies and Critical Perspectives,* ed. Scott Cummings, 25–47. Albany: State University of New York Press.

Molotch, Harvey, and John Logan. 1984. "Tensions in the Growth Machine: Overcoming Resistance to Value-Free Development." *Social Problems* 31, no. 5: 483–99.

Monti, Daniel J. 1985. *A Semblance of Justice: St. Louis Desegregation and Urban Order in America.* Columbia: University of Missouri Press.

———. 1994. *Gangs in Suburbs and Schools.* Cambridge, MA: Blackwell.

———. 1999. *The American City: A Social and Cultural History.* Malden, MA: Blackwell.

———. 2009. "Civic Capitalism and the Leisure of the Theory Class." *Italian Journal of Sociology of Education* 1 (June): 28–53.

———. 2013. *Engaging Strangers: Civil Rites, Civic Capitalism, and Public Order in Boston.* Lanham, MD: Fairleigh Dickinson University Press.

Monti, Daniel J., Colleen Butler, Alexandra Curley, Kirsten Tilney, and Melissa F. Weiner. 2003. "Private Lives and Public Worlds: Changes in Americans Social Ties and Civic Attachments in the Late 20th Century." *City and Community* 2, no. 2: 143–63.

Muzzio, Douglas, and Robert W. Bailey. 1986. "Economic Development, Housing, and Zoning: A Tale of Two Cities." *Journal of Urban Affairs* 8, no. 1: 1–18.

Nasaw, David. 1979. *Schooled to Order: A Social History of Public Schooling in the United States.* New York: Oxford University Press.

Neckerman, Katherine M., and Florencia Torche. 2007. "Inequality: Causes and Consequences." *Annual Review of Sociology* 33 (August): 335–57.

O'Connor, Alice. 1999. "Swimming against the Tide: A Brief History of Federal Policy in Poor Communities." In *The Future of Community Development*, ed. Ronald Ferguson and William Dickens, 12–24. Washington, DC: Brookings Institution.

O'Connor, Thomas H. 1993. *Building a New Boston: Politics and Urban Renewal, 1950–1970*. Boston: Northeastern University Press.

———. 2001. *The Hub: Boston Past and Present*. Boston: Northeastern University Press.

O'Donnell, Lawrence. 1983. *Deadly Force: The True Story of How a Badge Can Become a License to Kill*. New York: William Morrow.

Oldenburg, Ray. 1999. *The Great Good Place*. New York: Marlow & Company.

O'Neill, Gerard. 2012. *Rogues and Redeemers: When Politics Was King in Irish Boston*. New York: Crown.

Osterman, Paul. 1991. "Gains from Growth? The Impact of Full Employment on Poverty in Boston." In *The Urban Underclass*, ed. Christopher Jenks and Paul Peterson, 122–34. Washington, DC: Brookings Institution.

Ostrander, Susan A. 2013. *Citizenship and Governance in a Changing City: Somerville, MA*. Philadelphia: Temple University Press.

Park, Robert E. 1915. "The City: Suggestions for the Investigation of Human Behavior in the City Environment." *American Journal of Sociology* 20, no. 5: 577–612.

Park, Robert E., Ernest W. Burgess, and Roderick D. McKenzie. 1967 [1925]. *The City*. Chicago: University of Chicago Press.

Patton, Michael Quinn. 2002. *Qualitative Research and Evaluation Methods*. Thousand Oaks, CA: Sage.

PBS. 2023. *The Busing Battleground: The Decades-Long Road to School Desegregation*. PBS. American Experience Films.

Perloff, Richard M. 2017. "Reconsidering Dennis Kucinich 40 Years after His Cleveland Mayoral Run." Cleveland.com. September 17.

Peterson, Paul. 1981. *City Limits*. Chicago: University of Chicago Press.

Pietila, Antero. 2010. *Not in My Neighborhood: How Bigotry Shaped a Great American City*. Chicago: Ivan R. Dee.

Porter, Michael E. 1995. "The Competitive Advantage of the Inner City." *Harvard Business Review* (May–June): 54–57.

Portes, Alejandro, and Alex Stepick. 1993. *City on the Edge*. Berkeley: University of California Press.

Portz, John, Lana Stein, and Robin R. Jones. 1999. *City Schools and City Politics: Institutions and Leadership in Pittsburgh, Boston and St. Louis*. Lawrence: University Press of Kansas.

Putnam, Robert D. 1995. "Tuning In, Tuning Out: The Strange Disappearance of Social Capital in America." *Political Science and Politics* 28, no. 4: 664–83.

———. 2000. *Bowling Alone: The Collapse and Revival of American Community*. New York: Simon & Schuster.

———. 2007. "E Pluribus Unum: Diversity and Community in the Twenty-First Century." *Scandinavian Political Studies* 30, no. 2: 137–73.

*Radical America*. 1983–1984. Vol. 17, no. 6–vol. 18, no. 1 (November–February). Special issue.

Ravitch, Diane. 1974. *The Great School Wars: New York City, 1805–1973*. New York: Basic Books.

———. 2010. *The Death and Life of the Great American School System*. New York: Basic Books.

Reville, S. Paul, ed. 2007. *A Decade of Urban School Reform: Persistence and Progress in the Boston Public Schools*. Cambridge, MA: Harvard Education Press.

Rhomberg, Chris. 2004. *No There There: Race, Class and Political Community in Oakland*. Berkeley: University of California Press.

Rich, Wilbur. 2023. *Boston Mayor Tom Menino: Lessons for Governing Post-industrial Cities*. Boston: University of Massachusetts Press.

Rury, John L., ed. 2005. *Urban Education in the United States*. New York: Palgrave Macmillan.

Rury, John L., and Jeffrey E. Mirel. 1997. "The Political Economy of Urban Education." *Review of Research in Education* 22: 49–110.

Sampson, Robert J., Heather MacIndoe, Doug McAdam, and Simon Weffer-Elizondo. 2005. "Civil Society Reconsidered: The Durable Nature and Community Structure of Collective Civic Action." *American Journal of Sociology* 111, no. 3: 673–714.

Schmoke, K. L. 1995. "Medicalizing the War on Drugs." *Academic Medicine: Journal of the Association of American Medical Colleges* 70, no. 5: 355–58.

Shaw, R. 1998. "Tenant Power in San Francisco." In *Reclaiming San Francisco: History, Politics, Culture*, ed. J. Brook, C. Carlsson, and N. J. Peters, 287–300. San Francisco: City Lights.

Small, Mario Luis. 2004. *Villa Victoria: The Transformation of Social Capital in a Boston Barrio*. Chicago: University of Chicago Press.

Somers, Ed, and Elena Temple Webb. 2014. "Income Inequality, Early Childhood Education, Broadband, Focus of 'Commitment to Action." *U.S. Mayor* 81, no. 12 (August 18).

Stack, John F., Jr. 1979. *International Conflict in an American City: Boston's Irish, Italians, and Jews, 1935–1944*. Westport, CT: Greenwood.

Stone, Clarence. 1989. *Regime Politics: Governing Atlanta, 1946–1988*. Lawrence: University Press of Kansas.

———. 1993. "Urban Regimes and the Capacity to Govern: A Political Economy Approach." *Journal of Urban Affairs* 15, no. 1: 1–28.

Stone, John, and Polly Rizova. 2014. *Racial Conflict in a Global Society*. Malden, MA: Polity.

Strauss, Anselm, and Juliet Corbin. 1990. *Basics of Qualitative Research: Grounded Theory Procedures and Techniques*. Newbury Park, CA: Sage.

Suttles, Gerald D., 1968. *The Social Order of the Slum*. Chicago: University of Chicago Press.

———. 1972. *The Social Construction of Communities*. Chicago: University of Chicago Press.

———. 1984. "The Cumulative Texture of Local Urban Culture." *American Journal of Sociology* 90, no. 2: 283–304.

Swanstrom, Todd. 1985. *The Crisis of Growth Politics: Cleveland, Kucinich, and the Challenge of Urban Populism*. Philadelphia: Temple University Press.

Tager, Jack. 2001. *Boston Riots: Three Centuries of Social Violence*. Boston: Northeastern University Press.

Taylor, Steven. 2001. "Appointing or Electing the Boston School Committee: The Preferences of the African American Community." *Urban Education* 36, no. 1: 4–26.

Tebbetts, Charlie. "Changes in Boston from 1885 to 1949." *Historical Journal of Massachusetts* 32, no. 1 (Winter 2004): 1–34.

Thernstrom, Abigail, and Stephan Thernstrom. 2003. *No Excuses: Closing the Racial Gap in Learning*. New York: Simon & Schuster.

Thernstrom, Stephan. 1973. *The Other Bostonians: Poverty and Progress in the American Metropolis, 1880–1970*. Cambridge, MA: Harvard University Press.

Tough, Paul. 2009. *Whatever It Takes: Geoffrey Canada's Quest to Change Harlem and America*. New York: Houghton Mifflin.

Tyack, David B. 1974. *The One Best System: A History of American Urban Education*. Cambridge, MA: Harvard University Press.

Viteritti, Joseph P., ed. 2009. *When Mayors Take Charge: School Governance in the City*. Washington, DC: Brookings Institution Press.

Vrabel, Jim. 2004. *When in Boston: A Time Line and Almanac*. Boston: Northeastern University Press.

———. 2014. *A People's History of the New Boston*. Boston: University of Massachusetts Press.

Wallace, Brian P. 2022. *A Remarkable Life*. Boston: Y42K Publishing.

Weinberg, Martha Wagner. 1981. "Boston's Kevin White: A Mayor Who Survives." *Political Science Quarterly* 96, no. 1 (Spring): 87–106.

Waldinger, Roger. 2005 [1996]. "The New Urban Reality." In *Cities and Society*, ed. Nancy Kleniewski, 110–26. Malden, MA: Blackwell.

Warner, Sam Bass, Jr. 1962 [1978]. *Streetcar Suburbs: The Process of Growth in Boston (1870–1900)*. Cambridge, MA: Harvard University Press.

White, Theodore. 1978. *In Search of History: A Personal Adventure*. New York: Harper and Row.

Whyte, William Foote. 1993 [1943]. *Street Corner Society*. Chicago: University of Chicago Press.

Willie, Charles Vert. 1978. *The Sociology of Urban Education*. Lexington, MA: Lexington Books.

Wilson, William Julius. 1978. *The Truly Disadvantaged: The Inner City, the Underclass and Public Policy*. Chicago: University of Chicago Press.

———. 1996. *When Work Disappears*. New York: Random House.

———. 2009. *More Than Just Race: Being Black and Poor in the Inner City*. New York: Norton and Company.

Wirth, Louis. 1928. *The Ghetto*. Chicago: University of Chicago Press.

———. 1938. "Urbanism as a Way of Life." *American Journal of Sociology* 44, no. 1: 1–24.

Wong, Kenneth K. 2003. "Big City Mayors and School Governance Reform: The Case of School District Takeover." *Peabody Journal of Education* 78, no. 1: 5–23.

Wong, Kenneth K., and Francis X. Shen. 2002. "Do School District Takeovers Work." National Association of State Boards of Education. *State Education Standard* 3, no. 2 (Spring): 19–23.

Worthy, William. 1976. *The Rape of Our Neighborhoods: And How Communities Are Resisting Take-Overs by Colleges, Hospitals, Churches, Businesses, and Public Agencies.* New York: William Morrow and Company.

Zukin, Sharon. 1995. *The Cultures of Cities.* Malden, MA: Blackwell.

## REPORTS: BOSTON REDEVELOPMENT AUTHORITY

Boston Redevelopment Authority. 1964. "General Plan for Boston and the Regional Core, 1965–1975."

———. 1986. "Resolution of the Boston Redevelopment Authority Regarding Disposition Policies for the Kingston-Bedford Garage, Essex Street Lot and Parcel 18." Submitted by Stephen Coyle to BRA board on September 26.

———. 2003. "The Boston Economy." October.

———. 2008. "Demographic Profile of the Foreign-Born in Boston."

———. 2011. "Demographic and Social Trends in Boston."

City of Boston Planning Board. 1950. "General Plan for Boston 1950."

O'Brien, Margaret, and Deborah Oriola. 1985. "Boston at Mid-Decade: Results of the 1985 Household Survey II: Income and Poverty." Boston Redevelopment Authority.

## CITY OF BOSTON ARCHIVES

Boston Police Department. "2008 Crime Summary Report." Office of Research and Development, Office of Police Commissioner.

Boston Public Schools (BPS). 2011. *Boston Public Schools at a Glance 2010–2011.*

City of Boston Archives. 1984a. Flynn Statement on Approval of Downtown Development Projects, press release, and talking points. West Roxbury, MA. October 31.

———. 1984b. Memo from Detective George L. Sheridan, Community Disorders Unit, to Lieutenant Francis M. Roache, Community Disorders Unit. Subject: Breakdown (by Types of Crime) of Racially Motivated Incidents for 1983 and 1984. December 26. Box 1, West Roxbury, MA.

Mayor Kevin White's Inaugural Address. 1980. *Boston Globe.* January 8.

"Mayor Walsh Files Boston Residents Jobs Policy Update." 2016. City of Boston. November 28. https://www.boston.gov/news/mayor-walsh-files-boston -residents-jobs-policy-update.

"Mayor Wu Marks Creation of New City Planning Department with Signing Ceremony." 2024. Mayor's Office. April 2.

Neighborhood Housing Trust Report, City of Boston, Martin Walsh, Mayor. 2017. boston.gov.

*Redlining in Boston: Black People, Place and Policy*. 2023. BPDA Research Division. February.

Reports of the Boston Election Commissioners. 1949–2013.

## OTHER SOURCES

Bernadeau-Alexandre, Marjorie C., Tracy Kenney, and Lalita Pulavarti. 1975. "School Desegregation in Boston." US Commission on Civil Rights.

Biden, Joseph R. 2022. Remarks by President Biden at the National League of Cities Congressional City Conference. March 14.

The Boston Foundation. 2011. "The Measure of Poverty: A Boston Indicators Project Special Report."

Broadman, Richard, dir. 1978. *Mission Hill and the Miracle of Boston*. Educational Resources.

Broadman, Richard, John Grady, and Don Gillis, dirs. 1982. *Down the Project: The Crisis of Public Housing*. John Pennington.

CBS Boston. 2014. "Robin Williams Remembered Fondly in Boston." August 12.

Chapter 636, Racial Imbalance Law of 1965. https://repository.library .northeastern.edu/downloads/neu:rx914f96w?datastream_id=content.

Clinton, William Jefferson. 2024. Letter to Flynn Fortieth Anniversary Celebration. April 5.

Cronin, Joseph M. 1989. "Business Assistance to Urban College-Bound Students: Models That Work." Educational Resources Information Center.

Economic Justice Research Hub. 2013. "Boston Mayoral Vote 2013 Analysis." http://www.ejresearch.org/boston-mayor.

*Equality of Educational Opportunity* (The Coleman Report). 1966. National Center for Educational Statistics. https://files.eric.ed.gov/fulltext/ED012275.pdf.

Ferriabough, Joyce. 2024. Personal communication with author. January 4.

Flynn, Raymond. 2014. Personal communication with author, on his receipt of an award from the West End Museum. March 31.

HBO. 2013. *Murder in Boston: Roots, Rampage and Reckoning*. HBO Documentary Films.

HUD (US Department of Housing and Urban Development). 2022. *Annual Homeless Assessment Report*. December 19.

Jones, Hubie. 2024. Personal communication with author. October 9.

Judge Paul Garrity Receivership Files. n.d. University Archives and Special Collections, Joseph P. Healey Library, University of Massachusetts–Boston.

Mass Historical Society. 2024. "Italian Influence on Boston's Culture, Economy and Politics." April 10.

Muñoz, Ana Patricia, Marlene Kim, Mariko Chang, Regine O. Jackson, Darrick Hamilton, and William A. Darity Jr. 2025. "The Color of Wealth in Boston." A Joint Publication of Duke University, the New School, and the Federal Reserve Bank of Boston. March 25.

National Archives Voting Rights Act of 1964. https://legacy.catalog.archives.gov/id/1622796.

Nee, Mary. 2023. "Rebuilding Boston." Personal communication with author. February 12.

Osterman, Paul, and Anna Faith Jones. 1989. "In the Midst of Plenty: A Profile of Boston and Its Poor." Boston Foundation, Boston Persistent Poverty Project. December.

PBS. 2023. *The Busing Battleground: The Decades-Long Road to School Desegregation.* American Experience Films.

Powers, John E. 1967. Recorded interview by John Stewart. John F. Kennedy Library Oral History Program. March 9.

Scott, Esther. 1984. Kennedy School of Government, Harvard University Case Study: "Bailing Out Boston: The Tregor Legislation" (C-14-84-585).

Spar, Karen, and Monique C. Austin. 1984. "The Homeless: Overview of the Problem and the Federal Response." Report to the US Department of Housing and Urban Development. September 14.

"Statement of Demands." n.d. Boston: Boston Black United Front. SC1, Box 1, Roxbury Community College Library Special Collections.

"Suffolk University / Boston Herald Mayoral Poll Shows Connolly, Walsh Leading Pack." 2013. Suffolk University, MA Polls. July 15.

Sum, Andrew. 2013. Personal communication with author on poverty rates in Boston.

US Civil Rights Commission. 1975. *Desegregating the Boston Public Schools: A Crisis in Civic Responsibility.* A Report of the United States Civil Rights Commission. August. http://files.eric.ed.gov/fulltext/ED115706.pdf.

———. 1975. *Twenty Years after Brown: Equality of Educational Opportunity.* March. https://files.eric.ed.gov/fulltext/ED102285.pdf .

## Court Rulings

*Brown v. Board of Education of Topeka,* 347 U.S. 483 (1954).

*Brown v. Board of Education of Topeka,* 349 U.S. 294 (1955).

*Citizens United v. FEC,* 588 U.S. 310, 130 S.Ct. 876, 175 L.Ed.2d 753 (2010).

*Citizens United v. Federal Election Commission,* No. 08-205, 558 U.S. 310 (2010). http://www.supremecourt.gov/qp/08-00205qp.pdf.

*Hurley v. Irish-American Gay, Lesbian, and Bisexual Group of Boston, Inc.,* 515 U.S. 557 (1995).

*Jane Doe No. 1, et al., Plaintiffs, v. The City of Boston and the Boston Housing Authority, Defendants,* Agreement and Order, 1999.

*Morgan v. Hennigan,* 379 F. Supp. 410 (D. Mass. 1974).

*NAACP v. Boston Housing Authority,* 723F. Supp. 1554 D. Mass. 1989.

*Perez vs. Boston Housing Authority,* 368 Mass. 333 (masscases.com).

*Plessy v. Ferguson,* 163 U.S. 537 (1896).

*Swann v. Charlotte-Mecklenburg Bd. of Educ.,* 402 U.S. 1 (1971).

*Tregor v. Board of Assessors of City of Boston,* 377 Mass. 602 (1979).

# INDEX

Numbers in *italics* indicate charts and figures.

**Don Gillis, PhD,** is a community organizer and longtime activist in Boston. He has advised mayors of several cities and led economic and workforce development agencies. He holds a PhD in urban sociology and the sociology of education and an MA in community sociology from Boston University. He has taught sociology courses such as Boston's People and Neighborhoods, Race and Ethnicity, Occupations and the Workplace, Racial and Social Inequality in Schools, and the Sociology of HBO's *The Wire.*

# POLIS: Fordham Series in Urban Studies

Edited by Daniel J. Monti, Saint Louis University